Tourism and Ethnodevelopment

Ethnodevelopment is a well-established concept in the field of development studies. Despite its relevance to tourism initiatives and processes in the Global South, it continues to be an underutilised concept in the field.

This book bridges this gap, presenting an original conceptual framework to study the relationship between tourism and ethnodevelopment. It focuses on the processes of inclusion, empowerment, self-expression and self-determination to explore the effects of tourism initiatives on the identities, cultural resilience, livelihoods and economic opportunities of ethnic minority communities. Chapters explore a range of concepts and issues such as gender, authenticity, indigenous knowledge, tradition, the commodification of culture, community-based tourism, local entrepreneurship, cultural heritage, and tourism and the environment. Drawing on rich primary research conducted across South East Asia and South and Central America the book offers detailed evaluations of the successes and failures of various tourism policies and practices.

This book makes a valuable contribution for students, scholars, practitioners and policy-makers alike interested in tourism, development studies, geography and anthropology.

Ismar Borges de Lima is Professor of Regional Development and Population Studies at the Federal University of Southern and Southeastern Pará (UNIFESSPA), Brazil. He is also Director of the International Foundation for Research on Science, Nature and Tourism, RECINATUR, Brazil and Member of the MULTIAMAZON/UERR Lab for Research in the Amazonian Basin. He holds a PhD in Geography and Tourism from the University of Waikato, New Zealand, and has held positions as a postdoctoral researcher and Adjunct Lecturer at the School of Business and Tourism, Southern Cross University, Australia.

Victor T. King is Emeritus Professor in the School of Languages, Cultures and Societies, University of Leeds, UK; Professorial Research Associate in the Centre of South East Asian Studies, School of Oriental and African Studies, University of London, UK; Adjunct Professor in the Center for Ethnic Studies and Development, Faculty of Social Sciences, Chiang Mai University, Thailand; and Distinguished Visiting Fellow in the Institute of Asian Studies, Universiti Brunei Darussalam, Brunei.

Routledge Advances in Tourism and Anthropology
Series Edited by Dr Catherine Palmer and Dr Jo-Anne Lester

Dr Catherine Palmer (University of Brighton, UK) C.A.Palmer@brighton.ac.uk
Dr Jo-Anne Lester (University of Brighton, UK) J.Lester@brighton.ac.uk

To discuss any ideas for the series please contact Faye Leerink, Commissioning Editor: faye.leerink@tandf.co.uk or the Series Editors.

This series draws inspiration from anthropology's overarching aim to explore and better understand the human condition in all its fascinating diversity. It seeks to expand the intellectual landscape of anthropology and tourism in relation to how we understand the experience of being human, providing critical inquiry into the spaces, places, and lives in which tourism unfolds. Contributions to the series will consider how such spaces are embodied, imagined, constructed, experienced, memorialized and contested. The series provides a forum for cutting edge research and innovative thinking from tourism, anthropology, and related disciplines such as philosophy, history, sociology, geography, cultural studies, architecture, the arts, and feminist studies.

Published

Tourism and Ethnodevelopment
Inclusion, Empowerment and Self-determination
Edited by Ismar Borges de Lima and Victor T. King

Everyday Practices of Tourism Mobilities
Packing a Bag
Kaya Barry

Forthcoming

Post-Humanitarian Slum Tourism
Informal Urbanism, Affect and Subalternity
Tore E. H. Holst

Tourism and Indigenous Heritage in Latin America
Casper Jacobsen

Tourism and Ethnodevelopment

Inclusion, Empowerment and Self-determination

Edited by Ismar Borges de Lima and Victor T. King

LONDON AND NEW YORK

First published 2018 by Routledge

2 Park Square, Milton Park, Abingdon, Oxfordshire OX14 4RN
52 Vanderbilt Avenue, New York, NY 10017

Routledge is an imprint of the Taylor & Francis Group, an informa business

First issued in paperback 2019

British Library Cataloguing in Publication Data
A catalogue record for this book is available from the British Library

Library of Congress Cataloging in Publication Data
A catalog record for this book has been requested

ISBN: 978-0-415-78844-1 (hbk)
ISBN: 978-0-367-36229-4 (pbk)

Typeset in Times New Roman
by Cenveo Publisher Services

Contents

Figures

Tables

Contributors

David Barkin (PhD Yale, 1966) is Distinguished Professor at the Universidad Autónoma Metropolitana, Mexico City. He was a founding member of the Eco-development Centre in 1974 and a recipient of the National Prize in Political Economy in 1979. A Member of the Mexican Academy of Sciences, he was appointed an Emeritus Member of the National Research Council. He is the 2015 Winner of the Alexander von Humboldt Foundation-Georg Forster Research Prize for climate relevant research. He was awarded the 2016 CROP International Studies in Poverty Prize. His current work focuses on ecological economies, political ecology, solidarity-based economy and the construction of post-capitalist societies with a focus on Latin America.

Cecilia de Bernardi is a PhD Candidate at the University of Lapland. She also holds a Bachelor's degree in Tourism and a Master's degree in History from Linköping University (LiU). Furthermore, she holds a Bachelor's degree in Communication Sciences from the University of Milan (UniMi). She teaches courses in tourism research and destination development at the Multidimensional Tourism Institute, University of Lapland. Her research focus is on certifications and their use in tourism, collaboration in tourism, indigenous/Sámi tourism and tourism marketing representations.

Rosana Bignami holds a PhD in Literature from Mackenzie University (Universidade Presbiteriana Mackenzie – UPM) and a Master's degree in Communication Sciences from the University of São Paulo (USP). She is a Professor of Communication and Linguistics at the Language and Communication Center of Mackenzie University (CCL/UPM) and a Certified Sworn Translator for JUCESP (the Board of Trade of the State of São Paulo). She is also conducting research at the University of São Paulo (post-doctoral degree in Tourism, Social Capital and Communication) on the following themes: the Paraiba Valley, social capital, communications, ethnodevelopment and cultures, among others.

Robyn Bushell holds a PhD in Planning from the University of Sydney. She is an Associate Professor in Critical Heritage and Tourism Studies in the School of Social Sciences and Psychology and the Institute for Culture and Society,

Western Sydney University. Her research deals with the interface of heritage, tourism and community, with particular interest in the effect of World Heritage designation and subsequent tourism development on community development and poverty alleviation.

Márcia Teixeira Falcão holds a PhD from the Bionorte/Biodiversity Post-graduate Program at the Pará Federal University and Emilio Goeldi Paraense Musuem. She has a Master's degree in Natural Resources Management from the Roraima Federal University, UFRR. Currently, she is a Professor at Roraima State University, teaching subjects in the field of Geography, Tourism and Natural Resources at undergraduate and graduate levels. Her research interests are: geography, ethnodevelopment, ethnic and cultural tourism, indigenous community in the northernmost Amazonia (*Ingarikós*), environmental education, geomorphology and biodiversity conservation. Website: www.uerr.edu.br.

Clarissa Gagliardi has Bachelor's and Master's degrees in Tourism from the Ibero-American University Center (UNIBERO), a Master's in Management and Valorization of Historical Centers from the Università La Sapienza in Rome, and a Master's and PhD in Sociology from the Pontifical Catholic University of São Paulo. She is a Researcher at the São Paulo Metropolitan Observatory and at the Center for Tourism and Social Development Studies (CETES) at the School of Communications and Arts of the University of São Paulo (ECA USP), Professor at the Department of Public Relations, Propaganda and Tourism at the School of Communications and Arts of the University of São Paulo and at the Interunits in Museology Postgraduate Program of the University of São Paulo (PPGMus – USP).

Tuhina Ganguly holds a PhD from the Department of Sociology and Anthropology, University of Canterbury, New Zealand. Her dissertation is titled, 'Imagining India as a Spiritual Place: Life-journeys of Western Spiritual Practitioners in Pondicherry'. She was the recipient of the UC Doctoral Scholarship from 2013–16. Her research interests include tourism, guru movements, spirituality and lifestyle migration.

Mike Grimshaw (PhD Otago University) is Associate Professor in Sociology at the University of Canterbury. He is a series editor for *Radical Theologies* (Palgrave Macmillan) and founding co-editor of *Continental Thought and Theory* (http://ctt.canterbury.ac.nz/about-ctt/). He works at the intersections of radical and political theology, continental thought and critical social and cultural theory.

Mary Hawkins has a PhD in Social Anthropology from the University of Sydney and is an Associate Professor in Sociology and Anthropology at Western Sydney University. Her research focus is on identity, social change and globalisation in Indonesia and Iceland, and she is the author of a number of articles, book chapters and books, among them *Race and Ethnicity* (with Farida

Fozdar and Raelene Wilding, Oxford University Press, 2009), *Global Structures, Local Cultures* (Oxford University Press, 2014) and *Identity and Belonging* (editor, with Kate Huppatz and Amie Matthews, Palgrave Macmillan, 2016).

Sangkyun Kim (PhD) is Associate Professor of Tourism at the School of Business and Law at Edith Cowan University. His work is international and interdisciplinary at the boundaries of social psychology, cultural studies, media studies, geography and tourism. Associate Professor Kim's research includes film tourism, community empowerment and quality of life, tourist experience, and visual and mixed methods. He is on the editorial boards of the *Journal of Travel and Tourism Marketing*, the *Journal of Tourism and Cultural Change*, *Anatolia*, *Tourist Studies* and the *Journal of Hospitality and Tourism Research*.

Victor T. King (PhD) is Emeritus Professor in the School of Languages, Cultures and Societies, University of Leeds; Professorial Research Associate in the Centre of South East Asian Studies, School of Oriental and African Studies, University of London; Adjunct Professor in the Center for Ethnic Studies and Development, Faculty of Social Sciences, Chiang Mai University; and Distinguished Visiting Fellow in the Institute of Asian Studies, Universiti Brunei Darussalam. His recent publications include an edited volume, *UNESCO in Southeast Asia: World Heritage Sites in Comparative Perspective* (2016), and co-edited volumes, *The Historical Construction of Southeast Asian Studies: Korea and Beyond* (2013), *Rethinking Asian Tourism: Culture, Encounters and Local Response* (2014), and *Tourism and Monarchy in Southeast Asia* (2016). For a list of publications and career details: http://www.victortking.org; http://www.victortking.co.uk.

Outi Kugapi is a PhD Candidate at the University of Lapland (ULAP), Faculty of Social Sciences, Multidimensional Tourism Institute (MTI). She holds a Master's degree in Tourism research from ULAP as well as a Bachelor's degree in Tourism and Hospitality Management from Lahti University of Applied Sciences. She is a part-time teacher at the MTI, ULAP. Her research interests include tourist experience, handicraft tourism, indigenous tourism and indigenous cultures, among others.

Ismar Borges de Lima has a PhD in Geography and Tourism from the University of Waikato, New Zealand, is a Postdoc and Adjunct Lecturer at the School of Business and Tourism, Southern Cross University, SCU, Australia, and Professor of Regional Development and Population Studies at UNIFESSPA, Brazil. He has a Master's degree in International Relations from the International University of Japan (IUJ), completed a Post-graduation training course in 1995 at Radio and TV Nederland, RNTC, and was an intern in 2001 at UNESCAP, in Thailand. Currently, he is also director in Brazil for the International Foundation for Research on Science, Nature and Tourism (RECINATUR), and a Member of the MULTIAMAZON/UERR Lab for Research in the

Amazonian Basin. He is editor-in-chief of the books on *Wildlife Tourism* (Springer) and *Rare Earths* (Elsevier) and author of several book chapters and journal articles. He is a member of the editorial boards of eight journals, including *Ateliê Geográfico*, IESA-UFG. Former scholarship awards include: NUFFIC (The Netherlands government); Mombukagakusho (Japanese government); NZAID (New Zealand government); and CNPq, FAPEG and CAPES (Brazilian government). His research interests are: regional development, ethnodevelopment, tourism resources, wildlife tourism, tourism planning, ecotourism, environmental governance, environmental interpretation and education, and human-nature related topics within the Human and Social Sciences realms. Website: https: br.linkedin.com/in/ismarlimaphd www.multiamazon.weebly.com. SCU: www.scu.edu.au

Monika Lüthje holds a PhD in Social Sciences (Tourism Research) from the University of Lapland (ULAP), Finland. She is a senior lecturer of tourism research at ULAP. Her research interests include tourist cultures, tourist experiences, travel photography, rural tourism, indigenous tourism and ethics of tourism.

Thaís Alves Marinho holds a PhD in Sociology from the University of Brasília (UnB) and a post-doctoral degree in Social Sciences from the University of Vale dos Sinos (Unisinos). She is a Professor of Sociology at the School of Teacher Training and Humanities at PUC Goias and Coordinator of the Master's Programme in History/PUC Goiás. She is also editor of *Mosaico Magazine* and assistant editor of CMD *Archives Magazine*. Her research covers the following themes: creative economy, ethnodevelopment, traditional communities, consumption and subjectivity, among others.

La Mingqing is Professor and Dean at the Tourism and Historical Culture School at Southwest University for Nationalities, China and is also a member of the Ethnic Tourism Institute of China. He was born among the Mosuo People in Lugu Lake of Southwest China. His research interests are mainly ethnic culture and tourism development.

Lorraine Nicholas (PhD) is currently employed as a Tourism Specialist at the Organisation of Eastern Caribbean States (OECS) Commission. For the past 15 years, Lorraine has enjoyed a combination of education, training, lecturing, research and technical experience in the tourism field. In 2003, she was awarded a Fulbright Scholarship to pursue a doctorate in Tourism at the University of Florida. She also holds a Master's degree in Tourism and Hospitality Management with distinction from the University of the West Indies' Mona Campus and a Bachelor's degree in Tourism Management from the University of the West Indies. Dr, Nicholas pioneered research on the Piton Management Area. She has published several articles, primarily in international journals on the PMA. In her current position she is responsible for facilitating a regional approach to the development of the tourism sector in the OECS.

Yang Ningdong holds a PhD in Tourism Management from Sichuan University, China. Currently she is an Associate Professor of Tourism Management at the Tourism and Historical Culture School at Southwest University for Nationalities, China. She has been studying tourism development in ethnic areas of China, especially in the Southwest of China, for over ten years and her research focus is on community tourism, cultural tourism, ethnic tourism and ethnodevelopment, among others.

Ingeborg Nordbø is an Associate Professor at the Department of Economics and IT at the University College of Southeast Norway, and is the leader of the research group on sustainable tourism. Nordbø holds a PhD in Tourism/Entrepreneurship and an MSc in International Economics and Business Administration from the University of Aalborg, Denmark, and has specialised in tourism development, sustainability and entrepreneurship in rural areas. She has worked as an advisor and manager of various projects within tourism and local community development and in a number of international settings, such as Denmark, Chile, Guatemala, Kyrgyzstan, China and Norway.

Carlos Alfredo Ferraz de Oliveira is a doctoral candidate in Geography from the Postgraduate Program in Geography (PPGG) of the Federal University of Espírito Santo (UFES) and scholarship holder from CAPES of the Brazilian government. He has a Master's degree in Culture and Tourism from the State University of Santa Cruz (UESC), a *lato sensu studies* in Ecotourism from the Federal University of Lavras (UFLA), has graduated in tourism from the University Anhembi Morumbi (UAM) and is a park ranger with the National Commercial Apprenticeship Service (SENAC). He has been a casual lecturer in Geography at UFES, teaching Geography of Agrarian and Socio-environmental Conflicts. He develops research and consultancy on the following themes: territorial and environmental management of indigenous lands, ethnodevelopment, traditional communities and protected areas (conservation units and indigenous lands) and community-based ecotourism.

Eerang Park (PhD) is a Lecturer at the School of Management in Victoria University of Wellington, New Zealand. She has been developing her research in a wider tourism context that includes tourist experience and behaviour, community development and tourism, community empowerment, and visual analysis of tourism research.

Anoop Patiar holds a PhD in Hotel Management from Griffith University. He is an associate Professor of Tourism and Hotel Management in the Department of Tourism, Sport and Hotel Management, also at Griffith University. His research interests are in the areas of sustainable practices in hotels and tourism entrepreneurship. He serves on the editorial board of key hospitality and tourism journals.

Toulakham Phandanouvong is a Technical Official at the Tourism Marketing Department in the Ministry of Information, Culture and Tourism, Laos. She holds a Master's of Tourism from Flinders University in South Australia. Her research interests include community development, poverty alleviation, tourism policy and stakeholders.

Nantira Pookhao has a PhD in Tourism from the Western Sydney University and a Master's degree in International Hospitality Management from Leeds Beckett University, UK. Currently, Dr Pookhao is Head of Department, Hospitality and Tourism Studies, Siam University, Bangkok, and Lecturer at Western Sydney University, School of Social Sciences and Psychology, New South Wales, Australia. Her research interests and expertise are: hospitality and management, tourism, cultural tourism, social and cultural anthropology, culture, ethnography, social theory, and qualitative analysis.

Sacha Reid holds a PhD in Business from the University of Queensland. She is the HDR Convenor for the Department of Tourism, Sport and Hotel Management at Griffith University. Her research interests are in the areas of vertical communities, high-rise living, rural community development and event management. She is the Chair of the Griffith University Strata Title Conference and sits on a number of industry and academic boards.

Akhmad Saufi holds a PhD in International Tourism and Hospitality Management from Griffith University. He is a Senior Lecturer of Tourism Management in the Department of Management at the Faculty of Economic and Business of Mataram University, Indonesia. His research interests are in the areas of sustainable practices in tourist destinations and tourism entrepreneurship.

Russell Staiff holds a PhD from the University of Melbourne and is an Adjunct Fellow in Critical Heritage and Tourism Studies in the School of Social Sciences and Psychology, Western Sydney University. His research deals with the interface of heritage, tourism and community, with particular interest in heritage interpretation, the geographies of travel, representation and imagination.

Kennedy Rolando Lomas Tapia is a PhD holder in Environmental Education from the Universidad Pedagógica Libertador de Venezuela and has a Master's from the same university. He is a Research Professor at the State Polytechnic University of Carchi (UPEC), in Ecuador, and teaches graduate and postgraduate academic subjects at the Technical University of North Ecuador. He is also editor of the Terra Infinita Tourism Magazine. His research interests are: cultural tourism, ethnodevelopment, traditional communities, environmental education, and other topics within the Human and Social Sciences sphere.

Brijesh Thapa (PhD) is a Professor in the Department of Tourism, Recreation and Sport Management at the University of Florida, USA. Overall, his research theme is within the nexus of tourism, conservation and sustainability. He has been involved in numerous projects in various capacities in over 30 countries. Recently, Dr Thapa has been focused on capacity building and institutional development projects through curriculum development, research and training

training in tourism, nature and cultural heritage conservation, and natural resources management in several developing countries.

Carmen Amelia Trujillo is a PhD holder in Environmental Education from the Universidad Pedagógica Libertador de Venezuela and she also has a Master's degree from the same university. She is the Director of the Post-graduation Program of the Technical University of North Ecuador. Her main research topics are: cultural tourism, ethnodevelopment, traditional communities and environmental education, among others.

Gerda Warnholtz is a PhD researcher at the ICRETH, Leeds Beckett University. She is a Professor of Development Through Tourism and Sustainable Tourism at the Tourism School of the Autonomous University of Morelos. She has a Master's degree from the Universidad Latina in Cuernavaca, Morelos. She is an independent consultant for tourism-based social development interventions and policies. She is a reviewer for *PASOS*, Revista de Turismo y Patrimonio Cultural, and for *Teoría y Praxis*, a journal edited by the Sustainable Development Division of the University of Quintana Roo. She develops research on the following themes: sustainable development and poverty alleviation through tourism, ethnodevelopment, indigenous/rural communities and communality, among others.

Shirley Worland gained her PhD in Social Work from the University of Queensland, Australia in 2010 and is an Honorary Research Fellow with the Australian Catholic University, Sydney. She is a Lecturer in graduate and undergraduate international programmes in the Faculty of Social Science, Chiang Mai University, Thailand. Her current research interests include the nexus of adult literacy and development of Karen refugees, issues relating to ethnodevelopment in highlander communities in Northern Thailand and the portended repatriation of Karen refugees from the Thai–Myanmar border to Karen State, Myanmar.

Phouvanh Xaysena is a Deputy Director at the Tourism Marketing Department in the Ministry of Information, Culture and Tourism, Laos. She holds a Master's of Tourism from Flinders University in South Australia. Her research interests include community-based tourism, community empowerment and tourism policy.

Abbreviations

ABIPA	Pataxó Indigenous Buggy Conductors Association of Barra Velha
ADB	Asian Development Bank
AIEST	International Association of Scientific Experts in Tourism
ASEAN	Association of Southeast Asian Nations
ASEC	Ecuadorian Ecotourism Association
BEST	Business Enterprises for Sustainable Travel
BEST EN	Building Excellence for Sustainable Tourism – an Education Network
BEV	Ecuadorian Housing Bank
CANARI	Caribbean Natural Resources Institute
CAUTHE	Council for Australasian Tourism and Hospitality Education
CBET	Community-based Ecotourism
CBT	Community-Based Tourism
CBT-I	Community-Based Tourism Institute (former TVS-REST: Thailand Volunteer Service – Responsible Ecological Social Tours Project)
CDD	Community Development Department, Ministry of Interior
CDI	Commission for the Development of the Indigenous Peoples – a Mexican Agency of the Federal Public Administration.
CEI	Centre for Environmental Interpretation
CFN	National Financial Corporation
CODENPE	Council for the Development of Nationalities and Peoples of Ecuador
CODESPA	Foundation for Cooperation in Development and Promotion of Assistance Activities
CONAIE	Confederation of Indigenous Nationalities of Ecuador
CU	Conservation Unit (a Protected Area)
DADE	Department of Support to the Development of Tourism Resorts of the State of São Paulo
DCCED	Dirección de Capacitación de Cuadros y Estudios de Dirección

DED	German Development Service
DFID	Department for International Development, UK
DICT	Department of Information, Culture and Tourism (Laos)
DNP	Department of National Parks, Wildlife and Plant Conservation (Thailand)
DOT	Department of Tourism, Ministry of Tourism and Sports
EE	Environmental Education
ENCORE	Environmental and Coastal Resources Project
FIT	Free Independent Traveller; Free Independent Tour; Foreign Independent Tour; Foreign Individual Travel; Fully Independent Traveller
FOSIS	Social and Solidarity Investment Fund
FUNAI	Fundação Nacional do Indio (National Foundation for Indigenous People)
GMS-STDP	Greater Mekong Subregion – Sustainable Tourism Development Project
GPT	Gros Piton Tours
GPTGA	Gros Piton Tours Guide Association
GRDP	Gross Regional Domestic Product
IBAMA	Brazilian Institute for the Environment and Non-Renewable Resources
IBDF	Brazilian Institute for Forest Defense
IBGE	Brazilian Institute of Geography and Statistics
I-CBT	Indigenous Community-Based Tourism
ICMBio	Instituto Chico Mendes de Conservação da Biodiversidade
IDB	Inter-American Development Bank
IEPÉ	Instituto de Pesquisa e Formação Indígena (Brazilian Institute for Research and Indigenous Capacity Building)
IIED	International Institute for Environment and Development
IL	Indigenous Land
ILO	International Labour Organization
IN	Normative Instruction
INI	National Indigenous Institute
IPHAN	Instituto do Patrimônio Histórico e Artístico Nacional (Brazilian Institute for National Historic and Artistic Heritage)
IR	Indigenous Reserve
IWG	Interministerial Working Group
IWGIA	International Work Group for Indigenous Affairs
JICA	Japan International Cooperation Agency
KCC	Khiriwong Cooperative Center
KEC	Khiriwong Ecotourism Club

LBE	*La Barra Espaciadora*
LNTA	National Tourism Administration of Lao
MAE	Ministry of the Environment
MIES	Ministry of Social Welfare, now Ministry of Economic and Social Inclusion
MINTUR	Ministerio de Turismo (Ministry of Tourism)
MIT	Massachusetts Institute of Technology
MLC	Migrant Learning Centre
MMA	Ministério do Meio Ambiente (Ministry for the Environment)
MOP	Ministry of Public Works
MOTS	Ministry of Tourism and Sports
MPO-BID	Ministry of Public Works and Inter-American Band
NESDB	National Economic and Social Development Board
NESDP	National Economic and Social Development Plan
NGO	Non-governmental Organisation
NPA	Natural Protected Areas
ODI	Overseas Development Institute
OECD	Organisation for Economic Co-operation and Development
OIT	Organização Internacional do Trabalho (ILO)
OTOP	One Tambon One Product
OVC	OTOP Village Champion
OVOP	One Village One Product
PA	Preservation Area /Protected Area
PATA	Pacific Asia Travel Association
PCU	Project Coordination Unit
PKKNPA	Phou Khao Khouay National Protected Area
PMA	Pitons Management Area
PMDB	Brazilian Social Democratic Movement Party
PNGATI	National Policy for Environmental and Territorial Management of Indigenous Lands
PNHMP	Monte Pascoal National Heritage Park
PPD	GEF Small Grants Programme
PPG	Pro-Poor Growth
PPT	Pro-Poor Tourism
PTAZI	Programme for Alternative Tourism in Indigenous Zones
PTT	PTT Public Company Limited
RESEX	Extractive Reserves (one of the Brazilian categories for Protected Area)
RFD	Royal Forest Department
RRCAP	Regional Resource Centre for Asia and the Pacific
SAO/TAO	Subdistrict (*Tambon*) Council and Subdistrict (*Tambon*) Administration Organisation
SD	Sustainable Development
SEP	Sufficiency Economy Philosophy

SI	Social Intervention
SRDF	Soufrière Regional Development Foundation
STD	Sustainable Tourism Development
ST-EP	Sustainable Tourism – Eliminating Poverty
STM	Short-Term Mission
TAT	Tourism Authority of Thailand - Ministry of Tourism and Sports
T-BSDI	Tourism-Based Sustainable Development Intervention
THB	Thai Baht (Thai currency)
TI	Terra Indígena (Indigenous Land – IL)
TRF	Thailand Research Fund
TVS-REST	Thai Volunteer Service – Responsible Ecological Social Tours Project
UC	Unidade de Conservação (Conservation Unit/ Protected Area Unit)
UN	United Nations
UNAM	National Autonomous University of Mexico
UNCED	United Nations Conference on Environment and Development
UNDP	United Nations Development Programme
UNESCO	United Nations Educational, Scientific and Cultural Organization
UNWTO	United Nations World Tourism Organization
USAID	United States Agency for International Development
WCED	World Commission on Environment and Development
WTO	World Trade Organisation
WWF	World Wildlife Fund (World Wide Fund for Nature)

Introduction

1 Tourism and ethnodevelopment

An introduction

Victor T. King and Ismar Borges de Lima

The concept of ethnodevelopment

A brief history of origins

The concept of ethnodevelopment, sometimes rendered as ethno-development, is now well established in the development studies literature, though it is not so well known in the field of tourism studies. It attained an increasing position and popularity from the 1980s in studies of the relationships between development processes and ethnic identity, particularly with reference to the marginalisation and disempowerment of minority groups in the context of national development policies and nation-building in the developing countries of Latin America, Africa and Asia. An early use of the term is to be found in the important work of Rohini Talalla; she examined the difficulties experienced by the Semai-Senoi, comprising small groups of rural-based aborigines in Peninsular Malaysia, in sustaining their cultural identities and heritage, territorial integrity and livelihoods and sharing in the benefits of economic growth generated by the policies of the Malaysian political elite both to modernise minorities and also integrate them into a constructed national identity and a national strategy of development and economic growth (1980, 1984). However, the genesis of the concept of indigenous and endogenous approaches to local and regional development had already begun to emerge in the late 1970s in development studies circles (Todtling 2011: 333).

The concept was further popularised by a UNESCO Conference in 1982 to discuss ethnicity, development and ethnocide in Africa where ethnodevelopment, as a policy, process and practice, was referred to and debated as a means to address government approaches and development strategies that threatened ethnic identity, cultural resilience and self-determination (UNESCO 1982). The discussions focused on ethnicity, development and ethnocide in Africa and the importance of identifying, maintaining and deploying indigenous cultural values to strengthen local identities and to secure the confidence of minority populations in engaging in nationally generated development programmes and projects.

Janet Chernela, in developing our thinking about ethnodevelopment, has also considered the discussions in the UNESCO forum, which, as she emphasises, provided 'the foundational principles' of the relationship between ethnic identities and development (2011). She makes direct reference to the notes of the UNESCO meeting as follows:

> If we adopt the definition of ethno-development proposed by those responsible for this project, to the effect that it is a means of countering ethnocide by enabling ethnic, minority and/or exploited groups to revive the fundamental values of their specific culture with a view to strengthening their ability to resist exploitation and oppression and in particular, their independent decision-making power through the more effective control of the political, economic, social and cultural processes affecting their development, then we can safely affirm that the golden rule by which any ethno-development policy ought to abide, should be to ensure that all citizens of African countries, irrespective of their ethnic origin, enjoy the fundamental freedom to live their distinctive cultural lives. This is what we may term the principle of cultural democracy and the right to be different.
>
> Two general approaches may guide this policy: to begin with, suitable procedures should be devised for determining the part assigned to culture in the vast undertaking aimed at ensuring the overall development of peoples; secondly consideration should be given to the establishment of original cultural spaces in the light of our knowledge of the cultural heritage in question and the need to protect it; this is the essential foundation for a creative process free from the shackles of centralising and standardising ideology. (UNESCO 1982, cited in Chernela, 2011: 93–4)

For Chernela then what is needed is 'to rethink the assumptions underlying conventional development models', and, in her review, she refers to a broad range of writers who have worked in the field of ethnodevelopment from the 1980s into the 1990s, mainly in the disciplines of sociology, anthropology, geography, politics, economics and the combined field of political economy and social science-based development studies (Chernela 2011: 94) (see, for example, Bonfil Batalla 1982; Wright 1988; Bengoa 1993; Stavenhagen 1986; Partridge *et al.* 1996; Davis 2002).

The UNESCO Meeting in Africa, combined with the publication of the important work of Bonfil Batalla in a Latin American context (1982), coincided with the establishment of the Working Group on Indigenous Peoples in the same year which focused its attention on the protection of indigenous peoples worldwide. In 1985, as a result of its deliberations, the Working Group prepared a *Draft Declaration on the Rights of Indigenous Peoples* agreeing a set of core principles, and since 1987 the Working Group has continued to meet in order to give further consideration to proposals that enable the development of the original *Draft Declaration* (Iorns 1993). The work of Bonfil Batalla combined with the *Draft Declaration* and together with Rodolfo Stavenhagen's reviews and studies since the mid-1980s have formed the main guidelines in constructing an alternative development model from an ethnic perspective (see below). The World Bank also subsequently adopted the concept in the 1980s and 1990s, particularly in its funded projects among indigenous populations in Latin America (see, for example, Davis 1993; Davis and Ebbe 1993; Davis and Partridge 1994; Uquillas and Rivera 1993).

Ethnodevelopment and its continuing conceptualisation

The concept of ethnodevelopment therefore has served to recognise the importance of the cultural dimension in identity formation, the need for the empowerment of marginalised groups, and for the encouragement of local involvement in decision-making, as well as the recognition of the crucial roles that culture and indigenous or traditional knowledge and skills play in the local acceptance and success of development projects and therefore, in consequence, the sustainability of local livelihoods. In particular, ethnodevelopment has been used by Stavenhagen (1986) to refer to a type of development which must be concerned with the maintenance of ethnic diversity in that this provides a basic resource for addressing the endogenous needs of specific ethnic groups and minority communities. Following Stavenhagen and Bonfil Batalla these issues have been examined in their greatest detail in Latin America (see, for example, Andolina, Radcliffe and Laurie 2005; Chernela 2011; Hogue and Pilar 2008; Van Nieuwkoop and Uquillas 2000), and more recently there has been increasing interest in Latin American research in the relationships between tourism, ethnicity and development (Grünewald 2006 [2003]; Rivera 2012).

In the 1990s key statements emerged in social science circles to reorient development thinking in the direction of ethnic issues; these were also a clear response to the need to address dramatic increases in cases of ethnocide, ethnic violence, ethnic conflicts, ethnic marginalisation and ethnic exploitation (Hettne 1996: 21–4; Clarke 2001). Denis Dwyer coined the term 'ethnochaos' to capture the prevalence of 'ethnic discontent' and 'agitation' brought about by the encounters between politically dominant majority populations and subject minorities or between a privileged political-economic elite and dependent populations within the nation-state, as well as inter-ethnic interaction and tensions generated by migrations and diasporas and the ethnic dimensions of the intensification of resource competition, territorial displacement, environmental exploitation, uneven development and mass poverty (1996: 4).

Nevertheless, it should be noted that interest in issues of ethnic identity, as distinct from the concept of race, was certainly active in anthropology from the 1960s, but it took some time to register in other social sciences and then even longer to make an impact in the development studies literature (Dwyer 1996: 3). As Azril Bacal says in tracing the emergence and consolidation of studies of ethnicity up to 1990, 'The notion of ethnic identity is shown to have displaced acculturation in the realm of anthropology, while in sociology the focus has changed from immigration and marginality to recognition of ethnicity as a major structural dimension of society' (1991: 54).

Ethnicity and development: Hettne and its elaborations

Björn Hettne, in an important chapter in a volume on geographical perspectives on the relationship between ethnicity and development, a relationship which Hettne referred to as 'elusive' (1996: 15–44), argued that up to then ethnicity had been a neglected dimension in development theory, a view supported strongly by David Drakakis-Smith in the same edited book (1996: 277; see also Dwyer and Drakakis-Smith 1996); Western preoccupations with modernisation, and related assumptions about cultural obstacles to development, the nation-state as the primary unit of analysis and the homogeneity of development processes based on Western models and experiences have gradually been replaced by a focus on the encouragement and support of cultural diversity and sub-national and minority identities (Hettne 1996: 15, 1993; see also Clarke 2001; Stavenhagen 1986, 1990; Willis 2005).

Hettne identifies four dimensions or principles of this re-orientation in academic research and in development policy and engagement with regard to the concept, process and practice of ethnodevelopment:

- *cultural pluralism or ethnic pluralism* which entails mutual respect for other 'codes of behaviour and different value systems', including, in the case of minorities, 'the right to use their own language, practice their religions and to carry out cultural practices forming part of their identity and socialization process' as against the hegemonic approach to culture which sees it as only operating at the national level (and see Picard and Di Giovine 2014);
- *internal self-determination* or 'the collective capacity to control one's destiny in a situation of interdependence' but within the context of negotiation and give-and-take with those who exercise power in the nation-state, particularly with regard to resources within a given territory;
- *territorialism and territorial definition* which refers to 'an attachment to a specific habitat or a territory' and the control and maintenance of local natural resources, ecology and environment by those who inhabit a particular territory; and finally
- *sustainability*, embracing issues of protection, ecological balance and the maintenance of biodiversity in that the decrease in natural resources and 'environmental degradation' has been a significant underlying cause of 'human conflicts both between and within states'; in particular, development should not compromise the capacities of future generations to secure their livelihoods in a particular territory.

(1996: 24–9)

In this connection, Willis proposes that 'the spatial concentration of groups enables a construction of ethnic identity linked to a particular territory, making the notion of "ethnodevelopment" through self-determination a logistical possibility, if not a politically-favoured one' (Willis 2005: 123). Hettne also argues that an essential precondition for the realisation of these four principles of ethnodevelopment is the emergence of regionalism or the 'grouping of states' as 'the defensive bulwark, against the anarchy of the world market and the global forces of homogenization and ethnocide' and against the exploitation and oppression of minority populations (1996: 29–30).

Moreover, Hettne also suggests that our conception of ethnicity and cultural pluralism should not lead to the perception that ethnic identities present obstacles or barriers to modernisation, which was a commonly held view in early post-war economistic development thinking and the preoccupation with economic growth based on a Western model of transformation (see, for example, Rostow 1960; see also Agrawal 1995; Edelman and Haugerud 2005, 2007; Haugerud 2003; Radice 2015). But rather he proposes that indigenous communities have served as a means to counter and modify nation-state projects which act to undermine local or sub-national identities and resilience, and the capacity of ethnic groups to engage positively and successfully in the development process (Hettne 1996: 40–2). He therefore refutes the value of a globalised, market-driven reasoning that has acted to marginalise indigenous knowledge and culture, which in turn requires us to conceive of culture and identity as not 'rigid' but 'adaptable' and that if these qualities are recognised then development may not undermine but instead 'enhance broadly cherished cultural aspects' (Ascher and Heffron 2010: 238). Indeed, there has been a strong movement among anthropologists in particular to question the very premises of development policy and practice (Gardner and Lewis 2011).

But his review of the 'major theoretical traditions' up to the 1990s, Hettne proposed that 'ethnicity and development belong to different worlds … [in that] … development theory is concerned with 'states' and 'national economies' as basic units which precludes a serious treatment of the ethnic factor'. In his use and elaboration of the concept of ethnodevelopment he therefore attempts to elucidate the relationships between identities and development and to provide a 'model of development that releases the potential inherent in different ethnic groups' (1996: 16). The potential is also underpinned by the principles of participation, inclusion, self-determination and empowerment, and the recognition of the importance of local decision-making in the context of the development process.

However, we should not be seduced into thinking that ethnodevelopment is a panacea for all the complex problems that ethnic minorities face, located as they are within nation-states. It is easy to romanticise and essentialise the bold ideas which the proponents of ethnodevelopment, post-development and alternative development express. These ideas comprise principles responding to the needs of a global humanity which no one could easily deny (Edelman and Haugerud 2005: 49; see also Agrawal 1995; Haugerud 2003). But the ideas and principles have to be implemented and, as we shall see in several of our case studies in this volume, there have been successes and partial successes as well as failures.

Ethnodevelopment programmes still have to operate within a globalised economy, in interaction with powerful financial and corporate interests and within nation-states that often have national priorities other than the protection and support of ethnic minorities. But some of our cases do demonstrate that in translating public policies into praxis and focusing on the importance of ethnicity and ethnic resilience, there have been successful institutional interventions and financial support from, for example, the government of Ecuador (in the case of the Peguche Falls area), the United Nations Development Program (UNDP) and a range of NGOs and community-based indigenous groups.

A series of international laws and conventions to address indigenous rights have also been promulgated (Anaya 2004). Some of these interventions have helped to establish the basis of community-based, collaborative and participatory decision-making while encouraging cultural and ethnic revival, the positive evaluation of local culture and identity, the inclusion of local communities in the development of their own futures and their involvement in environmental stewardship. Some of these initiatives have managed to achieve these objectives without creating ethnic enclaves and by maintaining dialogue both within and beyond the local communities.

One developmental sector which concerns us in this volume and has shown some promise, though it is not without its problems, is that of tourism, focusing particularly on ethnic, cultural, heritage and ecotourism activities. But little has been elaborated to harness indigenous empowerment through tourism engagement, and internationally the role of the United Nations World Tourism Organisation (UNWTO) should become fundamental in this regard. However, it was the World Trade Organisation that highlighted the issues of local populations and equitability in relation to tourism: Article 5 of the WTO-OMT *Global Code of Ethics* states that local populations 'should be associated with tourism activities and share equitably in the economic, social and cultural benefits they generate, [and the] benefit from ... tourism policies should be oriented towards improving their standard of living' (Rangan 2005: 37).

Tourism and ethnicity

In earlier excursions into the relationships between ethnicity and development there was not much evidence of the realisation of the importance of tourism as a major agency of political, economic and cultural change. As Picard and Wood noted even as late as the mid-1990s and with the continuing global growth in the tourism industry, 'its importance for the understanding of ethnicity in the modern world has been generally neglected within the field of ethnicity studies' (1997: vii–viii). They then elaborate their contention that 'in most of the major journals on race and ethnicity or in the periodic literature reviews of the field, apart from an occasional dismissal as an agent of the commoditisation and, therefore, the degradation of ethnic culture' that tourism as an agent and a medium of encounter between representatives of different cultures, expressing different identities, is 'rarely mentioned' (1997: viii). However, they do refer to some exceptions to this generalisation in the work of Pierre van der Bergh and Charles Keyes in a special issue on 'Tourism and Ethnicity' in the *Annals of Tourism Research* (1984a, 1984b) and the early statements on tourism and identities in Dean MacCannell's seminal study of modern tourism in *The Tourist: A New Theory of the Leisure Class* (1976a, 1976b) and Valene Smith's very widely quoted anthropological compilation *Host* and *Guests: The Anthropology of Tourism* (1977), the latter so widely quoted and used that a second revised and expanded edition appeared in 1989.

Gradually the role of tourism was conceptualised in the context of the growing importance of cultural and ethnic tourism (or ethno-tourism) and its implications for the construction, maintenance and transformation of identities within the nation-state and within an increasingly globalised world (Picard and Wood 1997). In this respect the policies and actions of political elites in nation-building and national identity formation and specifically in the related field of policy-making in tourism (Richter 1989) tended to focus on local responses to the tourism encounter, and especially issues to do with ethnic and national identity. In this mode of analysis researchers developed such concepts as 'touristification' or the emergence of tourist-influenced and generated (touristic) cultures and identities (Picard 1996), and also explored such issues as 'authenticity', 'staging', 'invention' and 'hybridisation' in the context of cross-cultural encounters (see King 2009).

As Robert Wood indicated in his examination of the relationships between tourism and identities, 'Both ethnic and national identities will continue to be contested … and tourism will continue to be an important arena in which this contestation is played out' (1997: 24). This theme has continued to be expressed in that 'indigenous communities can also use tourism as a means of transmitting their culture, values and beliefs, and their ways of relating to the world of visitors' (Campos *et al.* 2014: 143). In addition, Wood makes the distinction between ethnic identity or ethnicity and national identity, although the two concepts are intimately interrelated. Moreover, political elites may well express a national identity in ethnic terms, and ethnicity and national identity are both cultural constructions which focus on establishing similarities and differences between groups and categories. However, they usually operate at different levels or scales of magnitude (Hitchcock and King 1997). In the context of the nation-state, which in spite of globalisation processes remains a vitally important decision-making body and one which exercises power, control and influence, minorities are frequently incorporated into political, economic and cultural processes generated at the national level.

Ethnic identity therefore comprises a form of social cleavage and serves as a means of organising social and cultural relations in terms of similarity and difference (Du Gay *et al.* 2000a). As Barth noted in what has become a pioneering work in the study of 'ethnic groups' that identities and differences entail the establishment and maintenance of boundaries and are generated in encounters and interactions across boundaries (1969). In this formulation identity cannot exist apart from the establishment and maintenance of 'cultural difference' and the formation and operation of boundaries; it is constructed and sustained in relationships, both at the level of ideas and in practice with others who are perceived to be and categorised as 'not us' or 'other'. The way in which ethnicity operates is therefore 'relational' and is constructed in relationships of 'opposition' and 'comparison' (Boulanger 2009: 19).

Identities can also be relatively 'contingent, fragile and incomplete' (Du Gay *et al.* 2000b: 2). In the 1970s anthropologists were examining the ways in which identities (using such alternative terms as 'tribal', 'indigenous', 'native', 'minority') are not straightforwardly carried unchanging from the past and anchored reassuringly in some distant ancestral time and space, but they are instead constructed and transformed. Indeed, as a resource they can be 'switched', 'manipulated' and 'deployed'. Many anthropological studies, especially in Asia, focused on the fluid and strategic ways in which particular communities adopt and discard identities, and the role-playing and behaviour associated with them, according to circumstances, needs and interests (Leach 1954; Nagata 1975, 1979; Dentan 1975). Individuals can also carry multiple identities and activate these as different situations and interactions demand (Dentan 1976: 78; King and Wilder 2003: 196–200; Nagata 1979). This is especially so in situations where minority populations have to come to terms with more powerful majorities (Dentan 1975).

However, we must recognise that notions of contingency and fragility should not be overemphasised, that some identities are more viable and enduring than others and that in certain political-economic contexts minority populations have come together to form overarching ethnic categories (Kahn 1992: 159). Furthermore, in cases where identities have been politicised and where indigenous communities have defined themselves and have also been defined in official and sometimes constitutional terms, and where they have been prepared to engage in political struggle then some groups have managed to secure recognition and respect for their territorial rights, their 'constructed' identities and their cultures, and their role in tourism development, as in the case of the Maori of New Zealand and some of the aboriginal populations of Australia and Oceania (Cooper and Hall 2005; Hayward 2012; Myers and Corrie 2006; Ryan and Aicken 2005; Zeppel 2003, 2006).

The establishment of identities can also entail a range of active interactions (cultural exchange and encounters in the context of tourism, social intercourse including possibly intermarriage, trade and commerce, political alliance and even peaceful assimilation) across the boundaries between different or separate groupings or they may involve processes of exclusion, avoidance, non-recognition or hostility, the latter sometimes resulting in political subjugation, economic exploitation, forced acculturation or in extreme cases genocide. In the case of the construction of national identities we shall see in this present volume how politically dominant groups, or in more abstract terms representatives of the state or nation-state, attempt to promote, disseminate and sometimes impose on others their notions of identity and what that identity comprises in the context of tourism development and national development more generally. The agencies of the state may give official support to some cultural markers and elements of identity while disapproving of, constraining or prohibiting others. But these agencies, though very significant, are not the only image-makers and there is a host of others who present and indeed construct cultures and identities and are participants in the forces and processes of ethnodevelopment – tourist guides and agents, interpreters, private promoters, travel companies, hoteliers and other entrepreneurs, and travel writers. Importantly the identities constructed, maintained and developed by local indigenous communities are also being increasingly emphasised in policies of ethnodevelopment and in public attempts to empower minority populations.

The chapters in this volume explore the complex interactions between national tourism development policies, local and minority responses, and the successes and failures of ethnodevelopment in the context of tourism policies and practices. They explore the rhetoric of sustainability, empowerment and ethnodevelopment in relation to what has happened in on-the-ground practice; they also examine critically the tendency to emphasise the business, entrepreneurial and economic dimensions of tourism development and mass tourism rather than those to do with local identities, resilience and benefits, as well as issues concerning the maintenance of cultural heritage and diversity.

Chapter summaries

We have organised the first section of the book into a collection of chapters under the title 'Institutionalised Ethnic Tourism and Advances in Ethnodevelopment: Policies, Communities, Organisations', which examines in some detail programmes and projects at the interface between tourism and ethnodevelopment. Gerda Warnholtz and David Barkin, in their chapter 'Development for Whom? Tourism Used as a Social Intervention for the Development of Indigenous/Rural Communities in Natural Protected Areas', focus on the failure of tourism programmes as sustainable development tools, and they then question the language of the objectives and policies of development agencies, which prioritise the sustainability of the tourism sector over that of the host communities in the context of tourism. They demonstrate that most Indigenous Community-Based Tourism (I-CBT) projects inserted as elements in national development policies have failed, and that researchers partly explain this failure from a tourism-business perspective, reaching business- and management-related conclusions. In evaluating these findings and conclusions it is clear that the study of I-CBT interventions from the perspectives of the host community on the one hand, and those of the development policy-formulators and practitioners on the other hand, is still scarce. The authors argue that, in contrast, a more detailed fieldwork approach indicates that the issues in determining the success or failure of I-CBT projects necessary to design successful interventions on behalf of the host community are much more complex than have hitherto been realised in the context of the generally accepted tourism development paradigm. In order to begin to address this crucial problem the focus of policy-thinking and planning should incorporate spaces for local empowerment and self-determination in order to meet the needs and expectations of the host community, along with those of the tourists. Using evidence from the evaluation of the Alternative Tourism Programme for Indigenous Zones the chapter demonstrates that the projects need to be based more firmly on the concept of local community-based development and on a more comprehensive and inclusive definition of tourism as a multifaceted and multi-dimensional phenomenon.

The chapter by Carlos Alfredo Ferraz de Oliveira, Ismar Borges de Lima and Márcia Teixeira Falcão, on 'Territorial Management and Brazilian Public Policy for Ethnotourism and Ecotourism in Indigenous Lands: The Pataxó Case in Bahia' reviews the major Brazilian government policies in regard to indigenous people and their territories in the Amazon and Northeast region of the country with a focus on the advances and drawbacks for ethnic tourism development. The process of increasing dialogue between indigenous organisations and representatives and the Brazilian government authorities was initiated decisively with Brazil's ratification of Convention 169 of the International Labor Organisation (ILO) in 2002 and the formal recognition of the rights of indigenous people, in addition to the need for prior consultation with them and to secure their consent in any intervention in indigenous lands.

The analysis includes specifically a critical review of the Brazilian Policy for Environmental and Territorial Management of Indigenous Lands (PNGATI) as a milestone in terms of formulating and recommending ethnodevelopment projects based on the principle of environmental and cultural advocacy, and indigenous environmental and territorial management and the sustainability of biodiversity. The PNGATI was approved and implemented in 2012 as an ethnic governance tool to contribute to indigenous land management, ethnic self-determination and empowerment, and community well-being. The policy sets out guidelines to regulate indigenous tourism initiatives and practices in Brazil as a potential activity to help ethnic groups, particularly in forest and rural areas, to create income generation and to facilitate the enhancement and protection of their culture. The analysis is predominantly qualitative participant observation with the provision of some statistical data and an evaluation of primary and secondary sources among the Pataxó who live in Barra Velha Indigenous Land, in the southernmost part of Bahia State; they were the first indigenous community in the Brazil tourist visitation programme to become involved in tourism practices and in the tour-guiding of visitors to their homeland.

Nantira Pookhao, Robyn Bushell, Mary Hawkins and Russell Staiff in their engagement with the subject of 'Empowerment through Community-based Ecotourism in a Globalised World: Global-local Nexus – Three Thai Villages as Case Studies' argue that a bottom-up approach to tourism development in the form of Community-based Ecotourism (CBET) is a viable means to improve sustainability and the quality of life for indigenous people. However, most research on CBET and local empowerment is considered to be too simplified and generalised. What is recommended is that place-based ethnographic studies are necessary and should be linked to the broader context of supranational institutions, governmental organisations, NGOs, tourists and local entrepreneurs, all of which greatly influence the success or otherwise of the tourism development projects. Given that local empowerment is regarded in the sustainable tourism literature as a key objective of CBET, this chapter endeavours to provide an improved understanding of the processes and conditioning factors involved in intra-community participation and their connection to self-determination in relation to community empowerment as a whole.

The chapter focuses on the ways in which communities may collaborate or reject support from external agencies in CBET development projects and the transformational processes involved in a globalised, modernised and capitalised world that act to influence rural lives in developing countries. Three CBET communities located in different regions of rural Thailand agreed to participate in a study employing ethnographic techniques over a period of four months. Prior to immersion in these communities, secondary data relating to CBET was reviewed and in-depth interviews were conducted with Thai policy-makers in order to gain a holistic understanding of the Thai programme. The findings demonstrate various experiences of exercising local community power to achieve environmental, political, psychological and economic empowerment. The chapter provides valuable lessons for other CBET communities, particularly in developing countries. What is also of especial interest is that it demonstrates the advantage of globalisation as a tool towards simultaneously achieving the objectives of empowerment, development and conservation.

The following chapter focuses on case material from Latin America. Rolando Tapia Lomas, Carmen Trujillo and Ismar Borges de Lima in their chapter on 'Environmental Stewardship, Indigenous Tourism Planning and the Fakcha Llakta Community: An Ethnic Endogenous Development Model in Otavalo-Imbabura, Ecuador' identify and critically discuss the indigenous traditions of the Kichwa Otavalo together with the maintenance of the natural ecosystem, an enterprise which had been abandoned by the local community. The revival of these cultural elements, the restoration of the indigenous environmental assets, community action and the strengthening of ethnic entrepreneurship in relation to local tourism activities appear as the most obvious achievements in the implementation of ethnodevelopment actions in Otavalo-Imbabura. This has been achieved through community engagement in the Environmental Management and Tourism Plan through educational and participatory approaches. The Plan has identified and set down as its objectives sustainable tourism, ethnic ecotourism and cultural tourism as the means to improve the quality of life of the Fakcha Llakta community located next to one of the most sacred locations in the country, known as Peguche Falls, an important cultural site dedicated to the worship of water since ancient times. The Plan was part of a project with financial support provided by the United Nations Development Program, UNDP-PPD, and by the MOP-BID Environmental Management and Tourism Plan. This chapter makes an important contribution to our understanding of the major challenges faced by governments, agencies and local communities in the implementation of a holistic ethnodevelopment model that can serve to harness social, cultural, environmental, business and economic elements for the benefit of indigenous peoples. Overall it is demonstrated that the programme has achieved a significant measure of success.

The following chapter on Thailand by Shirley Worland examines a rather different dimension of tourism and ethnodevelopment. In her chapter entitled

'Missio-tourism Among Ethnic Karen in Thailand: A Bridge to Empowerment, Development and Self-Determination or Promotion of "Assistencialism"?' Worland poses a set of questions about the relationships between missio-tourism, a relatively new field of academic research in anthropology and sociology and in the field of tourism development, and the processes of empowerment and self-determination. However, she indicates that in the last decade, the field of missio-tourism has attracted considerable interest with an increasing number of ethnographic studies. This is a growing global phenomenon, whereby in excess of two million individuals annually are being sent out from Christian churches in the so-called Global North to ethnic communities in the so-called Global South to carry out a variety of development-focused activities including medical, educational, vocational and evangelical training. Worland lived in an ethnic Karen community in a rural Thai village for six years and gathered in-depth ethnographic material, while simultaneously carrying out fieldwork in identity studies and teaching in a community school. In that time, she observed many short-term Christian mission teams coming and going. Utilising the tenets of an action research paradigm, she evaluates the impact from both ends of the spectrum – the sending community and the receiving community of her village.

Her findings demonstrate that, in the main, the sending community arrives with altruistic motives; however, often they lack the necessary cultural competence with little or no understanding of the socio-economic and socio-political issues impacting on their receiving community. With the demands on their time in the Global North, they come for increasingly shorter periods of time, mostly during their work or school vacation, with set ideas of their one- to two-week programme that they believe will improve the lives of the poor rural community to which they come. For the receiving community, there are mixed responses. Community leaders also have goals and visions of how to improve the life of their communities. However, many factors hamper meaningful dialogue of the actual needs of the community, often resulting in the priorities of the sending churches barely corresponding to those of the receiving community. The chapter critically analyses these issues and seeks to identify whether empowerment and self-determination have been promoted among the ethnic Karen in the context of missio-tourism, or whether it has only been a case for occasional 'assistencialism' with overly ambitious expectations in achieving local development.

The final chapter in this section by Eerang Park, Toulakham Phandanouvong, Phouvanh Xaysena and Sankyun Kim entitled 'Empowerment, Participation and Barriers: Ethnic Minority Community-based Ecotourism Development in Lao PDR' continues the focus on Asia and the community-based ecotourism (CBET) approach. Our collection of essays demonstrates that CBET has gained increasing attention from tourism researchers and practitioners involved in rural and/or ethnic minority community-based development, particularly in developing countries. The chapter investigates how community empowerment plays a vital role in encouraging ethnic minority communities to become more active in taking part in the CBET development and thereby increase their positive perceptions towards its impacts on their communities. It also identifies and discusses factors which present barriers to community-based participation and empowerment.

The findings are based on two case studies of CBET projects in Lao PDR – Ban Na village in Bolikhamxay province and Houay Kaeng village in Sayabouly province. The first project is an ecotourism development in Phou Khao Khouay National Protected Area (PKKNPA) established in 2003 by the National Tourism Administration of Lao PDR (LNTA) in collaboration with the Management of Phou Khao Khouay National Park, the Department of Forestry and the German Development Service (DED). The latter is a more recent CBET project as part of the Greater Mekong Sub-Region – Sustainable Tourism Development Project (GMS-STDP) funded by the Asian Development Bank (ADB). The chapter unravels the dynamics and complexities of community empowerment, local participation and the barriers faced by local communities in the context of CBET in Lao PDR.

While the first section of our volume focuses on collective and organisational responses to development projects and to the changes which ensue from government and other policy and practical interventions in ethnic tourism and ecotourism, the second section covers the theme of 'Ethnic Entrepreneurship, Tourism and Ethnodevelopment'. It examines individual and entrepreneurial engagements with the opportunities provided by the tourism industry. Entrepreneurship and the encouragement of small businesses in such areas as tourism is, on a global scale, increasingly promoted as a prime motor for economic development, not least in rural areas where there has often been a dramatic decline in primary industries and there are few viable alternatives.

In the first chapter in this section we move to Latin America. Ingeborg Nordbø in 'Indigenous Micro Tourism Businesses, Ethnodevelopment and NGOs: Projectitis in Lago Budi in Chile' focuses on government activities which are encouraging local citizens, through a number of policy instruments and supporting initiatives, to establish and develop entrepreneurial activities and organise their own private tourism businesses and projects. In this chapter, qualitative interviews and concepts and theories from institutional theory on organisations and social origins are used to shed light on an NGO-initiated rural tourism entrepreneurship project in an indigenous development area in Lago Budi, in the south of Chile. Particular attention is devoted to ethnic empowerment and inclusion as conceptual elements of ethnodevelopment. It is argued that NGOs are embedded in a set of relationships with stakeholders, particularly donors, and they have to work with rural communities whose historical circumstance and trajectories, and, in this case the continued influence of patron–client relations make the introduction of entrepreneurial values and practices exceedingly difficult. The case study demonstrates that the fostering of a spirit of independence rather than dependence and the encouragement of a forward-looking attitude rather than one of passivity have presented the NGO involved in the project with particular challenges.

Then Akhmad Saufi, Sacha Reid and Anop Patiar in 'Understanding Host Community's Experiences of Creating Small Autochthonous Tourism Enterprises in Lombok, Indonesia' consider how entrepreneurship might provide the means to stimulate host community participation in tourism development, particularly in developing countries. However, they argue that to stimulate the emergence of indigenous tourism entrepreneurs it requires an understanding of the entrepreneurial process itself. Unfortunately, our understanding of this process in tourism, especially among host communities and indigenous entrepreneurs, continues to remain unclear due to the lack of research on community-based participation in tourism development.

This chapter seeks specifically to provide insights into the indigenous entrepreneurial process in the tourism industry, the context in which the process occurs, and the entrepreneurial strategies that support the process. The study was conducted in five tourist destinations on the island of Lombok in Indonesia. There is a commonly experienced tourism entrepreneurial journey among indigenous entrepreneurs in Lombok throughout the lifecycle of an enterprise, from identifying an orientation towards entrepreneurial activity, through to the establishment and development of tourism businesses. However, host communities and local entrepreneurs are influenced by entrepreneurial cultures unique to locales and must employ coping mechanisms to navigate their way on this journey. This research has identified a range of entrepreneurial coping patterns employed by indigenous tourism entrepreneurs. Overall the study's wide-ranging investigation highlights the important role played by indigenous tourism entrepreneurs and the strategies they implement to build and maintain successful enterprises. This is particularly relevant in providing an understanding of small-scale entrepreneurship in tourism from which other host communities and cultures can hopefully learn.

We then return to Asian experiences in Yang Ningdong and La Mingqing's chapter entitled 'Community Entrepreneurship, Female Elite and Cultural Inheritance: Mosuo Women's Empowerment and the Hand-Weaving Factory'. The Mosuo people are located in the southwest of China. They have a unique matrilineal kinship and marriage system combined with the traditional handicraft of weaving undertaken by Mosuo women. In the past 30 years a place called Lugu Lake in the Mosuo homeland has become a famous tourist destination and tourists have shown an increasing interest in their hand-woven fabrics. To take advantage of this development a local Mosuo woman, A Qi Du Zhi Ma, established a weaving factory to produce traditional manually woven handicrafts using the skills inherited from their ancestors. Under her leadership and with the help of the local government and some third-party organisations, the factory has become a famous ethnic tourism enterprise in that area. The chapter critically presents this enterprise as an excellent example of indigenous entrepreneurship within the framework of an ethnodevelopment programme. This type of family ethnic enterprise points the way forward to the possibilities for income generation and subsequently empowerment in a locally fragile economy of an indigenous minority population.

In the following chapter we move to a European case study. Cecilia de Bernardi, Outi Kugapi and Monika Lüthje in their chapter 'Sámi Indigenous Ecotourism Empowerment in the Nordic Countries through Labelling Systems:

Strengthening Ethnic Enterprises and Activities' argue that tourism can have both positive and negative outcomes for indigenous Sámi communities. They acknowledge that ethnic tourism has been charged in many studies with having negative effects on local communities. For example, it has been argued that tourism has exploited natural and cultural resources and excluded local communities from the decision-making process. However, the authors argue, as we have seen in earlier chapters, that community-based ecotourism (CBET), although it too has its problems, could be a solution to this kind of dilemma. The main issue is to find a positive balance between tourism and local communities, for example by introducing an eco-label as a means of the certification of locally produced products and services. In drawing attention to labelling the authors have in mind the formulation and agreement of a set of predetermined criteria to which companies decide to adhere in order to gain visibility so that indigenous products and services can be easily identified.

A labelling system could be the means to empower indigenous communities, give more grounds for self-determination and benefit the local populations economically. It might also make the tourists, as well as the indigenous populations themselves, aware of the local culture and heritage by learning from each other. Furthermore, the authors argue that both parties can also learn about nature and how to respect and not exploit it. This chapter discusses different aspects of the adoption of labelling systems in indigenous CBET companies and activities. With the help of labelling, tourists have the possibility to consciously choose to visit Sámi-managed enterprises, which would provide them, not only with meaningful tourism experiences, but also with a story of Sámi culture told by the Sámi themselves.

The final section of the book entitled 'Empowerment Approaches in Ethnic Tourism: Issues of Authenticity, Cultural Commodification and Gender' addresses crucial conceptual issues in tourism studies, that is debates about the staging and invention of culture and authenticity, and the effects of the commodification on culture and the changing role of gender in tourism development. The first chapter in the section, which is an excursion into cross-cultural encounters by Tuhina Ganguly and Mike Grimshaw entitled 'Exotic Tourist, Ethnic Hosts: A Critical Approach to Tourism and Ethnodevelopment', situates itself within studies of the commodification of 'the Other' in ethnic tourism. Where ethnic minorities are marketed by governments and the tourism industry specifically for their 'exotic' appeal, issues arise around cultural consumption and unequal power relations in host–guest interactions. Based on Ganguly's auto-ethnographic record of a trip to Cuzco and Machu Picchu in Peru, this chapter focuses on ethnodevelopment in the context of the Quechua people. However, previous studies on the commodification of 'the Other' are primarily contextualised within the distinction between white Western tourists and exotic non-white hosts. This represents a problematical gap in tourism studies because middle-class tourists from so-called exotic countries like India are increasingly travelling to overseas destinations due to their enhanced consumption power. This chapter addresses the gap in existing literature by examining power relations between Ganguly as an Indian outbound tourist to Peru and the indigenous hosts. It shows that commodification of the ethnic hosts is generated by both Western and non-Western tourists (Ganguly specifically) even as the latter is treated as the 'exotic Other' by her Western fellow-tourists. Using post-colonial theory, this chapter argues the case for tourism studies to undertake a detailed examination of the power dynamics between tourists and hosts where such interactions are clearly transgressing the white tourist/non-white tourist binary. These new developments also have important ramifications for determining host agency and self-determination, and for addressing cultural consumption within changing tourism situations. The authors suggest that measures to support the empowerment of the Quechua people through tourism must go beyond recognising the politics involved in First World/Third World interactions to envisage complex tourism exchanges brought by a rapidly expanding and diverse global middle class.

Clarissa Gagliardi's and Rosana Bignami's chapter on 'The Legacy of Black People and Dialectic Inclusion-Exclusion in the Building of the Cultural Heritage of a Tourist Destination in Vale do Paraíba' analyses to what extent the neglect of Black history related to the slave period in the Paraíba Valley, a Brazilian coffee-producing region during the nineteenth century, has hindered the recognition of this territory as a historic place as well as its consolidation as a tourist destination shared between different social segments, despite having a wealth of natural and cultural attractions. Articulated here are Bourdieu's concepts of field, social space and symbolic capital (Bourdieu 1989; Hilgers and Mangez 2014). From the discourses of different social segments, the study of the transformations in the Paraíba Valley as the result of tourism development and the discussion of how the construction of tourism public policies is established, we can begin to appreciate how local identity is produced and which social relations are capable of generating empowerment, inclusion and the self-determination of populations. What is in focus is also the capacity of local actors to recognise themselves as subjects in the construction of networks necessary for tourism development. What we need to analyse is the reassignment of the meaning of places and memories from the point of view of tourism, as well as its capacity to boost confidence as an important pillar in the construction of social capital. The chapter supports the findings of research which has been conducted by the authors since 2003 and aims to support their analysis regarding the planning and management of tourist destinations based on the use of cultural heritage. Above all the chapter contributes to the studies of ethnodevelopment in relation to the processes of inclusion/exclusion of black ethnicity in the process of heritage enhancement through tourism.

Lorraine Nicholas and Brijesh Thapa's chapter entitled 'Tourism in the Fond Gens Libre Indigenous Community in Saint Lucia: Examining Impacts and Empowerment' considers the small remote, rural community of Fond Gens Libre situated in the southwest region of the Caribbean island of Saint Lucia, near the town of Soufriere. Literally translated from the local Creole language as 'valley of the free people', Fond Gens Libre is an old settlement dating back to the 1700s and is known as the home of the descendants of the Brigands (runaway slaves). A major attraction of the community is the Gros Piton Nature Trail which is a unique attraction endowed with a blend of natural, cultural and historical resources which has generated the development of tourism in the community. In addition to the tours and group hikes, a visitor and interpretive centre is located in the community to educate domestic and international visitors about the cultural and natural resources to be found there. The evolution and transformation of the Fond Gens Libre community is to a large extent the result of tourism development. This chapter delineates the impacts of tourism in Fond Gens Libre; specifically, it provides a comparative analysis of the community pre- and post-tourism development, and examines the role of tourism in shaping the socio-cultural, economic and environmental landscape. This research utilises information gathered via primary and secondary sources.

Thais Alves Marinho, in the following chapter on 'Ethnodevelopment in Kalunga's Community-based Tourism: From a Past Marked by Slavery to Ethnic Group Struggles for Empowerment and Recognition', argues that the increasing cultural appreciation for maroon communities in Brazil has been evidenced from the current relationships established in the Kalunga community, the largest maroon community of the country, located in the northeast of Goias State. The traditional local organisation allowed the formation of a new market, whose essence is on refreshing the past into the present. The interest in this form of cultural and economic life, which once was thought extinct, is now consumed with nostalgia and romanticism by visitors, who are motivated by the absence of this authentic rural life in the ultra-technological routine of cities. Therefore the main focus of public policies among the maroon has been that of sustainable local development, which takes advantage of the opening and expansion of markets for handicrafts and for traditional and local ethnic-ecological organic products at both national and international levels. This chapter seeks to evaluate the elective affinities between this trend and the growing demand for ecotourism and for ethno-cultural tourism. Despite the fact that ethnodevelopment in this context favours the community's inclusion and empowerment, it has also brought new challenges to the ways of living developed in Kalunga territory, as it adds a culturalist and essentialist requirement for recognition of the value of the group, which in many cases acts to contradict self-determination. To understand this dynamic the results of an ethnographic study are used to demonstrate the identity and territorial reinterpretations that have occurred and are occurring in the processes of ethnodevelopment.

The volume reaches the conclusion with a very short chapter by Victor T. King and Ismar Borges de Lima which reflects on the core themes and concepts of the book and suggests that the case material from South and Central America, Europe and Asia fills a significant conceptual and empirical gap in our thinking about the issues surrounding ethnodevelopment. Although there is a considerable literature on tourism and its relationship to socio-cultural and economic development, there is still a lack of ethnographic research and comparative studies on tourism used as a development tool among marginalised, minority communities and as a means to enhance local identities and resilience within the context of the nation-state and in interaction with a range of interest groups and stakeholders.

References

Agrawal, A. (1995) Dismantling the divide between indigenous and scientific knowledge. *Development and Change* 26, 413–39.

Anaya, S. J. (2004) *Indigenous Peoples in International Law*. New York: Oxford University Press.

Andolina, R., Radcliffe, S. and Laurie, N. (2005) Development and culture: transnational identity-making in Bolivia. *Political Geography* 24(6), 678–702.

Ascher, W. and Heffron, J. M. (2010) Conclusions: intertwining cultural adaptation and economic development. In W. Ascher and J. M. Heffron (eds), *Cultural Change and Persistence: New Perspectives on Development*. New York: Palgrave Macmillan, pp. 233–44.

Bacal, A. (1991) *Ethnicity in the Social Sciences: A View and Review of the Literature on Ethnicity*, Reprint Papers in Ethnic Relations No. 3. University of Warwick: Centre for Research in Ethnic Relations.

Barth, F. (ed.) (1969) *Ethnic Groups and Boundaries: The Social Organization of Culture Difference*. Bergen and Oslo: Universitets Forlager and London: George Allen & Unwin.

Bengoa, J. (1993) Development with identity: the issue of indigenous development in Latin America. In J. E. Uquillas and J. Rivera (eds), *Indigenous Peoples and Development in Latin America: Proceedings from the Second Inter-Agency Workshop on Indigenous Peoples and Development in Latin America*. Washington, DC: World Bank Regional Office for Latin America and the Caribbean, pp. 58–66.

Bonfil Batalla, G. (1982) *El Etnodesarrollo: sus premisas jurídicas, políticas y de organización. América Latina: Etnodesarrollo y Etnocidio*. San José, Costa Rica: Ediciones FLACSO, pp. 133–45.

Boulanger, C. L. (2009) *A Sleeping Tiger: Ethnicity, Class and New Dayak Dreams in Urban Sarawak*. Lanham, MD and Plymouth, UK: University Press of America.

Bourdieu, P. (1989) Social space and symbolic power. *Sociological Theory* 7(1), 14–25.

Campos, M. V., Scott, N. and Breakey, N. (2014) Ecotourism: a new challenge for protected rainforest areas in Chile. In B. Prideaux (ed.), *Rainforest Tourism, Conservation and Management: Challenges for Sustainable Development*. London and New York: Earthscan/Routledge, pp. 134–45.

Chernela, J. M. (2011) Indigenous rights and ethno-development: the life of an indigenous organization in the Rio Negro of Brazil'. *Tipití: Journal of the Society for the Anthropology of Lowland South America* 9 (Special Issue 2, article 5), Available at: http://digitalcommons.trinity.edu/tipiti/vol9/iss2/5.

Clarke, G. (2001) From ethnocide to ethnodevelopment? Ethnic minorities and indigenous peoples in Southeast Asia. *Third World Quarterly* 22(3), 413–36.

Cooper, C. and Hall, M. C. (eds) (2005) *Oceania: A Tourism Handbook*. Clevedon, UK: Channel View Publications.

Davis, S. (1993) *Indigenous Views of Land and Environment*, World Bank Discussion Paper No. 188. Washington, DC: World Bank.

Davis, S. (2002) Indigenous peoples, poverty and participatory development: the experience of the World Bank in Latin America. In R. Sieder (ed.), *Multiculturalism in Latin*

America: Indigenous Rights, Diversity and Democracy. New York: Palgrave Macmillan, pp. 227–51.

Davis, S. and Ebbe, K. (eds) (1993) *Traditional Knowledge and Sustainable Development*, World Bank, Environmentally Sustainable Development Proceedings Series No. 4. Washington, DC: World Bank.

Davis, S. and Partridge, W. (1994) *Promoting the Development of Indigenous Peoples in Latin America – Report*. Washington, DC: World Bank.

Dentan, R. K. (1975) If there were no Malays who would the Semai be? In J. A. Nagata (ed.), *Pluralism in Malaysia: Myth and Reality*. Leiden: E. J. Brill, pp. 50–64.

Dentan, R. K. (1976) Ethnics and Ethics in Southeast Asia. In Banks, D. J. (ed.) *Changing Identities in Modern Southeast Asia*. The Hague and Paris: Mouton, pp. 71–81.

Drakakis-Smith, D. (1996) Ethnicity, development and geography. In D. Dwyer and D. Drakakis-Smith (eds), *Ethnicity and Development: Geographical Perspectives*. Chichester: John Wiley & Sons, pp. 273–82.

Du Gay, P., Evans, J. and Redman, P. (eds) (2000a) *Identity: A Reader*. London, Thousand Oaks, CA and New Delhi: Sage.

Du Gay, P., Evans, J. and Redman, P. (2000b) General introduction. In P. Du Gay, J. Evans and P. Redman (eds), *Identity: A Reader*. London, Thousand Oaks, CA and New Delhi, pp. 1–5.

Dwyer, D. (1996) Ethnodevelopment or ethnochaos? In D. Dwyer and D. Drakakis-Smith (eds), *Ethnicity and Development: Geographical Perspectives*. Chichester: John Wiley & Sons, pp. 3–12.

Dwyer, D. and Drakakis-Smith, D. (eds) (1996) *Ethnicity and Development: Geographical Perspectives*. Chichester: John Wiley & Sons.

Edelman, M. and Haugerud, A. (2005) *The Anthropology of Development and Globalization: From Classical Political Economy to Contemporary Neoliberalism*. Oxford: Blackwell.

Edelman, M. and Haugerud, A. (2007) Development. In D. Nugent and J. Vincent (eds), *A Companion to the Anthropology of Politics*. Oxford: Blackwell, pp. 86–106.

Gardner, K. and Lewis, D. (2011) Beyond development? In M. Edelman and A. Haugerud (eds), *The Anthropology of Development and Globalization: From Classical Political Economy to Contemporary Neoliberalism*. Oxford: Blackwell, pp. 352–9.

Grünewald, R. de A. (2006 [2003]) Tourism and ethnicity. *Horizontes Antropológicos* 9(20), 141–59, trans. Alberto Sanchez Allred, 2006.

Haugerud, A. (2003) The disappearing local: rethinking global-local connections. In A. Mirsepassi, A. Basu and F. Weaver (eds), *Localizing Knowledge in a Globalizing World: Recasting the Area Studies Debates*. Syracuse, NY: Syracuse University Press, pp. 60–81.

Hayward, J. (2012) *Biculturalism, Te Ara – The Encyclopedia of New Zealand*, http://www.TeAra.govt.nz/en/biculturalism (accessed 30 December 2016).

Hettne, B. (1993) Ethnicitiy and development – an elusive relationship. *Contemporary South Asia* 2(2), 123–49.

Hettne, B. (1996) Ethnicity and development: an elusive relationship. In D. Dwyer and D. Drakakis-Smith (eds), *Ethnicity and Development: Geographical Perspectives*. Chichester: John Wiley & Sons, pp. 15–44.

Hilgers, M. and Mangez, E. (2014) *Bourdieu's Theory of Social Fields: Concepts and Applications*. London: Routledge.

Hitchcock, M. and King, V. T. (eds) (1997) *Images of Malay-Indonesian Identity.* Kuala Lumpur: Oxford University Press.

Hogue, E. and Pilar, R. (2008) Troubled Water: ethnodevelopment, natural resource commodification, and neoliberalism in Andean Peru. *Urban Anthropology and Studies of Cultural Systems and World Economic Development* 37(3/4), 283–327.

Iorns, C. J. (1993) The draft declaration on the rights of indigenous peoples. *Murdoch University Electronic Journal of Law* 1(1). Available online at: http://www.austlii.edu.au/au/journals/MurUEJL/1993/2.html (accessed 28 December 2016).

Kahn, J. S. (1992) Class, ethnicity and diversity: some remarks on Malay culture in Malaysia. In J. S. Kahn and F. Loh Kok Wah (eds), *Fragmented Vision. Culture and Politics in Contemporary Malaysia*, Asian Studies Association of Australia, Southeast Asia Publications Series, 22. Sydney: Allen & Unwin, pp. 158–78.

King, V. T. (2009) Anthropology and tourism in Southeast Asia: comparative studies, cultural differentiation and agency. In M. Hitchcock, V. T. King and M. Parnwell (eds), *Tourism in Southeast Asia: Challenges and New Directions*. Copenhagen: NIAS Press and Honolulu, HI: University of Hawai'i Press, pp. 43–68.

King, V. T. and Wilder, W. D. (2003) *The Modern Anthropology of South-East Asia. An Introduction*, reprint 2006. London and New York: RoutledgeCurzon.

Leach, E. R. (1954) *Political Systems of Highland Burma. A Study of Kachin Social Structure*. London: G. Bell & Son.

MacCannell, D. (1976) *The Tourist: A New Theory of the Leisure Class*. New York: Schocken.

Myers Jr, S. L. and Corrie, B. P. (eds) (2006) *Racial and Ethnic Economic Inequality: An International Perspective*. New York: Peter Lang.

Nagata, J. A. (1975) Introduction. In J. A. Nagata (ed.), *Pluralism in Malaysia: Myth and Reality*. Leiden: E. J. Brill, pp. 1–16.

Nagata, J. A. (1979) *Malaysian Mosaic: Perspectives from a Poly-ethnic Society*. Vancouver, BC: University of British Columbia Press.

Partridge, W. L., Uquillas, J. E. and Johns, K. (1996) 'Including the excluded: ethnodevelopment in Latin America'. Unpublished paper presented at the Annual World Bank Conference on Development in Latin America and the Caribbean, Bogotá.

Picard, D. and Di Giovine, M. A. (eds) (2014) *Tourism and the Power of Otherness: Seductions of Difference, Tourism and Cultural Change*. Bristol: Channel View Publications.

Picard, M. (1996) *Bali: Cultural Tourism and Touristic Culture*, trans. D. Darling. Singapore: Archipelago Press.

Picard, M. and Wood, R. E. (eds) (1997a) *Tourism, Ethnicity and the State in Asian and Pacific Societies*. Honolulu, HI: University of Hawai'i Press.

Picard, M. and Wood, R. E. (1997b) Preface. In M. Picard, and R. E. Wood, *Tourism, Ethnicity and the State in Asian and Pacific Societies*. Honolulu, HI: University of Hawai'i Press, pp. vii–xi.

Radice, H. (2015) *Global Capitalism: Selected Essays*. New York: Routledge.

Rangan, V. (EED/Equations) (2005) *A WTO-GATS-Tourism Impact Assessment Framework for Developing Countries*, Sector Research Report. Bonn: EED/Equations.

Richter, L. K. (1989) *The Politics of Tourism in Asia*. Honolulu, HI: University of Hawai'i Press.

Rivera, I. A. K. (2012) 'Unpacking Ethno-Tourism: "Development with Identity", Tourism and Mapuche Struggles in South-Central Chile'. Unpublished MA thesis, University of Oregon, Environmental Studies Program. Available online at: https://scholarsbank.uoregon.edu/xmlui/bitstream/handle/1794/12518/KrellRivera_oregon_0171N_10499.pdf;sequence=1.

Rostow, W. W. (1960) *The Stages of Economic Growth: A Non-communist Manifesto.* Cambridge: Cambridge University Press.

Ryan, C. and Aicken, M. (eds) (2005) *Indigenous Tourism: The Commodification and Management of Culture*, Advances in Tourism Research Series. New York: Routledge.

Smith, V. L. (ed.) (1977 [1989]) *Hosts and Guests: The Anthropology of Tourism*, 2nd edn. Philadelphia: University of Pennsylvania Press, expanded and revised, 1989.

Stavenhagen, R. (1986) Ethnodevelopment: a neglected dimension in development thinking. In R. Apthorpe and A. Krahl (eds), *Development Studies: Critique and Renewal.* Leiden: E. J. Brill, pp. 71–94.

Stavenhagen, R. (1990) *The Ethnic Question: Conflicts, Development and Human Rights.* Tokyo: United Nations University Press.

Talalla, R. (1980) *Ethno-development and the Orang Asli of Malaysia: A Case Study of the Betau Settlement for Semai-Senoi*, Fourth World Studies in Planning No. 15. Los Angeles: University of California School of Architecture and Urban Planning.

Talalla, R. (1984) Ethnodevelopment and the Orang Asli of Malaysia: a case study of the Betau Settlement for Semai-Senoi. *Antipode* 16(2), 27–32.

Todtling, F. (2011) Endogenous approaches to local and regional development policy, In A. Pike, A. Rodriguez-Pose and J. Tomaney (eds), *Handbook of Local and Regional Development.* Abingdon: Routledge, pp. 333–43.

UNESCO (United Nations Educational, Scientific and Cultural Organization) (1982) *Meeting of Experts on the Study of Ethno-development and Ethnocide in Africa.* Paris: UNESCO, Division of Human Rights and Peace.

Uquillas, J. E. and Rivera, J. (eds) (1993) *Indigenous Peoples and Development in Latin America: Proceedings from the Second Inter-Agency Workshop on Indigenous Peoples and Development in Latin America.* Washington, DC: World Bank, Regional Office for Latin America and the Caribbean.

Van den Berghe, P. L. and Keyes, C. F. (eds) (1984a) Tourism and ethnicity. *Annals of Tourism Research* 11(3), 339–501.

Van den Berghe, P. L. and Keyes, C. F. (1984b) Introduction: tourism and re-created ethnicity. *Annals of Tourism Research* 11(3), 343–52.

Van Nieuwkoop, M. and Uquillas, J. E. (2000) *Defining Ethnodevelopment in Operational Terms: Lessons from the Ecuador Indigenous and Agro-Ecuadoran Peoples Development Project*, Sustainable Development Working Paper No. 6. Washington, DC: World Bank, Latin American and Caribbean Regional Office.

Willis, K. (2005) *Theories and Practices of Development*, Routledge Perspectives on Development. London and New York: Routledge.

Wood, R. E. (1997) Tourism and the state: ethnic options and constructions of otherness. In M. Picard and R. E. Wood (eds), *Tourism, Ethnicity and the State in Asian and Pacific Societies.* Honolulu, HI: University of Hawai'i Press, pp. 1–34.

Wright, R. M. (1988) Anthropological presuppositions of indigenous advocacy. *Annual Review of Anthropology* 17, 365–90.

Zeppel, H. D. (2003) Sharing the country: ecotourism policy and indigenous peoples in Australia. In D. Fennell and R. K. Dowling (eds), *Ecotourism Policy and Planning.* Wallingford: CAB International, pp. 55–76.

Zeppel, H. D. (2006) *Indigenous Ecotourism: Sustainable Development and Management*, Ecotourism Series No. 3. Wallingford: CAB International.

Part I

Institutionalised Ethnic Tourism and Advances in Ethnodevelopment

Policies, Communities, Organisations

2 Development for whom? Tourism used as a social intervention for the development of indigenous/rural communities in natural protected areas

Gerda Warnholtz and David Barkin

Introduction

Although indigenous communities are a minority in the world's population, their distinct characteristics have drawn the attention of all kinds of development agencies for a long time. Within the high diversity of cosmologies and worldviews these communities have, they share a powerful interaction between poverty, ethnicity and natural environment, as well as strong internal social, cultural, economic and political organisations. These traits represent challenging factors for external social interventions (SIs) seeking their sustainable development (SD); the question is to privilege the communities' needs and expectations and their conception of development in concurrence with the theories of SIs, targeting the real mechanisms to trigger beneficial changes within these communities (Stavenhagen 2002). But the questions are what makes these social groups so important for international, national and local development agencies? Why are so many governmental and non-governmental organisations interested in providing these communities not only with survival alternatives, but also with SD opportunities? And why is tourism considered and used as a tool for this purpose? To answer these questions, it seems necessary to put into perspective what indigenous peoples represent for the future of the world's natural and cultural heritage, and the factors considered for the inclusion of tourism as an effective tool to improve their livelihoods.

The worldwide indigenous population is estimated at around 370 million, and represents about one-third of the global poor (United Nations, 2009). Many of them live in developing countries, in geographically isolated, rural areas and often in extreme poverty. Their traditional territories cover up to 24 per cent of the Earth's surface and around 80 per cent of the healthy ecosystems on the planet overlap with indigenous territories (Watanabe 2008). More importantly, they are the keepers of most of the world's cultural intangible heritage (Stavenhagen 2002).

It was only during the early 1970s, with the appearance of *The Limits to Growth*, a report prepared by the MIT for the Club of Rome, that attention was actively drawn towards the global environmental crisis. Natural protected areas (NPAs) and biosphere reserves were created with the purpose of conserving, protecting and eventually restoring the world's ecosystems, along with their correspondent management schemes (Chape *et al.* 2008; Bray *et al.* 2007). The establishment of these areas has generated specific management schemes implying control of the use of land and natural resources. Seeking to lower NPA inhabitants' dependence on farming, gathering and hunting, initiatives including the insertion of productive projects and activities that add value to local products have been implemented. The intention is to increase the communities' income in order to improve the communities' living conditions. Indigenous/rural communities living within NPAs have thus been forced to modify their living habits and traditional relationship with their territories; the centrally determined management policies have affected the communities' socio-cultural, economic and political structures, causing conflicts both internally as well as between them and the NPAs' management teams (Oltremari and Jackson 2006; Monterroso 2008).

The combination of poverty, indigenous peoples, cultural heritage at risk and endangered natural resources represent an important combination of issues which call for extremely carefully planned policies. SD and poverty reduction agencies, governments and NGOs have established a strong agenda of SIs following the SD paradigm to help indigenous communities in general out of backwardness, to preserve and protect their traditional knowledge and cultural heritage, and to preserve and protect biodiversity. The emphasis has been mostly set on the triple bottom-line approach, which seeks the balance of the social, environmental and economic dimensions of SD through social responsibility measures (Secretary-General of the UN Economic and Social Council 2016; Brundtland 1987; Parkin *et al.* 2003).

Given the natural and cultural assets available, and the rapid expansion of the activity in peripheral countries, tourism has been regarded as a possible trigger for the development of local host communities for a long time (de Kadt 1979b; Barkin 1976; van den Berghe 1994). The possibility of attracting investment, foreign currency, creating jobs and eventually creating the opportunity for economic growth for the host countries and communities has caused the incorporation of the activity as part of the poverty reduction and SD agenda, especially for peripheral countries with natural and cultural assets. Local governments have complied with the signature of international treaties through the inclusion of the development of tourism into their development programmes, at both the macro- and the micro-economic levels.

The idea of combining the expansion of tourism with the economic growth of host countries and communities made sense within the pro-poor growth (PPG) model. This model has been defined by several agencies as economic growth that effectively helps reduce poverty (OECD 2006; ODI 2008), while others specify that PPG can only be called so when the income of the poor has a stronger increase in relationship to that of the non-poor, making an important difference in the concept, but also leaving the benefit of the poor as a secondary issue (Kakwani and Pernia 2000). Derived from this general economic growth model, pro-poor tourism (PPT) and community-based tourism (CBT) were conceived as guidelines for developing tourism, and at the same time for relatively increasing the host community members' income (Chok *et al.* 2007; Saayman and Giampiccoli 2016). PPT was coined in a study commissioned in 1999 by the

Department of International Development (DFID) in the UK to assess the possibilities tourism has to contribute to poverty reduction and SD. This led to the inclusion of tourism in the International Millennium Goals Agenda as a tool for poverty alleviation and SD in 2002 (UN-WTO 2002; Bennett *et al.* 1999).

The inclusion of tourism as a tool for SD is based upon PPT, as is the Sustainable Tourism – Eliminating Poverty (ST-EP) programme, launched at the World Summit for Sustainable Development held in Johannesburg in 2002 (Scheyvens 2007). However, while PPT is basically concerned with the development of tourism and the eventual and relative benefit of the poor, the discourse of the development agencies proposes the actual use of tourism as a motor for the SD of the host communities. Although the difference of approach may seem insignificant, according to the definition of PPT the idea of equity for the host communities and their individual members is related to the definition of relative justice, which considers a more just distribution of given assets, such as education, income and communication, in contrast with that of absolute justice, which implies the existence of fundamental rights and freedoms, as well as capabilities necessary for the well-being of the social group and of the individual (Sachs 2010). Consequently, it can be suggested that PPT may be applied to the tourism sector and its development in general, but it is difficult to consistently relate it to the benefit of the host communities.

CBT in turn can be tracked back to the late 1970s/early 1980s. It emerges as a response to the mass tourism model, which had proven highly disruptive of the local socio-cultural and natural environments, and is closely related to the community-based development trend (de Kadt 1979a; Murphy 1983; Zapata *et al.* 2011). Although consensus has not been reached regarding its definition, CBT is naturally regarded as a for-profit economic activity, and has usually been associated with community-based enterprises. In CBT projects, terms like participation, self-determination, empowerment and inclusion are considered fundamental for their success, although there is dispute about what can be called CBT, depending on the degree of participation and decision-making of the host community's members (Mtapuri and Giampiccoli 2014; Manyara and Jones 2007; Strasdas 2005; Rojas and Martínez 2012). However, on the one hand, these concepts basically refer to individuals, or to the small group within the host community, which is/are in charge of the tourism project, rather than to the social group as a whole. On the other hand, they are rooted in the relative justice definition, giving more importance to economic growth and access to services and given assets than to the increase of rights and freedoms or to the communal well-being.

Even though there is still no agreed definition of CBT, or of PPT, they do share basic concepts such as *poverty alleviation* and *sustainable development* as well as the intention of generating positive environmental impacts. These approaches to tourism development share the PPG paradigm, as well as the idea of tourism as a for-profit economic activity, and have been regarded as effective elements to develop tourism in a more responsible manner. Accordingly, PPT and CBT have been used as fundamental conceptual premises, not only to plan, design and apply tourism development policies at a macro-economic level, but also at a micro-economic level, using tourism as a tool to alleviate poverty and foster the development of the host communities. Furthermore, these concepts have served as a basis for most of the research done to analyse both sustainable tourism development and the performance of tourism projects inserted into host communities for their benefit, focusing on tourism activity and its economic performance, failing to provide answers on the tourism project as an SI to trigger positive social change within the host communities (Warnholtz 2016).

The analysis of tourism as an SI for the benefit of a social group necessarily shifts the attention from the tourism business performance to the social change triggered by the intervention, and the scope moves from the business success/failure factors to the evaluation of highly complex SIs seeking social change involving at the same time social, economic, cultural and political betterment, as well as the protection of the natural environment. Consequently, the emphasis lies upon the community's needs and expectations rather than on the tourism project; the analysis needs to be carried out in terms of expected/unexpected outcomes of the intervention and of the social change to be achieved, with the success/failure of the business considered as a secondary issue. However, analysing tourism as an SI seeking social betterment poses important conceptual and methodological challenges. The task calls for an adequate conceptual framework as well as for a specific research toolbox that helps shed light upon the issue, and the first steps are to understand which are the indigenous communities living within NPAs and to clarify the basic concepts that underpin SIs' social objectives and their evaluation (see Figure 2.1).

Figure 2.1 Tapiscando, Chiapas, Mexico.
(Photo: Antonio Turok)

Indigenous communities and their internal organisation

The common traits of indigenous communities worldwide, in Latin America generally and Mexico in particular, is on the one hand their socio-cultural diversity, and on the other the particularities of their internal social, cultural, economic and political structures and institutions (Bohanon 1981; Douglas 1981; Barambah 2011; Díaz Gómez 1994). According to Díaz Gómez (1994), indigenous communities define themselves in two dimensions: the first is the concept of *community*, which is a complex system explained through its evident traits: a social group that, besides sharing a common history, also shares a present and a future, and is not just a compound of houses inhabited by individuals. It is understood in terms of the symbolic relationship of the group with its natural environment, beyond their mere physical location, and interaction between the social group and with the environment are considered above individual interactions and relationships; the rules of coexistence are established and interpreted based on nature itself and on experiences passed from one generation to another and collectively determined.

The second dimension is what is called *communality*, which is the support of what has been described as *community*. Communality is defined by intangible notions of land as mother earth and as traditional territory, decision-making through democratic consensus reached within the communal assembly, the social value of work, unpaid work in public service, and rites and ceremonies as the expression of the community's cultural heritage. In this sense, it is necessary to understand the notions of the *communal* as the collective, complementarity and completeness, to comprehend the apparent elements of the *community*. Without considering these notions, the understanding of the community and its internal workings will be limited. The interactions between these two dimensions and among the different elements represent the community's complex operating system. However, the communal way of life is not always explicit; it is always tacitly present in these communities, and usually becomes evident the moment an individualistic attitude emerges (Martínez Luna 2011; Rendón Monzón 2003; Díaz Gómez 1994). The collective essence defining indigenous communities has been amply documented by several anthropological studies (cf. Bonfil Batalla 1995b; Barthas 1997; Rendón Monzón 2003, among others).

Indigenous life is only possible in a specific territory, which is symbolically owned, understood and appropriated (Rendón Monzón 2003), inhabited by people and nature, and often by supernatural forces which interact within it, and whose interrelationships are ritually determined based on and explained through myths and other narratives. This territory is commonly owned and is home to the community, which is composed of families, intertwined by kinship, power and ritual links and which builds their community life based on reciprocity and participation as a fundamental rule. Reciprocity and participation are represented through common and voluntary labour, the exercise of power, and rituals and festivities, which have a communal character and are conceived to achieve collective goals and to solve collective problems (Rendón Monzón 2003;

Martínez Luna 2011). The family, inter-familial and inter-communitarian relationships are also determined by reciprocity and participation, and it is based on these and common and voluntary labour that collectivity is constructed: labour exercising power, labour in economic activities, and labour in festivities and rituals which give identity and rootedness to the social group (Barabas 2004).

These social groups also express their will of being part of their community through reciprocity and participation through common labour, which is never paid work. This, for them, is not only a duty, but also a sense of identity, engagement and rootedness: to symbolically and effectively collaborate and participate means to belong to the community. For this reason, those who refuse inter-familial labour or mutual help, which in different areas is called *tequio*, *faena* or *fagina*, or reject the charges they are elected for, or cease to participate in the festivities, imply that they do not want to be part of the community and hence are willing to lose their rights (Millán and Valle 2003).

It is possible for a member of the community to refuse to speak the local language, or wear traditional clothing and/or even to stop participating in common rituals, but to stop serving the community is absolutely unacceptable (Rendón Monzón 2003; Robles Hernández and Cardoso Jiménez 2007; Díaz Gómez 1994). Furthermore, those who have migrated and live somewhere else obviously cannot work within the community, but if they express their willingness to remain part of the collectivity they can do so by sending money to support the festivities or for the betterment of public infrastructure, or seek people who do their common labour for them. Some of them may even return to the community to take over charges for which they have been elected by the assembly, in which all heads of family have a voice and a democratic vote (Díaz Gómez 1994; Martínez Luna 2011).

This kind of social organisation is not exclusive of indigenous social groups. Many non-indigenous rural communities have the same traditions of reciprocity, participation and common labour, and decision-making through their assembly, and this may be explained through the historically common ownership of the land and the close relationship these social groups have with it. What distinguishes these communities from indigenous communities is their ethno-cultural elements: the local organisation based on the common language, their particular worldviews (which usually have their origins in pre-Hispanic times) and their corresponding rituals and festivities, the use of traditional clothing and the local cuisine, among many other issues. It could be stated that indigenous/rural communities base their social life upon the four fundamental elements of common life, and that the difference is defined by the degree of conservation or loss of the complementary elements (Rendón Monzón 2003; Bonfil Batalla 2012; Warman 2003; Zizumbo Villarreal 2013).

Common ownership of the land and/or the symbolic appropriation of the territory, along with the participatory and reciprocal character of labour and the ancient worldviews, not only shape the specific identity of an indigenous community, these elements, combined with the geographic isolation of indigenous/rural communities within or near NPAs, present a complex economic organisation weakly linked to the mainstream market, in which money and prices (fundamental for capitalist economic relations), are secondary issues (Kuokkanen 2011; Yates 2014; López Ángel 2001). They still barter among themselves and nearby communities as money is not their main exchange factor. The practical absence of paid labour gives their work a social value rather than a monetary price. Furthermore, the subsistence character of their economy prevents them from having a notion of accumulation or financial planning. Finally, their relationship with the mainstream market is marginal, as is their understanding of a service-based economic activity. For these social groups, money is useful only to relate with the *outside* and acquire goods or services that are not locally available. Hence, the insertion of tourism in these social structures may pose a serious challenge for the activity to succeed, as well as a huge risk of disruption for the local socio-cultural and socio-economic traditional structures.

Sustainable development versus ethnodevelopment

Development, sustainability and the combination thereof have been heavily contested concepts. While development within the neo-liberal paradigm is understood basically as economic growth and progress (OECD 2006; Bennett *et al.* 1999), under alternative economic theories, it refers to the qualitative improvement of the livelihood of a given social group, making the concept more complex and giving income a secondary role (Barkin and Lemus 2015; Esteva 2010; Guillén 2004; Barkin 2005). The concept of sustainability can also be defined at different levels of complexity; it may be simplistically related to environmental issues, or given a more holistic scope under the so-called triple bottom line, incorporating the notion of balance between social, environmental and economic aspects, or be brought to a more complex system that involves the entire ecosystem, including the communities living within it. This implies intricate internal/external political, economic and social relationships, along with the complex interaction between humans and the natural environment and the conservation and reproduction of their cultural heritage and cosmologies (Walters and Takamura 2015; Stanford 2008; Sutawa 2012; Milne and Ateljevic 2001).

Furthermore, the concept of development has consistently been related to a greater or lesser degree to those of self-determination, equity and empowerment (Duflo 2012; Moghadam 1990; Boley and McGehee 2014). The question is the degree of relevance these concepts have within the SI, and to what extent they apply to the individual rather than to the community as a whole. In the mainstream economic system, the well-being of the individual has become the centre of attention, while, as stated before, for indigenous communities the well-being of the individual depends on that of the community; collective well-being is considered above that of the individual, which leads to giving preference to concepts like autonomy, solidarity, self-sufficiency, productive diversification, participative decision-making, common labour and sustainable management. SI as tools for social change responding to centrally determined policy naturally focus on the individual's well-being and on the integration of the target population into the mainstream market (Secretary-General of the UN Economic and Social Council 2016; Le Blanc 2015).

Although for a long time the concept of development and sustainability was associated with social and economic progress, critical voices have appeared over the last 30 years, proposing alternative ways to development and sustainability. These alternatives define development as an intrinsic process to a given social group, and is determined by local needs and circumstances (Bustelo 1998). In this sense, Bonfil Batalla (1995a: 467) states that:

> Ethnodevelopment is the capacity of a social group to build its future, drawing on the lessons of their historical experience, as well as of their real and potential cultural resources, according to a project that corresponds to their own values and future aspirations; in consequence, the process of ethnodevelopment requires the compliance with a number of given conditions and requirements.

In concurrence with the concepts of indigenous community and communality, and with the absolute definition of equity, ethnodevelopment, emphasises diversity, rootedness and ethnicity; it integrates particular forms of cultural production and re-production, and claims the right to diversity and to cultural processes determined and managed by and for their social group. It privileges reciprocity, collective participation, common labour and the well-being of the community above that of the individual; all closely related with the determination of preserving and protecting local identity and tradition within their own structures and institutions, within a local context which needs to create linkages with the global. This poses in consequence a challenge to the Western definition of development and its underpinning values of the neo-liberal mainstream market, relative equity, self-determination and empowerment, which are terms derived from prioritising individual well-being and interests over those of the community.

In this sense, externally designed, funded and applied SIs may be conflicting with the internal and dynamic socio-cultural, socio-political and economic structures of the target communities, as well as with their most valuable tourism assets: their rootedness and identity. In concurrence with the concept of ethnodevelopment, Villoro (1998) states that a community has to be what it has always been in order to be able to become what it has chosen to be, and SIs can only achieve their aims if they consider these particular matters.

Social interventions and their evaluation

Generally speaking, SIs are organised efforts to improve human welfare; they seek a positive change within the community in which they are applied, through the use of specific strategies and intervention techniques. SIs are externally financed and/or supported programmes to generate pre-established social modifications in favour of the social group they target (Zorrilla-Vázquez 1999; Parsons 2007; Pawson 2013; Chen 2005), and as these use public or private donor funds, and as the resources invested are increasing, evaluation has become crucial to measure efficiency and efficacy in the achievement of their goals, and in generating knowledge to improve their performance (Shadish *et al.* 1995; Wholey *et al.* 2010). In this sense, tourism-based SIs are applied in highly complex contexts, and their evaluation poses methodological and conceptual challenges. While the choice of methods depends on what is being evaluated, the conceptual challenge needs to be solved in any case.

Although tourism – and sustainable tourism – is regarded as a socio-cultural and economic phenomenon, and should consider its environmental impacts, its definition focuses mainly on the tourist's and the market's needs and expectations, giving the host communities little importance. The three dimensions of sustainability are rooted in the neo-liberal paradigm, and concentrate on productivity and accumulation rather than on the actual development of the host communities (Guimarães 1994; Barkin 1993), whereas tourism as an SI for SD calls for a more comprehensive definition, one that puts the host community and its needs and expectations at the centre of the system in such a way that it allows the study of the development *of* tourism as well as development *through* tourism.

Coming across the problem of marginalisation of indigenous communities within natural protected areas, and at the same time protecting biodiversity and conserving cultural heritage as a crucial element of the social structure of the communities, represents an extremely complex challenge. Any intervention that directly or indirectly modifies any of the socio-political and cultural elements within indigenous social groups necessarily affects their interactions and equilibrium, rendering SIs as extremely delicate and complex issues. While SD comprises the management and balance of the interaction of social, political, cultural, economic and environmental issues (Secretary-General of the UN Economic and Social Council 2016), Bonfil Batalla (1995a) defines ethnodevelopment as 'a process which implies the capacity of a social group to evolve based on the lessons drawn from its past tradition, on their natural and cultural heritage, and on its values and future expectations'. This definition allows the understanding of the SD of a community from within, at the same time considering the conservation and evolution of the local culture, and integrating their structures and institutions into the process.

Towards a re-definition of the tourism phenomenon

The conflict emerged in the early 1980s, when Murphy (1980: 1) considered the host community as an important asset in the tourism scheme and defined the activity as 'an industry which uses the community as a resource, sells it as a product and, in the process, affects the lives of everyone'. This assumes the community as a possible product to be sold, rather than as an active stakeholder, giving way to the commodification of culture and evidencing the conceptual centrality of the market.

Sensing the conflict, several scholars have questioned the limitations of the definition of the tourism phenomenon from diverse perspectives (Tribe 2013,

2014; Jafari 2001; Williams 2004; Hall *et al.* 2004; among others), and based upon the mentioned authors' definition attempts, and considering the increasing complexity of the tourism phenomenon, the following more comprehensive definition of it is proposed as a synthesis of former definitions, particularly with regard to a 'host' and 'guest' relation and people mobility being a critical aspect of it. *The tourism phenomenon* is understood as

> a social, cultural, political, cultural, economic and environmental phenomenon which entails the movement of people to countries or places outside their usual environment for personal or business/professional purposes, as well as the reception of these people into communities and their cultural and natural environment. Moving people are called visitors (which may be either tourists or excursionists), and the people who receive them are called hosts. The tourism phenomenon is directly related with the interaction of these two social groups through the activities of visitors, as well as with the activities of the hosts, which may imply cultural interactions, provision of tourism services and commercial intercourse, but also the sustainable management of their natural and cultural heritage.

This working definition not only includes the market and the tourist's needs and expectations, but it also allows for the consideration of the community and of communality and ethnodevelopment into the analysis of tourism as an SI.

The case of the Mexican Tourism Programme in Indigenous Areas (PTAZI)

The National Indigenous Institute (INI), later the Commission for the Development of the Indigenous Peoples (CDI), as have many other development agencies throughout the world, has incorporated tourism into its development initiatives since the late 1980s and has funded hundreds of T-BSIs without consistent evidence available about how they have performed. In 2007 the Federal Government made the yearly evaluation of social programmes mandatory in the country, and that same year the first study on this issue appeared. It was commissioned and paid for by the CDI, and was carried out by the Institute of Economic Research of the National Autonomous University. The study's purpose was to determine the pertinence, efficiency, efficacy and accountability in the use of public resources, and the economic and social benefits achieved within the target population, as well as the identification of strengths and weaknesses in the operation of the programme, providing suggestions for improvement for the programme (Palomino Villavicencio and López Pardo 2007). The analysis considers tourism in the terms of PPT and the neo-liberal paradigm, and concludes that the programme coincides with the national interest in the development of tourism and the alternative tourism market niche, given the extraordinary natural and cultural heritage assets of these social groups. The study reports that the programme has evolved and changed names, but has remained practically the same. From an informal inclusion of tourism projects to support NPA management initiatives in the 1980s, the institution then formalised the initiative calling it the Indigenous Tourism Programme in the 1990s. In the 2000s it changed to the Ecotourism Programme in Indigenous Areas, and finally, since 2007, it has been operating under the name of the Alternative Tourism Programme for Indigenous Areas (PTAZI).

Coinciding with international research, the study has pointed to the high failure rate of the projects and explains these outcomes from the tourism business perspective, mentioning productivity, job creation, income increase and eventual improvement of the community members' livelihoods. Consequently, the study recommends providing community members with training in quality service provision and business management, as well as to help them with the promotion of their services. The evaluators suggest the creation of specific initiatives and sufficient budgets to reach their purposes. However, they do not focus on the actual needs and expectations of the host communities, their well-being or their collective values, but on the success of the tourism business.

After the release of the document in 2007 referred to above the programme was the subject of an apparently complete renewal: it was given new rules of operation and appointed a budget directly by the Federal Congress. Since 2007, the PTAZI is evaluated yearly in its performance and has undergone one programme design evaluation. The reports inform us that the resources have been applied primarily according to the operation rules, and that the resources have benefited a given quantity of individuals, distinguishing gender and age. Data are neatly presented in a logical frame, and conclusions state that the programme works within the established framework (Bensusán 2009; CDI 2013; Ahumada Lobo y Asociados 2011). However, the programme concentrates on the creation of infrastructure (cabins, hostels and restaurants), giving training and capacity building a secondary role, but always focusing on the development of tourism rather than on the enhancement of the host community's livelihood, and seeks the integration of the host communities into the mainstream market rather than prioritising the community's needs and expectations.

The programme assumes not only that the community's worldview and values coincide with those of the tourism business and service, but also that these social groups are familiar with the Western, urban way of life, and demands from them that they comply with the tourists' quality expectations in their services and products, which may be difficult for social groups which have never experienced these circumstances (i.e. sleeping in beds, having running water and/or electricity in their homes, etc.). The intervention thus forces the community to adapt to the business paradigm, and to deal with external tour operators in evident disadvantage, endangering their qualitative well-being as well as their highly vulnerable socio-cultural balances.

To illustrate this situation, the case of a tourism project which was being developed in the biosphere reserve of Montes Azules, in the State of Chiapas, with the purpose of restoring that part of the reserve and providing the community with income to improve their living is a good example. During the building process of a luxury ecolodge, which should provide a small group within the community with important income, the project manager was surprised that the people in charge of the ecolodge were not able to properly make a bed or to correctly clean the toilets. It never occurred to her that these people had never slept on a bed because they use hammocks or sleep on a *petate* (a kind of straw mat) and that they had never used a toilet with running water but use latrines placed outside their dwellings. She was also puzzled because they were unable to price their services and products adequately, disregarding that locally labour has a social value rather than a price.

It could be argued that learning to sleep in a bed and having electricity and running water might eventually represent an improvement in the livelihoods of the community, and it might be so if the climate, available public services and facilities allow the use of a bed, as well as if electricity, running water and sewerage disposal are there for the community as a whole. Moreover, practice evidences that the construction of infrastructure represents a disrupting issue for the community, for it is not clear who is responsible for the management and maintenance and how and why it is to be delivered, and, more importantly, how work is to be priced, how products are to be sold or services to be charged for. The question of the distribution of revenue, financial planning and economic benefits evidently conflicts with the community and its organisation, priorities and interests, and disrupts fragile socio-political and socio-cultural balances, making livelihood improvement very difficult.

Conclusion

In consequence, tourism-based policy designed to trigger development in indigenous/rural communities turns into a highly complex task. It requires full understanding of the particular traditional local social, political, cultural and economic structures and their inner workings. It needs to focus on the active participation of the community, but also, as stated earlier, to consider solidarity, diversity, rootedness and ethnicity, while integrating concepts like self-determination, autonomy, reciprocity, collective participation and common labour, and giving priority to collective over individual well-being. This implies real and deep-reaching communication between the stakeholders. In this sense, the degree of shared meaning in what is being discussed and done is fundamental for autonomous and democratic decision-making and self-determination, which underpin the cultural resources that give the community identity and rootedness, protecting the local cultural structures and institutions and allowing them to make decisions about their future based upon their past and present rather than on the tourism project's needs.

Furthermore, considering the importance of common land tenure, the importance of their social relations, the symbolic and symbiotic relationship with the natural environment along with local rituals and traditions, it is necessary to determine if the insertion of tourism is viable. In the end, their cultural heritage constitutes their identity and uniqueness. Their cultural identity is their main tourism asset, but at the same time tourism may be its greatest threat. This poses a complex paradox for policy-makers: the activity that may offer the possibility of a better livelihood for the community is at the same time a threat to their social and cultural identity and rootedness.

As stated before, indigenous communal social, economic, political and cultural organisation and structures respond to their particular cosmologies and traditions, presenting a paradox for tourism projects. The business nature of the tourism activity may represent a serious threat for the very same thing it offers as the basic attraction for the tourist to visit: their intangible cultural heritage and their natural heritage, which have been preserved through their symbiotic and symbolic relationship with it, and which are fundamental to their communal values and their reproduction as social groups with a shared identity.

References

Ahumada Lobo y Asociados, SA de C. V. (2011) *Evaluación en Materia de Diseño de los Programas F003 e I002 Promoción y Desarrollo de Programas y Proyectos Turísticos de/en las Entidades Federativas*. Mexico City, Mexico.

Barabas, A. M. (2004) La territorialidad simbólica y los derechos territoriales indígenas: reflexiones para el Estado pluriétnico. *Alteridades*, 14(27), 105–19.

Barambah, M. (2011) Relationship and communality: an indigenous perspective on knowledge. In B. Fitzgerald and B. Atkinson (eds), *Copyright Future Copyright Freedom. Marking of the 40th Anniversary of the Commencement of Australia's Copyright Act 1968*. Sydney: Sydney University Press, pp. 155–61.

Barkin, D. (1976) Dos milagros: monarcas y campesinos. In *Memoria: Conferencia Norteamericana sobre la Mariposa Monarca*. Mexico City and Montreal: Comisión para la Cooperación Ambiental, pp. 1–9.

Barkin, D. (1993) Superando el paradigma neoliberal: desarrollo popular sustentable. *Cuadernos de desarrollo rural* (4), 11–31.

Barkin, D. (2010) The Struggle for Local Autonomy in a multiethnic society: Constructing alternatives with indigenous epistemologies.. In S. L. Esquith and F. Gifford (eds.), *Capabilities, Power, and Institutions: Toward a more critical development ethics*. (pp. 142–61). College Station, PA: Pennsylvania State University Press.

Barkin, D. and Lemus, B. (2015) Construyendo mundos pos-Capitalistas. *Cultura y Representaciones Sociales* 10(19), 26–60.

Barthas, B. (1997) La Comunidad Indígena como Organización: El caso de la Huasteca. In *Encuentro de la Asociación de Estudios Latinoamericanos* (*LASA*). Buenos Aires: CLACSO, Consejo Latinoamericano de Ciencias Sociales, pp. 1–14. Available at: http://biblioteca.clacso.edu.ar/ar/libros/lasa97/barthas.pdf (accessed 16 April 2014).

Bennett, O., Roe, D. and Ashley, C. (1999) *Sustainable Tourism and Poverty Elimination Study. A Report to the Department for International Development*. London: DFID.

Bensusán, G. (2009) *Evaluación de Procesos 2009 del Programa de Turismo Alternativo en Zonas Indígenas* (*PTAZI*). Mexico City: Comisión Nacional para el Desarrollo de los Pueblos Indígenas (CDI).

Bohanon, P. J. (1981) El Impacto de la Moneda en una Economía de Subsistencia. In J. R. Llobera (ed.), *Antropología Económica*. Barcelona: Anagrama, pp. 189–200.

Boley, B. B. and McGehee, N. G. (2014) Measuring empowerment: developing and validating the Resident Empowerment through Tourism Scale (RETS). *Tourism Management* 45, 85–94. Available at: http://dx.doi.org/10.1016/j.tourman.2014.04.003.

Bonfil Batalla, G. (1995a) El Etnodesarrollo: sus premisas jurídicas, políticas y de organización. In *Obras Escogidas de Guillermo Bonfil Batalla*, Tomo 2. Mexico City: Instituto Nacional de Antropología e Historia/Instituto Nacional Indigenista, pp. 464–80.

Bonfil Batalla, G. (1995b) Etnodesarrollo: sus premisas jurídicas, políticas y de organización. In *Obras Escogidas de Guillermo Bonfil Batalla*, Tomo 2. Mexico City: Instituto Nacional de Antropología e Historia/Instituto Nacional Indigenista, pp. 464–480.

Bonfil Batalla, G. (2012) *México Profundo: Una civilización negada*, 7th edn. Mexico City: Random House Mondadori.

Bray, D. B., Merino, L. and Barry, D. (eds) (2007) *Los Bosques Comunitarios de México. Manejo Sustentable de Paisajes Forestales*. Mexico City: Instituto Nacional de Ecología/SEMARNAT.

Brundtland, G. H. (1987) *Report of the World Commission on Environment and Development: Our Common Future*. Oslo.

Bustelo, P. (1998) Macroeconomía Estructuralista y Neoestructuralismo Latinoamericano (desde 1983). In *Teorías contemporáneas del desarrollo económico*. Madrid: Editorial Síntesis, pp. 245–56. Available at: http://dialnet.unirioja.es/servlet/libro?codigo=213741 (accessed 31 August 2013).

CDI (2013) *Programa Turismo Alternativo en Zonas Indígenas* (*PTAZI*). Mexico City: CDI.

Chape, S., Spalding, M. and Jenkins, M. (2008) *The World's Protected Areas. Status, Values and Prospects in the 21st Century*. Berkeley, CA: UNEP World Conservation Monitoring Centre, University of California Press.

Chen, H. T. (2005) *Practical Program Evaluation: Assessing and improving Planning, Implementation, and Effectiveness*. Thousand Oaks, CA: Sage.

Chok, S., Macbeth, J. and Warren, C. (2007) Tourism and sustainable development: exploring the theoretical divide. *Current Issues in Tourism* 10(2), 144–65. Available at: http://www.tandfonline.com/doi/abs/10.2167/cit303 (accessed 22 August 2012).

de Kadt, E. (1979a) Social planning for tourism in developing countries. *Annals of Tourism Research* VI(1), 36–48. Available at: http://www.sciencedirect.com/science/article/pii/0160738379900938 (accessed 8 September 2013).

de Kadt, E. (1979b) *Tourism: Passport to Development? Perspectives on the Social and Cultural Effects of Tourism in Developing Countries*. New York: Oxford University Press.

Díaz Gómez, F. (1994) Comunidad y comunalidad. In *Antología sobre Cultura Popular e Indígena. Lecturas del Seminario Diálogos en la Acción, Segunda Etapa*. Mexico City: Consejo Nacional para la Cultura y las Artes (CONACULTA)/Culturas Populares e Indígenas, pp. 365–73.

Douglas, M. (1981) Los Lele: Resistencia al cambio. In J. R. Llobera (ed.), *Antropología Económica*. Barcelona: Anagrama, pp. 165–87.

Duflo, E. (2012) Women empowerment and economic development. *Journal of Economic Literature* 50(4), 1051–79.

Esteva, G. (2010) Development. In W. Sachs (ed.), *Development Dictionary*. New York and London: Zed Books, pp. 1–23.

Guillén, A. (2004) Revisitando la teoría del desarrollo bajo la globalización. *Revista Economía UNAM* 1(1), 19–42. Available at: http://www.economia.unam.mx/publicaciones/econunam/pdfs/01/03ArturoGuillen.PDF (accessed 16 April 2014).

Guimarães, R. P. (1994) Desarrollo sustentable: ¿Propuesta alternativa o retórica neoliberal? *Eure* 20(61), 31–47.

Hall, C. M., Williams, A. M. and Lew, A. A. (2004) Tourism: conceptualizations, institutions and issues. In C. M. Hall, A. M. Williams and A. A. Lew (eds), *A Companion to Tourism*. Malden, MA, Oxford and Victoria, Australia: Blackwell, pp. 3–21.

Jafari, J. (2001) The scientification of tourism. In V. Smith and M. Brent (eds), *Hosts and Guests Revisited: Tourism Issues of the 21st Century*. Putnam Valley, NY: Cognizant Communication Corp., pp. 28–41.

Kakwani, N. and Pernia, E. (2000) What is pro-poor growth? *Asian Development Review* 18(1), 1–16. Available at: https://www.researchgate.net/profile/Nanak_Kakwani/publication/253876792_What_is_Pro-poor_Growth/links/540ea4360cf2d8daaacd54a5.pdf.

Kuokkanen, R. (2011) Indigenous economies, theories of subsistence, and women: exploring the social economy model for indigenous governance. *American Indian Quarterly* 35(2), 215–40. Available at: http://muse.jhu.edu/journals/american_indian_quarterly/v035/35.2.kuokkanen.html (accessed 16 April 2014).

Le Blanc, D. (2015) *Towards Integration at Last? The Sustainable Development Goals as a Network of Targets*, DESA Working Paper No. 141, ST/ESA/2015/DWP/141, Department of Economic and Social Affairs, United Nations, New York. Available online at: http://www.un.org/esa/desa/papers/2015/wp141_2015.pdf.

López Ángel, G. (2001) Tenencia de la tierra y migración: el retorno y la pertenencia. *El Cotidiano*, 18(108), 31–7.

Manyara, G. and Jones, E. (2007) Best practice model for community capacity-building: a case study of community-based tourism enterprises in Kenya, *Tourism* 55, 403–16.

Martínez Luna, Jaime (2011) *Eso que llaman comunalidad.* Culturas Populares, CONACULTA/Secretaría de Cultura, Gobierno de Oaxaca. Colección Diálogos. Pueblos Originarios de Oaxaca, Serie. Oaxaca, Mexico: Veredas.

Millán, S. and Valle, J. (eds) (2003) *La Comunidad sin Límites. Estructura social y organización comunitaria en las regionaes indígenas de México*. Mexico City: Instituto Nacional de Antropología e Historia.

Milne, S. and Ateljevic, I. (2001) Tourism, economic development and the global-local nexus: theory embracing complexity. *Tourism Geographies* 3(4), 369–93. Available at: http://www.tandfonline.com/doi/abs/10.1080/14616680110070478 (accessed 11 August 2013).

Moghadam, V. (1990) *Gender, Development, and Policy: Toward Equity and Empowerment.* Helsinki: WIDER (World Institute for Development Economics Research of the United Nations University).

Monterroso, I. (2008) Comunidades locales en áreas protegidas: reflexiones sobre las políticas de conservación en la Reserva de Biosfera Maya. In G. Merino Alvarado *et al.* (eds), *Gestión Ambiental y Conflicto Social en América Latina*. Buenos Aires: CLACSO (Consejo Latinoamericano de Ciencias Sociales), pp. 227–63.

Mtapuri, O. and Giampiccoli, A. (2014) Winners and losers: a further exploration and reflection on the influence of external actors on community-based tourism. *Mediterranean Journal of Social Sciences* 5(14), 104–12. Available at: http://www.mcser.org/journal/index.php/mjss/article/view/3135.

Murphy, P. E. (1980) Tourism management in host communities. *Canadian Geographer* 24(1), 1–2.

Murphy, P. E. (1983) Tourism as a community industry – an ecological model of tourism development. *Tourism Management*, 4(3), 180–93.

ODI (2008) *Pro-poor Growth and Development*. London: ODI.

OECD (Organisation for Economic Co-operation and Development) (2006) *Promoting Pro-Poor Growth: Key Policy Messages*. Paris. Available at: http://www.oecd.org/dataoecd/0/61/37852580.pdf.

Oltremari, J. V. and Jackson, R. G. (2006) Un estudio de caso: conflictos, percepciones y expectativas de comunidades indígenas asociadas a áreas protegidas en Chile. *Natural Areas Journal* (26), 215–29.

Palomino, Bertha and López Pardo, Gustavo (2007) *Evaluación 2006 del Programa Ecoturismo en Zonas Indígenas*, Instituto de Investigaciones Económicas, Universidad Nacional Autónoma de México (UNAM), Informe Final. Mexico City: CDI-UNAM. Available online at: http://www.cdi.gob.mx/coneval/evaluacion_ecoturismo_2006.pdf.

Parkin, S., Sommer, F. and Uren, S. (2003) Sustainable development: understanding the concept and practical challenge. *Proceedings of the ICE – Engineering Sustainability*, 156 (March), 169–71.

Parsons, W. (2007) *Políticas Públicas: Una introducción a la teoría y la práctica del análisis de políticas públicas*. Buenos Aires: Facultad Latinoamericana de Ciencias Sociales, FLACSO-Sede México/Miño y Dávila, Srl.

Pawson, R. (2013) *The Science of Evaluation. A Realist Manifesto*. London: Sage.

Rendón Monzón, J. J. (2003) *La Comunalidad: Modo de vida en los pueblos indios*, Tomo I. Mexico City: Consejo Nacional para la Cultura y las Artes/Dirección General de Culturas Populares e Indígenas.

Robles Hernández, S. and Cardoso Jiménez, R. (2007) *Floriberto Díaz, Escrito. Comunalidad, energía viva del pensamiento Mixe*. In S. Robles Hernández and R. Cardoso Jiménez (eds), Mexico City: Universidad Utónoma de México (UNAM).

Rojas, M. and Martínez, I. (2012) *Measurement, Research and Inclusion in Public Policy of Subjective Wellbeing: Latin America*, Commission Report, Scientific and Technological Consultative Forum, Civil, Association, Mexico City.

Saayman, M. and Giampiccoli, A. (2016) Community-based and pro-poor tourism: initial assessment of their relation to community development. *European Journal of Tourism Research* 12, 145–90.

Sachs, W. (ed.) (2010) *The Development Dictionary. A Guide to Knowledge as Power*, 2nd edn. London: Zed Books.

Scheyvens, R. (2007) Exploring the tourism-poverty nexus. *Current Issues in Tourism* 10(2), 231–54. Available at: http://tandfprod.literatumonline.com/doi/abs/10.2167/cit318.0 (accessed 1 May 2012).

Shadish, W. R. Jr, Cook, T. D. and Levinton, L. C. (1995) *Foundations of Program Evaluation: Theories of Practice*. Newbury Park, CA: Sage.

Stanford, D. (2008) 'Exceptional visitors': dimensions of tourist responsibility in the context of New Zealand. *Journal of Sustainable Tourism* 16(3), 258. Available at: http://www.multilingual-matters.net/jost/016/jost0160258.htm (accessed 3 June 2013).

Stavenhagen, R. (2002) Identidad indígena y multiculturalidad en América Latina. *Araucaria* 4(7). Available at: http://www.redalyc.org/articulo.oa?id=28240702 (accessed 22 August 2013).

Strasdas, W. (2005) Community-based tourism: between self-determination and market realities. In *Tourism Forum International at the Reiseforum*. Hanover: The International Ecotourism Society (TIES, Germany).

Sutawa, G. K. (2012) Issues on Bali Tourism Development and Community Empowerment to Support Sustainable Tourism Development, International Conference on Small and Medium Enterprises Development (ICSMED). *Procedia Economics and Finance*, 4, 413–22. Available at: http://linkinghub.elsevier.com/retrieve/pii/S2212567112003565.

Tribe, J. (2013) Tourism knowledge and the curriculum. In J. Tribe and D. Airey (eds), *An International Handbook of Tourism Education*. New York: Routledge, pp. 47–60.

Tribe, J. (2014) The concept of tourism: framing a wide tourism world and broad tourism society. *Tourism Recreation Research* 24(2), 75–81. Available at: http://www.tandfonline.com/doi/abs/10.1080/02508281.1999.11014879.

United Nations (2009) *State of the World's Indigenous Peoples*, Department of Economic and Social Affairs, Division for Social Policy and Development, Secretariat of the Permanent Forum on Indigenous Issues, ST/ESA/328 UN Report, New York. Available online at: http://www.un.org/esa/socdev/unpfii/documents/SOWIP/en/SOWIP_web.pdf.

United Nations (2016) *Mainstreaming of the Three Dimensions of Sustainable Development Throughout the United Nations System*, Economic and Social Council Session 27 July 2016, A/71/76-E/2016/55 Report, New York. Available online at: http://www.un.org/ga/search/view_doc.asp?symbol=A/71/76&Lang=E.

UN-WTO (2002) *Tourism and Poverty Alleviation*. Madrid: UN-WTO.

van den Berghe, P. L. (1994) *The Quest for the Other: Ethnic Tourism in San Cristóbal, Mexico*. Washington, DC: University of Washington Press.

Villoro, L. (1998) Sobre la identidad de los pueblos. In *Estado Plural, Pluralidad de Culturas*. Mexico City: UNAM/Paidós, pp. 63–78.

Walters, F. and Takamura, J. (2015) The decolonized quadruple bottom line: a framework for developing indigenous innovation. *Wivazo Sa Review*, 30(2), 77–99.

Warman, A. (2003) *Los Indios de México en el Umbral del Milenio*, 1st edn. Mexico City: Fondo de Cultura Económica.

Warnholtz, G. (2016) Factores de éxito/fracaso de proyectos turísticos insertados en comunidades indígenas/rurales como oportunidades de desarrollo sostenible: una revisión de la literatura. In I. Magaña Carrillo and R. Covarrubias Ramírez (eds), *Competitividad, Sustentabilidad, Innovación: Logros y retos del turismo*. Colima, Mexico: Universidad de Colima/Puertabierta Editores, pp. 199–218.

Watanabe, Y. (2008) *Comunidades indígenas y biodiversidad*. Washington, DC: Fondo para el Medio Ambiente Mundial.

Wholey, J. S., Hatry, H. P. and Newcomer, K. E. (2010) *Handbook of Practical Program Evaluation*, 3rd edn. San Francisco, CA: Jossey-Bass.

Williams, S. (ed.) (2004) *Tourism: Critical Concepts in the Social Sciences. Vol. 1: The Nature and Structure of Tourism*. London and New York: Routledge.

Yates, J. S. (2014) Historicizing 'ethnodevelopment': Kamayoq and political-economic integration across governance regimes in the Peruvian Andes. *Journal of Historical Geography* 46, 53–65. Available at: http://linkinghub.elsevier.com/retrieve/pii/S0305748814001327.

Zapata, M. J., Hall, C. M., Lindo, P. and Vanderschaeghe, M. (2011) Can community-based tourism contribute to development and poverty alleviation? Lessons from Nicaragua. *Current Issues in Tourism* 14(8), 725–49.

Zizumbo Villarreal, L. (2013) *Las Paradojas del Desarrollo Local y del Turismo*. Mexico City: Universidad Autónoma del Estado de México, Miguel Ángel Porrúa.

Zorrilla-Vázquez, E. (1999) *Introducción al Diseño de Políticas para el Desarrollo*. Mexico City: Universidad Anáhuac del Sur/Miguel Ángel Porrúa.

3 Territorial management and Brazilian public policy for ethnotourism and ecotourism in Indigenous lands

The Pataxó case in Bahia

Carlos Alfredo Ferraz de Oliveira, Ismar Borges de Lima and Márcia Teixeira Falcão

Introduction

The Brazilian Constitution that was enacted in 1988 represents a significant landmark for the Indigenous groups of the country regarding the safeguarding of their rights and their lands, and also represents a legal and normative framework that sets up the basis and provides opportunities to consolidate aspects of an induced ethnodevelopment in Brazil under government assistance. Beyond defining special rights to the Indians, such as the right to a traditionally occupied land, the new Constitution represented a change in the conceptual and legal comprehension by the Brazilian government of the Indigenous people's role, no longer viewing them as incapable and living under the guardianship of the state, but as citizens with their own rights and duties to the Brazilian society (Brazil 1988). The acknowledgement of the special rights of the Indigenous people is no longer on account of them being considered inferior, fragile and in the process of integration into a society considered homogeneous, but it becomes justified by having their own cultural and social organisations (National Indian Foundation – FUNAI; Indian Formations and Research Institute – IEPÉ; Ministry Of Environment – MMA 2010). This legal and conceptual holistic understanding of the Indigenous people enables the creation, on a national, regional and local level, of Indigenous public policies that lead to concrete actions towards emancipation, self-determination and inclusion of the ethnic Indigenous minorities of Brazil. The Brazilian Policy for Territorial and Environmental Management of Indigenous Lands (PNGATI), as a national policy, will be reviewed in the context of two Indigenous groups, the Pataxó on Barra Velha Land, in Bahia, northeast region. The research reveals key aspects of Indigenous tourism in Brazil and ethnic group realities, and shows how PNGATI is an avenue for improving the overall situation of Indigenous communities by paving the road to advancing ethnodevelopment initiatives.

On a world level, advances in the conceptual and normative comprehension of Indigenous people can be seen. In 1989, the International Labor Organisation

(ILO) elaborated Convention 169 on Indigenous and Tribal People in Independent Countries, which was ratified by the Brazilian government in 2002. In that Convention it is emphasised the right of Indigenous people to have control and autonomy over their lives and over the land they occupy or use in any way (ILO 1989). Since the ratification of Convention 169 by the Brazilian State in 2002, the Indigenous people were granted the right to prior consultation and to free, informed consent regarding any interference that may occur in their Indigenous Lands (ILs) and lives (FUNAI, IEPÉ and MMA 2010).

The ILs in Brazil are protected areas delimited by the state that aim to protect and guarantee the right of the Indigenous people to survival, considering their activities, their physical and cultural reproduction, their autonomy and their access to and conservation of their natural resources (Brazil 1988). In order to reach these goals, the Indigenous people started, in the 1990s, a dialogue with non-governmental organisations (NGOs) and the Brazilian State about effective ways to observe what is prescribed in the Brazilian Constitution and in Convention 169 of the ILO regarding the demarcation of their lands and also about the Indigenous prerogatives in the management of their lands, as already observed in other nations (de Lima and Weiler 2016). In this same decade, during the United Nations Environment and Development Conference (ECO 92), through an approach between the Indigenous people and socio-environmental movements, the contribution of the Indigenous people to the biodiversity of their lands was recognised. This recognition generated between the decades of 1990 and 2000 projects and programmes directed at supporting the actions of conservation and environmental recovery integrated into income generation and cultural empowerment in the ILs of many different regions in Brazil. This period can be characterised as one of many conceptual changes in the Brazilian State's stance on Indigenous people, Indigenous organisations' empowerment, the recognition of the cultural and socio-environmental importance of those people and their lands, and the challenges for the next steps towards a higher autonomy and protagonism with regard to the management of their lands (Bavaresco and Menezes 2014).

Considering the challenges to the management of their lands, the Indigenous people movements established a dialogue with the Brazilian State. As a result of this dialogue an Inter-Ministerial Work Group (IWG) was created in 2008 with the goal of elaborating with Indigenous representatives from all over the country a public policy directed to Indigenous environmental and territorial management. This process involved five regional consultations with the participation of 1,300 people from the Indigenous communities from the north, northeast, southeast, south and centre-west of the country (Oliveira, A. R. 2011). As a result of this process of consultation and dialogue between the Indigenous organisations and the Brazilian State, on 5 July 2012 the Brazilian Policy for Territorial and Environmental Management of Indigenous Lands (PNGATI) was enacted by Federal Decree No. 7.747 that has as a goal to guarantee and promote together with the Indigenous people the sustainable management of their lands and territories, considering their socio-cultural autonomy and the current legislation

(Brazil 2012). According to the Brazilian Institute of Geography and Statistics (IBGE), the country has at least 225 Indigenous peoples that speak 180 distinct languages, and currently they total 734,000 indigenous individuals who live in rural and urban areas of Brazil, including the Amazon basin region. Some Indigenous groups live in lands that have hundreds of thousands of hectares and are as extensive as some European countries, and this reveals how relevant and sensitive the issue of 'land tenure', 'land ownership' and 'Indigenous land demarcation' is in Brazil.

> Indian culture and survival is closely linked to land. The plains Indians saw their territories ruthlessly invaded and usurped by cattlemen and farmers. They themselves had little understanding of legal ownership of land which they regarded as common to all mankind and were powerless to resist. During the past decade(s), their constitutional right to land has finally been recognised with the demarcation and protection of pockets of land around established *malocas*. The 1987 census of Indian lands listed 24 malocas occupying almost 400,000 hectares being ethnically formed by Makuxi and Wapixana, [and] 9,186 Ingariko [live in] 1,401, 320 ha [of] Raposa Serra do Sol [Indigenous land] … the Yanomami are the largest surviving tribe of forest Indians in South America … [with] around 17,000 Yanomami … half living in Brazil and half in Venezuela … Yanomami lands in Brazil amount to roughly 10 million hectares [which is double the size of Switzerland]. (Furley 1994: 1–22)

In the process of elaborating this policy, that took into consideration the demands of the Indigenous people on what they regard as being the adequate management of their territories and lands, three main themes were identified: territorial protection, environmental conservation and recuperation, as well as ethnodevelopment. These main themes and their interactions served as the basis for the PNGATI structure, constituted by seven axes and their specific goals (Bavaresco and Menezes 2014). Axis 5 stands out as the focus of this chapter. It involves the sustainable use of the natural resources and the Indigenous productive initiatives, presenting specific goals that correspond to the Indigenous ethnodevelopment demands.

Within Axis 5 of the PNGATI there is the specific goal of supporting ethnotourism and ecotourism in ILs which are considered to be sustainable productive activities as long as the Indigenous people are qualified for their management and their leadership and autonomy regarding the process of implementation and management and evaluation are respected (Brazil 2012). The activities of touristic visitation in ILs have already been happening in Brazil for a few decades, by Indigenous initiatives or by non-Indigenous activities or by both in an integrated way or not (de Grünewald 2001; Luindia 2007). During the contextualised process of securing the Indigenous rights over their lands and their autonomy in the use and management of those areas, during the last three decades, tourism in ILs has been part of the agenda and dialogue, but with little presence in legislation and policies.

The PNGATI represents the beginning of a steering of tourism in ILs by the state in response to a demand from the Indigenous peoples. During the elaboration and after the decree of PNGATI, the National Indian Foundation (FUNAI) has been conducting dialogue with the Indigenous people, institutions and tourism professionals aiming to create an IL tourism regulation. On 11 July 2015, FUNAI published the Normative Instruction (IN) No. 03 that establishes standards and guidelines related to the activities of visitation with touristic goals in ILs. The PNGATI and the IN No. 03 from FUNAI marked the first State initiative towards a regulation of tourism in ILs. Now, the challenge is its implementation in those areas and also an analysis of the effectiveness of its proposal.

This chapter aims at presenting historical, contextual and practical issues related to the Pataxó group of Barra Velha, in Bahia, with regard to Indigenous ethnotourism activities and ethnodevelopment advances. The chapter provides an overview of pertinent Indigenous public policies and of territorial and environmental management tools as evidence that Indigenous groups have experienced new paradigms as ethnic minorities in Brazil with segmented forms of development and autonomy.

Literature review

The Indigenous people in Brazil have, over a long period of time, through organisation, strategies and their own knowledge systems, been managing their territories aiming to ensure their economic, environmental and socio-cultural sustainability as a people. Since the contact with the Portuguese explorers, as well as during established colonialism and the post-independence period, Indigenous people and their territories have been suffering various external interventions that affect their physical survival, their own knowledge systems and their social organisation. Nowadays, the main external threats are identified as monocultures, the advance of urban areas, the implementation of potentially polluting projects such as industries, hydro-electric plants, harbours, mining plants and roads around the protected areas and, in some cases, roads and pipelines inside the ILs. The history of the impacts on Indigenous people and their territories caused a significant alteration in their way of life and in the Indigenous territories' management. The PNGATI was demanded by and elaborated with the Indigenous people, aiming to give those people the possibility to manage their territories alongside the current sustainability challenges of the threats posed for them, the increase of the Indigenous population, and the decrease of natural resources in the ILs (Bavaresco and Menezes 2014).

For a better understanding of the Indigenous socio-cultural changes generated and the PNGATI it is important to present the concept of territory, territoriality and territorial management that is being considered. For Haesbaert and Mondardo (2010) territory can be understood from the power relations point of view: the power in its strict material effects, or in the political administrative scope (laws, area demarcation, use and occupation regulation), or in the most symbolic cultural articulation, where the construction of identity itself is seen, mostly, as a power instrument. Considering this model of territory that has as its focus symbolic and material power relations, the Indigenous management of their territories implies the political control and management of the biophysical fluxes that exist there. In that way, Indigenous territorial management might be understood as the political control and environmental management of the territory by the ethnic groups that occupy that land and present its territoriality (Little 2006).

Territoriality can be defined as a 'multidimensionality of the territory lived on' expressed by a group in the context of the interaction in the material/functional and symbolic powers between society, space and territory (Haesbaert and Mondardo 2010). This territoriality can undergo processes of de-territorialisation and the creation of new relationships between man and territory, involving complex economic, political and cultural dimensions within a particular area (Haesbaert 2002). In this process of territoriality, de-territorialisation and re-territorialisation there is a strict relationship with the cultural dimension of the social groups inserted there promoting the creation of certain processes such as trans-culturalisation and cultural anthropophagy. According to Ortiz (1965, as cited in Cuccioletta 2001/2002), trans-culturalism is a transition process from one culture to another, and cultural anthropophagy is another process that consists of using elements of a foreign culture in a conscious transformation into a renewal and empowerment of the local culture, as originally defined in 1940 (p. 8). For Helena (1983), the term 'anthropophagy' as an 'ethos of Brazilian culture' (p. 91), therefore, constitutes a positive hybridism in which it symbolises either the destruction and impoverishment of past cultures on the one hand, or it can represent 'rejuvenation of cultures' on the other (Roca *et al.* 2016).

An important aspect to be considered in the territorial management, and in the cultural and territoriality processes strictly related to this issue, is the sustainability of the groups that have a relationship with a given territory. In the case of the traditional communities, ethnodevelopment emerges as a counterpoint to the developmental concept and discourse that in various instances prevails as a solution to the problems of those territories and communities. According to Little (2006), ethnodevelopment comprises productive, economic and political practices conceived and executed by the traditional people/communities corresponding to the group's projects and that guarantee their quality of life. Within this theme ethnotourism stands out as a socio-economic and socio-cultural activity conceived and managed by the receptive communities, which has as its motivation income generation, cultural exchange between the tourists and the Indigenous community and interaction with the natural environment presented from the Indigenous point of view (Luindia 2007).

Touristic visits to ILs in Brazil present various experiences, opinions and perceptions that diverge from those of Indigenous, Indian and non-Indian institutions (Leal 2009). According to Faria (2009) and Guimarães (2006) there are two predominant points of view about tourism in ILs in Brazil. One observes tourism as an activity developed through the influence of the external agents that threaten local cultures and the preservation of the natural areas of the Indigenous territory, while the other identifies ethnotourism, if it is conceived, planned and managed with the participation and determination of the Indigenous people, as an activity of ethnodevelopment which has the potential to generate income for distribution in the community, as well as cultural empowerment and interchange, along with the sustainable use of natural resources.

In Brazil one can observe cases in which tourism in ILs starts with a spontaneous demand of the touristic flow of a region, or with incentives from government agencies, NGOs and tourism companies. Many of these initiatives cannot or do not identify the necessity for Indigenous participation in the process. These cases generally result in a non-viable tourism model in relation to the local Indigenous context and social organisation and end up generating negative impacts on their ways of life in the visited IL areas (Guimarães 2006). There are also ethnotourism initiatives in ILs that were conceived and planned with Indigenous participation that are promoting a higher level of autonomy and self-determination of the Indigenous communities over development processes in their lands (Faria 2009; Luindia 2007). The initiatives of planned tourism in ILs, with Indigenous participation, in Brazil intensified during the decade commencing 2000. Due to the fact that they are recent initiatives, some limitations in the amount of information and results occur which impede an analysis of their impact on the Indigenous communities involved and their territories (Guimarães 2006).

Methodologically, the research with a focus on the Pataxó community was carried out by using a qualitative approach (Minayo 2004) using for the data collection and analysis the following procedures: (1) bibliographic and document studies (Gil 1987); (2) participant observation (Stacey 1977; Jones 1993); (3) analysis that systematises and establishes a dialogue between the data collected in the bibliography and documents with the results of participant observation carried out *in loco*, considering as a focus the categories of analysis defined for understanding the context and relations between ethnotourism and territorial management in Barra Velha IL.

The bibliographic and documentary study carried out covers the following themes and objectives: (1) public policies aimed at Indigenous rights to the territory and its management and to the development of ethnotourism in these areas, with the purpose of understanding the rights to the territory and its autonomy for management, especially with regard to ethnodevelopment; (2) territory and territoriality concepts, cultural anthropophagic hybridism, ethnodevelopment and Indigenous ethnotourism which aim at arriving at a better understanding of the topics addressed and related to the context of the Barra Velha IL and tourism there practised; (3) historical and current context of the Barra Velha IL and its surroundings, considering as a focus the descriptions and existing analyses of ethnotourism developed in the area.

The participant observation was carried out during 2008 and 2014, focusing on the understanding of the development and management of the touristic activities developed in Barra Velha and its relations with RESEX Corumbau and PNHMP. It was carried out through the follow-up of meetings, capacities and operation of the touristic activities and in dialogue with the agents involved where the following categories of analysis were considered: (1) the history of social, cultural and political relations of the Pataxó community with their territory; (2) the social and political organisation of the Pataxó community in territorial and touristic management; (3) relations between the Pataxó community and the institutional agents in territorial management and ethnotourism in the area.

The data collected were systematised considering the categories of analysis already referred to making it possible to establish a dialogue and interface between the narratives identified in the bibliographic and documentary survey with the narratives identified during participant observation.

Pataxó Indigenous tourism in Barra Velha Land, Bahia: issues of ethnodevelopment

The Barra Velha IL is occupied by Indigenous people of the Pataxó ethnic group, located in the municipality of Porto Seguro in the extreme south of Bahia, a region considered a priority for tourism development and identified as a Touristic Zone of the Discovery Coast. The IL has areas of Atlantic Forest and borders on two federal Preservation Areas (PAs), The Historical National Park of Monte Pascoal (PNHMP) and the Marine Extractive Reserve (RESEX) of Corumbau. It was created in 1980, prior to the regulation and current definition of ILs in the Constitution, through an agreement between the Brazilian Forest Defense Institute (IBDF), already extinct, and FUNAI. In this agreement the IBDF returned to the Pataxó community, the regional traditional inhabitants, 8,627 hectares that were considered part of the PNHMP area (Sampaio 2000).

The traditional means of production of the Pataxó families of Barra Velha IL are agriculture, vegetable extraction, fishing, shellfish and handicrafts. These activities were directed to Pataxó autonomy in food production and for household consumption and use. During the last four decades these productive activities suffered changes in production techniques and community organisation for its practice and objectives. In the course of the development of tourism, local crafts have been increasingly directed to commercialisation and are no longer for the domestic use of the Pataxó community. Income generation has become a necessity and of increasing interest to the Pataxó families (Cardoso and Pinheiro 2012).

Integrated into this handicrafts production, the Pataxó have been implementing ethnotourism in Barra Velha IL. The Pataxó consider ethnotourism an important mechanism for generating income and for establishing intercultural dialogue with non-Indians. Ethnotourism is observed by these Pataxó as an important activity for their ethnodevelopment and in the management of their territory (Oliveira 2014).

Brief history of Pataxó territory and ethnotourism in the Barra Velha Indigenous Land

From 1861 to 1951 the Pataxó along with five other ethnic groups that inhabited the south of Bahia and its proximities were established in hamlets and isolated between the mouth of Corumbau River, the current municipality of Prado area, and the Caraíva River, the current municipality of the Porto Seguro area, and the important village of origin of Barra Velha, also known by the Pataxó as 'Mother Village'.

The compulsory settlement of this Indigenous concentration was carried out by the Province of Bahia President as a strategy to ease the conflicts between settlers and Indigenous people and also to dominate the lands of that region that aroused the governing rulers' interest (Carvalho 1977). The Pataxó ethnonym prevailed over the natives there, probably due to the predominance of the Pataxó in the village and also due to the fact that it is located in part on this people's territory; 'some designations usually are not proper ethnic groups, but ethnonyms, that is, names attributed in the contact process, in which fragmented groups are reordered by war, reduction in settlements, and historical processes [e.g. of colonisation]' (de Resende 2013: 150). During this period the Pataxó established their means of production in agriculture, vegetable extraction, handicrafts, fishing and shellfish capture in an area that had the necessary natural resources to maintain their way of life (Sampaio 2000). In 1961 the PNHMP was created by Federal Decree No. 242 in 22,500 hectares of Atlantic Forest area and associated ecosystems, occupying the whole area of the Barra Velha village and places considered by the Pataxó as their territory.

From 1961 to 1980 there were conflicts between the organ responsible for the PA's management and the Pataxó, mainly referring to the functional and symbolic power over this territory, including its means of production and sustenance. The limitations imposed on the Pataxó livelihood in the area accentuated the dispersal of the Pataxó to the extreme south of Bahia coastal areas, including urban ones, causing de-territorialisation and the need for re-territorialisation in areas that were undergoing occupation and a development model focused on wood extraction from the Atlantic Forest, in which there were substantial transformations such as the construction and paving of roads, especially the BR-101, and tourism development (Sampaio 2000). This fact resulted in a Pataxó de-territorialisation that disregarded aspects of functional and symbolic power over its territory, and also in a cultural hybridisation characterised by the marginalisation of what is local and heterogeneous in favour of a Western and developmental hegemony. This de-territorialisation has negatively affected the ethnodevelopment programme established so far by the Pataxó. As a strategy for their survival the Pataxó began producing handicrafts geared at commercialisation for the tourist market which was increasing significantly in the region (Grünewald 2001).

In 1980 8,627 hectares of the PNHMP area were returned to the Pataxó, being regularised in 1982 as Barra Velha IL (Sampaio 2000). This period demonstrates a strategy of government protection of the Indians through guardianship, considering them as incapable of managing their own culture and territory. The Pataxó were considered to be Indigenes or savages 'integrated' or 'in the process of integration' within a 'national community' and they should be protected by FUNAI during its process of 'inclusion' in this attempt at cultural hegemony. The demarcation of Barra Velha IL characterises a territory with a material meaning that according to Haesbaert (2002) refers to the territorial concept of a state and administration focused on the power of the national government and its institutions in a delimited space and where its symbolic meaning is non-existent or secondary. For this reason from the 1980s to the present day the Pataxó of Barra Velha have struggled for the inclusion of a larger territory in the demarcation that surrounds the total area of the PNHMP, where their immaterial and symbolic senses are considered, besides the material and functional ones. This territory is also claimed to be a necessary area for Pataxó ethnodevelopment, in that it includes sites considered important for production and control (Cardoso and Pinheiro 2012).

Between the 1980s and 1990s the Pataxó faced different incisions in their territory in the extreme south of Bahia, which resulted primarily in the dispersion of the Indigenous people of Barra Velha during the conflicts generated by the creation and implantation of the PNHMP in the 1960s and 1970s. The legal recognition of a part of these territories, through the creation of ILs, has been occurring mainly after the promulgation of the Brazilian Constitution of 1988.

One of the Pataxó areas is the Jaqueira Indigenous Reserve (RI) where a group led by three women began a process of reinventing their traditions using elements still present in the memories of some, with the aim of enabling a way of life close to the origins of the 'Mother Village'. For this they have fought and still fight for an Indigenous education (formal and non-formal) aimed at cultural aspects considered important by this group and also the reintegration with natural and rural areas, counteracting the tendency towards closer relations with the urban environment that is increasingly available in some Pataxó areas of the region. In order to make this process feasible, the Pataxó, considering external guidelines and the tourist flows into the region, identified in ethnotourism a tool for income generation and also for ethnic affirmation and intercultural dialogue with non-Indians (Grünewald 2001; Luindia 2007). It should be noted that during the process of implementing this tourism programme in the 1990s, this group still came across the stance of some Brazilian public bodies of an incapacitated and protected Indian, which can be identified in the discourse of the Pataxó leadership when it was stated that 'We sought support from public bodies, but they told us that we did not have the capacity and conditions to set out and work with tourism in the reserve and that tourism was not allowed in the Indigenous area.'[1] In the absence of a public policy that guided these Indigenous peoples by which tourism could be developed to help them achieve their goals, they identified in the reinvention of their cultural elements and in the support of non-Indian partners the potential to invent and structure a Pataxó ethnotourism that enabled income generation, the strengthening of their internal organisation and Pataxó history and cultural diffusion to non-Indians. By then the Pataxó perceived ethnotourism as an important instrument for their ethnodevelopment.

In 2000 around the occasion of the commemoration of the 500th anniversary of the arrival of the Portuguese in Brazil, the Pataxó through an act organised by its leaders with the support of other ethnic groups, re-established the main guidelines of the PNHMP. This act is considered of great importance for the Pataxó movement in support of the struggle for the territory and resulted in a new agreement between the Ministries, involving FUNAI and the Brazilian Institute of Environment and Non-Renewable Resources (IBAMA),[2] promoted by the Union Prosecutor's Office. This agreement establishes the need for shared management of the park among the Pataxó, FUNAI and IBAMA (Sampaio 2000). From the agreement and the shared management attempt by PNHMP a Pataxó group established the Pé do Monte village, located near the main entrance of the park in its western sector. In this Pataxó village, with the support and participation of IBAMA and other external institutions, during this process of shared management, they started to structure a visitation to the PNHMP with a view to generating income and establishing a dialogue with the visitors to the conservation unit/protected area (CU). The format of the touristic activities developed there was directly influenced by the experience of the Jaqueira IR, which represents to these Pataxó a reference and a pioneering ethnotourism project that generated good results for the ethnodevelopment of the group involved (Oliveira, C. A. F. 2011). In the same period, groups from Barra Velha village, mainly young people, awakened to the possibilities, besides the production and commercialisation of existing handicrafts, of developing touristic activities that involve visits to places inside the IL, motivated by the tourist flow that increased in the localities of Caraíva and Corumbau and the experiences of the Pataxó in the RI of Jaqueira.

The tourism activities developed in Jaqueira IR, Pé do Monte village and Barra Velha village involve, besides commercial aspects and interests, a movement to recreate cultural elements and to disseminate information about its history and its rights to the territory. This is in front of an audience many of whom refer to them as 'false Indians' because they have mingled and become 'mestizos' and live using the utensils, tools and clothing of non-Indians, without understanding that they have passed through centuries of cultural hybridisation which have resulted from various forms of violence. Nowadays, in a process of socio-cultural and political resistance they are trying to transform this imposed hybridisation into an anthropophagic hybridism through a process of digesting foreign cultural elements, in this case non-Indian, selecting those of which are interesting for a conscious transformation of their culture directed also to improvements in local concerns. This process makes a connection with certain elements of local culture, resulting in a process of hybridisation where the traits of colonialism and hegemony diminish as new ones that serve consciously for renewal and the strengthening of culture and ethnodevelopment among the Pataxó are introduced (Andrade, cited in Haesbaert and Mondardo 2010). Through this process of resistance, the Pataxó have recognised the importance of ethnotourism as an instrument for local ethnodevelopment.

Currently, the Pataxó population totals approximately 9,000 individuals divided into 25 villages spread across five major Indigenous Lands alongside Bahia's shoreline, and the Pataxó reservations lie where Pedro Álvares Cabral anchored his ships when he 'discovered' [i.e. invaded] Brazil in 1500: 'Today, the Pataxó are a Portuguese-speaking group who are still fighting for land in the region [...]. Not surprisingly, the Indian population had difficulty living off their own lands' (Grünewald 2012: 163), and with the emergence of a tourism hub in Porto Seguro city in the 1970s the Pataxó started to produce their Indigenous handicrafts for tourist visitors.

Ethno-tourism management in the Barra Velha Indigenous Land

Currently at Barra Velha IL ethnotourism activities occur mainly in the villages of Pé do Monte, Barra Velha and Bujigão. The process of implementing ethnotourism in these villages underwent training, dialogue and definitions that involved the Pataxó, the Instituto Chico Mendes de Conservação da Biodiversidade (the Chico Mendes Institute for the Conservation of Biodiversity (ICMBio), formerly IBAMA, and FUNAI. During the initial attempt of the management of Barra Velha IL shared with the PNHMP, ethnotourism and ecotourism were identified as activities of community and institutional interest. Structural actions were taken for its implementation, such as Indigenous qualification for management and service provision, installation of a basic tourist visitors' infrastructure and definitions of conduct to minimise impacts on natural areas and local culture. In this process of implementing tourism in the IL the actions were not carried out in an integrated way between the ICMBio and FUNAI. FUNAI participated modestly in that it lacked an internal instrument to guide its actions on the theme of tourism.

The Pataxó Territorial Management Plan of Barra Velha and Águas Claras,[3] referred to by them as Aragwaksã,[4] was built during a four-year process of diagnosis and participatory planning that involved an intercultural dialogue between Pataxó, FUNAI and the technical team with the objective of thinking and jointly planning the Pataxó management of their territory. The plan was published in 2012 and the process of elaboration included the PNGATI political involvement at that moment; it was not yet sanctioned, but already had an influence on FUNAI's outlook and actions and also on the ICMBio. In this plan, the Pataxó of Barra Velha IL present the characteristics and demands of their ethnodevelopment, highlighting the necessity to revise the limits of their IL to enable the means of production practised and desired by them. This Pataxó ethnodevelopment is observed as the practice and management of its productive activities that are directed towards subsistence, income generation and the reproduction of its socio-cultural and socio-political practices (Cardoso and Pinheiro 2012). In Aragwaksã, ethnotourism is an important topic inserted in productive activities related to the Pataxó ethnodevelopment. This importance strengthens the need for FUNAI's more effective participation in the implementation and organisation of ethnotourism in Barra Velha IL. As for the relevance of tourism in regard to cultural revival, 'It is worth noting that a cultural revival has occurred in Barra Velha [triggered by tourism and visitors' interest in that ethnic group] encompassing not only craftwork, but also dances and songs and relying on both Indian names and a language still under construction' (Grünewald 2012: 163).

The FUNAI IN No. 3 published on 11 June 2015 represents the first legal instrument which provides guidance on the possibilities of developing tourism in ILs and the forms of state intervention required in order to monitor and support the process. The guidelines that relate to ethnotourism and ecotourism (the two touristic typologies addressed in the IN) specify the processes that need to be followed in the context of free and informed consultation of the Indigenous communities, provided for in the ILO Convention 169, and the actions of territorial and environmental protection of ILs involving control and inspection of non-Indian entry into the ILs.

It sets down that visits to ILs should aim at valorising and promoting culture and socio-biodiversity, through tourist interactions with the local population and the IL, with the objective of income generation and distribution, as well as respect for the Indigenous people, their way of life and their autonomy (Brazil 2015). IN No. 3 privileges the role of FUNAI as setting conditions and also as a means to plan and manage touristic activities in the IL, and the obligation to draw up a visitor plan to be sent to FUNAI by the Indigenous communities and organisations named as proponents. The process of elaboration and implementation of this plan should allow Indigenous people to manage their own activities on their ILs.

Taking IN No. 3 into consideration, the Pataxó people from Barra Velha IL face the challenge of elaborating and implementing its locally administered tourist visiting plan. In order to understand the challenges and possibilities of implementing IN No. 3 in the Barra Velha IL and its re-delimitation area, it is important to consider the current tourism context developed in the villages of Pé do Monte, Barra Velha and Bujigão.

The village of Pé do Monte is located in the western Barra Velha IL re-delimitation zone in the vicinity of Monte Pascoal and the main entrance to the PNHMP. The Pataxó of this village have developed and undertaken ethnotourism in this area of the park in conjunction with ICMBio which accompanies and supports them mainly through the installation of infrastructure and periodic training. The Pataxó entertain visitors from this area by driving them through interpretative trails in the Atlantic Forest and to Monte Pascoal, including cultural performances involving local cuisine using Pataxó agricultural and fishing products (see Figure 3.1).

The Pataxó people who had a connection with and influence upon the experiences in the Jaqueira IR, as well as capacity-building and training with the support of the ICMBio, developed the trails and the cultural performances. The Pataxó also established dialogue with non-Indians, based on their ethnic history and their knowledge of the natural areas and monuments visited. Of these monuments Mount Pascoal and the Monument of the Resistance are prominent and are considered by the Pataxó as symbolising their history, the violence that they suffered and the moments of struggle for the retaking of their territory. For the Pataxó these symbolic places are strategic for transmitting history to their children and also to inform and sensitise visitors about their history of struggle and ethnic resistance. It is worth mentioning the Monument of the Resistance, which was built by the Indians themselves at the time of the PNHMP's

Figure 3.1 Pataxó tourist guide at Jequitibá trail.
(Photo: Carlos Alfredo Ferraz de Oliveira)

intervention. It is shaped like the map of Brazil, together with instruments used by the Indians of Brazil, maraca and arrow. The map shows the names of several Indigenous ethnic groups in Brazil, located in their corresponding regions of the country, demonstrating that their presence has been evident all over the national territory and that their actions and claims for ethnic autonomy have not diminished.

Ethno-tourism in the village of Pé do Monte represents an activity that generates a significant income for families in conducting the visitors in the PNHMP, cultural their performances and the sale of handicrafts. Most of the families of this village are involved in ethnotourism practice and management. These Pataxó do not observe ethnotourism as their sole source of income but rather as a complement. The traditional activities, mainly agricultural, continue to be the main support for ethnodevelopment. Families of this village mention two major limitations in ethnotourism. Regarding income generation, village visits and the PNHMP have a concentrated touristic seasonality between December and February, a fact which generates an income concentrated in this period, with little involvement in the organisation and management of the activity during the rest of the year. The planning and management of village ethnotourism is done by the Pé do Monte Pataxó Village Association, involving leaderships and families, but there is still a need for external agents, FUNAI, ICMBio and others for technical support in professional qualification and management. There are also demands for external financial resources for the implementation of basic infrastructure to assist visitors.

The village of Barra Velha, also known as Aldeia Mãe, is located in the coastal area of Barra Velha IL. The activities of ethnotourism that take place in this village are buggy rides, beach and village visits, trails and Pataxó cultural performances. The beach of Barra Velha is the most visited place and tourists, usually hosted in the localities of Caraíva and Corumbau, travel there by hiking or buggy rides. Some of these tourists only go to the beach but others also visit the village to find out about the community or buy handicrafts. The participation in and control by the Pataxó of visitors does not occur when tourists walk from the beach to the village, only when the access is made by buggy. Many of the buggy conductors, wanting the organisation and representation of their work in the community and with external agents, founded the Pataxó Indigenous Buggy Conductors Association of Barra Velha (ABIPA). The most demanded buggy ride is the transport (and return) of tourists from Caraíva to Corumbau. If requested there is also the possibility of buggy rides to other villages of the IL, including the village of Pé do Monte in order to climb to Mount Pascoal, but these activities only occur sporadically.

Ethno-tourism in the village of Barra Velha represents an activity that complements the income of some families, through the sale of tours and buggy transport, cultural performances and the sale of handicrafts. These activities are managed in the village in a fragmented way. ABIPA manages the buggy rides, young people and cultural groups handle the staged performances and handicrafts are produced by the families, which also handle its management and commercialisation. In addition to indicating the same limitations as the Pataxó of Pé do Monte village, the families of Barra Velha village highlight the absence of a community dialogue about ethnotourism and its regulation in the village. This absence is observed as a barrier for autonomy, self-determination and Pataxó self-control over ethnotourism in the locality.

The village of Bujigão is located in the south of the re-delimitation of the Barra Velha LI area overlapping with PNHMP, specifically the banks of the mouth of the Corumbau river, a coastal area that borders the Corumbau RESEX. Its creation was due to the migration of Pataxó families to Corumbau and with the onset of real estate speculation from 2000 they were being pressured to move. They identified a site on the other side of the river Corumbau, an area traditionally occupied by the Pataxó, an appropriate place to settle and create a village. Soon after with the increase in population in the Barra Velha village, some families from this locality also migrated to Bujigão. During the establishment of the village they embraced tourism spontaneously as an opportunity for generating income. The touristic activities involve the transport of tourists from Corumbau to Caraíva or vice versa, buggy tours and boat tours on the Corumbau River and in the coral reefs, both inside the RESEX Corumbau. On these boat tours the conductor transmits the local Pataxó point of view about the sea and estuary and the symbolic places for this ethnic group, recounting stories and curiosities about the places visited. The provision for tourists also involves the local cuisine which uses fish and shellfish marketed by the fishermen of the village.

Ethno-tourism in Bujigão village has only begun in the last four years, but already it represents an important income supplement for the families living there that are engaged in fishing and shellfish collection as their main productive activity. Ethno-tourism is managed by the Bujigão Fishermen's Association, which contributes to community involvement in the planning, practice and management of this activity. This village also acknowledges the region's touristic seasonality and the need for external support, thus limiting both the development of ethnotourism and also greater community autonomy in its management. The current lack of definition of the land tenure situation that is currently superimposed on the PNHMP and awaits the determination of the Brazilian State on the re-delimitation of Pataxó ILs generates a perception in the community of a threat to its ethnodevelopment that depends on the guarantee of the demarcation of its territory, autonomy and self-determination regarding its use and management.

The three villages feature tourist activities developed by the Pataxó that provide ethnic experiences in relation to natural environments where the attractions of the cultural elements of the Pataxó and the rivers, beaches, sea and forests blend into an ethnic and ecotouristic experience. Ethno-tourism management in IL is undertaken by Pataxó associations in each village involved. The associations created by the Pataxó are seen by them as contemporary forms of collective organisation that aim to promote, plan and implement community projects, including those related to their ethnodevelopment. These associations have been conducting a dialogue with the village leaders about the involvement of other community members in the operation of the activities and also about the establishment of rules for developing ethnotourism, in order to minimise interference in the daily life of the community and to organise the sector. The Pataxó organisation of ethnotourism in the three villages is in its early stages, which necessitates a process of internal and external dialogue. Recently the initiatives in favour of the management of ethnotourism by the Pataxó have occurred in a concentrated way in periods of greater tourist flows, usually from December to February, though not during the rest of the year when tourism is less pronounced. This discontinuity of the dialogue on ethnotourism during the rest of the year generates an absence of agreements and internal determinations on tourism activities as well as only the occasional involvement of the different agents of the community. This factor is a limitation for the Pataxó to carry out proper participatory management of ethnotourism.

The Pataxó of Barra Velha IL have presented a perspective of ethnodevelopment based on agreements and internal determinations aimed at subsistence, the generation and distribution of income, practices that value local culture and their relationship with their environment, as well as their socio-cultural and socio-political strengthening to generate greater autonomy in the management of their territory and their lives. It is emphasised that the Pataxó regard ethnotourism as an activity that must integrate with the other productive arrangements to enable an overall ethnodevelopment process. In their ethnotourism planning and management practices, they demonstrate a strategy for the creation of touristic itineraries that offer products generated primarily from agriculture, fishing and handicrafts.

PNGATI and IN No. 3 can serve as mechanisms of technical and legal support for the process of organising ethnotourism in IL. The Aragwaksã Plan is a document that the Pataxó consider to be a guideline for a more autonomous management of their territory. The plan covers the principles of ethnodevelopment and ethnotourism, and can serve as an important tool for consultation and negotiation in the community. The process of drawing up a visitation plan for Barra Velha IL, foreseen in IN No. 3, has the challenge of promoting the participatory and integrated planning of ethnotourism in the territory. Considering PNGATI, IN No. 3, the Aragwaksã Plan and the opinions of the Pataxó observed in the field, we have systematised in Table 3.1 the main actions for an ethnotourism programme that favours the autonomy and self-determination of the Pataxó and the potential contributions of the PNGATI and IN No. 3 for this process.

The Pataxó case, as also observed in Fakcha Llakta tourism in Ecuador (see Chapter 5 of this volume), demonstrates the official recognition of Indigenous

Table 3.1 Main actions for Pataxó management of ethnotourism in Barra Velha IL

Actions required for Pataxó ethnotourism	*Potential contributions of PNGATI and NI No. 3*
Elaboration of the Visitation Plan for Barra Velha IL: mobilisation and effective involvement of the community in the process.	The PNGATI decree provides support for indigenous management initiatives on ethnotourism in their ILs. NI 3 requires the preparation of this plan. Use of these legal instruments to mobilise the community, guide the actions and request technical support from the State and partners in the process.
Strengthening and establishment of partnerships with institutions to implement the visitation plan.	Use of these legal instruments to require state support and establish partnerships for implementation.
Ongoing training for service delivery and activity management at the IL	Foreseen in the PNGATI, the promotion of continuous training of indigenous people for the management of ethnotourism and also of their territory.
Control of entry and exit of tourists in Barra Velha IL.	Foreseen in the PNGATI, the promotion of actions to protect, supervise and monitor IT and its limits. Provide strategies in the Visitation Plan, as directed by NI No. 3
Strengthening Pataxó associations to manage the activity and financial resources generated collectively.	PNGATI plans to strengthen and empower indigenous organisations to support IL management, which in the case of Barra Velha IL involves ethnotourism.

land by creating the legal mechanisms for Indigenous groups (or communities) to take decisions and manage their land according to their interests and needs, resulting in an enhanced proactivity with an increase in the sense of belonging, while strengthening group identity and culture (de Lima, 2011, 2014; de Lima and Weiler 2016); both cases reveal that these native groups have been part of a process of ethnodevelopment. PNGATI can be regarded as a milestone in the empowerment and inclusion of Indigenous groups by creating the framework, tools and a needed 'ethnic security' – some of the principles necessary for the materialisation of an ethnodevelopment structure.

Clarke (2001) and Willis (2005), in their work on the theories and practices of development, mention the four major 'principles' (what we also consider as 'conceptual dimensions') of ethnodevelopment as outlined by Bjorn Hettne (1995, 1996):

- *Territorialism*: the space where there is a concentration of ethnic groups in which decision-making on development is made within a particular territory based on the natural resources available in that specific area.
- *Internal self-determination*: the available means and mechanisms for a specific ethnic group to have control over their collective destiny within the context of a nation-state.
- *Cultural pluralism*: the recognition and mutual respect in regard to distinct cultures that coexist within one society; this involves a harmonious acceptance of an otherness vis-à-vis a particular self (group) identity (Picard and Di Giovine 2014).
- *Ecological sustainability*: development should take place without negatively impacting on the natural environment, its aesthetic elements (landscapes) and without compromising the environmental services while maintaining the conditions for future livelihoods. Within this context, 'the spatial concentration of groups enables a construction of ethnic identity linked to a particular territory, making the notion of "ethnodevelopment" through self-determination a logistical possibility, if not a politically-favoured one' (Willis 2005: 123).

Though not explicitly mentioned by Hettne, ethnic 'empowerment' and 'inclusion' are also principles (or conceptual dimensions) of an ethnodevelopment process. By examining the Pataxó case it was found that the key principles (or conceptual dimensions) of ethnodevelopment can be identified and the case does justice to the arguments presented in this chapter in that there has been a change of local self-perceptions, the valorisation of their own culture, and an increase in levels of self-determination. But tourism also brings with it other problems and complexities which the Indigenous groups need to be prepared to address, for example acculturation and staged indigeneity as underlined by Grünewald (2012), or they are subject to other external factors not related to tourism, for example beliefs that traditionally do not belong to their world context in that 'the

Pataxó have been concurrently converting to Pentecostalism at an ever steadier pace' (Bakker 2015: 304–27).

Conclusion

In this research study it has been identified that ethnotourism in Barra Velha IL is part of the recent history and the current daily life of the Pataxó communities of the three villages. It demonstrates that beyond expectations and effectively ethnotourism has become part of an ethnodevelopment process that involves strategies formulated by the Pataxó people for their sustainability and their territorial management. The PNGATI and IN No. 3 are legal landmarks that present guidelines for leadership and Indigenous autonomy in ethnotourism management in their territories. Because they are relatively recent decrees, it is not possible, at present, to analyse its effectiveness at Barra Velha IL. But it is possible to indicate them as instruments that can be coordinated with the Pataxó management of the ethnotourism programme that they have developed. At Barra Velha IL ethnotourism is part of a dynamic Pataxó process in the struggle for their rights to their own territory and its management. The construction of intercultural and inter-institutional dialogues and the cultural anthropophagy of the foreign elements that are inserted in the process of re-territorialisation and of regaining their rights to their lands are targets that present themselves as challenges to the Pataxó and their territorial management.

Acknowledgement

We want to thank Túlio Carlos de Moura Neves, MA in International Relations from the International University of Japan, currently serving in a diplomatic mission at the Brazilian Embassy, in Berlin, Germany, for kindly reviewing this paper and for proofreading the English language. Our thanks also goes to Prof. Dr Victor King for reviewing and copyediting this chapter.

Notes

1. Nitinawã Pataxó leadership speech during the Ethnotourism and Indigenous Peoples Dialogue held at the 'Pataxi Kuã: Knowledge Village' Meeting on 15 October 2015 in the municipality of Eunápolis-Bahia. Event organised by the State University of Bahia – UNEB
2. This is a federal organ responsible until 2007 for the management of federal CUs. During 2007 this competence was transferred to the Chico Mendes Institute for Biodiversity Conservation (ICMBio), an organ created specifically for the management of CUs.
3. Águas Claras IL is a Pataxó area that is located in the vicinity of Barra Velha IL and is bordered by its new delimitation.
4. Aragwaksã 'means conquest of the land, it is what all the elders have been dreaming for a long time, to have the land in our hands. It is also our dream' (Cardoso and Pinheiro 2012: 7). (It speaks of the chiefs and leaders of Pataxó in Barra Velha and Águas Belas in Aragwaksã.)

References

Bakker, A. (2015) Shapes of 'culture' and the sacred surplus: heritage formation and pentecostal conversion among the Pataxó indians in Brazil. *Journal of Objects, Art and Belief* 9(3), 304–27. Available at: http://dx.doi.org/10.2752/175183413X13730330868951.

Bavaresco, A. and Menezes, M. (2014) *Entendendo a PNGATI: Política Nacional de Gestão Territorial e Ambiental Indígenas*. Brasília: GIZ/Projeto GATI/FUNAI.

Brazil (1988) Brazilian Constitution and Indigenous Rights. *Direitos Indígenas na Constituição da República Federativa do Brasil de 1988*. Portal MEC, SECAD. Available online at: http://portal.mec.gov.br/secad/arquivos/pdf/cf.pdf.

Brazil (2002) Lei No. 9.985, de 18 de julho de 2000; Decreto No. 4.340, de 22 de agosto de 2002. *Institui o Sistema Nacional de Unidades de Conservação da Natureza – SNUC*, 58th edn. Brasília: MMA/SBF.

Brazil (2007) *Constituição da República Federativa do Brasil: promulgada em 5 de outubro de 1988*. São Paulo: Saraiva.

Brazil (2012) Decreto No. 7.747, de 5 de junho de 2012. *Institui a Política Nacional de Gestão Territorial e Ambiental de Terras Indígenas – PNGATI, e dá outras providências*. Brasília: FUNAI.

Brazil (2015) Instrução Normativa No. 3, de 11 de junho de 2015. *Estabelece normas e diretrizes relativas atividades de visitação para fins turísticos em Terras Indígenas*, available at: http://lex.com.br/legis_26886426_instrucao_normativa_n_3_de_11_de_junho_de_2015 (accessed 3 May 2016).

Cardoso, T. M. and Pinheiro, M. B. (2012) *Plano de Gestão Territorial do Povo Pataxó de Barra Velha e Águas Belas*. Brasília: FUNAI.

Carvalho, M. R. G. (1977) *Os Pataxós de Barra Velha: seu subsistema econômico*. Dissertação (Mestrado) – Programa de Pós-Graduação em Antropologia. Universidade Federal da Bahia.

Clarke, G. (2001) From ethnocide to ethnodevelopment? Ethnic minorities and indigenous peoples in Southeast Asia. *Third World Quarterly* 22(3), 413–36.

Cuccioletta, D. (2001/2002) Multiculturalism or transculturalism: towards a cosmopolitan citizenship. *London Journal of Canadian Studies*, 17. Available online at: http://www.canadian-studies.net/lccs/LJCS/Vol_17/Cuccioletta.pdf.

de Lima, I. B. (2011) *The Micro Geopolitics of Ecotourism: The Intricacies of Discursive Constructions, Power Relations and Partnership Models in Planning, Promotion and Management of (Eco)tourism*. North Charleston, SC: CreateSpace.

de Lima, I. B. (2014) *Etnodesenvolvimento e Gestão Territorial: Comunidades Indigenas e Quilombolas. Curitiba*. Brazil: Editora CRV.

de Lima, I. B. and Weiler, B. (2016) Indigenous protagonism in tourism operations and management in Australia, Brazil and New Zealand. *CMUJ of Social Sciences and Humanities 2(1)*, 1–31.

de Resende, M. L. C. (2013) Demonym cartography: native peoples and inquisition in Portuguese America (18th century). In S. Botta (ed.), *Manufacturing Otherness: Missions and Indigenous Cultures in Latin America*. Newcastle upon Tyne: Cambridge Scholars.

Faria, I. F. (2009) Ecoturismo, cultura e participação. In R. Bartholo, D. G. Sansolo and I. Bursztyn (eds), *Turismo de base comunitária: diversidade de olhares e experiências brasileiras*. Brasilia: Letra e imagem.

Fundação Nacional do Índio, Instituto de Pesquisa e Formação Indígena and Ministério do Meio Ambiente (2010) *Legislação ambiental e indígena: uma aproximação ao direito socioambiental no Brasil*. Rio de Janeiro: FUNAI/IEPÉ/MMA.

Furley, P. A. (1994) *The Forest Frontier: Settlement and Change in Brazilian Roraima*. London and New York: Routledge.

Gil, A. C. (1987) *Métodos e técnicas de pesquisa social*. São Paulo: Atlas.

Grünewald, R. de A. (2001) *Os índios do Descobrimento: tradição e turismo*. Rio de Janeiro: Contra capa livraria.

Grünewald, R. de A. (2012) Staged indigeneity and the Pataxó. In G. Lohmann and D. Dredge (eds), *Tourism in Brazil: Environment, Management and Segments*, Contemporary Geographies of Leisure, Tourism and Mobility Series. London and New York: Routledge, pp. 158–72.

Guimarães, R. G. (2006) Turismo em terras indígenas já é fato: quem se arrisca?, *Revista Dialogando no Turismo* 1(1), 5–42.

Haesbaert, R. (2002) *Territórios alternativos*. Rio de Janeiro: Eduff, Niterói.

Haesbaert, R., and Mondardo, M. (2010) Transterritorialidade e antropofagia: territorialidade de trânsito numa perspectiva brasileiro-latina-americana. *Revista Geographia/UFF* 12(24), 1–32.

Helena, L. (1983) *Uma literatura antropofágica*. Fortaleza, Brazil: Universidade Federal do Ceará, Editora UFC.

Hettne, B. (1995) *Development Theory and the Three Worlds: Towards an International Political Economy of Development*, 2nd edn. New York and Harlow: Longman.

Hettne, B. (1996) Ethnicity and development: an elusive relationship. In D. Dwyer and D. Drakakis-Smith (eds), *Ethnicity and Development: Geographical Perspectives*. Chichester: John Wiley.

ILO (1989) *Indigenous and Tribal Peoples Convention, 1989 (No. 169)*. Convention concerning Indigenous and Tribal Peoples in Independent Countries (Entry into force: 5 September 1991). Adoption: Geneva, 76th ILC session (27 June 1989). Available online at: http://www.ilo.org/dyn/normlex/en/f?p=NORMLEXPUB:12100:0::NO::P12100_ILO_CODE:C169.

Jones, P. (1993) *Studying Society: Sociological Theories and Research Practices*. London: Collins.

Leal, R. E. S. (2009) O turismo desenvolvido em territórios indígenas sob o ponto de vista antropológico. In R. Bartholo, D. G. Sansolo and I. Bursztyn (ed.), *Turismo de base comunitária: diversidade de olhares e experiências brasileiras*. Brasília: Letra e imagem.

Little, P. E. (2006) *Gestão territorial em terras indígenas: definição de conceitos e proposta de diretrizes*. Secretaria de Estado do Meio Ambiente e Recursos Naturais do Acre, Rio Branco, AC.

Luindia, A. L. (2007) *Ecoturismo indígena*. Quito: Abya-Yala.

Minayo, M. C. S. (2004) *O desafio do conhecimento: pesquisa qualitativa em saúde*, 8th edn. São Paulo: Hucitec.

Oliveira, A. R. (2011) *Processo de construção de Política Nacional de Gestão Ambiental e Territorial de Terras Indígenas – PNGATI: possibilidades, limites e desafios do diálogo entre estado e povos indígenas no Brasil*. Brasília: FUNAI/GIZ.

Oliveira, C. A. F. (2011) Ecoturismo étnico no Parque Nacional do Monte Pascoal: formas de comunicação entre condutores indígenas e visitantes da Unidade de Conservação. *Revista Brasileira de Ecoturismo* 5(1), 53–66.

Oliveira, C. A. F. (2014) *Diagnóstico sobre o turismo e uso público nas unidades de conservação federais do extremo sul da Bahia*. Caravelas, BA: Conservação Internacional Brasil.

Organização Internacional do Trabalho (OIT) (1989) *Convenção 169 da OIT: sobre povos indígenas e tribais*, available at: http://www.oitbrasil.org.br/info/download/conv_169.pdf (accessed 1 May 2016).

Picard, D. and Di Giovine, M. A. (2014) *Tourism and the Power of Otherness: Seductions of Difference*. Bristol: Channel View Publications.

Roca, Z., Claval, P. and Agnew, J. (eds) (2016) *Landscapes, Identities and Development*. New York: Routledge.

Sampaio, J. A. L. (2000) Breve história da presença indígena no extremo sul baiano e a questão do território Pataxó do Monte Pascoal. In *XXII Reunião brasileira de antropologia - Fórum de pesquisa 3*: 'Conflitos socioambientais e unidades de conservação', Brasília, pp. 1–19.

Stacey, M. (1977) *Methods of Social Research*. Oxford: Pergamon.

Willis, K. (2005) *Theories and Practices of Development*. New York: Routledge.

4 Empowerment through community-based ecotourism in a globalised world global-local nexus – three Thai villages as case studies

Nantira Pookhao, Robyn Bushell, Mary Hawkins and Russell Staiff

Introduction

Community-based ecotourism (CBET) is believed to improve the sustainability and quality of life for people living in the local area. However, most research into local empowerment suggests this form of tourism development is too simplified and generalised. Place-based studies are necessary to account for the specific influences of supranational institutions, governmental organisations, NGOs, tourists and local entrepreneurs, each of which greatly affect the success or otherwise.

Many studies within tourism research generally disregard the interrelationship associated with local communities and external bodies, but King (2009) has urged anthropologists to view tourism beyond the local realm and construct a more holistic understanding cognisant of globalisation, modernisation and socio-cultural change. Earlier, Agrawal and Gibson (1999: 630) argued that 'community-based conservation initiatives must be founded on images of community that recognise their internal differences and processes, their relations with external actors, and the institutions that affect both.' Blackstock (2005) has also expressed concern that studies of community-based tourism focus on functional approaches to community involvement and ignore community empowerment and change associated with community development, viewing 'community' as a homogeneous society. He also criticised the neglect of recognition of external power-bases and a sole focus on local control, leading to misunderstandings and ineffective development. Given that the construction of community identity revolves around the complexity of global processes of power relations and the interests of the state, these present challenges for the identity of local communities in addressing the 'tourist gaze' (Urry 1990). The commodification of ethnic identity can, in turn, empower local people to attract tourists by the increasing touristification of communities.

Since the sustainable tourism literature regards empowerment in a form of social framework as a key end goal of CBET (Foucat 2002; Gui *et al.* 2004; Laverack and Thangphet 2009; Reimer and Walter 2013), this chapter investigates the journey of intra-community participation and its connection to community empowerment in rural Thailand where local people are seen as uneducated and having limited voices and knowledge in relation to ecotourism management and operation.

Through three case studies located in different regions of rural Thailand this chapter addresses the issues above and the lack of research into the long-term operations of CBET, pointing to the complexity of intra-community operations in relation to self-motivation and inclusion, and the interrelationship of the notion of community empowerment in a broader context. To understand the transformative path towards empowerment, this study was conducted 19 years after the Thai government adopted sustainable tourism development (STD) embracing a bottom-up development approach, and urging local participation in both its policy and practice (Office of the National Economic and Social Development Board 2016; Tonami and Mori 2007). Prior to immersion in these communities, secondary data relating to CBET was reviewed and in-depth interviews were conducted with Thai policy-makers to establish a broader understanding of Thai CBET.

The Thai approach towards sustainable (tourism) development

The World Commission on Environment and Development (WCED) officially coined the term 'sustainable development' (SD) in the report *Our Common Future* in 1987, and guided the pursuit of environmental reform. In 1992, the United Nations Conference on Environment and Development (UNCED), known also as the Earth Summit, was held in Rio resulting in key documents and legal agreements such as the Rio Declaration on Environment and *Development*. These documents have led many local government agencies around the world, including the Association of Southeast Asian Nations (ASEAN), to implement countless plans related to SD. Among those agreements, Agenda 21 highlighted the formulation of environmentally sound and culturally sensitive tourism programmes as a strategy for sustainable development (United Nations, 1992). Agenda 21 became a blueprint for local communities to conform to the global objectives by proposing local actions with an emphasis on community participation in decision-making (UNCED 1992).

In principle, SD combines conservation and development with the driving force of communities and their active participation. Tourism sectors have embraced the concept of sustainable tourism development (STD) and the principles of Agenda 21, which led to a greater focus on decentralisation. Within the ASEAN region, the Manila Declaration of 1987 was the beginning of intra-collaboration, yet STD was not recognised until the Bangkok Summit Declaration in 1995, when the member countries agreed to promote STD in which ecotourism was included (ASEAN 2012). In developing the regional community, ASEAN has recently promoted community-based tourism and ecotourism (Kim *et al.* 2013).

Thailand has embraced the notion of SD in its policy as a guideline for the country's development after the Rio Earth Summit from its 7th National Economic and Social Development Plan (NESDP 1992–6) onwards, which created the establishment of the National Council for Sustainable Development and the formulation of National Sustainable Development Strategies in 2002 and 2003 respectively (UNEP, TEI and NESDB 2008). Due to the Asian financial crisis originating in Thailand in 1997, Plan 8 (1997–2001) shifted focus and evolved into a transition of human development and the strengthening of community by emphasising decentralised management. The government actualised the commencement of this by distributing a research budget to academics to assist in the implementation of CBET. The outcomes appeared in tourism policies related to government support of CBET (Sarobol *et al.* 2002).

The Sufficiency Economy Philosophy (SEP) or 'just-enough economy' (*Setthakit Pho Phian*), encouraged by His Majesty King Bhumibol Adulyadej of Thailand since the 1970s, has been heavily promoted and re-emphasised following the economic crisis in Asia. The SEP embraces the basic tenets of Buddhist ethical teaching in the context of self-reliance, moderation, and not less and not more than one needs. It is devoted to three principles: moderation, wisdom and resilience against internal and external risk according to self-immunity at the community level (United Nations Educational Scientific and Cultural Organisation 2013; United Nations Development Programme 2007). Many scholars believe that SEP is an alternative development path that places emphasis on the moral conditions of Buddhism that enhance immunity and resilience in a complex and changing world (for example, Prayukvong 2005; Darren 2011; Wibulswasdi *et al.* 2010). Dayley (2008: 4) proposed that SEP is a 'culturally-appropriate path to Thai development, especially rural development, through its agrarian application known as "The New Theory"'. Others suggest that SEP 'became the national brand of sustainable development' (Rossi 2012: 282).

In tourism, Buddhist ethics in SEP have been highlighted, promoting sociocultual mobilisation towards local tourism sustainability, particularly by the Thai scholar Theerapappisit (2003a, 2003b, 2009; Fennell and Malloy 2007; Theerapappisit and Cooper 2004). He suggested applying a Buddhist development model and principles as a socially appropriate approach to the planning and participation process for both policy-makers and local people.

Community-based ecotourism in a globalised world: experience, knowledge and power

Following the concept of STD, tourism scholars have categorised ecotourism – an alternative form of tourism – as a subset of sustainable tourism (Dowling 1995; Butler 1996, cited in Weaver 1998; Diamantis 1998, cited in Diamantis and Ladkin 1999; Weaver 2001). It involves nature-based, education-based and sustainability-based components operating in a small-scale manner (Blamey 1997, 2001, cited in Weaver 2002, 2005a, 2005b, and Weaver and Lawton 2007). With learning opportunities in ecotourism operations, participants are expected to gain more experience and knowledge in conservation and ecotourism management, in what Weaver (2005a: 441) termed the 'transformative effect'. Weaver categorised ecotourism into minimalist and comprehensive ideal types. Minimalist ecotourism fosters basic understanding about ecology but does not transform the values and behaviours of participants, while the second, being educational, fosters a deep understanding about the ecological and socio-cultural dimensions in a holistic way and, if effective, can transform the values and behaviours of participants. These transformative effects in ecotourism participation are instrumental in striving for sustainable development.

Accumulated knowledge gained from CBET operations is not only limited to shifting participants' worldviews towards ecology, but also increases the communities' capacity and interest in pursuing their attainment of becoming forest guardians, to raise local voices over land tenure issues and to strengthen local voices by emphasising local participation and cooperation through the formation of groups. In general, education and knowledge have the power to transform and can empower individuals towards self-determination.

Ecotourism scholars have proposed that ecotourism development requires a 'tailored approach' to work with local circumstances in order to achieve sustainability (Nault and Stapleton 2011; Cater 2006; Weaver and Lawton 1999). According to Cater (2006), the appreciation of nature must be considered in relation to its particular social, cultural, economic and political contexts, and not simply as ecotourism which is a Western construct. Fletcher (2009: 272) contends that 'many elements of ecotourism discourse are likely to be quite alien to members of rural communities in less-developed and often non-Western societies where ecotourism is promoted'. Therefore, some stakeholders may need capacity- building in order to be in a position to collaborate in decision-making (Carroll 1993, cited in Medeiros de Araujo and Bramwell 1999). Guidance and support from external stakeholders is vital for the CBET community in developing countries, where local people often have limited knowledge of tourism or ecotourism and the processes of CBET initiation, development and operation.

Community-based ecotourism emphasises small-scale, decentralised and locally-oriented development (Butcher 2007) that engages with the concept of "active participation" and demonstrates a bottom-up approach to development. In order to develop tourism towards sustainability, stakeholder support and involvement in tourism development is necessary (Timothy 1998; Medeiros de Araujo and Bramwell 1999; Andereck and Vogt 2000; Byrd 2007; Byrd *et al.* 2008, 2009; Graci 2012), because tourism stakeholder involvement is directed towards democratic empowerment and equity, operational advantages and an enhanced tourism product (Jamal and Getz 1995; Timothy 1998; Lane and Bramwell 2000; Murphy 2013).

In relation to empowerment, Scheyvens (1999, 2003) classified empowerment in ecotourism into four categories – political, economic, psychological and social empowerment – which leads local people to economic sustainability, self-confidence, self-determination, social integration and inclusion, and political influence on land rights. Butcher (2007: 86) defined empowerment as 'increas[ing] [the] ability of individuals or communities to influence their destiny'. From this notion, empowerment can encourage the means to achieve self-determination since local communities typically possess 'less power and less ability' (than other agencies they have been associated with) so they are in need of empowerment. This gives prominence to the issue of power relations between a local community and external stakeholders.

Three examples of Thai CBET: Mae Kampong, Ban Busai and Khiriwong

Mae Kampong is a small village in northern Thailand surrounded by mountainous terrain with over 400 villagers across 132 households (Huay Kaew Subdistrict Administrative Organisation (SAO) 2012). The village is a hundred-year-old community with the unique history of highlanders accompanied by close kinship. It is 60 kilometres away from Chiang Mai province, a well-known tourist city. The weather is cool all year round given its altitude of 1,300 metres above sea level (Huay Kaew SAO 2012). The area is covered by scenic mountainous evergreen and mixed forests which generate the water source for the Wang River and various small rivers and headwaters. A community forest is situated alongside Chae Son National Park. The prominent plant species found in the area is the wild terrestrial orchid and this has been domesticated for the purpose of selling to tourists. A seven-tiered waterfall, limestone cliffs, rocks and a stone garden are the natural capital resources of the village. Since Chiang Mai is a hub of Thai and foreign tourists, Mae Kampong also profits by receiving frequently a range of different visitors, including study trips of government organisations, students, academics and non-governmental organisations (NGOs), free independent travellers (FITs) and package tours.

The village of Ban Busai nestles by a rocky stream at the foot of the mountains that are part of an inscribed UNESCO World Heritage site, the Dong Phaya Yen–Khao Yai Forest, comprising Thap Lan National Park, Khao Yai National Park, Pang Sida National Park, Ta Phraya National Park and Dong Yai Wildlife Sanctuary (UNESCO 1992–2014). According to the Department of National Parks, Wildlife and Plant Conservation (DNP) of Thailand, abundant natural resources, such as evergreen forests, rainforests, mixed deciduous forests and grasslands, together with 800 species of mammals, birds and other wild animals, exist in the area (DNP, n.d.). The villagers at Ban Busai are a mixed group of people from nearby districts and provinces located in an area of Thailand northeast of the capital Bangkok. Around 295 households with close to 900 villagers live in Ban Busai (Thai Samakkhi SAO 2013). Travelling from Bangkok to Ban Busai village (210 kilometres) takes approximately three hours. Given the short driving distance, the majority of visitors are Bangkok residents. Since the village practices are in keeping with the principles of the Sufficiency Economy Philosophy (SEP) and the village has been promoted as a learning centre of the sufficiency economy, most visitors are government employees and students coming for agricultural workshops or school camps.

Khiriwong village is situated 30 kilometres from the southern Thai city of Nakhon Si Thammarat. Founded around 300 years ago in 1782 by settlers in the reign of King Rama I, the community is located adjacent to Khao Luang National

Park, which is the source of the downstream water supply to the Tapee River, Pak Phanang River and the canals of Krungching, Khao Kaew, Tapae, Lanae and Laeye. Khao Luang, the highest plateau in the southern part of Thailand, is covered by tropical evergreen forest and tropical rainforest. Khao Luang National Park is home to 327 species (DNP, n.d.). The community is comprised of four villages – Khiriwong, Khiri Thong, Khun Khiri and Khirithum – covering an area of approximately 8,173 *rai* (or 3 million square metres) in total. The total population is 3,120 across 1,070 households (Kamloan SAO 2013). Village kinship relations provide the key reason for participation and contribution toward the achievements of CBET operations at Khiriwong. Economically, Khiriwong has been practising integrated orchard farming, locally called *suan-somrom*. The communities' agricultural heritage consists of mangosteen, durian, bitter bean, langsat and longkong. The majority of tourists are Thai free independent travellers (FITs) and study tourists.

Ethnodevelopment in action: working with multiple stakeholders

With reference to the stakeholder approach, stakeholders should be continuously involved in the entire planning and management process, while active and dynamic participation along with information exchange will empower local stakeholders (Gunn 1994, cited in Byrd 2007; Mannigel 2008). Scholars have suggested that with stakeholder collaboration, the local knowledge capabilities of local stakeholders are recognised (Bramwell and Lane 1999; Yuksel *et al.* 1999) and this gives a voice to those who are most affected by tourism. It also provides an opportunity to gain resources from various actors (Jamal and Stronza 2009).

There are two perspectives on stakeholder theory (Byrd 2007). The first notion is that those who have more power gain more consideration. The other notion is that everybody should collaborate in making decisions in order to balance power, and that no stakeholders should be given higher consideration. However, the second perspective is naive – especially when local people have limited knowledge and experience in developing, managing and operating a CBT initiative. This issue of the capacity of stakeholders to participate has long been a matter for concern in the literature (Medeiros and Bramwell 1999; Simmons *et al.* 2006; Jamal and Stronza 2009; Simmons *et al.* 2010). Hence the external stakeholders who have more knowledge and power tend to suggest what is good for promoting the community as a tourism destination in order to sell it to the outside world, and what is good for the market (but not necessarily) for the local people in order to prolong the life of CBET.

A government project called One Tambon One Product (OTOP), or OTOP Village Champion (OVC), was a catalyst for CBET initiation and has benefited CBET operations. *Tambon* refers to the sub-district level in Thailand and one *tambon* includes many villages. OTOP was initiated by the Community Development Department (CDD), Ministry of Interior in 2001 and is a well-known marker of locally made products throughout Thailand. The project is consistent with SEP and aims to strengthen the local economy and community, promote local wisdom and human development, and encourage local creativity (CDD 2010). An individual village is expected to produce at least one standout product derived from local wisdom (*phumpanyaa tongtin*) and the product will be presented at the *tambon* level. This project is to promote local entrepreneurship to strengthen community self-reliance. OTOP was initiated by the Taksin government, based on and inspired by a Japanese initiative, One Village One Product (OVOP). Nevertheless, Curry and Sura (2007) and Prayukvong (2007) have noted that OTOP applies the concept of SEP.

Community-based ecotourism (CBET) in Mae Kampong was initiated in 1999 by the village headman (1996–2012) with the support of the Thailand Community-Based Tourism Institute (CBT-I), academics and the Thailand Research Fund (TRF) to pursue the research project called 'the model of sustainable management in conservation tourism', based on participatory action research. The community has received awards for their outstanding CBET operations. These include One Tambon One Product (OTOP Village Champion) as the Best Ecotourism Village (2006), the Thailand Tourism Award, the Excellent Community-Based Tourism Award (2007), the Best Northern Territory Homestay (2005), Homestay Thai Standard Award (2004) and the Pacific Asia Travel Association (PATA) Gold Award in cultural tourism (2012). The village has also received the accolade of the Best Sufficiency Economy Village in Chiang Mai (2010).

The village development has been implemented with the support of the Teen Tok Royal Project Development Centre, established in 1981 by the Royal Project Foundation of King Rama IX proposing the growing of alternative plants to replace opium plantations. This Centre has been responsible for the trading of local fresh coffee beans and helping villagers with overall agricultural issues. The core objectives of the foundation are to promote community self-reliance and local environmental rehabilitation, which conforms to the principles of the SEP (Royal Project Foundation 2015). Apart from the personal budget of the King, the Royal Project Foundation has received support from the United Nations (UN) under the project *UN/Thai Program for Drug Abuse Control*, from the Agriculture Research Service of the United States Department of Agriculture, and from cooperation between Thailand and Taiwan for agricultural research (Royal Project Foundation 2015).

In 1979, the King visited Mae Kampong and discovered that the villagers lacked electricity. In 1982, the Department of Alternative Energy Development and Efficiency supported and built a hydropower plant. Following the establishment of the plant, the community initiated the 'mini hydropower cooperative account' which became the core cooperative account used in managing and distributing CBET benefits to all community members. With the operation of hydropower plants and other community development projects related to conservation and self-reliance, the CBET operations of the village nowadays receive benefits from study tours by academics, students, government organisations, NGOs and their partners and entrepreneurs. These study tours also receive outstanding numbers compared with Thai or foreign FITs. The electricity generated by the plants has also been useful for the consumption of resources used in the CBET operations.

At Ban Busai, the villagers were afflicted by poverty. In 2000, the villagers were funded by the Office of Higher Education to collaborate with Suranaree University of Technology and Nakhorn Ratchasima Rajabhat University to develop a variety of seeds for local suitability. One of these agricultural collaborations with Suranaree University is the production of mushrooms. Consequently, the OTOP of the village includes mushroom paste and crispy mushrooms. The community has received numerous awards for their work including: Best Practices of Sufficiency Economy Philosophy Village: Happy and Peaceful Environment (2007), Greening Village (2007), Quality Community Development Plan at the provincial level (2008), Provincial Community-based Learning Centre (2009), Homestay Standard (2004, 2006 and 2008), and Community Wisdom of the Province (2009).

International and domestic NGOs have taken part in various local conservation initiatives boosting local environmental awareness. For example, the Japan International Cooperation Agency (JICA) cooperated with the Royal Forest Department (RFD) in conservation research and activities in the area along the border of Ban Busai and the National Park by establishing a demonstration plantation centre in 1991. This was to increase local collaboration and strengthen community-based forest management. The demonstration plantation centre was for developing seedlings, forestry extension, training, a demonstration plantation and nursery techniques. Despite the project ending, the centre has continued under the responsibility of the Royal Forest Department. The other example of conservation collaboration is a reforestation project of 1 million *rai* (approximately 395,369 acres) organised by the World Wildlife Fund Thailand (now known as the World Wide Fund for Nature) under the Royal Patronage of Her Majesty the Queen and the PTT Public Company Limited (PTT), along with support from various government agencies and the local people in Thai Samakkhi sub-district between 1997 and 2000.

In 1962, 1975 and 1988 respectively, Khiriwong encountered massive floods due to deforestation, which destroyed villagers' lives and property. Following the flooding disaster, the community received substantial external assistance from the state and NGOs. The villagers promoted ecotourism in 1992 with support from the Thai Volunteer Service – Responsible Ecological and Social Project (TVS-REST), now known as the Community-based Tourism Institute (CBT-I) by organising a tour programme to Khiriwong. The Khiriwong Ecotourism Club (KEC) commenced as a centre of community ecotourism management. In 2001, the Khiriwong Cooperative Center (KCC) was established to integrate community activities and alleviate internal and external conflict among the National Parks Office, the Tourism Authority of Thailand (TAT), KEC and SAO. Since Khiriwong has gained a reputation for being the first community-operated CBET operation in Thailand, various institutions have visited the village to learn about both self-reliant proficiency and ecotourism management. Khiriwong has received several awards, such as the National Honorary Mention Award of

Voluntary Development and Self-defense Village (*or por bpor*) in 1985–6, Best Ecotourism Award (1998), one of the first eight OTOP Tourism Villages in 2004 and the OTOP 5-star Award for its local products. Khiriwong has been widely acclaimed in various publications (for example, Division of Industry and Community Network 2009; Japan International Cooperation Agency 2008; Dechapimon 2001) as the effective practice community of SEP due to the reputation of its OTOP and its local way of life that is associated with SEP.

In 2001 and 2005 respectively, the Thai Research Fund (TRF) granted a budget to academics to conduct CBET and conservation research at Khiriwong (TRF 2002), and TAT provided funds to researchers to conduct participatory ecotourism development planning for the community in 2006 (TAT 2015). The Japan International Cooperation Agency (JICA) also took part in the development at Khiriwong. Likewise, the PTT Public Company Limited (PTT) has played a great role in supporting SEP at Khiriwong.

According to Rossi (2012: 282), SEP has also been represented from the perspective of romanticism. He notes:

> This regime of representation [SEP] is nurtured with a visual imaginary centred on the presentation of didactic pictures and movies reproducing Thai villages in a romanticised and static perfection. This imagery represents the ideal rural order as it is imagined by the royal elite and by institutions like the Office of Royal Development Projects and other foundations set up by members of the royal family. It has also become a key ideological framework for the activities of many NGOs and public institutions engaged in land and forest issues.

In the same vein, the study of Chanyapate and Bamford (2009) pointed to the notion of participatory democracy and the collective action of local communities interrelating with SEP to achieve self-immunity. In so doing, practising SEP can empower the communities examined, such as receiving budgets and a certificate of successful SEP practice.

Community identity and empowerment

According to the complex context of a globalised world, Bauman (2000) describes the continued, constant and relentless change (development) within society in the modern world as very rapid and where solidity is replaced by liquidity, which he terms 'liquid modernity'. Global assemblages in liquid modernity merge institutions, NGOs and supranational organisations into a global 'common' with global governance through the connectivity, interactivity, mobility and virtuality of people and society. While community self-governance and multiple selves are new challenges for the nation-state, this causes the nation-state to manage a multi-layered polycentric network of governance (Bauman 2000). This fluidity has an impact on the notion of community. Delanty (2003) proposed that community might not be in one physical place or necessarily have shared history among its people: ‘As real communities decline, identity replaces it around a new understanding of community’ (Delanty 2003: 118). Bauman (2000: 15) calls this ‘reinvented identity’. It can be the shared interest of people and it may be about developing new power relationships and drawing on the concept of empowerment through the concepts of community and sense of belonging.

The application of SEP in Thai CBET is relevant to what Hitchcock (1999) describes as the relationship of ‘ethno-nationalism’ employed in the promotion of tourism. The notion of ‘sufficiency economy village’ and the CBET communities encourage various institutions, particularly the study tours organised by government agencies, to visit the community in order to learn about proficiency in self-reliance and ecotourism management. Mae Kampong, Ban Busai and Khiriwong each represent themselves as a picturesque ideal of a Thai self-reliant, collective and cohesive community that can resist the modern regime of power related to modernisation and capitalisation and, correspondingly, conforming to the state’s direction.

With improved reputations and publicised awards of acknowledgement, the community identity has accordingly been constructed. Thus the identity of CBET has been aligned to the community strengths stated in the policy and the characteristics of SEP. The commodification of these characteristics is largely determined by the domestic market of study trips, whereas the FITs and inbound visitors are benefits after the communities gain a good reputation and market know-how.

The quote from Lertwicha (1989, cited in Winichakul 2008), one of the disciples of Chattip, an influential Thai scholar, illustrates this portrayal:

> Khiriwong is a real village which is identical to the one imagined by villagers … not penetrated by state and capitalism. We might think that this kind of community existed only in the peasant millennialism of the past. Or it might be just a wish of a utopian thinker. But this is real.

This work has been critiqued by Winichakul (2008) on the grounds of Chatthip’s romanticisation of the ‘authentic’ village as the site of anti-capitalism. Not only this study, but a lot of other research has been conducted, ranging from community studies and ecology to the human–nature relationship, forest management and tourism at Khiriwong in relation to its achievement (these include Puan-Auam and Sukphongsri 2000; Tungchawal 2001; Opasruttanakorn *et al.* 2006; Leksakundilok and Hirsch 2008; Rungklin 2009; Sukholthajit 2009). This idealisation of the village and community as a place firmly rooted in its past heritage and the recent achievements in the everyday life of Khiriwong, as well as the ideal of the ‘primitive’ as an ethnic community, are saleable to outsiders and support their tourism enterprise.

There have been many study tours to Khiriwong to learn about group collaboration and cooperation, and how local people manage a fair distribution of benefits from these groups, which is contradicted by ethnographic work in the community. Nevertheless, because these attributes can sell they become the front-stage performance for the tourists, but not enacted in their everyday lives – a scenario MacCannell (1973) describes as 'staged authenticity'. Commodification of culture has revolved around the notion of authenticity (MacCannell 1976; Cohen 1988; Greenwood 1989), which is a fake representation of a real world that takes place in what Boorstin (1964) described as 'pseudo-events' constructed by the tourism industry. Local people play 'natives' for tourists (Cohen 1979). This turns tourism into a stage for local plays. Thus the commodification of the tourist space leads to the creation of 'staged authenticity', explained by MacCannell (1973, 1999), who adopted the concept from Goffman (1974). The 'front' is the meeting place of hosts and guests, while the 'back' is a private space for the hosts. Therefore commodification of ethnicity, cultural identity and nature (in a form of cultural construction) become the tools of local people to attract tourists by increasing the touristification of communities which interrelate with 'the process of transformation' to match with the 'tourist gaze' (Urry 1990).

MacCannell (1984) elucidated the issues of ethnic tourism when the host community becomes associated with the image recognised by outsiders and perceives itself as an ethnic attraction. This is implicated in how the intangible – ethnicity and cultural identity – becomes a tangible value to tourism destinations as touristic attractiveness, particularly for the CBET destination. Associated with the idea of the 'tourist gaze' Urry (1990) noted the way that local people are represented and reinvented, or are creating and recreating themselves and their cultural identity. The image is maintained by the hosts with tourism influencing local conceptions of self (Picard and Wood 1997). Picard and Wood (1997) proposed that the state's interest is to promote national integration, which can challenge the identity of local communities within the nation that embeds diversity. Local people may respond to this either with resistance or take advantage of cultural promotion for touristic purposes (Hitchcock *et al.* 2009). However, according to Wood (1997), ethnic labels are issued and regulated by the state depending upon the level of state intervention. According to the research data, Mae Kampong, Ban Busai and Khiriwong have learned to reject or to accept support and intervention in order to gain benefits toward environmental, political, psychological and economic empowerment.

The construction of CBET identity revolves around the complexity of global processes of power relations. Wood (1997: 2–3) remarked:

> The relationship between tourism, states and ethnicity is dynamic and ongoing, with highly variable outcomes … These three interacting processes of change may be seen as parts of a broader process of globalisation … not only in its massive movement of people to virtually every corner of the world but also its linkage of economic, political and sociocultural elements … Ethnicity is also increasingly recognised as shaped by contemporary global processes, rather than by residue from parochial pasts.

The dynamic character of the global–local relationship influences 'the transformation (shape and reshape) of local image and identity'. This image and identity of local communities also influences the way local communities commoditise their way of life to gain power in the competitive market, domestically and internationally.

Conclusion

This chapter has explored the relationship between globalisation, national policy directions and multi-tourism-related stakeholders in relation to local CBET communities. It illustrates the shaping of CBET identity, which is influenced by the complexity of the global-local nexus and globalisation simultaneously achieving the objectives of empowerment, development and conservation. This chapter argues that local communities know how to benefit from specific identities and are willing to construct and reconstruct these to suit their purposes. From the surface, the communities are seen as followers and victims of the streams of top-down development. In reality, the communities have learned throughout the development and operational process to exercise their power in order to accept or reject the interaction of external stakeholders.

The differences between Thai and foreign tourists, particularly Westerners, create greater understanding of the way local communities commoditise different packages for Thai and foreign tourists, while the front and back stage are applied by local communities to empower themselves for CBET management. With this power, CBET communities can choose to espouse or neglect particular images urged by government agencies. Finally, this chapter contends that communities have learned throughout the development and operational process the way that they exercise their power when interacting with external agencies and know how and in what way to acquire power as a result of the experience gained from the operation.

References

Agrawal, A. and Gibson, C. C. (1999) Enchantment and disenchantment: the role of community in natural resource conservation. *World Development* 27(4), 629–49.

Andereck, K. L. and Vogt, C. A. (2000) The relationship between residents' attitudes toward tourism and tourism development options. *Journal of Travel Research* 39(1), 27–36.

Association of Southeast Asian Nations (ASEAN) (2012) *Plan of Action on ASEAN Cooperation in Tourism*. Retrieved from http://www.asean.org/?static_post=plan-of-action-on-asean-cooperation-in-tourism.

Bauman, Z. (2000) *Liquid Modernity*. Cambridge: Polity Press.

Blackstock, K. (2005) A critical look at community based tourism. *Community Development Journal* 40(1), 39–49.

Boorstin, D. J. (1964) *The Image: A Guide to Pseudo-events in America*. New York: Harper & Row.

Bramwell, B. and Lane, B. (1999) Collaboration and partnerships for sustainable tourism. *Journal of Sustainable Tourism* 7(3–4), 179–81.

Butcher, J. (2007) *Ecotourism, NGOs, and Development: A Critical Analysis*. Abingdon: Routledge.

Byrd, E. T. (2007) Stakeholders in sustainable tourism development and their roles: applying stakeholder theory to sustainable tourism development. *Tourism Review of AIEST – International Association of Scientific Experts in Tourism* 62(2), 6–13.

Byrd, E. T., Bosley, H. E. and Dronberger, M. G. (2009) Comparisons of stakeholder perceptions of tourism impacts in rural eastern North Carolina. *Tourism Management* 30(5), 693–703.

Byrd, E. T., Cárdenas, D. A. and Greenwood, J. B. (2008) Factors of stakeholder understanding of tourism: the case of Eastern North Carolina. *Tourism and Hospitality Research*, 8(3), 192–204.

Cater, E. (2006) Ecotourism as a Western construct. *Journal of Ecotourism* 5(1–2), 23–39.

Chanyapate, C. and Bamford, A. (2009) On recent projects and experiences of the Sufficiency Economy: a critique. In U. Brand and N. Sekler (eds), *Development Dialogue*. Uddevalla: Mediaprint, Vol. 51, pp. 143–56.

Chartrungruang, B. (2011) The model of Sufficiency Economy Philosophy: application for tourism industry in Chiang Mai, Thailand. *International Journal of Asian Tourism Management* 2(2), 134–44.

Choibamroong, T. (2009) *Roles of Local Government in Developing Sustainable Tourism Based on Sufficiency Economy Philosophy*. Bangkok: King Prajadhipok's Institute [In Thai].

Cohen, E. (1979) A phenomenology of tourist experiences. *Sociology* 13(2), 179–201.

Cohen, E. (1988) Authenticity and commoditization in tourism. *Annals of Tourism Research* 15(3), 371–86.

Community Development Department (CDD) (2010) *One Tambon One Product*. Retrieved from http://www.cdd.go.th.

Curry, R. L. Jr and Sura, K. (2007) Human resource development (HRD) theory and Thailand's sufficiency economy concept and its 'OTOP' program (One Tambon One Product). *Journal of Third World Studies* 24(2).

Darren, N. (2011) Thailand's Sufficiency Economy: Origins and comparisons with other systems of religious economics. *Social Compass* 58(4), 593–610.

Dayley, R. (2008) *Imagined Futures: Sufficiency Economy and Other Visions of Rural Thailand.* Paper presented at the 10th International Thai Studies Conference, Thammasat University.

Dechapimon, S. (2001) Self-Reliance Community Development: A Case Study of Kiriwong Community, Nakhonsrithammarat. Unpublished Master's thesis, Ramkhamhaeng University, Bangkok.

Delanty, G. (2003) *Community*, 2nd edn. London: Routledge.

Department of National Parks, Wildlife and Plant Conservation of Thailand (DNP) (n.d.) Available online at: http://www.dnp.go.th/index_eng.asp.

Diamantis, D. and Ladkin, A. (1999) The links between sustainable tourism and ecotourism: a definitional and operational perspective. *Journal of Tourism Studies* 10(2), 35–46.

Division of Industry and Community Network (2009) *BJIM Bulletin: Visit to Walailak and Suratthani Rajabhat University, Thailand.* Retrieved from http://icn.usm.my/index.php/en/component/phocadownload/category/38-e-bulletin?download=42:december-2009.

Dowling, R. K. (1995) *Ecotourism Development: Regional Planning and Strategies.* Paper presented at the International Conference Eco-tourism: Concept Design and Strategy, Ambassador Hotel, Bangkok.

Fennell, D. A. and Malloy, D. C. (2007) *Codes of Ethics in Tourism: Practice, Theory, Synthesis*, Vol. 33. Clevedon, Canada: Channel View Publications.

Fletcher, R. (2009) Ecotourism discourse: challenging the stakeholders theory. *Journal of Ecotourism* 8(3), 269–85.

Foucat, V. S. A. (2002) Community-based ecotourism management: moving towards sustainability, in Ventanilla, Oaxaca, Mexico. *Ocean and Coastal Management* 45(8), 511–29.

Goffman, E. (1974) *Frame Analysis: An Essay on the Organization of Experience*. New York: Harper & Row.

Graci, S. (2012) Collaboration and partnership development for sustainable tourism. *Tourism Geographies* 15(1), 25–42.

Greenwood, D. J. (1989) Culture by the pound: an anthropological perspective on tourism as cultural commoditization. In V. L. Smith (ed.), *Hosts and Guests: The Anthropology of Tourism*, 2nd edn. Philadelphia: University of Pennsylvania, pp. 171–85.

Gui, Y.-L., Fang, Y.-G. and Liu, J.-S. (2004) Community-based ecotourism in nature reserve of China. *Chinese Geographical Science* 14(3), 276–82.

Hitchcock, M., King, V. T. and Parnwell, M. J. G. (2009) *Tourism in Southeast Asia: Challenges and New Directions*. Copenhagen: NIAS.

Jamal, T. B. and Getz, D. (1995) Collaboration theory and community tourism planning. *Annals of Tourism Research* 22(1), 186–204.

Jamal, T. and Stronza, A. (2009) Collaboration theory and tourism practice in protected areas: Stakeholders, structuring and sustainability. *Journal of Sustainable Tourism* 17(2), 169–89.

Japan International Cooperation Agency (JICA) (2008) *Thailand: Regional Development Project (II)*. Retrieved from http://www.jica.go.jp/english/our_work/evaluation/oda_loan/post/2008/pdf/e_project11_full.pdf.

Kim, S., Kang, M. and Sukmajaya, D. (eds) (2013) *Opportunities and Challenges of Ecotourism in ASEAN Countries*. Seoul: Jungmin Publishing.

King, V. T. (2009) Anthropology and tourism in Southeast Asia: comparative studies, cultural differentiation and agency. In M. Hitchcock, V. T. King and M. J. G. Parnwell (eds), *Tourism in Southeast Asia: Challenges and New Directions*. Copenhagen: NIAS, pp. 43–68.

Lane, B. and Bramwell, B. (eds) (2000) *Tourism Collaboration and Partnerships: Politics, Practice, and Sustainability*. Buffalo, NY: Channel View Publications.

Laverack, G. and Thangphet, S. (2009) Building community capacity for locally managed ecotourism in northern Thailand. *Community Development Journal* 44 (2), 172–85. Available online at: https://doi.org/10.1093/cdj/bsm058.

Leksakundilok, A. and Hirsch, P. (2008) Community-based ecotourism in Thailand. In J. Connell and B. Rugendyke (eds), *Tourism at the Grassroots: Villagers and Visitors in the Asia-Pacific*. London and New York, Routledge, pp. 214–35.

MacCannell, D. (1973) Staged authenticity: arrangements of social space in tourist settings. *American Journal of Sociology* 79(3), 588–603.

MacCannell, D. (1976) *The Tourist: A New Theory of the Leisure Class*. Berkeley, CA: University of California Press.

MacCannell, D. (1984) Reconstructed ethnicity tourism and cultural identity in Third World communities', *Annals of Tourism Research* 11(3), 375–91.

MacCannell, D. (1999) *The Tourist: A New Theory of the Leisure Class*, 2nd edn. Berkeley, CA: University of California Press.

Mannigel, E. (2008) Integrating parks and people: how does participation work in protected area management? *Society and Natural Resources* 21(6), 498–511.

Medeiros de Araujo, L. and Bramwell, B. (1999) Stakeholder assessment and collaborative tourism planning: the case of Brazil's Costa Dourada project. *Journal of Sustainable Tourism* 7(3–4), 356–78.

Murphy, P. E. (2013) *Tourism: A Community Approach*, 2nd edn. London: Routledge.

Nault, S. and Stapleton, P. (2011) The community participation process in ecotourism development: a case study of the community of Sogoog, Bayan-Ulgii, Mongolia. *Journal of Sustainable Tourism* 19(6), 695–712.

Office of the National Economic and Social Development Board (NESDB) (2016) *The Eighth Plan*. Retrieved from http://www.nesdb.go.th/nesdb_en/main.php?filename=develop_issue.

Opasruttanakorn, O., Buddharat, C. and Tongkhundum, T. (2006) Needs of Khiriwong people to study English for tourism business. *Journal of Yala Rajabhat University* 1(2), 112–19.

Picard, M. and Wood, R. E. (eds) (1997) *Tourism, Ethnicity, and the State in Asian and Pacific Societies*. Honolulu, HI: University of Hawaii Press.

Prayukvong, W. (2005) A Buddhist economic approach to the development of community enterprises: a case study from Southern Thailand. *Cambridge Journal of Economics* 29(6), 1171–85.

Prayukvong, W. (2007) A Buddhist economic approach to happiness and capability linkage in OTOP craftsmen in southern Thailand. *Kasetsart Journal: Social Science* 28, 161–76. Retrieved from http://kasetsartjournal.ku.ac.th/kuj_files/2008/A080401160147.pdf.

Puan-Auam, K. and Sukphongsri, S. (2000) *Ecotourism: The Study Area, the Khiri Wong Community, Tambon Kamlon, Amphur Lan Saka, Nakhon Si Thammarat Province*. Retrieved from http://kb.hsri.or.th/dspace/handle/11228/1223.

Reimer, J. K. and Walter, P. (2013) How do you know it when you see it? Community-based ecotourism in the Cardamom Mountains of southwestern Cambodia. *Tourism Management* 34, 122–32.

Rossi, A. (2012) Turning red rural landscapes yellow? Sufficiency Economy and Royal Projects in the hills of Nan province, Northern Thailand. *Austrian Journal of South-East Asian Studies (ASEAS)* 5(2), 275–91.

Royal Project Foundation (2015) *About Us*. Retrieved from http://royalprojectthailand.com/about [in Thai].

Rungklin, D. (2009) Consumer Behavior and Marketing Factors: Buying Tie-dye of Ban Khiriwong's Natural Color Tie-dye, Community Nakhon Si Thammarat Province. Unpublished Master's thesis, Walailak University, Nakhon Si Thammarat.

Sarobol, S., Wongtabtim, U. and Songpornvanich, S. (2002) *Community-based Tourism: Concepts and Experiences (KarnTongTiew Doe ChumChon: NaewKind Lae Prasobkarn)*. Chiang Mai: Upper Northern Research Administration Network (UNRN).

Scheyvens, R. (1999) Ecotourism and the empowerment of local communities. *Tourism Management* 20(2), 245–9.

Scheyvens, R. (2003) *Tourism for Development: Empowering Communities*. London: Prentice Hall.

Simmons, B., Bushell, R. and Scott, J. (2010) Fostering responsible tourism business practices through collaborative capacity-building. In J. Sarkis, J. J. Cordeiro and D. Vazquez Brust (eds), *Facilitating Sustainable Innovation Through Collaboration*. The Netherlands: Springer, pp. 185–201.

Simmons, B., Scott, J., Bushell, R., Sinha, C., Desailly, M. and Baillie, B. (2006) Environmental management partnerships: a research case study from the tourism industry. In R. Welford, P. Hills, and W. Young (eds), *Partnerships for Sustainable Development*. Hong Kong: Centre of Urban Planning and Environmental Management, University of Hong Kong, pp. 74–93.

Subdistrict Administrative Organisation (SAO) (2012) *Tourism Information of MaeKampong*. Huay Kaew Subdistrict Administrative Organisation.

Subdistrict Administrative Organisation (SAO) (2013) *General Information of Kamsloan Subdistrict*. Kamloan Subdistrict Administrative Organisation.

Subdistrict Administrative Organisation (SAO) (2013) *Three Years Development Plan of Thai Samakkhi*. Thai Samakkhi Subdistrict Administrative Organisation.

Sukholthajit, P. (2009) Khiriwong: a self-reliant community (*Ban Khunnam Khiriwong: Chumchon Peungtonaeng*). *Romphruekj*, 27(1), 93–123. Retrieved from http://romphruekj.krirk.ac.th/books/2552/1/04.pdf [in Thai].

Thailand Research Fund (TRF) (2002) *eLibrary*. Retrieved from http://elibrary.trf.or.th/ [In Thai].

Theerapappisit, P. (2003a) Mekong tourism development: capital or social mobilization? *Tourism Recreation Research* 28(1), 47–56.

Theerapappisit, P. (2003b) Buddhist ethics: planning towards sustainable community-based tourism. *Journal of the Faculty of Architecture, Silpakorn University*, 19, 159–69.

Theerapappisit, P. (2009) Pro-poor ethnic tourism in the Mekong: a study of three approaches in Northern Thailand. *Asia Pacific Journal of Tourism Research*, 14(2), 201–21.

Theerapappisit, P. and Cooper, C. (2004) *Degradation or Enhancement Through Tourism: A Role for Ethical/Religious Approaches.* Paper presented at the 14th International Research Conference of the Council for Australian University Tourism and Hospitality Education (CAUTHE), Brisbane Convention and Exhibition Centre.

Timothy, D. J. (1998) Cooperative tourism planning in a developing destination. *Journal of Sustainable Tourism* 6(1), 52–68.

Tonami, A. and Mori, A. (2007) Sustainable development in Thailand: lessons from implementing Local Agenda 21 in three cities. *Journal of Environment and Development*, 16(3), 269–89.

Tourism Authority of Thailand (TAT) (2015) *Thailand Tourism Research Database 2002–2012*. Retrieved from http://tat.plushours.com/research/research_grid/rc_research_document/view/rc_research_document/12749?advance_search=Trueandcategory=44.

Tungchawal, K. (2001) Sustainable Ecotourism in the Village of Khiriwong and the Khao Luang National Park, Thailand. Unpublished Master's thesis, University of Wisconsin-Stout.

United Nations Conference on Environment and Development (UNCED) (1992) *Agenda 21: Programme for Action for Sustainable Development, Rio Declaration on Environment and Development.*

United Nations Development Programme (UNDP) (2007) *Thailand Human Development Report 2007: Sufficiency Economy and Human Development*. Retrieved from http://hdr.undp.org/sites/default/files/thailand_2007_en.pdf.

United Nations Educational Scientific and Cultural Organization (UNESCO) *Agenda 21*. Retrieved from: https://sustainabledevelopment.un.org/content/documents/Agenda21.pdf.

United Nations Educational Scientific and Cultural Organization (UNESCO) (1992–2014) *Dong Phayayen-Khao Yai Forest Complex*. Retrieved from http://whc.unesco.org/en/list/590.

United Nations Educational Scientific and Cultural Organization (UNESCO) (2013) *Towards a Sufficiency Economy: A New Ethical Paradigm for Sustainability*, UNESCO Future Lecture. Retrieved from http://unesdoc.unesco.org/images/0022/002230/223026E.pdf.

United Nations Environment Program (UNEP), Thailand Environment Institute (TEI) and the National Economic and Social Development Board (NESDP) (2008) *National Sustainable Development Strategy: A Guidance Manual*. Bangkok: Royal Government of Thailand, UNEP, TEI and NESDB.

Urry, J. (1990) *The Tourist Gaze: Leisure and Travel in Contemporary Societies*. London: Sage.

Wattanawannarat, S., Meanyoung, A., Jaruswong, W., Chaichana, W., Boontor, R., Sangasri, A. and Seneewong Na Ayuthaya, A. (2014) *The Way Out for Thai Workers*, Report of Group 3. Retrieved from http://www.tja.or.th/index.php?option=com_rokdownloadsandview=folderandItemid=27andid=332:–1 [in Thai].

Weaver, D. B. (1998) *Ecotourism in the Less Developed World.* Wallingford: CAB International.

Weaver, D. B. (2001) Ecotourism as mass tourism: contradiction or reality? *Cornell Hotel and Restaurant Administration Quarterly* 42(2), 104–12.

Weaver, D. B. (2002) Asian ecotourism: patterns and themes. *Tourism Geographies*, 4(2), 153–72.

Weaver, D. B. (2005a) Comprehensive and minimalist dimensions of ecotourism. *Annals of Tourism Research* 32(2), 439–55.

Weaver, D. B. (2005b) Mass and urban ecotourism: new manifestations of an old concept. *Tourism Recreation Research* 30(1), 19–26.

Weaver, D. B. and Lawton, L. J. (1999) *Sustainable Tourism: A Critical Analysis*, Research Report 1. Retrieved from Gold Coast: http://ckwri.tamuk.edu/fileadmin/user_upload/docs/WAGSO/Discussion_Topics/Ecotourism/Comprehensive_and_minimalist_dimensions_of_ecotourism.pdf.

Weaver, D. B. and Lawton, L. J. (2007) Twenty years on: the state of contemporary ecotourism research. *Tourism Management* 28(5), 1168–79.

Wibulswasdi, C., Piboolsravut, P. and Pootrakool, K. (2010) *Sufficiency Economy Philosophy and Development*. Retrieved from http://thaiembassy.de/site/images/download/suff_econ_book.pdf.

Winichakul, T. (2008) Nationalism and the radical intelligentsia in Thailand. *Third World Quarterly* 29(3), 575–91.

Wood, R. E. (1997) Tourism, ethnicity, and the state in Asian and Pacific societies. In M. Picard and R. E. Wood (eds), *Tourism, Ethnicity, and the State in Asian and Pacific Societies*. Honolulu, HI: University of Hawaii Press, pp. 1–34.

Yuksel, F., Bramwell, B. and Yuksel, A. (1999) Stakeholder interviews and tourism planning at Pamukkale, Turkey. *Tourism Management* 20(3), 351–60.

5 Environmental stewardship, Indigenous tourism planning and the Fakcha Llakta community

An ethnic endogenous development model in Otavalo-Imbabura, Ecuador

Kennedy Rolando Lomas Tapia, Carmen Amelia Trujillo and Ismar Borges de Lima

Introduction

This chapter presents a case study of the engagement of the Fakcha Llakta community in the ecological restoration of the Cascada de Peguche Forest Protected Area (Peguche Falls), and its role in an Indigenous cultural-historical revival and in ecotourism activities in Imbabura province, Otavalo district, Ecuador. A change in their ethnic welfare status and the 'environmental stewardship' role of the Fakcha Llakta have been evident after the Management Plan implementation in the 1990s. For implementing the Plan, a participatory and inclusionary Indigenous approach was used to improve the environment and the welfare of the community while empowering the ethnic group. The objective of the chapter is to examine the main autochthonous elements that have historically been embodied in the Ecuadorian Fakcha Llakta community and have been considered for implementing an ethnic-based development model to conserve cultural and natural assets. Attention is drawn to evidence of self-determination, ethnic empowerment and inclusionary actions that are critical for constructing an ethnodevelopment model. The relevance of (eco)tourism development for empowering the Indigenous community is also addressed. This chapter seeks to fill gaps in the literature on tourism and ethnodevelopment by presenting a genuine empirical case of development based on ethnicity.

Indigenous populations have increased in size since the mid-1970s, not only as a matter of biology but also of identity choice, and currently it is estimated that there are more than 350 million Indigenous people who have become increasingly more organised 'as well as winning a series of battles over land and cultural autonomy' (Friedman 2005: 162). Indigenous peoples have also been referred to as 'natives, aborigines, tribes, autochthons, pueblos originarios (original people), and many other labels … such as Indians, First Nations, and Adivasis … but they have received little attention in the human rights discourse before the late 20th Century' (Stavenhagen 2013: 45). However, to address Indigenous issues within the perspective of tourism and ethnodevelopment is not a simple task, particularly with regard to the controversial and complex Indigenous themes involved (Zeppel 2006;

Hughes *et al.* 2015) in Latin America, especially in Ecuador. This has occurred due to a series of past and current events faced by the native communities, such as social upheavals in a struggle to gain fair access to water resources; territorial and tenure disputes over the ownership and management of ancestral lands and sacred sites; bio-piracy of Indigenous traditional knowledge to exploit plant and animal species by illegally appropriating long-standing traditions and practices and claiming patents to restrict their general use, overwhelmingly disregarding any Indigenous culture and intellectual property (Simpson 1997): 'the concept among Andean Indigenous peoples of patenting their own knowledge, resources and products is virtually non-existent … [due to] extremely high costs and … cultural values' (IIDE 2006: 6). Moreover, external influences on daily Indigenous activities such as agriculture with imposed or introduced techniques and technologies aim exclusively to be responsive to an economic-driven development that undermines cultures and autochthonous peoples (Mowforth and Munt 2009; Zeppel 2006).

Distinct models of development have been imposed on countries over the years (Radice 2015), and consequently on native communities, blurring Indigenous concepts and knowledge by intercalating them with non-native developmental experiences – excessively exploitative ones – during the colonisation period undermining autochthonous cultures, and later on the basis of the premises of a modernisation and globalisation approach in the twentieth century (Edelman and Haugerud 2005). It is an economic and developmental reasoning that has negatively affected Indigenous living standards by gradually imposing rules, norms and extraneous ways of production highly disadvantageous to Indigenous peoples (López 2005).

Bonfil Batalla, in 1982, proposed his ethnodevelopment conceptions of cultural control based on a number of proposals. The first is the question of power, which refers to levels of cultural autonomy of Indigenous peoples; it has to do with the ability of Indigenous people to safeguard their own culture against acculturation processes: 'Ethnic groups undergoing an acculturation process have slowly, over past centuries, incorporated external material and spiritual values', gradually replacing their traditional life patterns (McNeely *et al.* 1994: 347–50). Indigenous peoples from every continent still experience the consequences of a colonisation process that has historically discriminated against them generally because of the otherness, that is their cultural specificities, such as distinct clothing, worldviews and physical appearance (Stavenhagen 2007, 2013).

For a fair and genuine ethnodevelopment, Indigenous rights and welfare must be a core concern for policies and actions. In 1985, as the result of three years of meetings, debates and research, the United Nations Working Group on Indigenous Rights prepared a Draft Declaration on the Rights of Indigenous Peoples agreeing on a set of principles that reflect much of Bonfil Batalla's conceptualisations for an ethnodevelopment model that considers the emancipation, empowerment, self-determination and inclusion of ethnic groups and communities. In regard to these elements, the Draft Declaration addresses them in six (5, 6, 7, 8, 9 and 14) of its 18 principles as follows:

5. Concerned that Indigenous peoples have been deprived of their human rights and fundamental freedoms, resulting, *inter alia*, in their

colonisation and dispossession of their lands, territories and resources, thus preventing them from exercising, in particular, their right to development in accordance with their own needs and interests;.

6. Recognising the urgent need to respect and promote the inherent rights and characteristics of Indigenous peoples, especially their rights to their lands, territories and resources, which derive from their political, economic and social structures and from their cultures, spiritual traditions, histories and philosophies.
7. Welcoming the fact that Indigenous peoples are organising themselves for political, economic, social and cultural enhancement and in order to bring an end to all forms of discrimination and oppression wherever they occur.
8. Convinced that control by Indigenous peoples over developments affecting them and their lands, territories and resources will enable them to maintain and strengthen their institutions, cultures and traditions, and to promote their development in accordance with their aspirations and needs.
9. Recognising also that respect for Indigenous knowledge, cultures and traditional practices contributes to sustainable and equitable development and proper management of the environment. […]
14. There is the acknowledgement that the Charter of the United Nations, the International Covenant on Economic, Social and Cultural Rights and the International Covenant on Civil and Political Rights affirm the fundamental importance of the right of self-determination of all peoples, by virtue of which they freely determine their political status and freely pursue their economic, social and cultural development […].

To study a situation subject to continuous changes requires the assumption of an ontological position that helps to interpret and understand its complexity, especially when addressing the Andean worldview and its hidden, hybridised and adopted knowledge, which constitutes a guide to address the nexus between ecotourism and ethnodevelopment. Therefore learning from within the community is still a relatively new interdisciplinary approach to science that recognises the limitations of traditional scientific knowledge to address the complex relationships between social institutions and ecological systems (Oberg 2011). This new interdisciplinary science was needed to build bridges and fill gaps between two worlds that have traditionally evolved independently: the 'knowledge' of the academy and the 'doing' of the government to reach the 'know-how' (Febres-Cordero 2013) for paving the way towards an all-encompassing 'Indigenous well-being' that can be integrated into contemporary globalised trends. Of particular interest is to understand community-based tourism as a tool for keeping the uniqueness of native cultures – their world values and views, their ecological ways of dealing with natural resources and of perceiving the landscapes as an intrinsic and valuable part of them (Mowforth and Munt 2009), and their environmental stewardship and ethical behaviour enhanced by a natural and cultural heritage legacy of a particular attraction to outsiders.

A pragmatic definition of 'environmental stewardship' is adopted in this chapter by considering it as a full commitment to continuously work on the mitigation and reduction of any negative effects and impacts on natural resources at an operational, managerial and developmental level by optimising well-being and economic outcomes grounded in sustainable practices and choices. For Worrell and Appleby (2000), environmental stewardship is 'the responsible use (including conservation) of natural resources in a way that takes full and balanced account of the interests of society, future generations, and other species, as well as of private needs, and accepts significant answerability to society' (p. 263). In their book entitled *Indigenous Peoples and the Collaborative Stewardship of Nature*, Ross *et al.* (2011) explain that 'in many Indigenous cultures people have lived in and managed (and often modified) their surrounding ecosystems for hundreds if not thousands of years. Over time their knowledge evolves to deal with newly emerging problems presented by environment' (p. 25), and based on these premises, Indigenous knowledge relates to 'environmental stewardship', which leads to conservation, and 'such knowledge should not be ignored by environmental mangers today' (p. 26). With regard to Peguche communities, there has been an array of practices with the potential to implement a balanced environmental equation by blending 'human well-being', 'economic reasoning' and 'nature conservation' through [eco]tourism activities.

Human and ethnic resources in the Cascada de Peguche Forest Protected Area

In the area of the Cascada de Peguche there are important Indigenous populations with cultures that enrich the National Cultural Heritage. These communities are: Agato, Peguche, Quinchuquí, Ariasuco, Yacupata, Pucará, La Compañia, Rey Loma, Monserrat, La Bolsa, Guanansi and Cotama. The main economic activities are subsistence farming, the production of cotton fabrics, synthetic fibre and sheep wool, embroidery and animal husbandry. The vision of land ownership is collective and ancestral; the local populations practise the sustainable use of natural resources such as the collection of firewood, grass and fodder for smaller animals, medicinal plants for traditional medicine and plants for human consumption.

In the Fakcha Llakta community, the usufruct of the land has been exercised in a communitarian way through an ecological ethno-tourism – with ethnic stakeholders playing the role of custodians of culture and biodiversity (Kelles-Viitanen, 2008), activities that emerged to incorporate this field into the productive sector of the province through community and international cooperation. These were strategies that then served to decrease the labour migration of young men and women to other countries.

So far, little research has been carried out on the Fakcha Llakta community, located in the Otavalo district, Imbabura province, despite being a relevant centre for ecotourism, and a site that brings together ethnic, cultural and historical resources of great touristic appeal. More recently the community's culture, traditions and homeland have been affected by both positive and negative external influences. As for the negative aspects, the community has lost its own language (Kichwa, language family: Quechuan) and the ability to orally transfer environmental knowledge among the generations, and undermined community perceptions of their traditions and common group understandings about the values of nature. However, daily experiences have been developed through community ecotourism. Even though some of these experiences remain invisible, intangible assets, they have been shaped by a cumulative environmental knowledge. These experiences constitute 'cultural capital' expressed in their clothing, cosmology, agriculture, religion and ecotourism activities – for example, interpretive tour guiding – as part of the systemic thinking of the community. This Indigenous cultural capital (de Lima and d' Hauteserre 2011) has been taken into account by the Ecuadorian government and authorities in legislation and public policies for community and collective improvements (Trujillo and Lomas 2014).

This chapter examines the main autochthonous elements of the Ecuadorian Fakcha Llakta community (see Figure 5.1), and the status changes and knowledge acquisition with regard to decision-making and inclusion within an ethnodevelopment perspective by contextualising it as part of 'community assets', an ethnic transformation that has empowered the native groups and the role of (eco)tourism practices in this process. The chapter also considers cultural and environmental developments, especially after the Peguche Management Plan of the 1990s, which has given an 'environmental stewardship' status and role to members of the Fakcha Llakta community. In addition, this chapter sets 'environmental education' as a critical element intertwined with cultural knowledge as part of a holistic empirical model of ethnodevelopment; this approach can help fill gaps in the literature (Berger and Luckmann 2001; Martínez 2007; Boff 2013; Bonfil Batalla 1982; Stavenhagen 2007; Leff 2013). The chapter also addresses some issues related to the PPD-UNDP/MPOD-BID Environmental Management and Tourism Plan that was conceptually and financially implemented to assist the Fakcha Llakta community to improve its overall quality of life through collaborative *participatory* projects. The financial support and interventions of other institutional donors are also considered.

This study was developed by considering as a legal foundation the regulations of Articles 56, 57, 58 and 59, Chapter IV, of the current Constitution of Ecuador 2008, which recognises and guarantees the collective rights of peoples, communities, *montubios*, Indigenous peoples and Afro-Ecuadorians in their cultures and traditions, by preserving their identity, protecting their ecosystems and supporting the provision of tourism services as set by law and regulations for nationalities and peoples. The *montubios* are Indigenous mestizo people who mostly occupy the coastal areas of Ecuador, and were recognised by the government in 2001.

The preparation of the Environmental Management Plan and Community Tourism for the Flakcha Llakta from the late 1990s into the 2000s was possible due to the work of Carmen Trujillo and Rolando Lomas as they received funds to develop it. They are Indigenous individuals themselves, university professors and environmentalists, who have close links to Peguche communities, and their

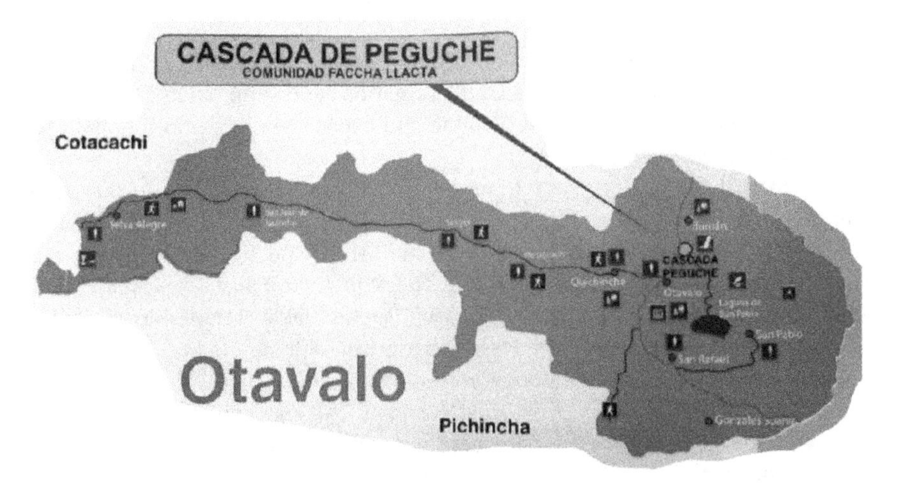

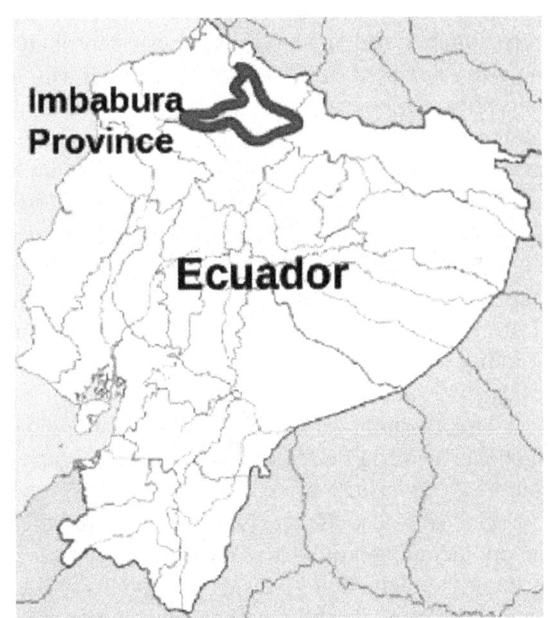

Figure 5.1 Location of Fakcha Llakta Community, in Imbabura province, Otavalo district, on the Peguche Waterfall site, Ecuador.

Source: Map assembled by Ismar Borges de Lima with images from the Cascada de Peguche map from Trujillo and Lomas (2014) and a plain Ecuador map from Creative Commons with additions.

collaborative work and support to members of the community is long-established and ongoing in order to rescue and revive Indigenous traditions as well as to strengthen ecotourism capabilities and environmental stewardship in the Otavalo district. Their concerns included the creation and implementation of an Environmental Interpretation Programme and capacity-building in this field for the Flakcha Llakta community.

The role of Ismar Borges de Lima in this chapter is not linked to that early period of the Management Plan implementation; instead, he undertook a technical visit to Peguche in November 2014 accompanied and assisted by Lomas and Trujillo when he had the opportunity to check in person and assess the current state of the Cascada de Peguche and of the Flakcha Llakta community, as well as the improvements achieved with regard to tourism, culture and heritage revivals, including the restoration of historical relics. This visit together with Trujillo's and Lomas' critical insights have furnished the empirical, conceptual and intellectual elements for assessing the Peguche case within the realms of an ethnodevelopment premise, even though the initial management projects of the 1990s had not been specifically designed within this conceptual and ideological framework. Since then the programmes and actions have largely contributed to paving the way for Indigenous development from within by backing it with inclusionary and participatory conceptions and managerial strategies.

The projects and actions developed are described and examined in this chapter in order to understand their role in promoting ethnodevelopment in the Imbabura-Otavalo region. There are lessons to be learned from these interventionist actions that became of the utmost relevance for these communities to form an institutional community-centred platform and framework to transform their lives. This way, there is empirical evidence of ethnic empowerment, self-determination and inclusion that bring together environmental, cultural, social and ethnic issues underpinned by Indigenous ecotourism activities, cultural and heritage revival, and environmental conservation with the direct participation of the Fakcha Llakta community. These lessons significantly help to outline an endogenous development model which can serve to be replicated elsewhere. Zeppel (2003) defines 'Indigenous ecotourism' as 'nature-based attractions or tours owned [managed] by Indigenous people, and also Indigenous interpretation of the natural and cultural environment including wildlife' (p. 56).

For this case study the methodology resides in reviewing the relevant literature, considering the historical formation of Peguche, and assessing the steps and actions and the participation of institutions and community engagement taken to improve the quality of life of the Flakcha Llakta, as well as its natural and cultural assets. Environmental stewardship in ecological ethno-tourism planning and implementation is a core ethnic aspect in this study.

Background

In the period 1996–8 in the Fakcha Llakta community, an environmental training programme was developed as the result of a project presented to the United

Nations Programme, which addressed issues related to environmental conservation and a curricular design for inclusion in the Institutional Reform of the Ministry of Education of Ecuador (MEC 2008). Likewise, the Ecuadorian Foundation for Social Development – Funedes, whose Director was Carmen Trujillo, developed an Environmental Management Plan for the development of educational and environmental programmes in the area of the Peguche Waterfall, which included the elaboration of participatory projects, as well as community-based ecotourism activities, ecological restoration and conservation actions, through 'environmental education' (EE). In order to achieve its goals, distinct communities engaged in the activities to implement projects financially supported by a series of international and domestic Institutional donors from 1999 to 2004. These projects helped the communities to organise themselves in order to solve local problems and capacity demands such as in community training and learning in environmental education for solid waste management, water irrigation, sustainable land use, reforestation, production and planting of native species, interpretive trails construction and skills development, as well as environmental knowledge and signage for visitors. It is worth noting that these projects and actions, even though not initially conceptualised within an ethnodevelopment framework, have served to guide and produce significant changes in the life of the Indigenous community.

The initial efforts made by both Funedes and PPD-UNDP to promote the acceptance of and conscious attitude change by the community can be regarded as the key 'gears' to strengthen the community assets (Kronik and Verner 2010; de Lima and d'Hauteserre 2011) such as its cultural heritage, the waterfall site, and other every-day and traditional knowledge. Other important institutional projects were developed later to support further community ecotourism initiatives that directly benefited the Imbabura province, such as the Runa Tupary project, legalised in 2008 by the Community Tourism Association and the Ministry of Tourism of Ecuador. This institutional partnership helped to create a Community Tourism Network supported by a Dutch NGO project, 'Aid in Action 2000' (ONG de Holanda 'Ayuda en Acción 2000'), an entity that supports rural communities in community projects, and by the Ecuadorian Ecotourism Association (ASEC 2006).

In this context, sustainable development in tourism requires the informed participation of all agents of the community as well as a strong and legally constituted political leadership, committed to the establishment of consensus on integration and sustainable management. Therefore the achievement of sustainable tourism requires a continuous process of technical-pedagogical and environmental accompaniment to propose preventive or corrective measures to the possible ecological impacts of this activity (Ross *et al.* 2011; Buckley 2004). This precept has given priority to ecological processes essential for conserving bio-diversity while respecting the socio-cultural authenticity of the host communities.

Community sustainability can be understood as a process for solving, mitigating or preventing sustainable tourism problems and for achieving harmonious human development, so individuals can consciously use their biophysical and cultural heritage abiding by the laws of Indigenous territoriality in order to manage and respond in a sustainable way to emerging environmental challenges (Carayannis 2013; Trosper and Parrotta 2012). The objective of community management in sustainable development is to achieve self-determination (Simpson 1997), protect resources, avoid degradation of the environment and improve the quality of family and community life, and this process must be integrated with local economic objectives based on environmental ethics (Pojman *et al.* 2015; Larrère 2002) and the identification of opportunities for its members.

It is necessary to generate interest and genuine motivations in the new environmental measures and initiatives at all community levels to promote the search for innovative local and regional solutions in human and social development (Carayannis 2013). Likewise, competencies must be ranked in an eco-interrelated way that allows the individuals to rethink the importance of the 'society-nature-globalisation-local-sustainability-management' relationship in all its spheres (Cabrera 2000). However, the decline in conservation practices due to 'altered ideologies of nature, loss of secure tenure over lands and resources, and centralized authority are not mutually exclusive effects and often work together to undermine "community sustainability" and "human–environment relations"' (Carayannis 2013).

Therefore it must be taken into consideration that the advance of the tourism industry coincides with the world crusade for the conservation of the environment (Pigram 2000). It is worth noting that a tourist destination unfamiliar with environmental sustainability measures can condemn itself to failure; this is because by affecting its own natural resources and assets (de Lima and d'Hauteserre 2011) there are great risks of a destination becoming disapproved by the tourists, who are even more sensitive nowadays, displaying appreciation and care for the natural world and cultural heritage (Zeppel 2006). Lopez (2005) points out that community environmental management, as well as environmental education in the community, must be founded on five epistemological and ideological pillars – learning: (1) to know; (2) to exist; (3) to make; (4) to live together; and (5) to transform oneself. This last pillar deals with socio-ethical changes for the consolidation of creative capacities, capacity-building, research and innovation.

Community tourism is not something that can be succinctly defined or easily recognised from external observation (Gartner and Lime 2000: 312). As stated in the *Acuerdo Ministerial 16/Registro 154* (2010), it is a type of tourism through which the locals have a chance to be agents of their own improvements in living conditions and economic development. Li (2006) says that 'the most simultaneously accepted concept of community tourism is perhaps the well-known advocacy of community involvement'. And community tourism is only valid if the activity evolves itself and has an answer to the challenges of economic, environmental, social, educational and cultural growth. 'It is a process that must yield a fair exchange of value between the host and the hosted, preserve the community's sense of place and bring dignity and pride to the host' (Jamal and Dredge 2015: 203). Taylor (1995) queries whether 'in the end, [community tourism] is different from any other kind of tourism development' (p. 489); it should be seen as a process rather than a product (BEST 2003; Beeton 2006). For it to become a reality, 'the destination communities should get involved in, rather than being excluded from, tourism development within the boundary of the destination area where they are settled' (Li 2006: 43).

So what is 'community'? For Terry (2011), 'community' constitutes the physical space that gives rise to the formation of culture through an identity, a paradigm of values, interests and traditions, a group or people who share common elements, such as territory, resources, language, customs, values, tasks, and worldview (p. 112). For this reason, community tourism development involves shared work and identity, governed by principles, values and norms of harmonious natural and cultural coexistence. Rocchio (2013) indicates that the economic factor drives the productive activities of the rural environment since the supply is based on community actions and allows them to generate additional and complementary incomes by increasing employment opportunities through fair trade while reducing migration and rural depopulation.

In the environmental field, community-based tourism can help promote the conservation and sustainable use of natural elements (Buckley 2004; Zeppel 2006) and the preservation of environmental values, which can become a space for education and environmental awareness (Mowforth and Munt 2009). In the social sphere, community-based rural tourism nourishes and promotes the continuity of ancestral forms of social organisation for the sustainable management of common natural resources (Zeppel 2006; de Lima and d'Hauteserre 2011); it can help to improve community living standards by implementing tourism infrastructure and services, and it can generate opportunities for the participation and leadership of women, young people and the elderly.

In terms of culture and education, visitors have given the utmost importance to local culture (Zeppel 2006). Therefore, the conservation and long-term recovery of expressions of traditional society and culture should be included in ethnic tourism planning and development. Similarly, community-based tourism strengthens local, regional and national identity through the recognition of multiculturalism, multilingualism and local biodiversity (Garner 2016). In short, community rural tourism is a space for research and learning in rural environment and local culture (Carayannis 2013; Mowforth and Munt 2009).

This type of tourism therefore requires a set of conditions for its optimum development:

- elements linked to the rural, cultural and natural environment that can attract visitors;
- planned as a complementary economic activity associated with rural traditions, business alliances, traditional knowledge and the community commitment to consider techniques that can minimise risks and negative impacts on the natural and cultural heritage of the communities as well as on its human resources;
- the existence of connectivity, minimum sustainable basic infrastructure and complementary local activities to strengthen the cultural product vis-à-vis the demands of tourism related to identity and intrinsic values.

In this context, Ecuador has been one of the first countries in the development of this type of Andean rural tourism. But the government has contributed to revive customs and the preservation of native community identity, and to ensure the participation, commitment and consensus of the communities by the means of co-responsibility as underlined by the National Plan for Good Living (2009–13).

Endogenous development and sustainable community tourism

Theoretically, endogenous development comprises the development of policies, systems and structures based on the idea that 'local and regional development should be driven in a bottom-up manner by Indigenous and endogenous forces and factors'. But there is a borderline between Indigenous and endogenous development concepts as the former refers to 'nurturing ... home-grown assets and resources that may be more locally and regionally embedded' (Todtling 2011: 333) while the latter is more broadly defined as the 'focus more on internal factors and processes of local and regional development instead of external ones' (Stohr 1990, as cited in Todtling 2011: 333). Endogenous approaches to local and regional development first emerged in the 1980s linked to certain concepts such as local entrepreneurship, regional learning and regional innovation systems (Todtling 2011: 337). Paez and Arias (2006) indicates that the objectives of the endogenous development model include: fostering the capacity to dominate the modes and means of production in a way that, from a self-managed and autochthonous perspective, can cover the basic needs of its members; the organisation of communities to eliminate poverty, improve the quality of life of the populations, and promote participatory, proactive and productive actions in society; and to guarantee and promote endogenous development consistent with national policies, plans and projects. According to Paez and Arias (2006), endogenous development is strengthened by attempting to empower the communities, so they can develop their potential in the agricultural, industrial and tourism sector of the region.

Within an endogenous model sustainable growth must be pursued through ecological capital, human–environment relations and human–society relations in order to respect the natural environment (not only as a supplier of immediate human needs); to enrich and diversify the means to achieve development; to seek various opportunities for sustainable use of resources; to mitigate differences between rich and poor; to reduce consumption and waste; to broaden the participation of citizens and local leaders in decision-making; and to raise local, regional, intergovernmental and international cooperation (Gardner and Lewis 2005; Haugerud 2003). Based on these principles and considerations, it is possible to establish a theoretical framework that defines, in general terms, the minimum conditions for a settlement pattern to generate sustainability.

In order to achieve the principles of endogenous development, it must be assumed that: oil is finite; cities do not guarantee better holistic living conditions and the potential of ecosystems is exhausted; the primary productive systems have been erroneously managed based on other extraction models; and the guidelines for managing the rural-ethnic areas are still based on top-to-bottom decision-making by following (centralised) market and taxation patterns (Job and Li 2006: 51), so there must be investment in decentralised systems and models that can multiply the creative potential of each community. An important current dimension is to analyse endogenous development as a model that originates from 'development policies concerned with local interests' (Pigram 1992: 92), so that each region discovers its productive resource potential by finding alternative ways of interacting with and exploring their natural resources (Fernández 2004).

According to the Foundation for Cooperation in Development and Promotion of Assistance Activities (CODESPA) (2011), the following attributes and variables should be taken into account in order to assess the potential of tourism recreation within an endogenous development model:

- *scope:* as the territorial space of tourism;
- *management:* the definition of a community-based rural enterprise, where community participation in management and operation is in strategic alliance with other actors (local governments, NGOs, international cooperation, private companies) with similar and complementary objectives;
- *supply:* identification of the natural and cultural products offered, after analysing the profile of rural community-based tourism, and the characteristics and compatibility of supply and demand;
- *interaction:* participation and host-visitor interaction in rural activities related to the product;
- *behaviour:* the responsible attitude of all the actors involved in the tourist activity during its management and operation, including community organisations, partners, local governments, service providers and visitors for the sustainable management of territories through community-based rural tourism;
- *value of experience:* the compatibility between the visitors' expectations and the products offered in terms of the diversity of authentic cultural and natural elements, as well as the genuine experiences of the visitors.

The Fakcha Llakta community, its characteristics and geographic location

According to historical data, the Indigenous community of Fakcha Llakta has its origins from the sale of the 'Peguche' farm to the Ecuadorian Housing Bank (BEV) in 1986, which undertakes the sale of lots of 300m^2 to the *comuneros* (members of a community) who were in possession of the property (Trujillo and Lomas 2014). This community is located in the Miguel Egas parish of the Otavalo canton, in the province of Imbabura. It has easy access within the protected area of Cascada de Peguche (see Figure 5.1) and is an ideal natural space for ecotourism with recreational and cultural activities that have been well-visited by domestic and foreign tourists. This ethnic community maintains cultural traditions and ancestral knowledge, and it is considered a natural bastion of local identity.

Landscapes and recreation

The landscape of Otavalo, comprising lakes, lagoons, waterfalls, mineral sources, forests and mountains, in combination with the local cultural universe, is the basis for the development of community-based sustainable tourism. In this area, the cascade is part of a set of historical and cultural elements, attractive to tourists and expressed in its *obrajes*, fulling mills, and a sixteenth-century hacienda house, declared as cultural heritage, where hundreds of Indigenous people worked their looms (Truillo and Lomas 2014). In addition there are the thermal mineral pool, the colonial bridge over the Jatun-Yacu River and the solar clock, formerly called the *bohío cacical* by the archaeologist César Fuller in 1982. Also, there is the water mill, the giant eucalyptus of 1830, guided interpretive trails, and ornamental and ethnobotanical gardens.

The waterfall is formed from the 'San Pablo' lake, comprising two waterfalls with a height of 15m respectively, forming the Upper Río Napo, called locally Jatun-Yacu, originally from the Kichwa language meaning 'Big Water' (Krahenbuhl 2011), which in conjunction with the presence of exotic and native trees results in both a colourful and unique landscape for tourists, as well as for shamanic teachers, who guarantee the healing power of the waters, as a sacred site in the Andean worldview of Kichwa communities; the waterfall continues as a place of celebration of solstices and equinoxes, especially in June during the Festival of the Sun or Intyraimi (Oviedo, quoted by Trujillo and Lomas 2014).

It is worth mentioning that the waterfall is named 'Peguche' or 'Peguchi' in the old Cara language, spoken by the elders of the area; it means 'sacred water vapour that falls or bathes from above' (Lema 1995). For some historians such as Oviedo (1983) and Vásquez (1987) as well as for local people, 'Peguche' is also a tribute to a representative of those called 'Tío Peguche', literally 'Peguche Uncle'. The term 'uncle' is commonly used among the natives, which means very respectable man or lady.

In 2002, the community organisation gained funding from the United Nations under the Small Grants Programme for the environmental recovery of the area, especially by the reforestation of native species, community organisational strengthening, environmental education training, as well as the construction of the environmental interpretation centre and the trail infrastructure with support from the Inter-American Development Bank and the Public Works Ministry. The Peguche area and Fakcha Llakta also received financial aid and training for socio-environmental and tourism projects by the Embassy of Japan and by the Ministry of Social Welfare (MIES).

As the restorative and capacity-building work progresses, the Fakcha Llakta community is regaining its leadership in environmental management, changing its name and administrative status from Community Development Committee to *Communa*, a legal organisational level that empowers the locals as a Forest

Protector administration for training in environmental and tourism issues. For the management of the natural resources, a legal agreement was signed between the Ecuadorian Ministry of the Environment and the Municipality of Otavalo (2000) with the establishment of different Commissions in order to optimise the operational capacities of its members and thus to contribute significantly to the sustainable development of the community and its environment.

The Peguche Waterfall is still considered a sacred place for local people, where shamans acquire spiritual strength and energy through the rituals at the site that are performed at certain times of the year. According to Vásquez (1987), the Cascada was part of a vast complex of worship that was complemented by the 'Lechero of Pucará and Laguna de Imbacocha' located in the parish of San Pablo, Imbabura. Verschuuren (2010) outlines the main arguments for developing biocultural conservation approaches for sacred natural sites, as observed by the Flakcha Llakta community.

During the colonial period, with the formation of the hacienda (farm) system, this whole area was integrated into the Quinchuquí-Peguche hacienda, where one of the most famous *obrajes* had been operating, called San José de Peguchi Obraje, founded in 1622, and which lasted for 40 years (Rueda 1988); it consisted of 300 natives working with eight looms, seven for adult clothes and one for slingshots (Rueda 1988: 75). According to Freile (1981), since 1709 because of inadequate management, the Peguchi hacienda was frequently auctioned off and run by several owners, the last being Carlos Barba, who faced an uprising of the natives from several neighbouring communities, risking their lives to take possession of the farm. The property was then sold to the Ecuadorian Bank of Housing which chose to divide it into lots for community members (Trujillo and Lomas 2014).

The architectural remnants of the San José de Peguchi Obraje can still be seen, although other historically relevant constructions have disappeared or are hidden by vegetation. The *obrajes* were places where Indigenous people were first trained in textile production and then worked in the craft workshops as makers of textiles in cotton, wool and silk. In the early 1960s, the Indigenous community was underdeveloped and excluded, as explained by Alberto Muenala in an interview with Diego Cazar Baquero, a reporter working for *La Barra Espaciadora* (*LBE*) (September 2016); Muenala is considered the film-maker of the Indigenous peoples of Ecuador. His film focuses on languages, practices and symbols of the Indigenous world. Part of Alberto's life was in Otavalo, Cascada de Peguche:

> When little Alberto was sitting in front of the waist loom, Peguche was barely a small hamlet set up along the road, a few miles north of the small town of Otavalo. There was no electric light and racism on the part of the mestizo people towards the natives of the Kichwa Otavalo people was very marked, so much so that they lived far from the urban centre, dedicated to agriculture and artisanal textile manufacturing. In the buses, the natives could only occupy the back rows and they were not allowed to enter certain bars. In those years, as an inheritance of the elders, whole families spent their days working

> looms, like enchanted spiders among their own threads. In their houses, still built with barley straw and cow manure, they baked bread and cooked corn to give their bodies the necessary energy.
>
> But little Alberto had different plans, so when he turned twenty-one in 1980, he looked north and went to Mexico to study film at the University Center for Cinematographic Studies of the Autonomous University of Mexico (UNAM).
>
> Somehow, Alberto continues to knit. For Don Jose, 'he is always surrounded by cameras and making his films for all of us.' It relates, for us, to the Indigenous peoples and nationalities of Ecuador. As a member of the Confederation of Indigenous Nationalities of Ecuador (CONAIE), Alberto carries on a tireless struggle to make the reality of his people visible through film. 'Cinema is one of the few ways you can tell the reality of what you feel, I think it is much more effective than writing, because everyone now sees, and you can make them understand what you mean.' The cinematographic work of Alberto is made by Indigenous Kichwa Otavalo and reveals his own experiences in daily life. 'From the beginning I needed to express myself and communicate with people,' recalls Alberto, 'because I want to transmit that knowledge, to recover that memory so that our knowledge will not be lost ...' (Diego Baquero, *LBE online*, 21 September 2016)

According to Farinango, one of the oldest people living in Peguche, the 'Bosque' was in the past – as a prohibited place for the local Indigenous communities because of the sacredness of the Peguche Forest and Waterfall – and it also reveals the significant transformations of Peguche as it returned to the hands of the native peoples and became a tourist destination.

> According to Farinango, he was barely a child, and the Peguche waterfall in Otavalo and its forest were 'a forbidden place' for local Indigenous communities, even though they considered it a sacred place. The owner of that farm (the Peguche farm) raised cows and horses at the site instead, while the children of Peguche community only could watch behind the fences and 'keep away' signs that Peguche was private property. Today, Farinango, 63 years-old, proudly tells the fantastic legends about the energy of Peguche water, the musical stone, and the Inca pool at the place. [in contrast to its 'private land'], Peguche receives more than 1,000 visitors per month and who are astonished at the site, considered one of the main attractions of Imbabura. (*El Comércio*, Redacción Ibarra, Las Cascada y el Bosque de Peguche están cuidados, regional newspaper, archives by Trujillo and Lomas 2014)

This evidence confirms that the Cascada de Peguche has great cultural and scientific importance (Trujillo and Lomas 2014). The community has currently run labour commissions comprising men, young women and older adults who are legally organised, based on the principles of ethnic and cultural participation supported by a normative-Indigenous chapter, and backed by the parish government. It is also important to mention the advantages of the 'Indigenous *communas*', the organised social groups that can make use of large community areas through consensual agreements.

The ancestral knowledge for the environmental education management of community tourism

In order to understand the Indigenous reality of the Fakcha Llakta community, we need to look back at history (see Figure 5.2) in which observation is an element driven by the original culture, particularly because Ecuador is geographically located in the middle of the planet with the privilege of observing the sky from different angles, and being favourably positioned to discover relevant elements of the cosmos, which influence and determine the aspects, activities and behaviour of the members of the community. From ancient times, the community has been placed at the centre of a 'spiral model' that has the power to rule the lives of human beings following and replicating in many aspects the spiral calendar for agriculture based on the three worlds (Figures 5.2, 5.3 and 5.4).

Life for the Aborigines is embodied in the *pachakutic* (Indigenous time spiral) or, as they call it, the *churo* (snail) that has great influence on their everyday lives. In Figure 5.2, historical and archaeological relics can be observed supporting the spiral model and its conceptualisation.

The historical construction based on the 'spiral model' is an environmental-educational reference for the communities of Ecuador, particularly in community-based tourism. A spiral model indicates the beginning of life and the daily activities of the *comuneros* (members of the community) as it depicts distinct aspects of Imbabura province (Figures 5.2, 5.3 and 5.4); it embodies and expresses their beliefs, agriculture and environmental protection. The model represents the Indigenous worlds within Andean cosmogony, directly related to the cosmos (*Hanan Pacha*), mother earth (*Kay Pacha*) and the subsoil (*Uku Pacha*) (Figure 5.3). From an ethno-historical perspective, Shady (2014) explains that the model relates to the Andean ideological concept of the three worlds: the world above of the stars and the gods; the world of humans; and the underworld of the ancestors. Each of the three worlds is looked after by its respective deities (p. 88; Strong 2012). Likewise, as also explained by following a spiral reasoning, the Andean native person has no past, present or future; the Andean Indigenous understanding is that there is only the 'current moment', the 'place here', because the world is cyclical. It regenerates, reproduces itself, is activated and reactivated – everything revolves, grows and advances in relation to human lived experiences, and by following the spiral dynamics in a synchronous way it represents the modelling of current life, ecotourism activities and an environmental stewardship based on the ancestral agricultural calendar. By taking this axiomatic native thought into account an ethnodevelopment model should function through an ethno-historical perspective by using cumulative tangible and intangible native knowledge to centre ethnicity as critical for the well-being of ethnic minorities.

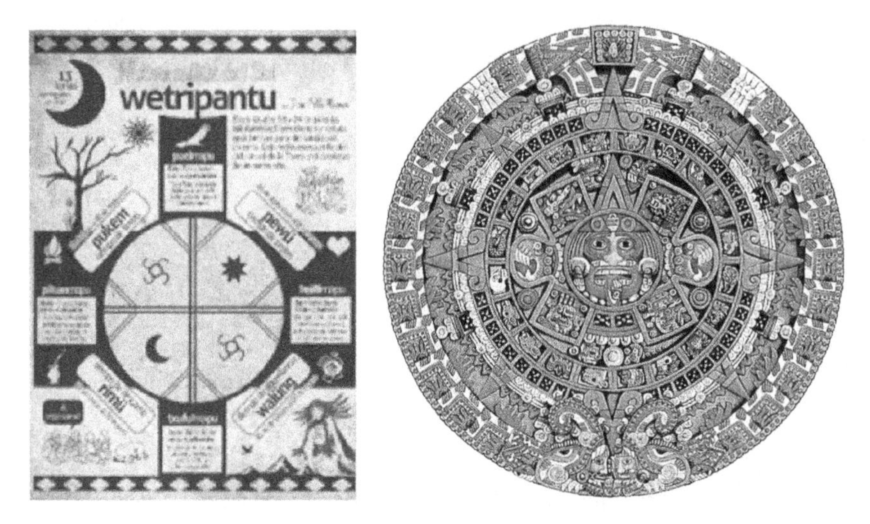

Figure 5.2 Indigenous spiral model to determine planting time, harvest, and periods of drought and abundance.

Source: Rolando Lomas' research materials.

Thus this investigation describes social phenomena and seeks to analyse meanings and to make interpretations about the social reality of the Indigenous people of Fakcha Llakta, because community knowledge is neither aseptic nor neutral; it is a relative knowledge with regard to the meanings of humans in their 'spiral' interactions. This knowledge establishes the basis for decision-making on the fundamental aspects of daily life, the responsible use of resources, appropriation and respect for community values, which are largely shared with visitors, particularly during interpretive sessions and trails. This knowledge is an integral part of

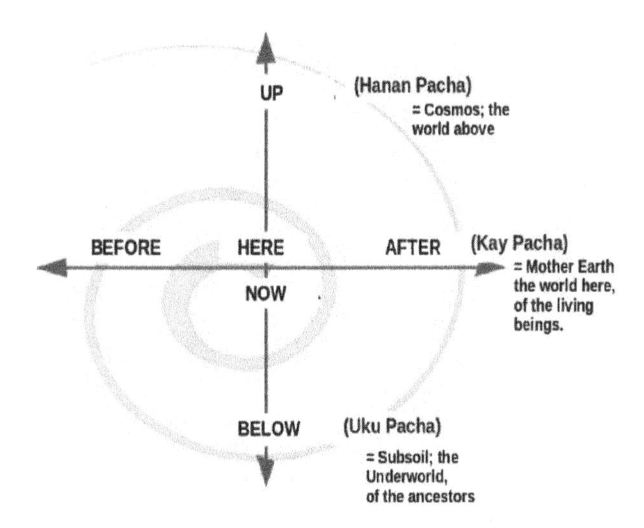

Figure 5.3 Indigenous spiral model to determine time, past (traditional knowledge), after (mother earth), above (cosmos, the world of gods), down (subsoil), here and now (where the living beings are).

Source: Lomas and Trujillo, this chapter.

the cultural system of the community that allows visitors to get to know some of the details of the native way of life (Figure 5.4).

Local knowledge is part of the historical culture of the Fakcha Llakta community, which has been communicated to visitors through different tourist activities. Local history is a pedagogical means to ensure that, with the cumulative knowledge on the most significant natural and cultural events and processes acquired locally, the tourism products of the Fakcha Llakta community can be managed in a sustainable way. Figure 5.4 shows the interrelations between local knowledge and other community elements relevant to constructing an educational model for the management of community-based tourism.

The environmental, social and cultural resources management plan sought to integrate technical-ecological actions with the needs, concerns, interests and participation of the Fakcha Llakta community, with the purpose of revaluing, enhancing and restoring the natural and cultural potential of the Cascada de Peguche as a heritage site of utmost relevance for Ecuador. The main ecological goals of the plan were:

- to conserve and rescue the natural and cultural heritage of the sector;
- to determine the interpretive potential of the entire protected area of the Cascada de Peguche;
- to carry out a socio-economic and cultural study of the Fakcha Llakta community and visitor profile;

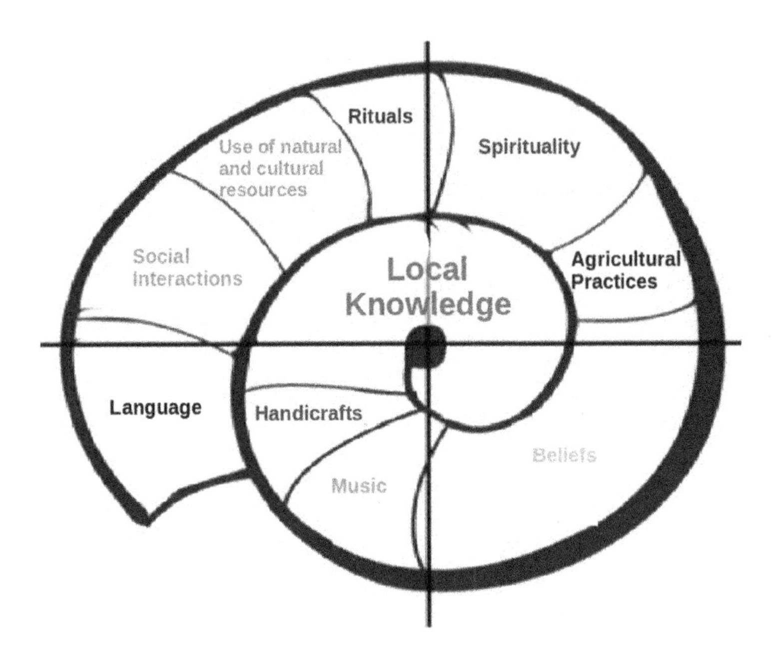

Figure 5.4 Incorporation of local knowledge that emerged from the Fakcha Llakta community into the environmental education model for community tourism management.

Source: Lomas and Trujillo, this chapter.

- to determine the composition of the flora and fauna of the natural area;
- to elaborate and execute the environmental management plan of the whole area with programmes of forest management, recreation and sports activities, interpretation and environmental communication, botanical gardens, environmental and tourism training, solid waste management, as well as community land management, agricultural land, water sources, tourism infrastructure, environmental sanitation and historical sites.

For achieving the goals of the Management Plan, the direct participation, engagement and commitment of the local communities was fundamental. Their actions included the creation of a 'Development Committee' and capacity-building through seminars and knowledge transfer for the holistic improvement of Cascada de Peguche. It required collaborative work for improving its infrastructure, access, trails, signage, promotion and zoning:

Community actions:

- Organisation and strengthening of the Fakcha Llakta community: formation of a 'Community Development Committee' (later transformed into *Communa*).

- Participatory action-research workshops, environmental and tourism training seminars, hands-on workshops and observation tours to community tourism enterprises in Ecuador.
- Visibility of strategic sites of the natural area in three languages (signage).
- Adequacy of the parking lot and extension of the main entrance to the community.
- Occasional cleaning of the forest, Jatun-Yaku River, natural causes, historic swimming pool and solar clock.
- Adequacy of trails towards the small waterfall (woman waterfall).
- Protection of centenary trees.
- Eviction of construction debris and burners in poor condition within the area.
- Involvement of older adults, young people and children in ancestral knowledge and community oral history.
- Editing of advertising material (first triptych with the help of Daizen Oda, United Nations volunteer).
- Acquisition of forest species (in donation) for vegetative recovery of the area.
- Delimitation of interpretive trails (previous diagnosis of the interpretive potential of the area).
- Geo-referencing and zoning of the area (CON-NOR).
- Implementation of basic services and environmental sanitation.
- Training of environmental interpreters to members of the community.
- Visibility of the project in the mass media of the province.

Beneficiaries and participation

The Fakcha Llakta community as a direct beneficiary, being located within the Cascada de Peguche area, allowed 90 per cent of its members to be included (children, young people, men, women and older adults) who contributed with field information and viable solutions to the various problems of the natural area and provided labour in all programmes in cooperation with Funedes and institutions of secondary and higher education. The surrounding communities in the Otavalo canton and the province of Imbabura are indirect beneficiaries of incorporating the Peguche Waterfall into the local tourism economy.

It is important to point out the democratic and decisive participation of Indigenous and mestizo women in this environmental process in terms of decision-making and empowerment. Their presence is reflected in the creative work of textile craftsmanship, which captures the attention of the tourist, and also in agricultural work.

The community organisation that had registered its statutes in the Ministry of Social Welfare, and in the Council of Development of Nationalities and Peoples of Ecuador (Codenpe), is in charge of the management of the Cascada de Peguche together with technical support from interns of the Technical University of the

North and from other entities committed to rebuilding the area through environmental education, conservation and ecological restoration.

Natural, cultural and heritage zoning as part of the Cascada de Peguche Management Plan

One important aspect for consolidating the environmental management and stewardship of the Cascada de Peguche region through community participation was a site zoning for defining the relevance and attribute of each area of the Protected Forest. The zoning functioned to identify the main elements of community, ecology/conservation and tourism interests as strategies for the implementation and effectiveness of the Management Plan (see Figure 5.5 and Table 5.1). Five Macro Zones were established as an initial step for knowing the area by categorising it according to its major attributes, restorative demands, infrastructural or logistic relevance and tourism attractiveness: (a) cultural and historical interest zone; (b) tourism and recreation interest zone; (c) zone for conservation, research and restoration of ecosystems; (d) environmental education and interpretation zone; and (e) production and buffer zone. Subsequently more zones were defined totalling 14 to better accommodate the managerial and restorative demands of members of the community, institutions, and tourists. However, cultural-ethnic tourism and ecotourism translate themselves into a genuine and authentic ethnic experience for the visitors as there is not a fabricated culture for tourism neither is there a 'Disneyization' (Bryma 2004) of an Indigenous community performance, or staged authenticity through the commoditisation of local cultural products (MacCannell 1973; Wang 1999; Xie 2011; Mostafanezhad 2016). The zoning system was essential for successfully developing nine management programmes, among them: Environmental Interpretation and Education; Ethno-Botanic Gardens; Forestry; Environmental Capacity; Solid Waste Management; Historical Site Restoration; Handicraft and Traditional Indigenous Food Sales Stands; Traditional Vegetable Gardens; and, Tourism and Environmental Infrastructure Construction (see Table 5.1 for details).

Historical-cultural zone

In this category are considered important sites within the Andean worldview of the Kichwa Otavalenõs peoples, such as: the solar clock, the fulling mills, the watermill, the terminal pool, the set of slopes, legendary cascades of purification, the caves, the tree of fertility of Venus, the musical stone and the colonial bridge. Many of these components belong to aboriginal and colonial times and aroused investigative interest by archaeologists and anthropologists in 1979 as an area of special scientific interest, due to the discovery of prehistoric remains such as stone and ceramic axes near the ritual waterfall. The large (male) and small (female) waterfalls, according to the Indian tradition, are sacred purification sites which Yachacs and Shamans frequent during the winter and summer solstices and equinoxes to perform the 'holy bath' and initiate the festivities of the Four Raymikunas.

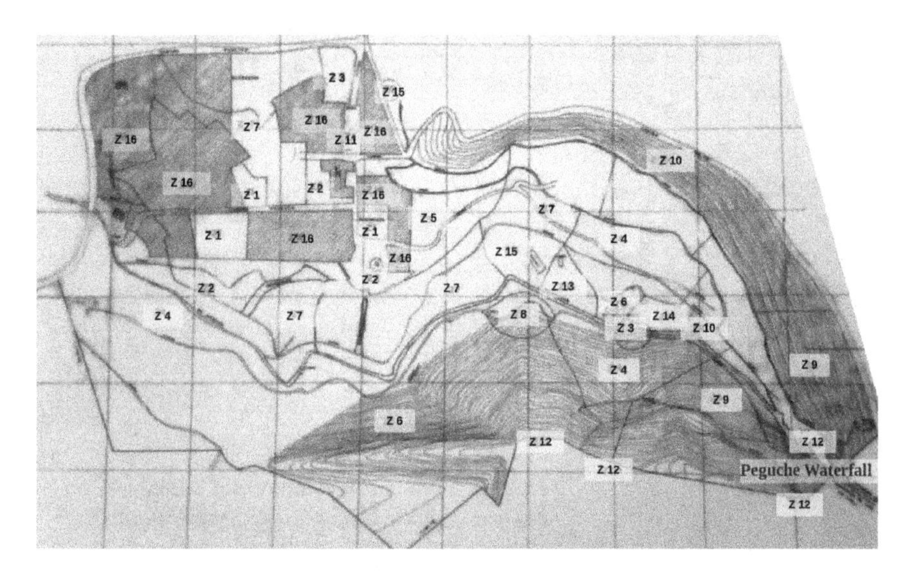

Figure 5.5 Zoning map of the Cascada de Peguche for organisation of the area, natural-cultural assets and territorial management in the Environmental Programmes.

Source: Zoning map edited from Trujillo and Lomas (2014).

Key to Cascada de Peguche zoning and its categories.

Nomenclature (Zones Description) 'Cascada de Peguche' Forest Protector Area			
Z 1	Community Integration Zone	**Z 9**	Biodiversity and Walks Zone
Z 2	Historical Archaeological Interest Zone	**Z 10**	Cultural and Specific Interest Zone
Z 3	Cultural Zone	**Z 11**	Parking Zone
Z 4	Recreation Zone	**Z 12**	Blackberries Zone
Z 5	Botanic Testing Zone	**Z 13**	Tourist Services Zone
Z 6	Afforestation and Reforestation Zone	**Z 14**	Historical Traces and Remnants Zone
Z 7	Tree Planting and Ornamentation Zone	**Z 14**	Religious Mythical Zone
Z 8	Ferruginous Water Zone	**Z 16**	Dwellers' Lots and Housing Zone

Source: Trujillo and Lomas (2014).

Table 5.1 Programmes, goals and activities of the Management Plan* for the Cascada de Peguche area

	General Framework		
	Programmes	*Goals*	*Activities*
1	**Environmental Interpretation and Communication Programme** ***General objective:*** to design interpretive paths and an Environmental Interpretation Centre so that the visitor can enjoy, know and value the heritage of the place.	(a) To meet the needs of knowledge, learning and environmental experiences of visitors and society in general. (b) To interpret the historical-cultural sites and natural resources for the conservation of the location. (c) Cultural, historical and environmental recovery of the Cascada through the interpretive action.	• To study the interpretive potential of the site. • To design interpretive itineraries (trails). • To carry out topographical survey and designs of architectural plans • To design of interpretive elements and labelling. • To promote training in environmental interpretation.
2	**Ethnobotanical Gardens Programme** ***General objective:*** to rescue ancestral and traditional medicine, through customs of use and application of native plants.	(a) To create a natural space with ethnobotanical species and raise awareness about the cultural value of native species with medicinal properties.	• To perform ethnobotanical study • To obtain native ethnobotanical species. • To design of the garden.
3	**Forestry Programme** ***General objective:*** construction of a Forest Nursery for the production of native species and to recover the vegetal cover.	(a) Production of forest species, reforestation, protection, forest management and water sources. (b) To recover the dynamics of the forest.	• To prepare the communal land for installation of the nursery. • Seed collection and nursery construction. • Production of native species, maintenance and reforestation.
4	**Environmental Training Programme** ***General objective:*** to educate environmentally the Fakcha Llakta community, surrounding communities and educational institutions of the canton Otavalo and visitors.	(a) Promote a change of attitude and environmental valuation of existing resources through sustainable actions of empowerment and collective participation.	• To develop instructional materials. • Environmental training workshops for the community. • Observation tours for environmental learning. • Community and business leadership trainings.

5	**Solid Waste Management Programmes** ***General objective:*** to reduce and recycle solid waste and to generate healthy and environmental conditions in the sector.	(a) Generation of an ecological behaviour for the environmental preservation of the sector through the production of organic fertilisers. (b) Sessions of collective voluntary work of permanent communal cleaning. (c) Establishment of codes of ethics and environmental culture policies for residents and tourists.	• To train the community in the collection and use of organic waste: earthworms culture and compost. • To raise awareness to avoid plastic consumption.
6	**Recovery Programme of Historical Sites** ***General objective:*** tourist value of the historical heritage of the Fakcha Llakta community.	(a) Conservation and promotion of historical sites for incorporation into the cultural heritage of the province of Imbabura.	• To conduct field and documental studies. • To rebuild the solar clock (Autonomous Government of Otavalo). • To rebuild the old mill. • To refurbish the historic stone bridge. • To rebuild the entrance of the *obraje* (knitting building) and old road. • To rebuild the historic pool (Autonomous Government of Otavalo).
7	**Typical Gastronomic Handicraft Construction Programme** ***General objective:*** to build a craft market and generate added value to the tourist activity of the sector by demonstrating artisan and gastronomic techniques	(a) Exhibition, demonstration and sale of handicrafts and typical and local food. (b) Construction of the craft market.	• Elaboration of architectural plans – CON-NOR. • Use of materials in harmony with the natural environment. • Advertising: triptychs, posters, T-shirts, key chains. • Assignment to heads and heads of household (craft positions and for typical gastronomy).

(*Continued*)

Table 5.1 Programmes, goals and activities of the Management Plan* for the Cascada de Peguche area (Continued)

	General Framework		
	Programmes	*Goals*	*Activities*
8	**Traditional Orchards Programme** ***General objective:*** to promote agritourism through ancestral farming techniques.	(a) Demonstration of traditional agricultural practices to domestic and foreign tourists. (b) Organic and biodynamic production to guarantee the health of the family nucleus and visitors.	• Traditional crops. • Organic food preparation.
9	**Programme of Construction of Tourism and Environmental Infrastructure** ***General objective:*** to build tourism infrastructure and environmental sanitation in accordance with the needs of the Cascada considering the principles of sustainable development.	(a) Environmental Interpretation Centre in operation. (b) Interpretive trails: stone platform with wood protection for guided trails. The pathways are named as follows: *manto blanco*, 'white mantle'; *reliquias del bosque*, 'relics of the forest'; *sendero del picaflor*, 'path of the hummingbird'. (c) Sanitary sewage system with recycling and purification of waste water. (d) Bridge of the waterfall in wood. (e) Parking lots. (f) Landscape lookouts.	• Health services. • Educative centre. • Housing for internships and cabins. • Adventure tourism. • Restaurant. • Children games. • Museum of the *obraje* and specialised library. • *Note: these activities are still pending.*

*The Management Plan was implemented from 1999 to 2002.

Source: Trujillo and Lomas (2014).

Area of tourism and leisure

Included in this designated area are the guided and self-guided interpretive trails named 'blanket white' and 'relics of the forest', the camping sector, the thermal swimming pool, the Jatun-Yaku River, landscape lookouts and the sports areas. Currently these are equipped with the respective signage and codes of behaviour. Children's playgrounds set up for the physical and motor development of children, with swings, sub-balances, slides, hanging bridges, natural labyrinths made from environmentally friendly materials, and the design of animal figures, are the complement to recreation.

Area of environmental education, training and interpretation

Taking into account the trend of tourism in this sector, and with it the alteration of the ecosystem, being in an area of high environmental sensitivity, interpretive trails were constructed based on the interpretive potential of the location, the profile of the visitors and the socio-economic study of the communities involved. Thus this area includes 12 technical stops with messages that afford a pleasant and pre-established route, with the support of environmental communication materials related to local knowledge, valuation and conservation of the natural and cultural heritage. The Centre for Environmental Interpretation (CEI), a key component in environmental education for the public and for visitors, is also part of this area because environmental education contributes to the generation of an integrated attitude change regarding the conservation of the biological diversity of natural and cultural spaces.

Production and buffer zone

The dispersed houses located within the area of influence of Peguche belong to this category, with traditional orchards kept in check by dairy plants (*Euphorbia latazi*) and alders (*Alnus acuminata*). This agricultural land is intended for horticulture, forestry and smaller animals. A variety of ornamental plants concentrated in small winding paths with stone and wood edges give colour to the cultural landscape.

This area also includes community infrastructure and social services such as the artisan and gastronomic market, parking, school and basic services that are important for the development of daily community life and tourism. This area is considered of high social sensitivity and requires permanent attention in terms of maintenance and collective and community commitment.

Peguche management strategies

The management of the Cascada de Peguche Forest Protected Area was carried out based on consultations with the social actors and the analysis of environmental and economic sustainability during the process of elaboration, execution and evaluation of the environmental and tourist project.

The functional administrative structure for the period 1999–2002 highlights the intervention of Funedes in the direction and coordination of the rest of the functions relating to Fakcha Llakta. Currently, the overall administration of the natural area is in charge of the Fakcha Llakta community chapter governed by the Indigenous Communes Act and by the environmental authority of the Ecuadorian Ministry of the Environment (MAE), and chaired by an Indigenous representative of the community advised by team members.

Institutional involvement

Funedes, the managing Institutional agency of the Management and Restoration Plan, carried out the majority of environmental and infrastructure programmes (including the reconstruction of the thermal pool, the solar clock and the suspension bridge), together with the Fakcha Llakta community and with the support of *mingas* (collective voluntary work sessions). The financing by national and international donors was as follows:

- funding in 2002 for the community organisation gained from the GEF Small Grants Programme, under the United Nations Development Programme (UNDP), for environmental recovery;
- topographic survey and elaboration of structural and architectural plans by the Consortium of Autonomous Provincial and Municipal Decentralised Government Councils of the North of the Country (CON-NOR);
- Construction of the Handicrafts Market, Ministry of Social Welfare, now Ministry of Economic and Social Inclusion (MIES);
- construction of sanitary sewerage system financially supported by the Japanese Embassy;
- construction of the interpretive trails and first parking area, Ministry of Public Works, (MOP) and Inter-American Development Bank (IDB);
- training in leadership, entrepreneurship and interpretive labelling, National Financial Corporation (CFN) and HANSIEDEL.

All these Institutions printed their commitment and support for the sustainable management of the different natural resources in this important area of life (Trujillo and Lomas 2014).

Discussion and final considerations: the evidence of an ethnodevelopment process in Peguche

The direct hands-on participation of the Fakcha Llakta community in the execution of the nine programmes of the Management Plan undoubtedly helped to increase a community sense of ownership, conservation and responsibility for the well-being of Cascada de Peguche and its cultural-historical elements. It is worth noting that the creation of participatory Indigenous Development Committees, later transformed with the increased decentralisation of decision-making

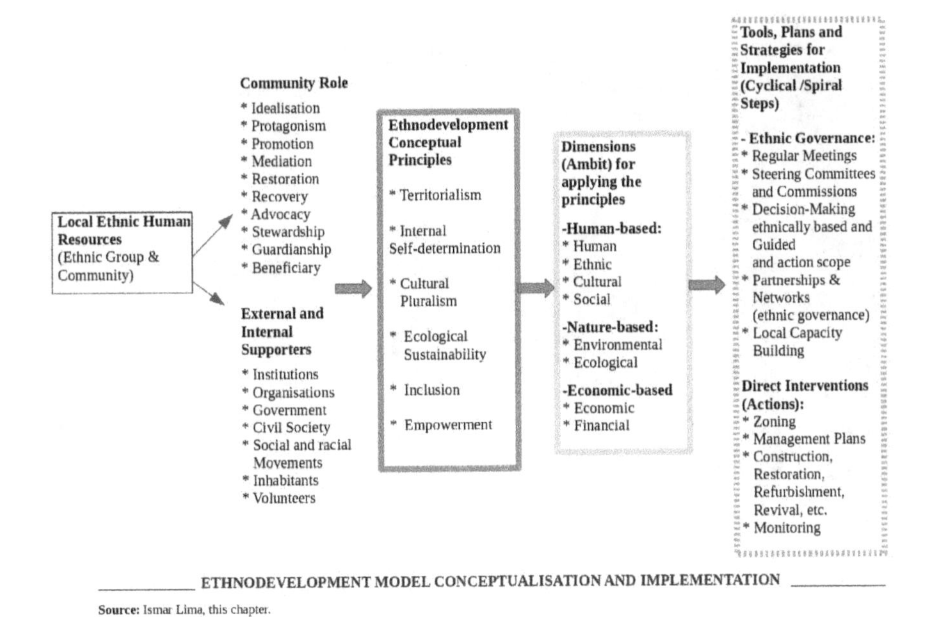

Figure 5.6 Main aspects and elements to be considered in an ethnodevelopment model and its implementation.

(*self-determination*) and an Indigenous-based managerial system (*empowerment*) with strong concerns for Indigenous culture and ethnic issues (*inclusion*), makes evident the materialisation of an ethnodevelopment model for Peguche communities. We can mention 'ethnic empowerment' and an 'ethnically centred decision-making process' within a certain geographical area that contributed to a status change of the ethnic minorities in a region where they had been *socially excluded, ethnically discriminated* and *highly exploited.*

Clarke (2001) and Willis (2005), in their work on the theories and practices of development, mention the four major principles of ethnodevelopment as outlined by Bjorn Hettne (1995, 1996):

- *Territorialism:* the space where there is a concentration of ethnic groups in which decision-making on development is made within a particular territory based on the natural resources available.
- *Internal self-determination:* the available means and mechanisms for a specific ethnic group to have control over a collective destiny within the context of a nation-state.
- *Cultural pluralism:* the recognition and mutual respect of distinct cultures that coexist within one society; this involves a harmonious acceptance of an otherness vis-à-vis a particular group identity (Picard and Di Giovine, 2014).

Figure 5.7 Ismar Borges de Lima, Peguche Waterfall Forest Protector's Entrance accompanied by Professors Dr Rolando Lomas and Dr Carmen Trujillo, and Lomas' grandson, 'Tomi', during a technical visit to Cascada de Peguche, November 2014.

Source: Ismar Borges de Lima – personal collection.

- *Ecological sustainability:* development should take place without negatively impacting on the natural environment and landscapes, and without compromising the conditions for the feasibility of future livelihoods.

Within this context, 'the spatial concentration of groups enables a construction of ethnic identity linked to a particular territory, making the notion of 'ethnodevelopment' through self-determination a logistical possibility, if not a politically-favoured one' (Willis 2005: 123). Though not explicitly mentioned by Hettne, *ethnic empowerment* and *inclusion* are also principles (or conceptual dimensions) of ethnodevelopment.

By examining the Cascada de Peguche case, it was found that all the principles of ethnodevelopment can be identified by examining the concrete actions taken by the Indigenous communities for ecologically and culturally rebuilding the Cascada de Peguche area for domestic and international visitors, besides learning about the local ecosystem, fauna and flora. Other tangible evidence of an ethnodevelopment matrix was the way the programmes and the Management

Figure 5.8 Ismar Borges de Lima during his technical visit to Peguche, Otavalo, Ecuador, in 2014, with companions Profs. Rolando Lomas and Carmen Trujillo. (pictures also of local Indigenous students and dwellers).

Plan were designed by positioning ethnicity at the centre of the ideological conception while looking for strategies to transfer power to ethnic groups through an endogenous institutionalisation of decision-making. More importantly, community (eco)tourism became the main arena for combining the ethnic, social, cultural and environmental demands and strengths.

All these factors support the notion of an endogenous development by empowering the Fakcha Llakta from within the community by transferring to its members the whole decision-making and management process, even though the financial support has come from external sources. This is therefore a type of externally induced endogenous development process, which, though externally supported, can still be seen as 'endogenously generated' (see Figure 5.6).

It should be noted that the connections between ethnicity and territory do not always occur easily, though (eco)tourism has been considered by some governments, institutions and organisations (including the native groups and representatives) dealing with indigenous issues as a type of tourism able to promote income generation and visitor-native interactions that can enhance indigenous cultural practices (de Lima and d'Hauteserre 2011; Zeppel 2006; Buckley 2004; Campos *et al.* 2014: 143).

Figure 5.9 Historical pictures of the Bosque de Peguche.

Figure 5.10 Construction, restoration and improvement of tracks at Peguche Forest, and the production of informative signs, etc.

Figure 5.11 Historical pictures of Peguche: pictures of local children, a local community meeting and a cultural event, Peguche, Otavalo, Ecuador.

Figure 5.12 Solar clock and visitors at Peguche, peforming a Fakcha Llakta solar clock ritual, accompanied by Carmen Trujillo.

Figure 5.13 Current state of the Cascada de Peguche. Some of the visitors' areas such as the natural thermal pool, restored tracks and pristine landscapes. These pictures provide proof of a great transformation and successful social-environmental work done at Peguche, in Ecuador.

It is therefore advocated that a strengthened, conscious and practical knowledge, the base for a community environmental stewardship, make up the collective cement to achieve self-determination, self-management and communal self-confidence, because it is the local people who make their own decisions and initiatives based on their socio-cultural and environmental realities.

The role of (eco)tourism practices in the process of ethnodevelopment has been of the utmost importance. The community advanced itself, especially after the Peguche Management Plan of the 1990s, which has given an 'environmental stewardship' status and role to members of the Fakcha Llakta. In addition, 'environmental education' has been regarded as a critical element intertwined with culture for the consolidation of a genuine conservationist model of ethnodevelopment. Compared to periods before the implementation of the Indigenous community participatory Management Plan, the Fakcha Llakta community has had a relative improvement in its overall quality of life through collaborative participatory projects.

By taking into account the autochthonous elements that have historically permeated the Ecuadorian Fakcha Llakta community in the Otavalo-Imbabura region, the environmental education process has an important role as the Indigenous communities generally have traditional knowledge and native experiences about the different ways of interpreting the natural phenomena.

Tourism in Cascada de Peguche has had the potential to provide genuine Indigenous experiences to visitors in a protected area that can serve as places for exercising the decolonisation of legacies through honouring indigenous knowledge and worldviews, challenging the stereotypical representations of Native people and serving as sites of knowledge-making and remembering for their own communities and the general public (Eller 2016: 310). More importantly, a site for mutual learning (visitor-local) about the cultural, historical, ethnic and environmental assets of the Fakcha Llakta is provided constituting the contemporary cumulative legacy of Indigenous elements.

The consolidation of an ethnodevelopment model in Otavalo-Imbabura can take place through environmental stewardship and advocacy, ethnically based local environmental governance and tourism development and entrepreneurship fully controlled and managed by the ethnic group(s) with benefits returning to members of the community as collective assets;. These benefits are either directly used by local families or for keeping a permanent state of conservation and of ecological restoration of natural settings, as well as conservation and enhancement of historical-cultural-ethnic assets. In fact, an ethnodevelopment model and its implementation demand 'spiral/cyclical steps' founded on an *ethnic governance structure* (Figure 5.6) constituted of human and social capital with regular meetings, a steering committee and commissions, decision-making processes that are ethnically based and guided, partnerships and networks, local capacity-building and constant knowledge transfer.

Ethnic governance is not a new concept and since the 1980s it has been thoroughly and intensively debated by planners, developers, governments and United Nations staff, as well as researchers in the field of policies, institutional framework-building, ethnic conflict resolution, ethnic and racial democracy construction, ethnic and environmental advocacy, management and conservation, multiculturalism and anthropological understandings. An ethnic governance perspective usually includes 'a body of norms (e.g., customary law and practice), procedures (e.g., decision-making processes, conflict management and dispute settlement), specific knowledge, and individuals playing specific roles (often the traditional representatives)' (Borrini-Feyerabend *et al.* 2004: 285). However, 'ethnic governance' is regarded as a very complex structure because it elicits multiple stakeholder participation, particularly for resolving issues on land tenure which is normally ascribed at the same time to several actors, which include households, extended families, villages, lineages and clans (Borrini-Feyerabend *et al.* 2004, and see Breton 1991; Shoup 2007; and Marxer 2012). Figure 5.6 demonstrates the main aspects and elements to be taken into account to conceptualise and implement an ethnic endogenous development model. It is advocated that 'ethnic governance' is crucial for forming human and social capital and the institutional framework in an ethnodevelopment process while enabling the model to effectively work on an operational level.

In the following pages Figures 5.7–5.13 provide a series of pictures taken at Cascada de Peguche showing the work of Indigenous dwellers and volunteers helping to implement the nine Programmes of the Management Plan. There are also more recent pictures showing visitors and local tourism infrastructure. Readers will be able to visually identify the huge difference with regard to the environment, structure and local landscape before the Master Plan and the Fakcha Llakta interventions, and the current state of Peguche with attractive, well-preserved natural and built tourism structures, including signage; specifically, visitors' experience an enhanced cultural and ethnic experience at Peguche, guided by interpretive interventions from native people. As part of a cultural-historical and Indigenous sacred experience, the visitors can participate in the reproduction of a solar clock ritual. There is also a collection of pictures taken during Ismar Borges de Lima's technical visit to Peguche in 2014 accompanied by Rolando Lomas and Carmen Trujillo (Figure 5.7).

References

Acuerdo Ministerial 16/Registro 154, 2010, Reglamento para los Centros Turísticos Comunitarios. Ecuadorian Government. Available online at: http://www.turismo.gob.ec/wp-content/uploads/2016/04/REGLAMENTO-PARA-LOS-CENTROS-TURISTICOS.pdf.

Baquero, D. C. (2016) Alberto Muenala y el tejido del tiempo. *La Barra Espaciadora (LBE)*. Available online, http://www.labarraespaciadora.com/culturas/alberto-muenala-y-el-tejido-del-tiempo/ (accessed 25 December 2016).

Beeton, S. (2006) *Community Development Through Tourism.* Collingwood, VIC: Land Links – CSIRO Publishing.

Berger, P. L. and Luckmann, T. (2001) *La construcción social de la realidad.* Buenos Aires: Amorrortu.

Boff, L. (2005) *La Carta de la Tierra: una promesa*. Online at: http://www.servicioskoinonia.org/boff/articulo.php?num=141 (accessed 7 November 2009).

Boff, L. (2012) *La sostenibilidad, que es y que no es*. Petrópolis, Brazil: Editora Vozes.

Bonfil Batalla, G. (1982) *El Etnodesarrollo: sus premisas jurídicas, políticas y de organización. América Latina: Etnodesarrollo y Etnocidio*. San José de Costa Rica: Ediciones FLACSO, pp. 133–45.

Borrini-Feyerabend, G., Pimbert, M., Farvar, M. T., Kothari, A. and Renard, Y. (2004) *Sharing Power. Learning by Doing in Co-management of Natural Resources Throughout the World*. Tehran: IIED and IUCN/CEESP/CMWG/CENESTA.

Breton, R. (1991) *The Governance of Ethnic Communities: Political Structures and Processes in Canada*. Ottawa: Greenwood Press.

Bryman, A. (1999) The Disneyization of society', *Sociological Review* 47(1), 25–47.

Buckley, R. (2004) *Environmental Impacts of Ecotourism*, Vol. 2, Ecotourism book series. Wallingford: CABI Publishing.

Business Enterprises for Sustainable Tourism (BEST) (2003) The Community Tourism Summit, BEST Summary Report, 13–15 May.

Cabrera, A. (2000) *Política de Desarrollo de Varadero. Capítulo Medioambiente. Ministerio de Turismo*. Varadero, Cuba.

Campos, M. V., Scott, N. and Breakey, N. (2014) Ecotourism: a new challenge for protecting rainforest areas in Chile. In B. Prideaux (ed.), *Rainforest Tourism, Conservation and Management: Challenges for Sustainable Development*. Oxford: Routledge, pp. 134–45.

Carayannis, E. G. (2013) *Creating a sustainable social ecology using technology-driven solutions*. Information Science Reference, Hershey, PA, USA.

Clarke, G. (2001) From ethnocide to ethnodevelopment? Ethnic minorities and indigenous peoples in Southeast Asia. *Third World Quarterly* 22(3), 413–36.

de Lima, I. B. and d'Hauteserre (2011) Community capitals and ecotourism for enhancing Amazonian forest livelihoods. *Anatolia – An International Journal of Tourism and Hospitality Research* 22(2), 184–203.

Edelman, M. and Haugerud, A. (2005) *The Anthropology of development and globalization: from classical political economy to contemporary Neoliberalism*. Oxford: Blackwell Publishing.

Eller, J. D. (2016) *Cultural Anthropology: Global Forces, Local Lives*. New York: Routledge.

Febres-Cordero, M. (2013) *Tendencias y escenarios de la educación ambiental*. Conferencia UPEL, Venezuela, November.

Fernández, D. (2004) *Colombia: Desarollo económico reciente en infraestructura: Balanceando las necesidades sociales y productivas de infraestructura*. Washington, DC: World Bank, Finance, Private Sector and Infrastructure Unit.

Freile, J. Granizo (1981) Numeraciones del Repartimiento de Otavalo, 2 vols. Otavalo Ecuador: Instituto Otavaleño de Antropología.

Friedman, J. (2005) Globalization, dis-integration, re-organization: the transformations of violence, In M. Edelman and A. Haugerud (eds), *The Anthropology of Development and Globalization: From Classical Political Economy to Contemporary Neoliberalism*. Oxford: Blackwell, pp. 160–8.

Gardner, K. and Lewis, D. (2005) Beyond development? In M. Edelman and A. Haugerud (eds), *The Anthropology of Development and Globalization: From Classical Political Economy to Contemporary Neoliberalism*. Carlton, VIC, Australia: Blackwell, pp. 253–9.

Garner, B. (2016) *The Politics of Cultural Development: Trade, Cultural Policy and the UNESCO Convention on Cultural Diversity.* London and New York: Routledge.

Gartner, W. C. and Lime, D. W. (eds) (2000, *Trends in Outdoor Recreation, Leisure and Tourism*. Wallingford and Cambridge, MA: CABI Publishing, pp. 373–82.

Haugerud, A. (2003) The disappearing local: rethinking global-local connections. In A. Mirsepassi, A. Basu and F. Weaver (eds), *Localizing Knowledge in a Globalizing World: Recasting the Area Studies Debates*. Syracuse, NY: Syracuse University Press, pp. 60–81.

Hughes, M., Weaver, D. and Pforr, C. (eds) (2015) *The Practice of Sustainable Tourism: Resolving the Paradox*. Abingdon: Routledge.

IIDE (2006) *Protecting Indigenous Knowledge Against Biopiracy in the Andes. Sustaining Local Food Systems, Agricultural Biodiversity and Livelihoods*. London: International Institute for Environment and Development (IIED). Available online: http://pubs.iied.org/pdfs/14531IIED.pdf (accessed 28 December 2016).

Iorns, C. J. (1993) The draft declaration on the rights of Indigenous peoples. *Murdoch University Electronic Journal of Law* 1(1). Available online: http://www.austlii.edu.au/au/journals/MurUEJL/1993/2.html (accessed on 28 December 2016).

Jamal, T. and Dredge, D. (2015) Tourism and community development issues. In R. Sharpley and D. J. Telfer (eds), *Tourism and Development: Concepts and Issues*. Bristol: Channel View Publications, pp. 178–204.

Job, H. and Li, J. (2006) *Natural Heritage, Ecotourism and Sustainable Development: Potentials and Pitfalls for China*. Contributions delivered at the Sino-German Symposium on Natural Heritage, Ecotourism and Sustainable Development, Zhangjiajie, China, 4–11 November 2004.

Kelles-Viitanen, A. (2008) *Custodians of Culture and Biodiversity: Indigenous Peoples Take Charge of Their Challenges and Opportunities*. Rome: IFAD Innovation Mainstreaming Initiative and Government of Finland.

Krahenbuhl, P. (2001) *Ecuador's Amazon Region*. Quebec and Montreal: Ulysses Travel Publications.

Kronik, J. and Verner, D. (2010) *Indigenous Peoples and Climate Change in Latin America and the Caribbean*. Washington, DC: World Bank.

Larrère, C. (2002) Philosophy of nature or natural philosophy? Science and philosophy in Callicott's metaphysics. In W. Ouderkirk and J. Hill (eds), *Land, Value, Community: Callicott and Environmental Philosophy*. Albany, NY: University of New York Press, pp. 151–70.

Leff, E. (2013) *Saber ambiental. Sustentabilidad, racionalidad, complejidad, poder*, Cuarta reimpresión Siglo XXI editores. México.

Lema, G. (1995) *Los otavalos: cultura y tradición milenarias*, 1st edn. Quito: Editorial Abya-Yala.

Li, Y. (2006) Contradictions of modernization in China and the implications for community tourism development. In T. V. Liu (ed.), *Tourism Management: New Research*. New York: Nova Science Publishers, pp. 41–63.

López, G. (2005) El turismo como actividad emergente para las comunidades rurales. *XXI Seminario de Economía Mexicana. La política económica del gobierno actual: análisis y perspectivas. ¿Hacia dónde va México?* Mexico: Instituto de Investigaciones Económicas (IIEc) – Universidad Nacional Autónoma de México (UNAM).

Lovelock, B. and Lovelock, K. M. (2013) *The Ethics of Tourism: Critical and Applied Perspectives*. London and New York: Routledge.

MacCannell, D. (1973) Staged authenticity: arrangements of social space in tourist settings. *American Journal of Sociology* 79, 589–603.

Martínez, M. (2007) *Ciencia y arte en la Metodología Cualitativa*. Mexico: Col. Pedro María Anaya.

McNeely, J. A., Harrison, J. and Dingwall, P. (eds) (1994) *Protecting Nature: Regional Reviews of Protected Areas*. Gland, Switzerland and Cambridge, UK: IUCN.

Marxer, W. (ed.) (2012) *Direct Democracy and Minorities*. Bandern, Liechtenstein and Germany: Springer.

MEC (2008) *Ministerio de Educación de Ecuador. El Desarrollo de la Educación. Informe Nacional del Ecuador*. October. Available online at: http://www.ibe.unesco.org/National_Reports/ICE_2008/ecuador_NR08_sp.pdf.

MINTUR (2012) *Plan de Turismo del Ecuador*. Quito, Ecuador: Ministerio de Turismo (Gobierno de Ecuador).

Morín, E. (1990) *Introducción al Pensamiento Complejo*. Barcelona: Gedisa Editorial.

Mostafanezhad, M. (2016) *Volunteer Tourism: Popular Humanitarianism in Neoliberal Times*. New York: Routledge.

Mowforth, M. and Munt, I. (2009) *Tourism and Sustainability: Development, Globalisation and New Tourism in the Third World*. London and New York: Routledge.

Naciones Unidas Informe Brundtland (1997) *Nuestro Futuro Común*. Available at: http://worldinbalance.net/intagreements/1987-brundtland.php.

Oberg, G. (2011) *Interdisciplinary Environmental Studies: A Primer*. Oxford: Wiley-Blackwell.

Ortiz Ordaz, F. C. (2009) Metodología para desarrollar los valores asociados a una cultura organizacional en el turismo sostenible. *Folletos Gerenciales*. Cuba: Dirección de Capacitación de Cuadros y Estudios de Dirección (DCCED), p. 11.

Oviedo, C. (1983) *Estudio de aguas de la provincia de Imbabura, Cascada de Peguche, Otavalo*. Otavalo, Imbabura, Ecuador.

Paez, M. P. and Arias, A. E. O. (2006) El Desarrollo endógeno y la necesidad de generar procesos de aprendizaje comunitario. In A. E. O. Arias (eds), *Aprendiendo en torno al Desarrollo Endógeno*. Venezuela: FUNDACITE Mérida/ULA, pp.121–40. Available online at: http://www.rebelion.org/docs/35115.pdf.

Pardo, M. (2006) *Cambio global. Impacto de la actividad humana sobre el sistema Tierra*. Madrid: Divulgación.

Petry, F. (1995) Sustainability issues in agricultural and rural development policies. *Training Materials for Agricultural Planning*, Vol. 2. Rome: Food and Agriculture Organization of the United Nations (FAO).

Pigram, J. J. (1992) Alternative tourism: tourism and sustainable resource management. In V. Smith and W. R. Eadington (eds), *Tourism Alternatives: Potentials and Problems in the Development of Tourism*. Philadephia: University of Pennsylvania Press, pp. 76–87.

Pigram, J. J. (2000) Tourism and sustainability: a positive trend. In W. C. Gartner and D. W. Lime (eds), *Trends in Outdoor Recreation, Leisure and Tourism*. Wallingford: CABI Publishing, pp. 373–82.

Plan Nacional para el Buen Vivir (2009–13) *Construyendo un Estado Plurinacional e Intercultural*, 2nd edn. Quito.

Pojman, L. P., Pojman, P. and McShane, K. (2015) *Environmental Ethics: Readings in Theory and Application*, 7th edn. Boston, MA: Cengage Learning.

Radice, H. (2015) *Global Capitalism: Selected Essays*. New York: Routledge.

Rocchio, D. (2013) *Sustentabilidad ambiental. Estrategias y proyecto arquitectónico.* Quito: Corporación para el desarrollo de la educación universitaria Codeu.

Ross, A., Sherman, K. P., Snodgrass, J. G., Delcore, H. D. and Sherman, R. (2011) *Collaborative Stewardship of Nature: Knowledge Binds and Institutional Conflicts.* Walnut Creek, CA: Left Cost Press.

Rueda, R. (1988) *El Obraje de San Joseph de Peguchi.* Quito: Ediciones Abya-Yala.

Ruíz, F. (2009) *Cultura, comunidad y turismo: ensayos sobre le turismo comunitario en Ecuador.* Quito: Abya-Ayala.

Shady, R. M. (2014) Living conditions, social system and cultural expressions of the Caral and Chinchorro populations during the archaic period. In N. Sanz, B. T. Arriaza and V. G. Standen (eds), *The Chinchorro Culture: A Comparative Perspective. The Archaeology of the Earliest Human Mummification.* Mexico City: ARICA and UNESCO.

Shoup, B. (2007) *Conflict and Cooperation in Multi-ethnic States: Institutional Incentives, Myths and Counterbalancing.* London and New York: Routledge/Taylor & Francis Group.

Simpson, T. (1997) *Indigenous Heritage and Self-determination: The Cultural and Intellectual Property Rights of Indigenous Peoples.* Copenhagen: International Working Group for Indigenous Affairs (IWGIA).

Stavenhagen, R. (1986) Ethnodevelopment: a neglected dimension in development thinking. In R. A. Krahl (ed.), *Development Studies: Critique and Renewal.* Leiden: E. J. Brill, pp. 71–94.

Stavenhagen, R. (2007) *Los pueblos indígenas y sus derechos.* Mexico: UNESCO.

Stavenhagen, R. (2013) *The Emergence of Indigenous Peoples.* New York and London: Springer.

Strauss, A. and Corbin, J. (2005) *Bases de la investigación cualitativa. Técnicas y procedimientos para desarrollar la teoría fundamentada.* Antioquia: editorial universitaria de Antioquia.

Strong, M. (2012) *Art, Nature, and Religion in the Central Andes: Themes and Variations from Prehistory to Present.* Austin, TX: University of Texas Press.

Taylor, G. (1995) The community approach: does it really work? *Tourism Management* 16(7), 487–9.

Terry, G. (2011) *Cultura, identidad cultural, patrimonio y desarrollo comunitario rural: una nueva mirada en el contexto del siglo XXI latinoamericano.* Eumed.net, España.

Todtling, F. (2011) Endogenous approaches to local and regional development policy. In A. Pike, A. Rodriguez-Pose and J. Tomaney (eds), *Handbook of Local and Regional Development.* Abingdon: Routledge, pp. 333–43.

Trosper, R. L. and Parrotta, J. A. (2012) *Introduction: The Growing Importance of Traditional Forest-related Knowledge.* Dordrecht, Heidelberg, London and New York: Springer, pp. 1–36.

Trujillo, C. and Lomas, R. (2014) *Gestión sostenible en turismo comunitario: programas de manejo, interpretación ambiental y senderismo.* Caso cascada de Peguche, 1st edn. Quito: Dimex publicidad.

Vásquez, C. (1987) *El culto fálico: contribución al estudio de la teogonía en Imbabura (Estudios y ensayos).* Otavalo, Ecuador.

Verschuuren, B. (2010) Arguments for developing biocultural conservation approaches for sacred natural sites. In B. Verschuuren, J. McNeely, G. Oviedo and R. Wild (eds), *Sacred Natural Sites: Conserving Nature and Culture.* Abingdon and New York: Earthscan.

Wang, N. (1999) Rethinking authenticity in tourism experience. *Annals of Tourism Research* 26(2), 349–70.

Willis, K. (2005) *Theories and Practices of Development*, Routledge Perspectives on Development. London and New York: Routledge.

Worrell, R. and Appleby, M. C. (2000) Stewardship of natural resources: definition, ethical and practical aspects. *Journal of Agricultural and Environmental Ethics 12*(3), 263–77.

Xie, P. F. (2011) *Authenticating Ethnic Tourism.* Ontario: Channel View Publications.

Zeppel, H. (2003) Sharing the country: ecotourism policy and Indigenous peoples in Australia. In D. Fennell and R. K. Dowling (eds), *Ecotourism Policy and Planning.* Wallingford: CABI Publishing, pp. 55–76.

Zeppel, H. (2006) *Indigenous Ecotourism: Sustainable Development and Management*, Ecotourism Series No. 3. Wallingford: CABI Publishing.

6 Missio-tourism among ethnic Karen in Thailand

A bridge to empowerment, development and self-determination or promotion of assistencialism?

Shirley Worland

Introduction

The term 'missio-tourism' is a relatively new sphere of scholarly interest in anthropology and sociology. However, in the last decade, it has gained considerable interest with a number of ethnographic studies being carried out in Latin America, Africa and Southeast Asia (Priest and Howell 2013; Zehner 2006, 2013; Howell 2009, 2012; Wuthnow 2009; Ver Beek 2006). This is a growing global phenomenon, whereby in excess of two million individuals per year are being sent out as short-term mission (STM) teams from Christian churches in the so-called Global North to ethnic communities in the so-called Global South to carry out a variety of activities, including medical, evangelistic, vocational and academic training over periods ranging from one day to a number of months, with the average length being two weeks.

From 2007 to 2013, I lived in the majority ethnic Karen populated Mae La refugee camp and in rural ethnic Karen communities to the south of Mae Sot while simultaneously carrying out fieldwork in displaced Karen identity studies and teaching. Since moving to Chiang Mai in 2013 to take up an academic position, I continue to focus my research in these places. Throughout these years, I have observed many Christian short-term mission teams coming and going which has provided me with the opportunity to evaluate the impact from both ends of the spectrum – the sending community and the receiving community in the refugee camp, in the village where I lived and the nearby migrant learning centre (MLC).[1] As such, this research has utilised a phenomenological reflective approach, whereby my practical description and emotive first-person reflection and analysis provides readers insight into my lived experiences during this time. Webb (1992) emphasises the point that 'doing science' is a highly social enterprise making it natural and ethical for the use of the active first-person form of language to be used in reporting (pp. 748, 750). Dreby and Brown (2013) support this view, adding that a close eye to the personal and social positionality of the researcher is essential for the contribution of quality 'scientific knowledge' (p. 7).

The objective of this chapter is to analyse critically the impact the activities of Christian short-term missions has on the development and empowerment of ethnic Karen communities along the Thai–Myanmar border. Specifically, the question this research has sought to answer is: 'Are the activities of Christian short-term missions carried out in ethnic Karen communities creating opportunity or promoting assistencialism?' The central terms in this question are opposites – 'opportunity' encompasses the agency of empowerment and self-determination, enabling communities to identify their needs and actively participate in the realisation of those needs. 'Assistencialism' is a term coined by education reformer Paulo Friere in the early 1970s. Essentially, 'assistencialism' deprives agency from the community that outside organisations are trying to aid by treating the recipients of that aid as passive objects, incapable of participating in the process of their own development. It offers the community no responsibility or opportunity to make any decisions for their own development (Freire, 1973: 16).

The findings of this research show that, in the main, the teams from the sending community arrive with altruistic motives, a genuine desire to help; however, they often lack cultural competence with little to no understanding of the socio-cultural, socio-economic and socio-political issues impacting on their receiving community. With the increased pressure of work, study and family commitments experienced by many living in the so-called Global North, these teams come for increasingly shorter periods of time, mostly during their work or school vacation, with set ideas of their one- to two-week programme that they believe will improve the life of the poor rural community to which they come. For the receiving community, there are mixed responses. Community leaders also have goals and visions about how to improve the life of their communities. However, the lack of communication, often hampered by language, and cultural mores and norms whereby values of hospitality and desire to please the guest hamper meaningful dialogue of the actual needs of the community, often results in the priorities of the sending churches barely corresponding to those of the receiving communities where the author lived.

Literature review

This chapter explores the impact the concept of missio-tourism (in the form of Christian-oriented short-term mission teams) has on ethnic Karen communities along the central part of the Thai–Myanmar border. In many instances, the aims of the STM teams are to assist in the development of impoverished rural ethnic communities. Construction and repair of housing, schools and health clinics, teaching English and conducting medical and dental outreaches are identified as the most common development activities in which these teams engage (Probasco 2013; Zehner 2013; Ver Beek 2006). In considering the interrelationship of these STM teams and development of ethnic Karen communities, it is useful to explore meanings attributed to the wider constructs of missio-tourism and ethnodevelopment.

The massive increase of people involving themselves in short-term missions to the so-called Global South in the past five decades is difficult to fathom. Thomas Chandler (1972, cited in Wilder and Parker, 2010) noted that there were only

540 people from the United States of America who engaged in short-term missions in 1965. Later researchers in this area recorded an increase in this number to 120,000 in 1989. Just three years later, the same researchers recorded the figure at 240,000 and currently the figure is estimated to be in excess of one million, and this is only in the United States of America (Wilder and Parker 2010; Wuthnow 2009). Other nations such as the United Kingdom, Australia, Norway and South Korea are also major senders of short-term mission teams. Convenient and affordable air travel combined with an increasing exposure to media images of the plight of the Global South are credited as the drivers of this growing phenomenon (Priest and Howell 2013; Howell 2012).

Increasingly, these teams are concerned with spreading the social Gospel of Christ, defined by Rauschenbusch (1917) as '… the Kingdom of God in which all human beings are to labour for the common good of all humanity … Christ's teachings focus on love … characterised by service and equality.' The outworking of this 'social Gospel of Christ' can be seen with large groups of often younger people travelling to remote places fully equipped 'to do' something to better the life of the poor and oppressed of our global society.

It was with such ideals that I first joined a short-term mission team in January 2003. Our team had several pre-travel meetings that covered everything from travel medicine for ourselves, finances, a day-by-day, almost hour-by-hour itinerary and the resources needed. Our plan was very focused on 'what we would do' – there was no cross-cultural training or even consideration that our Western mindsets may be a hindrance to our being able to carry out 'this social Gospel of Christ' in a caring and culturally competent way. Our resources were such that they would be enough to run a vacation school in the majority ethnic Karen Mae Ra Ma Luang refugee camp for 600 children over 10 days – pencils, crayons, paper, paints, balls, musical instruments. Imagine our shock when arriving in the camp in the black of night (no electricity), the pastor told us there would be a minimum of 1,000 children as they would also come from the neighbouring camp, and on the actual morning of the first day, we were greeted by the expectant faces of 1,600 children! There was no shopping mall down the road; we had to hastily recalculate how we were going 'to do' for these children; a major challenge to our Western pre-conceived ideas of what was essential for working with children and sharing this 'social Gospel of Christ' for which we had planned so long and travelled so far.

The reality for both ourselves back then and the many STM teams that came to the Thai–Myanmar border is that we fall into the category of 'missio-tourists'. We had no long-term commitment to these people, we knew very little about them. We had some good motives and even some skill in working with children, but the ten days in Mae Ra Ma Luang camp was only one part of our trip to Thailand which also involved a further 10 days in a luxury hotel in Chiang Mai to 'recover from our exposure to the oppressed of our world'. Our situation resonates with Ver Beek's (2006) research findings into the proliferation of STM teams that arrived in Honduras in 1998 and 1999 after the devastation of Hurricane Mitch, in that our focus was only on a short-term fix rather than long-term solutions. Most of our 16-strong team understood very little of the struggle and trauma these refugees had experienced, of the more than 50-year-long civil war in Burma (now Myanmar) that had robbed them of their homes, livelihoods and families, forcing them to flee to the refugee camps on the Thai side of the border. Our focus was simply on developing the English skills of ethnic Karen children through different activities in a short space of time.

Howell's (2009) research into the explosive growth of the phenomenon of missio-tourism concluded that it merited a much closer social-scientific investigation as well as missiological reflection. His findings likened the mass commodification of the structure and expectations of STM teams to the creation of a 'missionary gaze', not unlike the 'tourist gaze' proposed by Urry (2002), a gaze that is dynamic and socially constructed, interpreted by one's own interpretation of one's surroundings, often unable to connect with the real meaning of what s/he actually sees. Howell contended that the increasingly shorter times that STM teams stay in a place results in an experience whereby a 'decontextualised otherness' is produced – with the Western country being 'the Other' and the developing country identified only as the 'undifferentiated Poor'. Howell concludes his paper with this statement:

> In order, however, for STM trips to meet the goals of sending bodies and for them to be beneficial to the receiving communities, a minimal requirement is surely that the trips foster real connections with real places throughout the world. (2009: 211)

Howell's findings are echoed by those of Zehner (2006, 2013) who observed that American STM members are often overly concerned with low living standards, viewing people and places from their own cultural lens. As a response to this, Zehner (2006) developed a field-oriented model to encourage a more empowering and inclusive relationship for both STM members and their host communities. Central to this model is the role of the STM member as a trainee under the supervision of the host community leaders. In this way, STM members will become experientially aware of the cultural diversity of themselves within their host community, learn the value of interdependence with the local people and develop an experiential empathy for their situation, the result being the development of a true partnership between the STM members and the community into which they enter.

A further criticism relating to STM development objectives in ethnic communities is that they often entrench communities in the trap of assistencialism, a cycle of dependency waiting for the next STM team to arrive with more injection of foreign capital. The Freiran concept of assistencialism is well described as 'saintly spirits' reflected upon by French philosopher, Jacques Lacan:

> Lacan … offers us some insights to understand this saintly spirit: it is as if there is an underlying desire to keep someone in the status of a victim, so that we can enact in ourselves the desire for helping. This mechanism allows people to

> ease their conscience, while at the same time assures that no fundamental change in the lives of the underprivileged or hindered occurs. (Pais 2014)

Missiology researchers such as Harries (2016) and Zehner (2013) reflect this criticism in their findings, recommending sending organisations of STM teams to study the true meaning of development and apply its principles to their outreach programmes.

Development as a term is in itself problematic, full of value-laden implications. Stavenhagen (2013) raises this issue by providing a definition as being a state of change, evolution and growth, but then proceeds to ask a series of questions, 'development from where to where, from what to what?', concluding that there are no adequate answers (p. 66). In his work on this subject, he calls on the need to re-evaluate the role of cultural values and social systems in development, placing particular emphasis on the rights of indigenous people to determine their own development. Emphasising this point further, Sahlins (1999) introduced the term 'the indigenisation of modernity', meaning that non-Western people have a right to develop their own cultural space in the global scheme of things (p. 410). These viewpoints have come to be known as ethnodevelopment, governed by the four principles of cultural pluralism, internal self-determination, territorialism and sustainability (Willis 2011; Clarke 2001), and over the past three decades has guided development policies sensitive to the rights of ethnic groups to participate (or not, as the case may be) in the modern development process on their own terms (Kassam 2002; van Nieuwkoop and Uquillas 2000).

My lived experience of living and working alongside ethnic Karen communities for nearly ten years has enabled me to gain an understanding of culture as described by Baldwin *et al.* (2008), as being historically situated, complex and socially constructed. Into this milieu, I have had the opportunity to observe first-hand the construct of missio-tourism alongside the development projects their team members have sought to initiate and carry out in these ethnic communities. Extremes of exclusiveness and inclusiveness, of power and control tensions versus genuine empowering relationships, have been evident in these varied encounters (see later in this chapter).

Method

The subject of this chapter is not the result of any formal research I have conducted. Rather, it results from the outcome of several years of lived experience. From 2007 to 2008, I lived and worked full-time in Mae La Refugee Camp situated on the Thai–Myanmar border, while simultaneously carrying out ethnographic fieldwork for my doctoral study. For the next six years, I lived between a Thai Karen village teaching in a Bible Seminary for refugee Karen youth in that place and a secondary-level migrant learning centre 30 kilometres further south. In 2013, I moved to the northern Thai city of Chiang Mai to take up an academic position but have maintained close ties to both the camp and village through personal relationships and ongoing research.

In this way, this work is both phenomenologically reflective (Van Manen 2016) and reflexively ethnographic (Boylorn and Orbe 2014). While phenomenological research always begins in the lifeworld, the reflection of the lived experience in that lifeworld should always be retrospective and recollective, so as to uncover and describe the internal meaning structures of the lived experience (Van Manen 2016: 10). Ellis and Bochner (2000) highlight that reflexive ethnography primarily focuses on culture and that, as researchers, we use our own experience in the culture reflexively to 'bend back on self and look more deeply at self-other interaction' (p. 740).

While living in Mae La Camp, the village and migrant learning centre, I recorded my many experiences – conversations, observations, interactions and anecdotal narratives – in personal journals. My research posture during this time and since has been one of reflexivity whereby I have become part of the social system in which my adopted community is located. My 'self' has become a source of and location for experience and action, thus enabling an inclusive approach to my work and community roles (Fook 2002). In so doing, my 'self' has become located within the Karen's existential and psychosocial reality and cannot be abstracted from that reality.

Over the past six months preparing to write this chapter, I have visited Mae La Camp and the village several times to discuss relative contents from my personal journals with community leaders, teachers and former students. Through ongoing relationships, I have also held discussions with a number of Christian based non-government organisations (NGOs) located in the border area that host short-term mission teams.

The data gained from my personal journals and more recent discussions has been analysed thematically in what Van Manen (2016: 79) states are derived from the 'structures of experience' and by 'the art of testing' (Gadamer 2004: 360). Themes derived from the structures of the experiences of both the receiving communities of STM teams and of the STM team members themselves are the lifeworld existentials of lived space (spatiality), lived time (temporality), lived body (corporeality) and lived other (relationality) (Van Manen 2016: 101–5). The 'art of testing' was achieved through the more recent meetings via discussion of relative contents from my personal journals.

In relation to the ethics of this research, I have sought to be guided by Clandinin's (2006) imperative of the need 'to imagine ethics as being about negotiation, respect, mutuality and openness to multiple voices' (p. 52).

Discussion

The ethnic Karen living along the Thai–Myanmar borderline are clearly not a homogeneous group. For the scope of this chapter, the focus is on refugee Karen originating from Myanmar and located in Thai-based refugee camps and migrant learning centres, and Thai Karen living in rural villages within a radius of 70 kilometres of the border town, Mae Sot. Relating to the latter group, researcher Assistant Professor Pinkaew Laungaramsi wrote that

> from a position of insignificant other outside the realm of the pre-modern state, the Karen have been relocated by the invented discourse of hill tribe. The shift to backward hill tribe has situated many Karen within a most vulnerable position … (2004: 39)

This position makes them an ideal target for the altruistic motives and projects of STM teams. Within the majority Karen migrant learning centres and refugee camps that are more accessible to the outside world, for example Mae La and Umphiem, STM teams are very visible.

Development activities that these teams are involved in are providing funds to erect classrooms and dormitories which some will actually assist in building and painting. Medical and dental teams carry out much needed procedures. Other teams conduct short-term teaching, often centred on English gospel songs, art classes and projects for micro-credit enterprises, for example sewing. Their sending organisations often continue to support the work of these places financially and return each year to evaluate progress.

The question can be asked, 'Are these ventures creating opportunity or promoting assistencialism for the receiving communities?' Another question (or more of a statement) that is often put forward by some of the more seasoned long-term volunteers I have worked with is, 'Perhaps they should stay at home and just send the money they spend in their coming.' This latter statement resonates with Corbett and Fikkert's (2009) observation that short-term mission has become a $1.6 billion annual enterprise in the United States of America with the average spending per person being conservatively estimated at $3,000 for a trip of less than two weeks.

In this study, the four existential themes pervading the life-worlds of all human beings as identified by Van Manen (2016) – lived other, lived body, lived space, lived time – correlate with the four principles of ethnodevelopment identified by Willis (2011) and Clarke (2001) – territorialism, ecological sustainability, cultural pluralism and internal self-determination. Further correlation exists in Zehner's (2006) four ideal outcomes of a field-oriented STM model as can be seen in Table 6.1.

Within this framework, three 'development'-based projects initiated by sending agencies of STM teams in ethnic Karen communities that I have observed are now presented for discussion and analysis.

Project 1

The Thoo Mweh River (in the Karen language), also known as the Mooei River (in the Thai language), forms part of the border between Thailand and Myanmar. In a Karen village on the Myanmar side, an international Christian non-governmental organisation (NGO) with a base in Mae Sot, Thailand has partnered with the local villagers to conduct development projects for several years now. Especially during the dry season when the river is low, they facilitate STM teams to visit this village with the focus on educational and health development. STM medical and dental teams carry out health education and training, provide treatment and donate much needed medical supplies.

Table 6.1 Empowerment development framework: correlated constructs of life-world themes, ethnodevelopment and field-oriented STM model

Life-world existential themes (Van Manen 2016: 102–4)	*Principles of ethnodevelopment (Willis 2011: 123)*	*Outcomes of STM field-oriented model (Zehner 2006)*
• Lived other – relationality – as we meet the other in the interpersonal space we share with them, we are able to develop relationships which allow us to transcend ourselves. • Lived body – corporeality – when meeting others in their landscape, we both reveal and conceal things about ourselves.	• Cultural pluralism – the existence of and mutual respect for a number of cultures within one society. • Internal self-determination – the ability for a particular ethnic group to control collectively its destiny within the context of a nation-state.	In a trainee (STM member) and supervisor (host community leaders) relationship, the trainee will: • become experientially aware of cultural diversity; • learn the value of interdependence with people; • learn to develop experiential empathy of the host community's situation; • leading to a learning of true partnership with people.
• Lived space – 'we become the space we are in' • Lived time – temporality – our lived experience. Time as we live it. The interrelationship of what we have done in the past, what we plan and enact in present and how we project ourselves into the future.	• Territorialism – the spatial concentration of ethnic groups, such that decisions about 'development' are made within a particular territory based on the resources of that particular area. • Ecological sustainability – development should progress with no significant destruction of the natural environment which would threaten future livelihoods.	

Source: This research.

Until recently, when children in this village finished middle school and wished to proceed to secondary school, they had to cross the river as undocumented migrants to the migrant learning centre six kilometres away. In the rainy season, this was very dangerous, resulting in the children having to remain in the dormitory for whole semesters on the Thai side. Through listening to the needs of the community, the NGO partnered with the village leaders to expand the school both physically and in a service-oriented manner. Buildings were constructed by villagers themselves from local-based materials; teachers were trained in partnership with a Karen ethnic community-based organisation and educational resources provided to expand the school to Grade Ten. For two years now, Western teachers who originally came as STM team members have remained in the village for whole semesters immersing themselves in the culture working alongside local teachers, resulting in development based on inclusiveness, mutual respect and beneficence to the ethnic Karen of this village.

Another Mae Sot, Thailand-based Christian NGO hosts many STM teams from their originating country to the Thai–Myanmar border. Over the past ten years, I have observed and discussed with the NGO staff the advantages and disadvantages of their development initiatives. This organisation has two specific development foci for ethnic communities located in Tak Province, Thailand – livelihood and education. Livelihood projects have involved setting up 'cow and pig banks' and fish farms in ethnic villages. Education development takes the form of building classrooms and providing books and computers in migrant learning centres. Both these foci have achieved varied success depending on whose viewpoint is taken.

Project 2

Take, for example, a livelihood project in an ethnic Karen village south of Mae Sot. The STM teams brought by the NGO to this village are largely young people with their church youth leaders on their school vacation. The focus is on cultural immersion. To this end, the STM teams sleep, eat and play with Karen young people who are from more remote areas and live in hostel type accommodation in this village so they can attend secondary school. Over several years, strong relationships have been built with STM leaders returning year after year. In consultation with religious and village leaders, it was agreed to initiate a 'cow bank' project some years ago. The home churches of the STM teams provided the initial capital; 11 cows were purchased with one cow given to local villagers wanting to participate (chosen by lot) with the aim of empowering the local ethnic community economically by generating extra income. Through artificial insemination, calves were born and sold and the cost of the initial cow gradually repaid, generating funds to buy additional cows for more villagers. Cow dung is sold as organic fertiliser in surrounding villages as well as used on local plots of land.

Project 3

Conversely, a classroom building project in an ethnic Karen migrant learning centre (MLC) initiated by an STM team working through this same NGO has had a very different outcome. Funding for this venture was secured from an STM team who visited the MLC and were concerned that existing buildings were of poor quality and not conducive to student learning. In keeping with the surrounding houses, these buildings were made from local materials of bamboo and thatch built on stilts to protect against flooding during the rainy season. However, regarding this project, the funding team operated only through the NGO which then passed on the requirements to the community leaders. The result was a six-classroom building of cement with a tiled roof built on a concrete foundation with fixed windows and electric ceiling fans and lights that would serve as the new primary school for the MLC. The STM team returned for the opening ceremony which I attended. Four years have passed and this building is now in a state of disrepair. Windows have fallen out and large cracks are evident in both the foundations and the walls. Electricity has been cut due to a lack of funds to pay for it. Water enters during the rainy season and during the hot season there is limited ventilation.

Comparing the tenets of the empowerment development framework in Table 6.1, an analysis of the development projects presented above can be conducted. In relation to the first two projects outlined above, both organisations hosting STM teams have facilitated development ventures that have served as a bridge to the empowerment and self-determination of ethnic Karen, as can be seen in Table 6.2.

In my many years of interacting with staff and STM teams coming from the NGO to facilitate Project 1, I have observed that they abide by a policy of providing orientation prior to STM teams visiting the villages and camps along the border. Their motto, 'Normal is over', aims to prepare STM teams to be aware of their own cultural nuances and the impact they may have on the culture they will be interacting with, and to respect and learn from the communities they enter. Many of their staff members are bilingual ethnic Karen, enabling training and support to be delivered in the community's own language, while at the same time able to understand and provide cross-cultural training with Western STM team members. Their educational development project in the ethnic Karen village on the Myanmar side of the Thoo Mweh River has achieved Sahlins' (1999) concept of the indigenisation of modernity, in that the local community has been empowered to raise the education level of its youth. Prior to this project, many of the youth dropped out of school at Grade Eight, leaving to search for employment as undocumented migrant workers in the agricultural, fishing or textile industries in Thailand, receiving low pay with often dangerous working conditions and risking detention if caught by the Thai authorities. Through a process of partnership with like-minded organisations and local authorities, this community is working to gain official recognition of its education standard, providing viable options for its youths' futures. The NGO and the STM teams they bring to this village have been the means by which this process started; however, the community is now empowered to determine its own ongoing educational development.

From the viewpoint of missio-tourism, the STM teams to this village are increasingly made up of returning members, especially those with teaching and medical skills. While their average time spent in the village is five to seven days, they have fostered real connections with the community through their return visits, a 'lived other' experience, thus achieving Zehner's (2006) ideal outcome of STM to truly partner with the people they come to serve. The STM members who return for longer-term volunteer posts can then expand their 'lived body and lived time' experiences in that they immerse themselves more fully in the culture in which they are living (Van Manen 2016).

Table 6.2 Projects 1 and 2: correlations of ethnodevelopment principles and STM field-orientation model

	Ethnodevelopment principles (Willis 2011)			
	Cultural pluralism	*Internal self-determination*	*Territorialism*	*Ecological sustainability*
Experientially aware of cultural diversity	**P1.** STM attend orientation training Many staff same ethnicity – able to share cultural mores and norms **P2.** STM youth live together with locals – share food, cultures	**P1&2.** Traditional and modern knowledge both respected		**P1.** STM teams participate in repair and building maintenance – shared learning of local environment
Value of inter-dependence with people		**P1.** Medical and educational resources in hands of Karen community **P2.** Village, religious and NGO leadership working together	**P1.** Teacher training partnered with local CBO – training in own language. Health education delivered in own language	**P2.** Respect of local agrarian knowledge
Experiential empathy with host community's situation	**P1&2.** Returning teams have time to understand community needs **P1.** Cultural immersion of long-term volunteers enables greater understanding of local issues	**P1.** Long-term volunteers and trained local teachers enabling school standards to rise to Burmese levels. More options for students' futures	**P2.** Project achieving socio-economic growth within local kinship structure	**P1.** Buildings constructed of local materials in keeping with village structure

In the case study of Project 2 situated in a Thai Karen village, there is a strong leadership structure with a good relationship between the Buddhist sangha and Christian church. Consultation with all these groups occurred from the beginning of the project with all principles of ethnodevelopment evident. Ownership of the project is village-based and eco-sustainability is a significant factor. The NGO facilitating the STM teams to this village have a long relationship with the Christian church and its youth ministry. As they are financial supporters of the youth hostel, their STM team focus has always been youth-based with the leaders and youth from churches in their home country coming during school vacation time. The cow bank project began with a low budget for which an STM youth team could raise funds. Initially, the village church leadership had identified this as a means to improve the socio-economic status of the whole village, so from the beginning, it was a project whereby local people determined their own development (Stavenhagen 2013).

I lived in this village for six years and return regularly. As the STM leaders stayed in our house while the youth would bunk in with our youth, I came to know some of these team members well as they returned year after year, sometimes twice a year. It was interesting to see the change of what Howell (2009) refers to as the 'missionary gaze' the more times they returned. At first, many focused only on the seeming poverty of the village and the lives of our youth living dormitory style as underprivileged, viewing themselves as simply donors to these 'undifferentiated poor'. However, in their preparedness to interact with our church members despite the lack of a common language, it was encouraging to see attitudes change as they realised the value of the kinship system of Karen culture and developed an experiential empathy (rather than sympathy) for our villagers' situation. This was not a one-way change; we learnt from each other's different cultures in a genuine partnership relationship.

For our youth, language never seemed to be a deterrent for building meaningful relationships. There is always enough English between them to communicate and the sharing of cultural music and dance has resulted in a cultural pluralism that does not depend on a mutual spoken language. The three to five days that the STM teams stay in our village are definitely viewed by their youth as a holiday, but a 'lived other' (Van Manen 2016) experience is achieved for all of those involved.

While Projects 1 and 2 can be seen to be bridges to empowerment, development and self-determination, Project 3 had a very different outcome. The NGO involved here facilitates STM teams from different backgrounds and funds many different development ventures. Some of their teams comprise mostly older Christian businessmen and women. It was such a team that came to the migrant learning centre I was teaching at in 2011. They came with a specific agenda to source what they considered to be a worthwhile development project that would advance the educational opportunities of ethnic Karen children. Over the course of four hours as I accompanied them, they struggled up and down bamboo ladders and entered classrooms where children sat cross-legged on the bamboo floor behind low wooden benches that served as desks. In a trilingual translation, they spoke words of encouragement to each class they entered and left.

Two weeks later, a staff member of the NGO visited the MLC and gave the good news to the pastor, headmaster and me that members of the STM team had chosen this MLC to build new classrooms for the primary school. The ethnic Karen community in this place are largely undocumented refugees and migrants who have built up the MLC on non-tenured land over several years with donor funds. However, this good news was clouded with a list of directives on every aspect of the development project of which they were given no say – it was presented to them as a *fait accompli.* Outside builders of a different ethnicity were employed because they submitted the lowest tender. Even when shortcuts such as the water/sand/concrete mix being watered down was observed by the local leaders and reported to the NGO, no action was taken. A year later, the same STM team returned to proudly open the new school. Again, with trilingual translation, students were encouraged to do their best.

In direct contrast to the livelihood project facilitated by this same NGO just 30 kilometres north, this project completely disempowered the local community, promoting assistencialism. There was no mutuality in this venture; the receiving community were treated as passive recipients of aid that was determined in a vacuum of decontextualised otherness (Zehner 2013). From a mission perspective, there was a distinct lack of respect for cultural diversity and lack of experiential empathy with the lives and needs of the MLC community, with no awareness of Van Manen's (2016) 'lived space' and 'lived other'. From an ethnodevelopment perspective, none of the four principles stated by Willis (2011) were evident. Neither internal self-determination nor issues of territoriality were taken into consideration, with no consultation or funds for maintenance and upkeep provided.

As with all the MLC's operating on this part of the Thai–Myanmar border, this MLC's existence has always been precarious. Its legal status in Thailand is tenuous and it is totally dependent on the generosity of donors to maintain the delivery of education to the children and youth of their community. These two facts combine to increase their vulnerability to assistencialism, whereby they believe they have limited power to influence the development of their own environment.

Conclusion

This chapter has been written in the spirit of temporality – lived time as I have lived it on the central Thai–Myanmar border in ethnic Karen communities, past, present and future (Van Manen 2016). The proliferation of missio-tourism in recent decades and its inextricable link with development through its missions to 'the poor and oppressed of our world' is the continuing focus of the phenomenological research elaborated on in this chapter – 'knots in the web of my personal experience' lived through and contributing to a meaningful whole (*ibid.*, p. 90). My findings show that, in the main, the sending community arrives with altruistic motives; however, they often lack cultural competence with little to no understanding of the socio-economic and socio-political issues impacting on their receiving community.

The question asked is this: 'Are the activities of Christian short-term missions carried out in ethnic Karen communities creating opportunity or promoting assistencialism?' The answer is sought by means of the analysis of three case studies utilising the tenets of an ideal model for short-term missions (Zehner 2006) and the principles of ethnodevelopment (Willis 2011). Through this analysis, it can be concluded that development ventures initiated by STM teams can be the bridge of opportunity to real development objectives of inclusiveness, empowerment and self-determination for ethnic communities when values of cultural diversity, interdependence and experiential empathy of those communities' situation and environment are incorporated into the whole mission from its inception planning stages to its conclusion – a desire for true partnership with those they come to serve.

However, my experience has shown that while values and mindsets are changing towards a more genuine understanding of ethnodevelopment principles, many STM teams continue to arrive with their preconceived 'tourist gaze' (Urry 2002) which results in the abrogation of the ethnic communities' rights to determine their own development needs and trajectories, promoting a cycle of assistencialism from which vulnerable communities have great difficulty escaping. It is noteworthy to emphasise that the work, aid and overall participation of volunteers in missio-tourism support a historically ethnic unprivileged minority on the border of Thailand and Myanmar. This support to the ethnic Karen community has contributed to mitigate the effects of an existing asymmetrical development that negatively imposes harsh living conditions on these people in Myanmar by the previous authoritarian regime.

By taking these aspects into account, this perception corroborates Fong's (2008) understanding that a holistic ethnodevelopment process would gain shape though state-oriented ethnic minority development strategies and policies that can permit the exercise of self-determination and thus neutralise such asymmetries. Fong (2008: 344) advances the scope of Stavenhagen's ethnodevelopment by perceiving that Karen liberation ethnodevelopment is also a development process, a bottom-up approach that is not incompatible with federalist and democratic processes. Within this context, my many years of observing the phenomenon of missio-tourism on the central Thai–Myanmar border has led me to conclude that community-based and non-governmental organisations facilitating STM teams have a pivotal role in developing a transitive consciousness in their members which will both enrich their STM tourist experience as well as break the cycle of assistencialism to the communities they seek to serve.

Note

1. Migrant learning centres are unofficial schools operated by community-based or non-governmental organisations for children and youth living in areas in Thailand where large numbers of migrants and/or refugees live. While the Ministry of Education, Thailand acknowledges the existence of these schools, they are not accredited within the official education system and they are totally dependent on donor funding for their operation.

References

Baldwin, J., Faulkner, S. and Hecht, M. (2008) A moving target: the illusive definition of culture. In J. Baldwin *et al.* (eds), *Redefining Culture: Perspectives Across the Disciplines*. Abingdon: Routledge, pp. 3–26.

Boylorn, R. M. and Orbe, M. P. (2014) Critical autoethnography as method of choice. In R. Boylorn and M. Orbe, *Critical Autoethnography: Intersecting Cultural Identities in Everyday Life*. Walnut Creek, CA: Left Coast Press, pp. 13–26.

Clandinin, D. J. (2006) Narrative inquiry: a methodology for studying lived experience. *Research Studies in Music Education* 44: 27–54.

Clarke, G. (2001) From ethnocide to ethnodevelopment? Ethnic minorities and indigenous peoples in Southeast Asia. *Third World Quarterly* 22(3): 413–36.

Corbett, S. and Fikkert, B. (2009) *When Helping Hurts*. Chicago: Moody.

Dreby, J. and Brown, T. M. (2013) Work and home in balance: finding synergy through ethnographic fieldwork. In T. M. Brown and J. Dreby (eds), *Family and Work in Everyday Ethnography*. Philadelphia, PA: Temple University Press, pp. 3–16.

Ellis, C. and Bochner, A. (2000) Autoethnography, personal narrative, reflexivity. In N. Denzin and Y. Lincoln (eds), *Handbook of Qualitative Research*, 2nd edn. Thousand Oaks, CA: Sage, pp. 733–68.

Fong, J. (2008) Revising the ethnodevelopment model: addressing Karen self-determination within the context of the failed ethnocratic state of military-ruled Burma. *Ethnic and Racial Studies Journal* 31(2): 327–57.

Fook, J. (2002) Theorising from practice: towards an inclusive approach for social work research. *Qualitative Social Work* 1(1): 79–95.

Freire, P. (1973) *Education: The Practice of Freedom*, trans. Myra Bergman Ramos. London: Writers and Readers Publishing Cooperative.

Gadamer, H. (2004) *Truth and Method*, 2nd edn. London: Continuum.

Harries, J. (2016) To compromise on missionary vulnerability in Africa? A response to critics of 'vulnerable mission'. *Global Missiology* 3(13).

Howell, B. (2009) Mission to nowhere: putting short-term missions into context. *International Bulletin of Missionary Research* 33(4): 206–11.

Howell, B. (2012) *Short-term Mission: An Ethnography of Christian Travel Narrative and Experience*. Downers Grove, IL: Intervarsity Press.

Kassam, A. (2002) Ethnotheory, ethnopraxis: ethnodevelopment in the Oromia Regional State of Ethiopia. In P. Stillitoe, A. Bicker and J. Pottier (eds), *Participating in Development: Approaches to Indigenous Knowledge*. Abingdon: Routledge, pp. 64–81.

Pais, A. (2014) *The Pedagogy of Freire, the Psychoanalysis of Lacan and the Trap of Assistencialism.* Paper presented at the European Conference on Educational Research, Porto, Portugal, 4 September.

Pinkaew, L. (2004) Construction marginality: the 'hill tribe' Karen and their shifting location with Thai state and public perspective. In C. Delang (ed.), *Living at the Edge of Thai Society: The Karen of the Highlands of Northern Thailand.* London: Routledge-Curzon, pp. 21–42.

Priest, R. and Howell, B. (2013) Introduction: theme issue on short term missions. *Missiology: An International Review* 41(2): 124–9.

Probasco, L. (2013) Giving time, not money: long-term impacts of short term mission trips. *Missiology: An International Review* 41(2): 202–24.

Rauschenbusch, W. (1917) *Theology for the Social Gospel*. New York, NY: Macmillan.

Sahlins, M. (1999) Two or three things that I know about culture. *Journal of the Royal Anthropological Institute* 5(3): 399–421.

Stavenhagen, R. (2013) Pioneer on Indigenous rights. In H. Brauch (ed.), *Springer Briefs on Pioneers in Science and Practice*, Vol. 2. New York, NY: Springer.

Urry, J. (2002) *The Tourist Gaze*, 2nd edn. London: Sage.

van Manen, M. (2016) *Researching Lived Experiences: Human Science for an Action Sensation Pedagogy*, 2nd edn. Abingdon: Routledge.

van Nieuwkoop, M. and Uquillas, J. (2000) *Defining Ethnodevelopment in Operational Terms: Lessons from the Ecuador Indigenous and Afro-Ecuadoran Peoples Project*. Washington, DC: World Bank.

ver Beek, K. (2006) The impact of short-term missions: a case study of house construction in Honduras after Hurricane Mitch. *Missiology: An International Review* 34(4): 477–95.

Webb, C. (1992) The use of the first person in academic writing: objectivity, language and gatekeeping. *Journal of Advanced Nursing* 17(6): 747–52.

Wilder, M. and Parker, S. (2010) *TransforMission: Making Disciples through Short-Term Missions*. Nashville, TN: B & H Publishing.

Willis, K. (2011) *Theories and Practices of Development*, 2nd edn. London: Routledge.

Wuthnow, R. (2009) *Boundless Faith: The American Outreach of American Churches*. Berkeley, CA: University of California Press.

Zehner, E. (2006) Short-term mission: toward a more field-oriented model. *Missiology: An International Review* 34(4): 509–21.

Zehner, E. (2013) Short-term mission: some perspectives from Thailand. *Missiology: An International Review* 41(2): 202–24.

7 Empowerment, participation and barriers

Ethnic minority community-based ecotourism development in Lao PDR

Eerang Park, Toulakham Phandanouvong, Phouvanh Xaysena and Sangkyun Kim

Introduction

This chapter investigates the extent to which, and indeed how, community empowerment plays a vital role in enhancing the active participation of ethnic minority communities, thus increasing the likelihood of positive perceptions of the impact of tourism on their communities in the context of community-based ecotourism (CBET) in Laos. It also identifies and discusses the factors that hinder community participation and empowerment, using two case studies of CBET projects in Lao PDR – in Ban Na Village in Bolikhamxay Province, and Houay Kaeng Village in Sayabouly Province. Two similar cases of CBET development in Lao PDR, approached differently, generated different sets of outcomes.

The significance of local community involvement in tourism development is frequently discussed in the sustainable tourism literature (Bramwell 2010; Lapeyre 2010; Park and Kim 2016; Spenceley and Meyer 2012; Stone and Stone 2011). It is, however, less likely to be accomplished in practical ways, particularly in the context of developing countries in which highly centralised governmental systems mean that the participation of local communities rarely goes beyond mere consultation and information exchange (Tosun 2000; Yuksel *et al.* 2005). This demonstrates that the active participation of the local community in decision-making processes about tourism planning and development is not yet apparent. It is even more challenging in ethnic minority areas that are remote and relatively inaccessible, as well as being disadvantaged socio-economically and politically due to power imbalances, economic inequality, limited economic capital, and low levels of education and service skills (Cohen 2016; Dogra and Gupta 2012; Ellis and Sheridan 2015; Timothy 1999; Tosun 2000).

Despite the above, there has been much development of ethnic and cultural tourism in ethnic minority areas across mainland South East Asia, in countries that are ethnically very diverse (Cohen 2016). Although the development of ethnic and cultural tourism in this region, particularly in China, Vietnam and Thailand, has been used as a political and cultural project to achieve poverty alleviation or eradication, its top-down approach, radical transformation and local community disempowerment are believed to have caused tensions and distortions (Cohen 2016).

In contrast, the development of ethnic minority tourism in Laos is a relatively recent phenomenon. Thanks to lessons learnt from neighbouring countries, the Lao government based its initiatives on the concept of community-based ecotourism (CBET); the transitional feature of community empowerment is particularly important in the CBET development approach, which aims to foster the communities' abilities and build capacity to develop and control their own affairs in relation to tourism (Zeppel 2006). Thus the CBET approach was chosen by the Lao government to facilitate a fairer distribution of the income generated by tourism to relatively poor and underdeveloped ethnic minority groups in rural areas, as well as community empowerment, placing indigenous ownership and control at the heart of ecotourism (National Tourism Administration of Lao PDR – hereafter LNTA n.d.). This approach was also aligned with the country's Poverty Eradication Strategy (Harrison and Schipani 2009).

Having acknowledged the above, this chapter aims to investigate the extent to which and indeed how community empowerment plays a vital role in encouraging ethnic minority communities to play a more active part in CBET development, thus increasing the likelihood of positive perceptions towards the impacts of CBET on their communities. It also identifies and discusses the factors that hinder community participation and empowerment. Scheyvens' (2003) four-dimensional empowerment framework (i.e. economic, psychological, social and political) is adopted due to its relevance to CBET development. The geographical focus is on Ban Na Village in Bolikhamxay Province and Houay Kaeng Village in Sayabouly Province, Laos. The primary data were gathered via a series of semi-structured in-depth interviews with 26 community members in Ban Na Village (10 from the tour guide group, 8 from the hand product group and 8 from the homestay group) in January 2014, and 20 community members in Houay Kaeng Village (3 community leaders and 17 local residents) in July 2013.

Backgrounds of the two CBET projects in Laos

The CBET project in Ban Na Village in Bolikhamxay Province was established in 2003 by the LNTA in the Phou Khao Khouay National Protected Area (PKKNPA) in collaboration with the Management of Phou Khao Khouay National Park, Department of Forestry, and the German Development Service (DED). Phou Khao Khouay has been designated a 'National Protected Area' since 1993, as it is home to 500 species of flora and fauna. There are two major herds of Asian elephant and more than 50 per cent of all orchid species can be found in the sandstone mountain range. Many forest dwellers and ethnic minority communities in the area utilise the park for their livelihoods through activities such as (unsustainable) agricultural practices, livestock grazing, timber extraction, forest burning, the collection of non-timber forest products, and hunting and fishing (LNTA, n.d.).

While residents in and around the park belong to different ethnic groups, including Lao-Tai and Mon-Khmer, the majority in Ban Na Village belong to the Hmong-Mieu group. As of January 2014, there were 126 households in this area. The total population was 667 people, 336 of whom were women. The majority of the households in the village participated in subsistence rice farming. The village grew rice in the rainy season, from June to December, whereas during the dry season, from January to May, the farmers were mainly involved in supplementary activities, such as making sticky rice containers. The women were engaged in weaving while the men provided the raw materials, which often involved gathering bamboo from the forest (LNTA 2009).

Meanwhile, the CBET project in Houay Kaeng Village in Sayabouly Province was a more recent CBET project which was part of the Great Mekong Subregion – Sustainable Tourism Development Project (GMS-STDP), funded by the Asian Development Bank (ADB) in 2009. Houay Kaeng Village, in the northern part of Laos, was home to Lao ethnic groups, namely 81 families consisting of 61 Hmong highlanders, 17 Khmu mid-landers and 3 Lao Loum lowlanders (Department of Information, Culture and Tourism – hereafter DICT 2012). Most of the villagers were engaged in farming, with an estimated average annual household income of US$1,000 (ADB-GMS 2011). Most households engaged in subsistence farming, mainly growing chillies and corn. Some of them engaged in other activities, such as raising cattle and chicken, collecting and selling bamboo shoots, and producing and selling craftwork such as bamboo baskets, tissue boxes and sticky rice boxes. In addition, some of the men worked in the city as construction workers.

Houay Kaeng Village was selected to be the main site for the establishment of the CBET in the Sayabouly District, not only because of the poor living conditions of its population, but also because of its potentially outstanding tourism resources, particularly the Namsai stream, the Houng River and the medicinal plant forest (DICT 2012). The Namsai stream is the most significant tourism resource in the village as it offers very clean water all year round. This water is used for the sauna (one of the CBET activities in Houay Kaeng), but is normally boiled before drinking to ensure cleanliness (ADB-GMS 2011). In addition, Ban Houay Kaeng is a Hmong village that maintains its ethnic character and traditions, and is able to utilise the Hmong reputation for herbal medicine to attract tourists to the area and provide services for the public (DICT 2012). Up to 100 traditional medicinal plants are located within the village's protected area of 35 hectares, which is covered by lush green forest on mountainous hillsides and where the Houng River meanders through the valley and is met by the Namsai stream gushing from the foot of the cliffs. This wide spectrum of medicinal plants was surveyed by the Provincial Health Department in 2003. It was then decided that this site should be preserved for the conservation of these medicinal plants (DICT 2012).

The case of Ban Na Village

Overview of CBE development in Ban Na Village and community initiatives

Ban Na Village in the PKKNPA implemented the CBET development as the forest dwellers' existence was seriously threatened by rapid deforestation and the overexploitation of resources. The elephant population now threatens agricultural livelihoods as they would often raid village fields containing sugarcane, pineapples, bananas and other crops. The large-scale resource extraction of the tropical forests has also had a tremendous ecological and environmental impact. With financial, technical and advisory support from the DED, the project prioritised the establishment of awareness of ecotourism development and the role and importance of community involvement in the project. Starting with education and training, the village residents received extensive information about the benefits and pitfalls of ecotourism development in their village as well as information about the conservation of the nearby National Protected Area. Having established sufficient understanding of the project among community members, various training programmes such as tour guiding, food preparation and serving (e.g. hygiene), and accommodation services were also provided to the residents so that they could run tourism businesses while ensuring that their culture and lifestyles are embedded and shared through tourism services.

The local villagers in Ban Na Village formed a village CBET unit called the Project Coordination Unit (PCU), managed by three sub-groups, namely the tour operators, the project secretary and the project assistant. The main purpose of the PCU is to monitor the operation and management of the CBET services; most of the residents' participation in tourism activities came through the tour operator sub-group. The project secretary was tasked with auditing records and preparing the monthly financial report for the project, whereas the project assistant's role was to assist the head of the project in inspecting the damage to household crops and rice fields caused by elephants. The latter was also tasked with reporting back to the project so that compensation for the households affected could be processed.

Tour guides and homestay providers are the key players in the CBET tour operator sub-group, along with producers of hand-made products. Ban Na Village is well-known as an elephant village. The community operates elephant trekking and observation programmes through the activities of the tour guides. The tour guides are also interested in extending this popular Ban Na ecotourism product by developing a walking trail that begins in the village and goes along the river to some cascades, where visitors can then travel by boat to Ban Yang Kuea and other river attractions. The local guides show tourists the region's wild orchids, traditional herbs, birds, insects and butterflies (PCU 2011). The responsibility of the homestay provider is to supply accommodation and hospitality for tourists. As of January 2014, there were eight households offering accommodation in the village and they were happy to share their unique lifestyles and engage in cultural exchange activities with the tourists. The local craftspeople in the handmade product team mainly produce woven bamboo handicrafts for sale.

Supporting the PCU's operational side, Ban Na Village established community-level service groups that are autonomously and collectively controlled by the villagers. The activities served to enhance active community engagement in the project's activities, guarantee the equitable sharing of benefits and increase efficiency in training delivery. These activities have also become a tool to not only improve local awareness of sustainability, but also to educate local people in the need for local control and management in order to secure long-term harmonious development. For example, the handicraft production team is encouraged to design and create its own handicrafts, and the producers are financially supported to attend the annual National Handicraft Festival and Exhibition in order to meet potential buyers and other important business contacts.

The annual number of tourists visiting the village dramatically increased from 128 people to 519 people between 2008 and 2011. The CBET project generated revenue for the village of around US$11,780 in 2011 (PCU 2011). As of January 2014, the project has been entirely handed over to the local community, and thus local villagers autonomously manage tourism in the area according to the principles of CBET planning and implementation. This small-scale CBET is still strong and well-managed by the villagers, who are enthusiastic and determined. They recruit and train new guides, and maintain the elephant tower. Restaurants in the village have also been improved, and the construction of a small guesthouse is under consideration. The Lao National Tourism Administration and the park administration also provide ongoing advice and technical support when requested (PCU 2011).

Community empowerment and positive perceptions toward tourism development

As demonstrated above, the inclusion and self-determination of the local community in the case of Ban Na Village was noticeable from the beginning of the CBET project development, which led to high-level community empowerment and more positive perceptions of and support for tourism development. Firstly, psychological empowerment generated by community pride and self-esteem in their ethnic culture and traditions, as well as their unique natural resources and environment, was visible. Most of the local villagers that participated in the project were proud of their cultural traditions and their uniqueness and authenticity, as reflected in tourists' sincere interest in and reverence for their ethnic culture. Such psychological empowerment was most evident from the homestay services and handmade products. For instance, the villagers' handmade products, especially the sticky rice containers, became the highlight of the crafts group and were very popular among tourists. This also inspired local people to maintain their skills and craftsmanship for later generations, and promote their products to tourists in a sustainable manner. As such, tourism activities enabled local villagers to be more aware of the significance of preserving their traditional lifestyles and ethnic culture. In this regard, a male local villager stated:

> Most of the villagers in Ban Na village belong to the Meui group. I am very proud to promote my traditional culture, such as our dress, our food, and our traditional language. For instance, I explain to the tourists that the local women usually wear a Lao skirt, we eat sticky rice, and the host and the guest usually eat together to promote harmony. Most of the tourists who visit our

village respect our ethnic culture, and their deference for our tradition can increase my self-esteem.

Secondly, while psychological empowerment ultimately underpins the success of the CBET development, another important aspect of this empowerment is the community's perception of the economic benefits of tourism. Local people believed that higher incomes ultimately improved their living conditions. In the past, the local average monthly income from growing and selling farm produce and livestock was about LAK 450,000 (equivalent to US$55). Since the launch of the CBET project, the local people engaged in tourism activities have attained more stable monthly incomes of more than LAK 1,100,000 on average (equivalent to US$135). They have even been able to save money to pay for their children's education, housing repairs and vehicle purchases.

The tourism activities of the CBET initiative have also developed the village. With steadier incomes, local people have been able to establish village funds to help members of the community and develop better conditions in the village. For example, the tour guide fund was established in 2005 with regular contributions from members of the tour guide group. This fund was set up to assist those members who needed loans with low or no interest due to sickness or to take temporary leave. A similar handicrafts fund was also created in the same year. Each member of the group contributes 3 per cent of their entire sales to the fund. The money is spent on the delivery of local craft products to merchants and to pay for the hiring of booths at annual handicrafts exhibitions. The fund is also used to lend money to group members who suffer from financial issues due to, for example, unexpected illness. In 2010, the homestay fund was established and is used to fix and improve the village infrastructure, including the school, bridges, roads and the electricity and water supply. As the villagers realise that their economic empowerment has, in many respects, improved their living conditions, their attitudes towards the CBET development in their village have also improved.

It is also noteworthy that the economic empowerment that followed the equal distribution of opportunities and responsibilities to men and women played a crucial role in building support among the villagers for the CBET project, as women in Ban Na Village were able to widen their horizons and challenge the status quo from being traditionally passive to active players. All ten of the female participants collectively stated that the equity of economic activities, and the economic empowerment that followed, significantly helped narrow the gap between men and women in the community (see Figure 7.1). Furthermore, such economic empowerment led to the engendering of a strong sense of self-esteem and pride, which is central to psychological empowerment in this context. Indeed, representatives of the village were encouraged to attend a gender focal point in the Project Implementation Unit, in collaboration with the Provincial Women's Union representatives. The Unit had elaborated upon and updated the Gender and Ethnic Minority Mainstreaming Strategies and Action Plans at the provincial level. The project's goal of supporting gender and ethnic equality is pursued through training and awareness-raising activities, as well as in the planning of other project activities (LNTA n.d.).

Figure 7.1 Woman and men villagers cooking together for tourists in Ban Na Village.
Source: Author.

Alongside psychological and economic empowerment, a strong sense of cohesion and harmony among the community's members could be seen, which is central to social empowerment (Scheyvens 2003), although it is worth remembering that strong and harmonious relationships already existed in Ban Na Village before the development of CBE. In particular, the local handicraft business boosted social harmony among the villagers, especially among women and the elderly, as they would spend most of their time together producing handicraft products. The social empowerment generated by such cohesion and attachment reached its peak when their sticky rice containers won a local government prize for an outstandingly high-quality ethnic-minority handicraft product. This prize bolstered the locals' pride and confidence in their abilities to create valuable products that are deeply embedded in their ethnic culture and traditions.

Finally, the residents of Ban Na Village were politically empowered to make their own decisions about the process of CBET development and its activities. From the very beginning, local involvement was welcomed at every decision-making stage with regard to the planning and implementation of tourism activities. In addition, through the use of village meetings and workshops, the entire community was able to stay informed, and was asked to share its opinions about the project activities. Each of the three tourism groups had monthly meetings during which they would report on the strengths and weaknesses of the activities in which they were engaged and on the progress of their jobs. Members would identify any issues that had arisen with their jobs and discuss possible solutions to these problems. In addition, they were empowered to express and share ideas for future plans and the further implementation of CBET development. Their participation in the development process generated a sense of ownership, which is seen as key to sustainability. Thus the above ultimately enhances community ownership of the initial tourism development and its subsequent operation and management (Ellis and Sheridan 2015).

The case of Houay Kaeng Village

Overview of CBET development in Houay Kaeng Village

Since 2009, the CBET project in Houay Kaeng Village has attempted to create jobs and income-generating opportunities for local villagers in order to improve their living conditions. Unlike in Ban Na Village, the ADB (GMS-STDP) and the Department of Information, Culture and Tourism (DICT) have worked with community leaders in Houay Kaeng to plan and develop a range of tourism service groups under its own CBET programme. This includes a sauna and traditional massage service group, a reception-hospitality and food service group, a tour guide service group, a homestay service group and an administration group. The core ecotourism product produced in this village is the sauna and the traditional massage service, which can be found at the Houay Namsai Medicinal Plant Preserve Centre, a community-operated healthcare centre. The pure water of the Namsai stream, which runs through the centre, is fed from an underground source and has a reputation as a sacred healing stream. Surrounded by up to a hundred different types of traditional medicinal plants, this centre is well placed for the conduct of most of the CBET activities and services. Tourists can experience the healing services of traditional Hmong medicinal practitioners before joining walking tours with local guides.

The processes of CBET planning and development in which local residents were involved included educational and information, economic and conservation activities. The aim of these activities was to encourage residents to participate in the development of tourism in their community, as well as to create opportunities for income generation to boost their standards of living. Although each service group was supposed to be given an equal opportunity to take part in these activities, it was revealed that the structure and delivery of each activity was insufficient to engage with all community members and to provide them with sufficiently deep knowledge and skills. The educational and information activities aimed to deliver essential knowledge and enhance local people's understanding of the CBET development through training sessions and study tours. However, few villagers participated in the sessions, and the activities were mainly focused on providing vocational knowledge such as handicraft production, operating the sauna and providing the massage service, and cookery. Although some sessions included tourism-specific training and despite the fact that the public participation process was held, the community leaders were the only ones that participated.

Economic activities were found to be the main form in which local resident involvement took place. These activities included operating the sauna and traditional massage services, food services, tour guide service, homestay services, and the selling of local handicrafts. However, most of the residents participating in the economic activities had already been trained in these tourism services. They believed that these activities could increase their income beyond that which they earned from working in the rice fields and thus enhance their living conditions. While some local residents were given responsibility for the protection of tourism resources, a number of residents volunteered to take part in this activity. They became involved through the training programmes on environmental and wildlife conservation organised by the tourism development authorities. Some expressed a desire to be part of the conservation of resources in their area, and were keen to learn about and become involved in this activity. In particular, the protection of natural resources was the main reason for their involvement as their lives were heavily reliant on these resources, as can be seen in the following comment:

> I decided to become involved in the CBET project as it allows me to learn about environmental conservation through the training programme, and enables me to protect the natural resources in my locality … I want to protect the rivers and forest in my village because these resources provide food and products for me to eat and sell …

Three levels of community participation, unequal opportunities and hindering factors

In contrast to the case of Ban Na Village, three different levels of community participation in the tourism planning and development process in Houay Kaeng Village were observed: active, passive and non-community participation. Only a few local residents, namely the community leaders as representatives of the village, had substantial responsibilities for the CBET development process. In this active participation group, five key responsibilities were identified, namely: participation in the consultation and decision-making process, the protection of tourism resources, the provision of a pleasant environment for tourists, the provision of essential information for tourism planning and development, and monitoring the progress of tourism development. It was clear that this group was the most proactively engaged in tourism planning and development activities compared to the rest of the community. It consulted with tourism officers about their expectations and concerns about the development of tourism in the village, such as the types of activities they wanted to create and provide for tourists, and how a safe environment for tourists could be ensured. In addition, the group was responsible for making decisions on the sharing of the benefits of tourism and the allocation of tourism development funding for the village. Accordingly, the members of this group had a higher level of awareness of the significance of their participation and had a strong willingness to participate in CBET activities.

In comparison, a large number of community members belonged to the passive participation group. The residents in this group were characterised as being marginally engaged, less aware of the importance of their participation and less willing to take part in the CBET development process. Although some sporadic participation was found, the passive participation group barely followed or implemented the tourism development plan that had been made on their behalf, and were not given equal opportunities to take part in the decision-making process. For some villagers categorised as being in the non-participation group, no actual participation and little awareness and willingness were discovered. It is not surprising that this non-participation group had no voice or ability to make decisions concerning any of the tourism development issues.

The above suggests that only a small number of local residents were satisfied with their participation and expressed a willingness to continue to participate in the process of CBET, whereas most residents were unwilling to participate at all. The main reasons why some residents were willing to continue participating are due to the financial benefits they see and their sense of community pride, which generate economic and psychological empowerment. The active participation group, in particular, claimed that, since becoming actively involved in the CBET, they had had more opportunities to share their views and to develop a stronger sense of ownership and autonomy in relation to their own futures and that of the CBET development. In addition, they had had the opportunity to work with their neighbours and the tourism development authorities to protect local resources and to create alternative forms of employment for other villagers in order to improve the overall well-being of the community. This resulted in increased self-esteem and allowed this group to feel that they were participating in the development of their community.

However, the vast majority of residents in Houay Kaeng Village belong to the passive- and non-participation groups, and were unaware of the significance of their potential participation. As noticed in previous studies (Marzuki *et al.* 2012; Scheyvens 2003; Tosun 2000), the major cause of this lack of engagement, particularly for ethnic minority groups, was inadequate information about the tourism development that was available to them and a more general lack of education. Indeed, lack of awareness of the significance of community participation appears to be most prevalent among poorly educated people, particularly those that had only received primary education. Some of the interviewees accepted that they had little idea of what 'community participation' meant, but that they took part in the CBET project as they had nothing else to do at the time and just wanted to follow the example of their neighbours. In addition, their limited literacy made it harder for them to properly understand the concept of community participation in the context of the CBET development programme.

As prior studies similarly confirmed (Hibbard and Lurie 2000; Marzuki *et al.* 2012), the local people in Houay Kaeng Village were hesitant to participate in the CBET project because of a lack of self-confidence; this could lead to undesirable consequences for the community. Consequently, the residents in these groups believed that the tourism development authorities were able to plan and develop the tourism industry without their support. They believed that these authorities had sufficient expertise and knowledge to formulate tourism development effectively. Although they had occasionally shared their ideas on a number of tourism issues, they did not expect their ideas to be considered or applied in future tourism development in the village. Hence, they maintained that it was unnecessary for them to participate in the process of development, particularly in the consultation activities as they believed they had nothing to contribute.

The second barrier lies in limited economic capital and spare time, due to poor living conditions. As most of the poor ethnic minority groups in this village had inadequate or underdeveloped facilities to offer tourists, they were reluctant to take part in tourism service activities. The majority of the respondents also commented that they did not have enough time to regularly participate in tourism-related activities, such as meetings or training sessions, as they had other essential work to do for their own survival, such as farming, fishing and finding bamboo shoots to sell. Indeed, those that had permanent jobs were reluctant to participate in the CBET project for the same reasons. The dominant attitude towards the CBET development among the passive and non-participation groups was, therefore, scepticism. For these members of the community, tourism was not the main economic activity, which conflicts with the aim of the CBET project.

The case of Houay Kaeng Village demonstrates a failure of the bottom-up approach of the CBET development by selecting community leaders and assigning responsibilities only to them. Although the community leaders were essential for facilitating communication between other community members and the tourism authorities, in this case the community leaders acted as local elites and thus genuine grassroots development using this bottom-up approach was not achieved. Inadequate understanding and awareness of tourism development among the vast majority of the community resulted in little community engagement. Despite the efforts made to counter this, the lack of engagement between local elites (i.e. community leaders) and residents hindered the building of community capacity and self-confidence, through which community empowerment could be achieved.

Conclusion

Community empowerment is essential, particularly in the context of remote ethnic minority communities, as community involvement not only provides a platform for long-term community capacity building, but also facilitates improved awareness and more positive perceptions of tourism among local residents. The CBET is meaningful when it assists the building of community capacity so that wider inclusion of local communities is possible through active participation and support or collaboration, thus establishing the essential components of community empowerment: community ownership and control over tourism development (Sofield 2003). In reality, particularly in the Lao context examined in this chapter, the actual practice of community participation in CBET development tends to be more complex than the theoretical concepts suggest. Although the above cases of

CBET development in Laos were initiated with a common goal – poverty alleviation and social and economic development through community building – the different approaches generated different outcomes.

The factors hindering CBET development, such as limited economic capacity, low educational levels and power inequality are also worth noting in order to understand the complexity of tourism development, community participation and empowerment, and community perceptions of the impacts of tourism. As noted in the second case, the matter of education and literacy is inevitably a significant challenge as literacy is related to the education and training needed as part of the first step in capacity building. This also becomes problematic when tourism development targets international markets rather than domestic markets; the latter raises fewer issues such as language barriers.

The first case, in Ban Na Village, demonstrates how the bottom-up approach was well balanced with a top-down approach. Before the transfer of decision-making powers, most of the villagers that were only engaged in agriculture were offered appropriate education and training to enable them to engage with tourism services and businesses. These training programmes not only boosted their self-confidence in participating in CBET development, but also increased their capacity to work more effectively and their awareness of the significance and purpose of their involvement (Alkan *et al.* 2009; Jim and Xu 2002). This was missed in the second case, in Houay Kaeng Village, in which the foundations were weak, which hindered the further engagement of more community members in the CBET project. The implementation process in the first case was also structured alongside local groups' operations and management, and continuing efforts were made, in consultation with other stakeholders (e.g. government authorities), by establishing local service groups that acted as bridges between the community and outsiders.

Although the evidence from the second case is limited, both cases demonstrate that a sense of community is a strong indicator of a community's active participation in tourism development; this can, in the first case, be explicitly explained with reference to psychological and social empowerment. The findings suggest the potential of CBET in terms of social capital building in the setting of rural ethnic minority communities, where a strong community network and sense of belonging can facilitate the sharing of knowledge and experiences and participation in CBET planning and development. A common perception of tourism, not as a secondary source of income but as a significant proportion of the economic activities engaged in by the rural ethnic minority community, would likely minimise the adverse effects of the identified barriers and thus establish high levels of community empowerment.

References

Alkan, H., Korkmaz, M. and Tolunay, A. (2009) Assessment of primary factors causing positive or negative local perceptions on protected areas. *Journal of Environmental Engineering and Landscape Management* 17(1), 20–7.

Asian Development Bank – Great Mekong Subregion (2011) *Houay Namsai Medicinal Plant Preserve and Service Centre Management and Development Plan 2012–2016.* Vientiane, Laos: Asian Development Bank.

Bramwell, B. (2010) Participative planning and governance for sustainable tourism. *Tourism Recreation Research* 35(3), 239–49.

Cohen, E. (2016) Ethnic tourism in mainland Southeast Asia: the state of the art. *Tourism Recreation Research* 41(3), 232–45.

Department of Information, Culture and Tourism (2012) *Sayabouly Tourism Development Strategy and Promotion 2012–2020.* Sayabouly Province, Laos: Department of Information, Culture and Tourism.

Dogra, R. and Gupta, A. (2012) Barriers to community participation in tourism development: empirical evidence from a rural destination. *South Asian Journal of Tourism and Heritage* 5(1), 129–42.

Ellis, S. and Sheridan, L. (2015) The role of resident perceptions in achieving effective community-based tourism for least developed countries. *Anatolia* 26(2), 244–57.

Harrison, D. and Schipani, S. (2009) Tourism in the Lao People's Democratic Republic. In M. Hitchcock, V. T. King and M. Parnwell (eds), *Tourism in Southeast Asia.* Copenhagen: NIAS, pp. 165–88.

Hibbard, M. and Lurie, S. (2000) Saving land but losing ground: challenges to community planning in the era of participation. *Journal of Planning Education and Research* 20(2), 187–95.

Jim, C. Y. and Xu, S. W. S. (2002) Stifled stakeholders and subdued participation: interpreting local responses toward Shimentai Nature Reserve in South China. *Environmental Management* 30(3), 327–41.

Lao National Tourism Administration (2009) *Protected Areas*. Available from: http://www.ecotourismlaos.com/protected_areas.htm (accessed 2 July 2016).

Lao National Tourism Administration (n.d.) *Lao PDR Tourism Strategy 2006–2020.* Available from: http://www.tourismlaos.org/files/files/Lao%20PDR%20Tourism%20Strategy%202006-2020%20in%20English.pdf (accessed 2 July 2016).

Lapeyre, R. (2010) Community-based tourism as a sustainable solution to maximise impacts locally? The Tsiseb Conservancy case, Namibia. *Development Southern Africa* 27(5), 757–72.

Marzuki, A., Hay, I. and James, J. (2012) Public participation shortcomings in tourism planning: the case of the Langkawi Island, Malaysia. *Journal of Sustainable Tourism* 20(4), 585–602.

Park, E. and Kim, S. (2016) The potential of Cittaslow for sustainable tourism development: enhancing local community's empowerment. *Tourism Planning and Development* 13(3), 351–69.

Project Coordination Unit (2011) *Annual Report of Implementation of Community-based Tourism for Sustainable Economic Development Programme in Lao PDR*, Report No. 1. Vientiane, Laos: Tourism Development Department, Ministry of Information, Culture and Tourism, p. 1–54.

Scheyvens, R. (2003) *Tourism for Development, Empowering Communities.* New Jersey: Prentice Hall.

Sofield, T. H. B. (2003) *Empowerment for Sustainable Tourism Development.* UK: Emerald Group.

Spenceley, A. and Meyer, D. (2012) Tourism and poverty reduction: theory and practice in less economically developed countries. *Journal of Sustainable Tourism* 20(3): 297–317.

Stone, L. S. and Stone, T. M. (2011) Community-based tourism enterprises: challenges and prospects for community participation: Khama Rhino Sanctuary Trust, Botswana. *Journal of Sustainable Tourism* 19(1), 97–114.

Timothy, D. J. (1999) Participation planning: a view of tourism in Indonesia. *Annals of Tourism Research* 26(2), 371–91.

Tosun, C. (2000) Limits to community participation in the tourism development process in developing countries. *Tourism Management* 21(6), 613–33.

Yuksel, F., Bramwell, B. and Yuksel, A. (2005) Centralized and decentralized tourism governance in Turkey. *Annals of Tourism Research* 32(4), 859–86.

Zeppel, H. (2006) *Indigenous Ecotourism: Sustainable Development and Management.* Wallingford: CAB International.

Part II

Ethnic Entrepreneurship, Tourism and Ethnodevelopment

8 Indigenous micro tourism businesses, ethnodevelopment and NGOs

Projectitis in Lago Budi in Chile

Ingeborg Nordbø

Introduction

Entrepreneurship and small business start-ups are, on a global scale, increasingly promoted as prime motors for economic development, not least in rural areas where the economic situation is often characterised by a dramatic decline in primary industries and where few other alternatives for economic development are seen as viable. Correspondingly, local citizens in both developed and developing countries are, through a number of policy instruments and support initiatives, stimulated to initiate entrepreneurial activities and to set up their own private businesses or projects. In the eyes of the author, entrepreneurship can be understood as a management trend in which the idea of entrepreneurship as a rural economic development strategy was developed in the West, and during the last few decades, has increasingly been diffused to other geographical areas and contexts by international organisations such as the World Bank, the EU, development consultants and NGOs. In this chapter, concepts and theories from institutional and social origins theory were combined in order to shed light on an NGO-initiated rural tourism entrepreneurship project in an indigenous development area in Lago Budi, in southern Chile. The fostering of ethnodevelopment and empowerment of the indigenous population through entrepreneurship and the establishing and running of a number of indigenous micro tourism businesses have been central elements of the project (Nordbø 2009). The focus of entrepreneurship as a development strategy springs out of economic theory where the unit of analysis usually is the individual and the firm, and not the collective or the group as traditionally has been found at the core among indigenous populations (Bonfil Batalla 2005). The central research question addressed in this chapter therefore centres around looking into what happens when entrepreneurship, as a management trend is diffused and implemented in an indigenous context, and furthermore by a third party (an NGO) which might not have a sufficient understanding of how the current forms of local organising are embedded into the broader historical, social and cultural context of the place and its people. In the context of other types of ideas that have been diffused and translated, such as sustainability and corporate social responsibility (CSR), studies have shown that such diffusions can also be problematic and result in unexpected consequences when actors from different contexts meet (Khan *et al.* 2007; Schwartz 2012; Berglund and Schwartz 2013). The empirical data referenced in the chapter are based on a qualitative longitudinal case study of the Lago Budi tourism project; more specifically, they are based on participant observations and 18 in-depth interviews with 12 indigenous tourism entrepreneurs, the local tourism organisation (run by the indigenous tourism entrepreneurs themselves), representatives from the NGOs involved in the tourism development in the area and the local and regional tourism authorities. The empirical findings, apart from looking into the consequences of the spreading of entrepreneurship as a management trend among indigenous populations, also allow the examination of the awkward role that such organisations might come to undertake in terms of ethnodevelopment.

Theoretical framework

Ethnodevelopment can in its most simple form be defined as the development of ethnic groups within the framework of the larger society (Stavenhagen 1986). More precisely it deals with allowing the extension and consideration of elements of the own culture, strengthening the ability to resist exploitation and oppression, and, especially, independent decision-making power through more effective control of the political, economic, social and cultural processes affecting their development (UNESCO 1981). Lacking most of the institutions usually connected with nation-states (Olsen 2003), ethnic groups often have to rely much more on external development agents such as NGOs. Within the field of NGO research there is in general a growing recognition of the role that NGOs play in economic, social and political life, as 'important agents of social and political coordination' and as 'knots' in social networks (Salamon and Anheier 1998: 46, 227). NGOs are also often important financial linkages between foreign donors and domestic groups (Jalali 2013: 56).

Since the 1980s, a great body of literature on organisations has been devoted to the study of the linkages between organisations (e.g. NGOs) and their environment. Within the 'new institutional organisational analysis', the concept of institutional environment is one of the most central concepts. The research and theories of institutional environment deal with how organisations are influenced by 'societal factors such as ideas, rules, fashions, knowledge, ideologies, norms, etc., as well as how these are created and disseminated between organisations and cultures' (Furusten 2013: 12). For instance, DiMaggio and Powell (1983) discussed the diffusion and imitation of ideas using the concept of isomorphism. Coercive isomorphism relates to formal and informal pressure, pursuant to which organisations are forced by the actions of governments or competitors to adapt to a regulatory framework. Mimetic isomorphism occurs when organisations imitate other organisations as a response to uncertainty. Normative isomorphism relates to professionalisation, as managers in the same profession tend to use the same models and methods. In the diffusion process, ideas are also translated into new contexts and organisations by a transformation of the original idea (Sevón 1996;

Czarniawska and Joerges 1996). NGOs are connected to a number of stakeholders, including financiers, suppliers, buyers, national and international authorities, etc., which, to a greater or smaller degree, place a number of demands on them. This implies, in the opinion of the author, that NGOs often are crucial disseminators of Western management trends, bonded as they are by, for example, donors' guidelines and politics. NGOs often work and depend on projects and project financing for their survival, and thus we can assume that in particular, a great deal of coercive isomorphism will take place.

Within the institutional environment field, the study of organisations and their networks, so-called network theory, has received the most attention, focusing on the interplay between organisations and their stakeholders, that is other actors with which they are connected. Furusten (2013) argued that such theories have their limitations in the sense that they are based primarily on an 'observable' dimension (p. 11) or what could also be labelled a 'present time' dimension, in which it is possible to observe, investigate and have dialogue with the actors with which an organisation is connected. He argued that these elements are important, but that it is not the least important to understand the more implicit elements of an organisation's environment, because, as he put it, 'organizations are not only governed by the observable' (p. 12). Furusten (2013) thus argued in favour of the usefulness of also studying the more implicit elements of the institutional environment, which he, in a pragmatic manner, defined as 'the legal, social and mental structures that individual organizations are embedded in' (p. 12).

Within the NGO literature, the institutional environment of NGOs has been a field that has attracted the attention of researchers in recent decades. Investigations of the social origins, as well as the institutional analysis of NGOs by researchers such as Salamon and Anheier (1998), Salamon *et al.* 1999), Kabalo (2009), Moore (2001), Wagner (2000), Suda (2006), and Ju and Tang (2010) thus represented a shift in the research on NGOs away from single unit theories toward an examination of the non-governmental sector's embeddedness in broader social, political and economic realities. The argument is that the non-profit sector cannot be properly understood or seen in isolation from its broader context. Salamon and Anheier (1998) have been accredited as the founders of the social origin approach within third-sector studies. Their main argument in their study of the origins of civil society was that the traditional and mostly single-factor approaches that have historically been applied to the study of the sector do not properly contemplate the historical past of societies, taking into account the impact of factors such as cultural traditions and historical trajectories.

Social origins theory argues that historical-contextual factors in general and power relations among social classes in particular influence the character and size of the NGO sector in each country. In his critique of the social origin approach, Wagner (2000) thus argued for the usefulness of institutional analysis, suggesting that non-profit organisations should be viewed 'not so much as forming a specific institutional sector but as part of a complex network of organisations that are linked together in what will be called *the public sphere*' (p. 542). The social origin approach is thus normally not thought of as belonging to the field of institutional analysis, although they share the central understanding of the embeddedness of organisations in a wider environmental context. The next section presents some of the key characteristics of Lago Budi and of the Mapuch-Lafkenche people, and it also seeks to examine critically the role of development-oriented NGOs for supporting and promoting the Indigenous entrepreneurship in Chile, and how effective ethnodevelopment has been within this context.

Lago Budi and the Mapuche-Lafkenche people

Lago Budi lies in the IX region in Chile, the Araucania Region, and borders the Pacific coast, approximately an hour's drive from the regional capital, Temuco. Lago Budi is the southernmost inland salt-water lake in the world; it is known for its rich fauna and is today a protected natural area (Nordbø 2009).

In 1993, the area surrounding Lago Budi was turned into one of two development areas for Indigenous people in Chile according to the Indigenous People's Act of 1993 (Aylwin 1997: 5). Lago Budi is populated by a branch of the Mapuche, Chile's largest group of indigenous people,[1] who are known as the Mapuche-Lafkenche ('the people by the lake'). Lago Budi borders on the municipalities of Puerto Saavedra and Teodoro Schmidt. The population in ADI Budi numbers some 13,000 (Impulsa 2002: 2).

Some of the existing descriptions from the colonial period about the area around Lago Budi tell of a numerous people who resided between the Imperial River and the Toltén River. Stories are told of *Cacikes* (traditional Mapuche chiefs) who kept up to 18 wives and of the 27 Spanish colonialists who settled around the Imperial River and were 'allotted' 8,000, 10,000 or 12,000 Indians during the introduction of the *encomienda* system.[2]

The earth was very fertile; people lived well and had a comprehensive source of food, including agriculture, fishing and animal husbandry.

Toltén was one of the most important areas in the Mapuche territory, and one of the bloodiest battles in the history of the colonial period was fought by the people surrounding Lago Budi. The killing of Pedro Valdivia[3] led the colonists to flee the area, and as with the rest of the area south of Bío-Bío, the area was self-governing for the rest of the colonial period (Flores Ch. 1997). However, after the formation of the Chilean republic, state land granted by the state to the Mapuche comprised only 500,000 hectares, slightly more than 5 per cent of their ancestral territory south of the Bío-Bío River (Bravo 1999). Furthermore, estimates indicate that during the first half of the twentieth century, approximately one third of this granted land had been further usurped by private individuals (Bengoa 1985), many of whom were European settlers who, after the formation of the Chilean nation-state, were given free land by the government.

In the 1980s, after the military dictatorship decreed that collective property must be divided, and titles of ownership were issued to individual Mapuche families as a result of the Indigenous Law of Pinochet (No. 2,568 of 22 March 1979), the number of Mapuche reservations decreased to 665 and the average size of the Mapuche peasant's land was 5.5 hectares (Calbucura 1994: 1). The reduction in

Figure 8.1 One of the Mapuche-Lafkenche families hoping to be part of the Nature and Ancestral Culture Project.
Photo: Ingeborg Nordbø.

their ancestral territory also implied much more intensive land use and a brutal rupture in the communities. The land deeds (*mercedes de tierra*) were also, in most cases, granted for the poorest soil, and in practical terms, the Mapuche were not prepared, either technologically or agriculturally, to take advantage of their small properties.

Saavedra municipality in ADI Budi, the municipality in Chile with the highest proportion (83 per cent) of Mapuche, was, at the beginning of the millennium, also Chile's poorest, with 59.9 per cent of the population living below the poverty line compared to a national average of under 20 per cent (Mideplan 2000). Ever since Pinochet's regime, the people of Lago Budi have, due to the high level of poverty, been a favoured target of a number of development-oriented NGOs. Even since the re-introduction of democracy in 1990 and the declaration that the area was an Indigenous people's development area in 1993, the presence of a number of national and international organisations (NGOs) and institutions with diverging goals has characterised the area (Nordbø, 2009).

At the beginning of the 1990s, public politics concerning small, rural agricultural producers in Chile started to focus on finding new and alternative sources of income for small producers such as those in ADI Budi through greater diversification, efficiency and access to 'non-traditional' markets. Rural and ethnic tourism have thus been regarded as plausible alternatives. The first initiatives, in part stimulated by foreign NGOs, arose from the grassroots and were later taken up by the state, which regarded rural tourism entrepreneurship as a strategic solution to the problem of poverty in rural areas in Chile. A number of programmes focused on developing entrepreneurial and tourism skills thus emerged. More systematic development of tourism in Lago Budi resulted in the project called Nature and Ancestral Culture, of which one of the main outcomes was the development of 15 tourism entrepreneurship initiatives in rural areas that surround the lake.

The project emerged in the wake of the Impulsa programme financed by the Social and Solidarity Investment Fund (FOSIS), a decentralised public agency of the Chilean government. The programme came to Puerto Saavedra in 1996 as a result of the national Plan to Combat Poverty, which was implemented by the government in 1995. From the local NGO Impulsa's side, the entrepreneurial empowerment involved in the Nature and Ancestral Culture project has focused on training and the development of skills related to self-governance, business start-up and administration, independence in terms of decision-taking and an understanding of the necessity for long-term thinking and development. However, some years into the project, the local NGO is struggling to implement the logic of entrepreneurship among the majority of the indigenous entrepreneurs. In the following, some of the 'present time' challenges related to implementing the logic of entrepreneurship will be presented. With the exception of the interview with the local coordinator of Impulsa all the participant observations and the voices presented below are of and with the indigenous Mapuche-Lafkenche tourism entrepreneurs themselves.

Present time situation

First money, then work

For entrepreneurship to flower, one of the main elements of empowerment is to stimulate a proactive attitude or personality (Crant 1996), and for Impulsa, the development of skills related to self-governance, decision-taking and independence was an explicit aim. However, a number of the reported challenges related to the tourism entrepreneurship project (Nordbø 2009) dealt with a shortage of just that. The leader of the local tourism organisation (established as part of the project), herself one of the indigenous tourism entrepreneurs, reported on the majority of members' passivity and lack of interest in and devotion to their work, as expressed in the following phrases referring to one of the other entrepreneurs: 'The only thing he's waiting for is for them to give him money, but he doesn't contribute anything himself.' In addition, the vice-leader of the organisation, herself also one of the Mapuche-Lafkenche entrepreneurs, expressed the same frustration with the other indigenous members of the organisation: 'When will they better themselves/make progress, these people? Do they expect just to get everything, for it to fall from the sky? If they don't make an effort themselves, what more can you do for them?' Both leaders have argued, however, that when it comes to obtaining some sort of financial gain, the members demonstrate a rather different attitude: 'But when a project or other benefits turn up, then the people who have almost never struggled, but who are members of the local tourist organisation, are first in line.'

The findings from the research undertaken showed that, among the indigenous tourism entrepreneurs, there seemed to be an attitude of 'first money, then work, rather than the other way around, which is visible in the following argumentation from two of the Mapuche-Lafkenche business owners: 'An incentive so that we can work really well … Impulsa still has not given us … for example they say to me, your project is ready, so now you can carry on working in peace … here a lot of things are still lacking', or 'but to start a project you need money … I still don't have a lot of things, a laundry which I have to make the foundations for and a rubbish dump/room. We also need to make some guestrooms and a bathroom in the house. We need support for this.' The local advisor for Impulsa, when confronted with these attitudes, argued that 'some people take their starting point from what they have and ask can I do this and this? But other people want to be given everything, whether the project can give them this and this, and that's not OK.' Thus Impulsa, in its report (2002), describing the indigenous tourism entrepreneurs involved in the project, stated that 'only some of the members are more independent, the majority are at a stage where they are awaiting what the program, other members of the community or the organisation suggest' (p. 14, author's own translation).

My little project

For Impulsa, in terms of fostering local development through entrepreneurship, it has been important to work both with self-determination and independent decision-making power, together with an understanding of the importance of cooperation. The first two are central elements of ethnodevelopment as already argued. The local leader of Impulsa thus explained:

> It is important for the families to be independent, but at the same time dependent on each other. That means that they think about their projects and their development, and that they are not dependent on others to develop, but also that they have contact between themselves, that they work in a more organised and efficient manner.

Another of the findings from the empirical material is the constant mention of a 'project': 'my project', 'their project', 'his project', etc. As one of the Mapuche-Lafkenche tourism entrepreneurs argued when speaking of one of the other entrepreneurs and a member of the local handicraft centre: 'She's just a member, she doesn't come to work now that she's got her own project.' Similarly, one of the other indigenous tourism entrepreneurs talked about obtaining a project as if it were to win the lottery: '[B]ecause of our culture we were favoured … and the projects *were won* due to this.' By virtue of the same investigation, it also became obvious that the leaders of the local tourism organisation, themselves indigenous entrepreneurs as already argued, to some extent, displayed elements of the same passive attitude as described in the previous section: 'Further on, there's … a new member, the idea is ready but there's still nothing there. They *lack the winning ticket*, as we put it, the money.' For several of the Indigenous entrepreneurs, the tourism project is thus just one of a variety of projects in which they are involved as a means of making a living: one of the entrepreneurs stated that she is involved in a number of projects financed by other institutions or NGOs.

Top-down decisions

For Impulsa, a central element of entrepreneurship as an ethnodevelopment strategy is to strengthen a bottom-up approach and to facilitate involvement from the indigenous entrepreneurs at all stages of the project or tourism business development: '[G]iving confidence and training is important, so they can be involved in the planning, developing and evaluating.' However, despite this goal, many important subjects related to the decision-making processes of the tourism entrepreneurship project have been rather top-down, which has resulted in a number of conflicts, as was seen in the development of some of the marketing material related to the tourism entrepreneurship project. The local coordinator of Impulsa explained how the conflict evolved among the indigenous entrepreneurs:

> Later, we were going to take more pictures, and I entrusted three people with the task of carrying on with this work. These people took photos of some of the projects, but people in the projects who hadn't been photographed felt very insulted and displeased … It wasn't important who was in the pictures, but the impression they gave. But they just didn't get it. Maybe because they had low self-esteem. Pictures are expensive, and you can't develop all those you take. I gave the group of three the task of picking out pictures with the photographer.

We can observe that instead of letting the local tourism organisation set up a committee that could work on the subject, and then, for example, have a meeting later at which the organisation as a whole decided which pictures to use, the local coordinator of Impulsa probably took a 'shortcut' which eventually provoked a rather extensive conflict. The leader of the local tourism organisation also brought up the conflict and argued: '[T]hey should still have asked us: How should we do this?' Clearly, the local coordinator of Impulsa did not really understand why the indigenous entrepreneurs were so disturbed, seemingly about nothing.

Patron/client relationships

For Impulsa, to implement entrepreneurship as an ethnodevelopment strategy has also been an explicit goal to strengthen the understanding of the relationship between private initiative and independent decision-making alongside the necessity for cooperation.

Another of the main internal conflicts between the indigenous entrepreneurs in the local tourism organisation is thus that the entrepreneurs from the municipality of Puerto Saavedra have, thanks to negotiations with the local mayor, managed to obtain a car and a driver to transport them to and from their monthly meetings, while the entrepreneurs from Pto. Dominguez municipality have not managed to obtain such a favour.

In the empirical data, there are several other traces of such patron/client relationships. It was observed, for instance, that the leader of the local tourism organisation, herself one of the indigenous tourism entrepreneurs as already mentioned, considered that her most important task as the leader was to 'knock on doors' on behalf of the other members to obtain support for their projects. We also observed that when referring to the regional or local government, they tended to refer to *el alcalde* or *el intendente*, rather than the names of the corresponding administrative bodies. The empirical material also showed that the relationship with the local advisor at Impulsa was rather patron/client in its nature, and that he acted as a sort of *father patria* who guided and advised the indigenous tourism entrepreneurs, even at the tiniest micro level. Such relationships clearly do not really foster self-determination and reveal the unequal power relations involved in such a clientelistic relationship, clearly not in best interest of real ethnodevelopment. This was visible, for instance, in the following comment made by the leader of the local tourism organisation in relation to the local advisor of Impulsa: 'I always say to him: "You are the advisor and we must obey."'

Discussion

What became increasingly clear from the research and follow-up was that the 'passive attitude', project-focus, top-down decision processes and patron/client relationships seemed to be of such a general character among the indigenous entrepreneurs in the Lago Budi area that it was legitimate to speak of it as a local cultural characteristic. Further, the research showed that this characteristic was hampering the implementation of entrepreneurship and thus the ethnodevelopment efforts by Impulsa.[4] Similar findings from the same area have also been reported by other researchers (e.g. Lambrou 1997; Barría 2001). In the following, we will discuss how the challenges can only be understood through an analysis of the more implicit elements of the external environment, as argued by institutional theory, and by including the NGO's embeddedness in a broader context including factors such as cultural traditions and historical trajectories, as argued by social origin theory.

The origin of paternalism and patron/client relationships

The land-granting that followed the colonisation of Chile was the inception of a system of large estates (*haciendas* or *latifundos*), which have been a characteristic feature of Chilean rural society ever since (see e.g. Hudson 1994 or Bauer 1975). The large Chilean landholders, the *latifundistas*, who had direct contact with the Spanish monarchy through the Viceroyal of Lima, the capital of Peru, soon became the Chilean local elite and have remained so until the present day. Pedro de Valdivia did not envisage, as did the Crown, a pattern of rural settlement where European-style farms would exist alongside villages of free-holding indigenous people. Rather, he imposed a feudal system in which the native workers would be subordinated to the eminent domain of a powerful lord and reside inside the legal boundaries of a great estate (Nordbø 2009). Bauer (1975), referring to Mario Góngora (1970), argued that this rather seigneurial aim among most of the conquerors was only achieved in Chile, which was related to the fact that Chile was considerably removed from the centres of imperial power. The system of Valdivia involved the subordination of the Indians to their patron (landlord), the 1608 Royal Decree making Indian slavery legal and giving minimal rights to the 'free' Indian in the seventeenth century, which blurred the distinction between them and those who were legally enslaved, exacerbating the already low social status of the indigenous population in Chile and strongly reinforcing the original bonds of a seigneurial society (Bauer 1975: 7–8).

This Chilean *hacienda* system developed a special character in many ways, and each *hacienda* functioned as a miniature version of a complex society. The large rural estates even had stores where people could buy a variety of goods, as well as chapels and dispensaries for primary medical attention. There were houses for the estate's administrators, mechanics, accountants, oenologists (if wine was produced), blacksmiths and others who constituted the professional and skilled labour force of the enterprise. Some of the labourers lived on the estate year round, and they or their family members worked when needed in exchange for the right to cultivate a portion of the land for themselves and to graze their animals on specified fields. These labourers' families, in general, enjoyed better living standards than the rest of the rural poor (Bauer 1975). This system laid the foundations for a hierarchical and classist society where the indigenous population was at the bottom. The hacienda system and the Portalian state, by virtue of their paternalistic character, also laid the foundations for a culture of 'giving' and 'awaiting' benefits, rather than one characterised by the acquisition of such benefits due to one's own efforts (Mosovich Pont-Leizica 1997).

Stavenhagen (2002) argues that 'when the Spanish-American republics achieved their political independence in the early nineteenth century most of them were populated by a majority of Indians, but the power holders, as is well known, were the *criollo* elite, the direct descendants of the Spanish colonial ruling class. Indians remained, as it were, at the bottom of the heap, as they had been since the European conquest' (p. 24). When Chile became an autonomous republic in 1818, the central part of the country, the metropolitan area, developed social, cultural and political institutions and practices similar to those of its European and North American counterparts, while at the regional and local level, the paternalism, under-representation and patron/client relationships inherited from colonial times continued to dominate. According to Mosovich Pont-Leizica (1997), the national arena was dominated by representative political systems and by political transactions involving the interaction of interest groups, while at the local level 'the goals of political transactions were, as occurs with clientelist relations, the obtaining of goods or personal favours in exchange for political support' (p. 199; see also Rehren 1991).

The NGOs and the culture of projectitis

In the southern part of Chile, the clientelistic model assumed a new and rather peculiar form under the dictatorship of Augusto Pinochet (1973–89). Lambrou (1997) argued that left-wing professionals who had held central positions under the socialist Salvador Allende government were 'kicked out of office' after 1973 and transferred to the South. She asserted that, due to the formation of a number of local NGOs which provided economic survival opportunities, they soon became a 'nucleus for resistance and expertise on solutions to local development problems' (p. 107). Due to the existence of a military government which was considered internationally to be both brutal and despotic, 'donor agencies were falling over each other to find alternative channels for their development assistance' (p. 109). A vast quantity of funds was channelled to peasant organisations, and the NGOs helped the local communities to set up development projects and to seek external funds and technical assistance. Lambrou (1997) thus argued that the external funding provided much needed resources, while creating 'a culture of reliance and a clientelistic middle class of professionals' (p. 107). She further highlighted that within the local communities, a culture of 'projectitis'[5] emerged which involved the local indigenous poor seeing 'their survival and salvation linked to having a project funded by an external foreign agency' (p. 110).

With the return of democracy to Chile, many things changed, but others did not; among the factors which did not change was the highly neo-liberal and profit-oriented local development model of Pinochet, where public services continued to be economic goods under the notion of 'what you pay for is what you get'. Lambrou (1997) concluded that one of the lessons learned from the Pinochet regime was that the state was not necessarily 'the only possible promoter of development' (p. 110), and that the democratic government was well aware of the role that the NGOs could play in the future as a means through which to channel international funds and to implement government policy. As a consequence, the NGOs, which had been wholly independent of the government under the military regime, suddenly became one of its closest allies. Thus, in the poor rural communities of southern Chile such as Lago Budi, a culture of 'giving' and 'awaiting' benefits still rules, but now the NGOs and their local advisors have become the new 'political brokers'. As argued by the local coordinator of Impulsa, 'The Mapuche are awful beggars.'

Conclusion

The findings from the case study confirm the claim that (tourism) entrepreneurship can be seen as a Western management trend, and the idea of entrepreneurship as a rural development strategy has been spread (diffused) to Lago Budi by the numerous NGOs presented in the area. It was later taken up (imitated) by the state as a solution to the poverty problem among Chile's indigenous population and funds were provided for NGOs to initiate ethnodevelopment projects such as the 'Nature and Ancestral Culture in Lago Budi' project presented and studied in this chapter. Looking at the diffusion of entrepreneurship in the Lago Budi area from a historical perspective, we can observe traces of coercive, normative and mimetic isomorphism. The case study also shows how entrepreneurship, in the diffusion process, has been adopted and translated into a new context by a transformation of the original idea. The fact that there is no universally accepted definition or theory of entrepreneurship, despite the extensive amount of published research and literature, is also likely to have had an impact on the speed and scope of the transformation.

However, perhaps the most important lesson from the research undertaken is that the implementation of any given management trend without the necessary understanding of the local historical context might be fatal and can, in the worst case, as shown in this study, prevent ethnodevelopment and instead foster the reinforcement of unfavourable cultural patterns. In terms of entrepreneurship as a rural development strategy, there are a couple of lessons from the study undertaken that are of special importance. First, where NGOs are involved in local development, it is fundamental to understand and avoid the development of a clientelistic relationship between the NGOs and the local people. As argued in the introduction, this is especially important for ethnic groups that have often relied heavily on external development agents and NGOs due to a lack of infrastructure often associated with the nation-state. Furthermore, another important lesson from the case study is the fact that NGOs are often dependent on project financing, and that this might hamper long-term sustainable development in local destinations. In the first place, this means that normally, no project is fully financed by one agency, and thus it might be difficult to have a long-term planning span. In the second place, NGOs always chase project money and must adapt to the strategies of the donors, meaning that a given project may be forced to change its focus during execution or, even worse, may never be finalised. In the third place, the project focus may imply that the local population will eventually compete against each other in terms of having their projects financed (and thus having money for survival), which clearly hampers cooperation and a collective spirit as traditional elements of indigenous culture. Finally, the case study shows that more research should be dedicated to the study of the diffusion of Western management trends, such as entrepreneurship, as well as the roles that NGOs, cultural patterns and historical trajectories play in this respect.

Notes

1. Numbering some 1.4 million people, they constitute one of the largest groups in Latin America, along with the Aymará, Quechua, Mayas, Cackchiquele, Mixteca, Nahuatle, Otomie, Pile, Quiché, Yacateco and Zapateco. About a million are located in Chile and the rest are in Argentina (Calbucura 1997).
2. Precious metals were scarce in Chile compared to most other Latin American countries, and the early Spanish settlers thus turned their focus basically on agriculture and ranching. During the process of colonisation, land grants (*merced*) were allocated to the conquerors as a way of rewarding their loyalty to the Crown through the *encomienda* system, through which a group of native Americans would also be consigned to their care (see, for example, Bauer, 1975).
3. Pedro Gutiérrez de Valdivia (*c.*1500–53) was a Spanish conquistador and also the first royal governor of Chile.
4. It should be noted, however, that although we can mention a local cultural characteristic, there were also clear exemptions. There seemed to be a generational difference whereby the younger indigenous entrepreneurs were more proactive and less clientelistic than the older ones.
5. Projectitis means 'small project' and refers to the Chilean habit of making everything 'smaller' by adding the diminutive suffixes *-ito* or *-ita* to words. According to Nordbø (2009), this habit is also traceable back to the patron/client relationship that developed with the hacienda system and beyond. The relationship of giving and receiving favours created a hierarchical power imbalance, where small favours were more easily fulfilled than bigger ones. Thus it is not a question of doing me 'a small favour' (*un favor pequeño*), but a question of 'a very small favour' (*un favor puequeñito*).

References

Aylwin, J. (1997) *Area de desarrollo indígena Lago Budi*. Temuco, Chile: Instituto de Estudios Indígenas, Universidad de La Frontera.

Bauer, A. J. (1975) *Rural Chilean Society: From the Spanish Conquest to 1930*. Cambridge: Cambridge University Press.

Bengoa, J. (1985) *Historia del Pueblo Mapuche Siglo XIX y XX*. Santiago: Ediciones Sur, Colección de Estudios Históricos.

Berglund, K. and Schwartz, B. (2013) Holding on to the anomaly of social entrepreneurship dilemmas in starting up and running a fair-trade enterprise, *Journal of Social Entrepreneurship*, online (accessed 9 April 2013).

Bonfil Batalla, G. (2005) *Mexico profundo: una civilización negada*. Mexico City: Random House Mondadori.

Brandt, B. and Haugen, M. S. (2005) *Farmers as Tourist Hosts: Consequences for Work and Identity*, Paper No. 2/05. Available online at: http://bf.publishpack.no/dynamisk/Publikasjoner_PDF/PAPER%2002.05.pdf.

Bravo, G. E. (1999) Areas de desarrollo indígena. Draft copy. Temuco, Chile: CONADI, Unidad de estudio y planificación.

Calbucura, J. (1994) *Legal Process of Abolition of Collective Property: The Mapuche Case*. Mapuche Documentation Center. Available at: http://www.soc.uu.se/mapuche/.

Calbucura, J. (1997) *Krönika om en förebådad etnisk utplåning*. Mapuche Documentation Center. Available at: http://www.soc.uu.se/mapuche/ (accessed 22 February 2006).

Crant, M. J. (1996) The proactive personality scale as a predictor of entrepreneurial intentions. *Journal of Small Business Management* 34(3), 42–50.

Czarniawska, B. and Joerges, B. (1996) Travels of ideas. In B. Czarniawska and G. Sevón (eds), *Translating Organizational Change*. Berlin: Walter de Gruyter.

DiMaggio, P. J. and Powell, W. W. (1983) The iron cage revisited: institutional isomorphism and collective rationality in organizational fields. *American Sociological Review* 48(2), 147–60.

Dogan, H. Z. (1989) Forms of adjustment: sociocultural impacts of tourism. *Annals of Tourism Research* 16, 216–35.

Faiguenbaum Ch., S. (2001) *El programa de turismo rural de INDAP. Un caso de empleo e ingresos rurales no agrícolas inducidos por políticas públicas*. Santiago: INDAP.

Fermandois, J. (2004) Catolicismo y liberalismo en el Chile del siglo XX. *Estudios Publicos* 93.

Flores Ch., J. (1997) Antecedentes históricos del territorio Lafkenche del Budi. In J. Aylwin (ed.), *Area de desarrollo indígena Lago Budi*. Temuco, Chile: Instituto de Estudios Indígenas, Universidad de La Frontera.

Furusten, S. (2013) *Institutional Theory and Organizational Change*. Cheltenham: Edward Elgar.

Hudson, R. A. (ed.) (1994) *Chile. A Country Study*. Washington, DC: Federal Research Division, Library of Congress. Available online at: http://www.country-data.com/cgi-bin/query/r-2383.html.

Impulsa (2002) *Informe de sistematización proyecto: Naturaleza y cultura ancestral en el Lago Budi*. Santiago: Fundación de desarrollo local Impulsa.

Jalali, R. (2013) Financing empowerment? How foreign aid to southern NGOs and social movements undermines grass-roots mobilization. *Sociology Compass* 7(1), 55–73.

Ju, C. B. and Tang, C. Y. (2011) Path dependence, critical junctures, and political contestation. The developmental trajectories of environmental NGOs in South Korea. *Nonprofit and Voluntary Sector Quarterly* 40(69), 1048–72.

Kabalo, P. (2009) A fifth nonprofit regime? Revisiting social origins theory using Jewish associational life as a new state model. *Nonprofit and Voluntary Sector Quarterly* 38(49), 627–42.

Khan, F. R., Munir, K. A. and Willmott, H. (2007) A dark side of institutional entrepreneurship: soccer balls, child labour and postcolonial impoverishment. *Organization Studies* 28: 1055–77.

Lambrou, Y. (1997) The changing role of NGOs in Rural Chile after democracy. *Bulletin of Latin American Research* 16(1), 107–16.

Lerner, M. and Haber, S. (2000) Performance factors of small tourism ventures: the interface of tourism, entrepreneurship and the environment. *Journal of Business Venturing* 16, 77–100.

Mideplan (2000) *Etnias y pobreza en Chile (2000) Análisis de la VIII Encuesta de Caracterización Socioeconómica Nacional*. Available online at: http://www.mideplan.cl/final/ficha_tecnica.php?cenid=30 (accessed 10 June 2016).

Moore, L. (2001) Legitimation issues in the state-nonprofit relationship, *Nonprofit and Voluntary Sector Quarterly* 30(4), 707–19.

Mosovich Pont-Leizica, D. (1997) Local politics and depolitisation in Chile. *Bulletin of Latin American Research* 16(2), 197–217.

Nordbø, I. (2009) *Living with Tourism: The Challenges and Constraints of Small Scale Rural Tourism Businesses in Norway and Chile*. PhD Dissertation, Aalborg Universitet, Aalborg.

Olsen, K. (2003) The touristic construction of the 'emblematic' Sami. *Acta Borealia* 1, 3–20.

Rehren, A. J. (1991) El impacto de las políticas autoritarias a nivel local. Implicancias para la consolidación democrática en Chile. *Estudios Públicos* 44, 207–46.

Salamon, L. and Anheier, H. K. (1998) Social origin of civil society. Explaining the Nonprofit Sector Cross-Nationally. *Voluntas: International Journal of Voluntary and Nonprofit Organizations* 9, 213–48.

Salamon, L. M., Anheier, H. K., List, R., Toepler, S., Sokolowski, S. W. and Associates (1999) *Global Civil Society: Dimensions of the Nonprofit Sector.* Baltimore, MD: Johns Hopkins Center for Civil Society Studies.

Schwartz, B. (2012) Societal entrepreneurship contextualized: dark and bright sides of fair trade. In K. Berglund, B. Johannisson and B. Schwartz (eds), *Societal Entrepreneurship: Positioning, Penetrating, Promoting.* Cheltenham: Edward Elgar.

Sevón, G. (1996) Organizational imitation in identity transformation. In B. Czarniawska and G. Sevón (eds), *Translating Organizational Change.* Berlin: Walter de Gruyter, pp. 49–67.

Stavenhagen, R. (1986) Ethnodevelopment: a neglected dimension in development thinking. In R. Stavenhagen (ed.), *Pioneer on Indigenous Rights.* Berlin and Heidelberg: Springer, pp. 65–86.

Stavenhagen, R. (2002) Indigenous people and the state in Latin-America: an ongoing debate. In R. Sieder (ed.) *Multiculturalism in Latin America. Indigenous Rights, Diversity and Democracy.* Basingstoke: Palgrave Macmillan, pp. 24–44.

Suda, Y. (2006) Devolution and privatization proceed and centralized system maintained: a twisted reality faced by Japanese nonprofit organizations. *Nonprofit and Voluntary Sector Quarterly* 35(3), 430–52.

UNESCO (1981) *UNESCO and the Struggle Against Ethnocide: Declaration of San José.* SS.82/WS/32.

Barría, R. V. (2001) Desarrollo local de las comunidades Mapuche-Lafkenche del lago Budi. Fundación de desarrollo local Impulsa. Comuna de Saavedra. IX Región de la Araucanía. In Javier Salina Garcia and Julia Cubillos Romo (eds), *Espacios locales y desarrollo de la ciudadania. 30 Innovaciones para construir democracia.* Santiago, Chile: Fundación Nacional para la Superación de la Pobreza y Centro de Análisis de Políticas Públicas, Universidad de Chile, pp. 443–66.

Wagner, A. (2000) Reframing 'social origins' theory: the structural transformation of the public sphere. *Nonprofit and Voluntary Sector Quarterly* 29(4), 541–53.

9 Understanding the host community's experiences of creating small autochthonous tourism enterprises in Lombok, Indonesia

Akhmad Saufi, Sacha Reid and Anoop Patiar

Introduction

Tourism is seen as a panacea for many developing destinations. However, development within these destinations is fraught with challenges and external influence that may impede host communities' support for tourism. Scheyvens (2002a) argues that in developing countries host communities need to be encouraged to actively engage in tourism development. 'Ethnodevelopment builds on the positive qualities of Indigenous culture and societies to promote local employment and growth' (Van Nieuwkoop and Uquillas 2000: 1). One way to directly involve host communities in ethnodevelopment is through tourism entrepreneurship (Kamsma and Bras 2000; Timothy 1999), for example by providing opportunities for the host communities to start their own small tourist enterprises (Hampton 2005; Scheyvens 2002b). However, the emergence of local small tourism enterprises is reliant on the willingness of the host communities to proceed and transform the local resources into products and services to meet the tourist's needs.

This book chapter explores the issues of ethnodevelopment in Indigenous tourism entrepreneurship on Lombok, Indonesia. The aim of this chapter is twofold. First, to highlight the opportunities and barriers to ethnodevelopment of small-scale tourism entrepreneurship within five local communities of Lombok. And second, it seeks to understand the factors influencing entrepreneurial culture for small-scale Indigenous tourism entrepreneurs. These findings, while unique to the research setting, have broader lessons for ethnodevelopment in tourism entrepreneurship in other developing countries.

Entrepreneurship, ethnodevelopment and tourism

To date, there is no single definition for entrepreneurship. The lack of consensus on defining entrepreneurship relates to the disparate discipline features and focus (Simpeh 2011). However, key definitions of entrepreneurship are centred on creating or developing a business activity that aims to fulfil the needs of an evolving market and is adaptive to future opportunities for advancement (Sharma *et al.* 1996). Regardless of the diverse definitions of entrepreneurship, Shane and Venkataraman (2000) assert that entrepreneurship requires the presence of two essential elements: entrepreneurial opportunity and a prospective entrepreneur whereas Koh argues that tourism entrepreneurship is different from general entrepreneurship. Specifically, Koh (2002) notes that tourism entrepreneurship differs in terms of product characteristic, the expertise needed and the market system.

Within the ethnodevelopment literature, entrepreneurship is 'thought to lead ethnically structured enterprises and production into 'steady income sources' and 'long-lasting financial autonomy', so those pertinent groups are financially enabled to govern their business initiatives' (de Lima *et al.* 2016: 17). The empowerment of Indigenous peoples for long-term community development and income generation is seen as central to ethnodevelopment.

Engaging Indigenous people in the identification of entrepreneurial opportunities to generate income is one way that fulfils ethnodevelopment objectives. Indigenous tourism entrepreneurs play important roles in the allocation of innate resources, the integration and transformation of those resources into the creation of a tourist attraction, and tourism promotion. In other words, entrepreneurs can establish a thriving local tourism destination that will contribute socio-economic benefit to the community (Koh 2002). At the same time, the tourism business can become an important ingredient in the tourism pull factor that is one of the factors attracting tourists to visit a tourist destination.

Locally established tourism enterprises also play a critical role in the distribution of the economic benefits to other local people (Kokkranikal and Morrison 2011; Page *et al.* 1999; Ryan *et al.* 2012; Thompson 2004). These local enterprises also limit the potential economic leakage from tourism activities (Kokkranikal and Morrison 2011; Scheyvens 2002b), as the money is redistributed within the local economy. Harrison and Schipani (2007) point out that most locally owned tourism enterprises, such as hotels and restaurants, meet their customers' needs with products (e.g. fruits, vegetables, and meat) purchased locally. Likewise, tour operators and tour agencies help to promote local products and services, such as local restaurants and the sale of locally produced art and souvenirs, to the tourists.

However, local tourism development and entrepreneurship is largely dependent on the host community. The importance of the host communities' participation has been widely discussed in the literature, for example: how host community members participate in tourism; what factors influence their participation; and what approaches facilitate positive involvement of community members in tourism development. Thus engaging the host community in tourism through ethnodevelopment and Indigenous entrepreneurship requires an understanding of the tourism entrepreneurial process, as well as the attitudes of the host community towards the entrepreneurial activities in tourism. Our research seeks to fulfil this gap by examining the entrepreneurial culture on Lombok, Indonesia facilitating or inhibiting Indigenous entrepreneurs within the tourism industry.

Research setting: Lombok, Indonesia

Lombok is an island within Indonesia that lies between three main tourist destinations (Bali in the West, Tana Toraja, Sulawesi in the North and Komodo in the East). The island is surrounded by beautiful beaches, crystal clear water and colourful marine life, making them ideal for tourist marine activities. Tourism development on Lombok has formally developed in the late 1980s when the first three-star hotel, Senggigi Beach Hotel, was built. Since then, tourism and agriculture have become the two most important sectors in Lombok's economy. The increasing contribution of the tourism sector to Lombok's gross regional domestic product (GRDP) indicates the growing importance of the tourism industry for Lombok's future economic growth.

Historically, the development of the tourism industry on Lombok is characterised by a lack of local people's involvement. The lack of involvement during the first decade of tourism development was evident by the low number of local people working in the industry, especially in hotels, restaurants and travel agents. Changes in Indonesian political policies since 1997 have brought a more supportive environment to the growth of micro-scale tourism businesses (Hampton 2005), particularly on Lombok (Fallon 2003). Nevertheless, several factors still challenge the engagement of the host community in small-scale tourism entrepreneurship.

Saufi's study of 2008 reported that, despite the host communities eagerness to participate in tourism development, they were still poorly engaged. This lack of participation was limited by the poor work performance of the government officials, as well as the lack of communication about entrepreneurial tourism opportunities. Moreover, many of the local resources, particularly land, have been speculatively acquired by outsiders who have little commitment to the well-being of the local economy. The outsider's speculation has caused a delay in tourism development on Lombok and distrust of tourism development from within the community (Fallon 2001). Additionally, social unrest and riots in the early 2000s reflected local people's uncertainty around fragmented plans for the island's tourism (Fallon 2003), as well as a lack of confidence among local tourism stakeholders. These events significantly impacted on the development of the tourism industry on Lombok.

Schellhorn (2010) added that, despite tourism growth in a village close to Rinjani National Park, Lombok, the local villagers responded passively to the obvious opportunities for tourism entrepreneurship. Schellhorn identified nine barriers to local tourism participation in the village including: culture, education, ethnicity, gender, political/historical background, location, socio-economic factors, mobility and tourism skill/knowledge. On the other hand, Saufi *et al.* (2014) discovered three factors hindering host community participation on Lombok, which ultimately influences the engagement process through small-scale entrepreneurship. These three factors were: poor work performance of tourism agencies, a lack of support from the private sector, and cultural limitation or host communities' lack of tourism knowledge. As a consequence, host community members are unaware of the island's tourism development potential and fail to engage in the tourism industry sector (Saufi 2008; Schellhorn 2010). Understanding the barriers to local people's participation can help authorities to develop appropriate policy and strategy to encourage small-scale tourism entrepreneurship within the host community members.

Methodology

The research adopted an Indigenous ethnographic qualitative research approach. Indigenous ethnography is an inquiry into the culture of a community, whereby the inquiry is conducted by a member of the community (Tomaselli *et al.* 2008). This is particularly pertinent to enable the ethnodevelopment perspective from those who are experiencing the phenomenon to be heard. In-depth interviews were conducted across five communities in Lombok. The five villages were chosen as they represented the main tourist destinations where the majority of tourism enterprises were located in Lombok. Figures 9.1. and 9.2 show some types of autochthonous business managed by locals in Lombok.

Purposive and snowball sampling to recruit research participants was undertaken. Firstly, purposive sampling identified individuals who were: (1) Indigenous entrepreneurs; (2) owned a tourism enterprise; (3) with a maximum of 50 employees (Storey and Greene 2010); and (4) had been established for at least 42 months (McGehee and Kline 2008). These sampling conditions enabled the

Figure 9.1 Local homestay and restaurant at Senggigi.
Source: Author.

Figure 9.2 Selling activity at Sade Village.
Source: Author.

participants to have experienced the entrepreneurial journey and process. Secondly, a snowball sampling approach enabled these initial participants to provide further contacts who fulfilled the criteria. In total 27 interviews with 21 participants were undertaken. Two interviews were conducted with six participants who had additional information on particular issues that emerged after the first interview.

The interviews were conducted in Sasak (the local language) and lasted between 30 minutes and two hours. This method encouraged the participants to express their beliefs, opinions and experiences and enabled the Indigenous stories to emerge. Interviews were digitally recorded, transcribed verbatim and pseudonyms assigned and then analysed and coded in NVivo. An open and axial coding process identified 53 emergent themes which were condensed into 15 primary concepts and three lower-order concepts. These themes, concepts and orders provide an overview of the entrepreneurial process that Indigenous tourism entrepreneurs journey through. This chapter presents the results for one of these themes, that of entrepreneurial culture.

Results

Entrepreneurship is dependent upon the entrepreneurial culture, which enables or otherwise the support for ethnodevelopment and entrepreneurial activities within a society. Entrepreneurial culture results from the interconnectivity between individuals, and between the tourism entrepreneurs and their environment, at the local, national and international levels, within a period of time. Entrepreneurial culture is also influenced by the micro and macro conditions of the tourism industry sector. Micro conditions are associated with the immediate conditions that the Indigenous entrepreneurs encounter in their daily tourism entrepreneurial activities. Macro conditions are related to specific conditions of the tourism industry sector in Lombok, namely the social and political conditions at the local, national and international level. When combined these factors shape the individual's perspective on ethnodevelopment and entrepreneurship, as well as the relationships between entrepreneurs and their environment.

Entrepreneurial culture is characterised by a set of problems that continuously threaten the success of the entrepreneurial process. The problems, incorporated into five major categories, of these three categories were influenced by micro conditions (*stereotypes of tourist and locality status*, *destructive competition* and *lack of encouragement*) and two categories were influenced by macro conditions (*decentralised government* and *security issues*). The results will report on the observations and discussions relating to each of these five major categories.

Micro conditions influencing entrepreneurial culture

Many local Lombok people have a long established negative perception about tourists and those who work within the tourism sector (Fallon 2001, 2003; Saufi 2008; Saufi *et al.* 2014; Schellhorn 2010). It was perceived by many locals that tourism workers were polluted by Western attitudes and behaviours, and were being disrespectful of their society. An online tour operator in Senggigi stated:

> After I had graduated from my college, I was banned from working in tourism by my parents. They perceived that if I was to work in tourism I would do negative things with female tourists. I finally stopped and have worked odd jobs ever since … My parents just did not allow me to work in tourism regardless of my two years of tourism education … If you live in a remote village, you get to listen to what others say about you. There is more to hear than to see in the village … Our neighbours told my parents that people who work for tourists were inhospitable towards our culture. They perceived that people who worked for tourists had loose sexual morals. They slept with female tourists even though they were not married. My people believed in such a stereotype … I could not do anything about my wish to work in the tourism industry until I got married in 1992. After that, my parents had no reason to forbid me from working in tourism anymore. (Basar)

As a result of such a stereotypical attitude, many local people, particularly the young and single, are discouraged from pursuing a career in tourism. This is because the Lombok people (the Sasaks) live communally, their way of thinking influenced by the common values adopted by the community. If the community perceives tourism negatively, then the community members respect this trend and avoid working in the tourism industry. These community perspectives influenced the willingness of locals to engage in tourism entrepreneurial activities and to attract and retain high-quality staff to work in this industry sector.

There was an additional stereotypical attitude among locals that tourists were wealthy and generous Westerners, with strong buying power that created differential tourist pricing. As one respondent noted:

> I mean local people still perceive that every tourist has much money … there is still much annoying behaviour directed towards the tourists and towards us, the tourism providers. (Leo)

This led to a number of situations where tourists and entrepreneurs became the victims of crime. These perceptions have also facilitated a secondary category of entrepreneur with the emergence of street vendors. The street vendors' lack of knowledge about positive selling techniques may result in their becoming aggressive towards tourists. The street vendors' perceptions that tour operators and tour guides inhibit their efforts to make sales from the tourists can result in their inappropriate behaviour towards these gatekeepers.

Another key finding of the research was where the entrepreneur originated from. The villagers call non-local entrepreneurs *pengusaha luar*, meaning that the entrepreneurs were not born in the village or location where they established their business. As one participant commented:

> I got very little support, except from pottery producers. Other art shop owners looked upon me as an outsider at that time. When I just started my art shop, my materials were stolen three times, and my fence was pushed over twice within a week. I was also gossiped about maliciously … (Husein)

This was despite Husein being an Indigenous Sasak entrepreneur, the level of 'locality' being defined by the villagers at the village level. The non-local entrepreneur stereotype is similarly exploited by local entrepreneurs to control local resources in order to compete more effectively against non-local entrepreneurs. Therefore it is difficult for non-local entrepreneurs to establish and develop their tourism enterprises outside of their home village.

The research identified that the entrepreneurial culture of Lombok led to the potential for destructive competition among tourism entrepreneurs, with the pursuit of short-term business profits being prioritised by some. Indigenous tourism entrepreneurs establish business relationships with other entrepreneurs in order to sell their products and services. These relationships are managed on a commission basis rather than a formalised contract. For example, a hotelier in Senggigi describes the process as follows:

> I always pay ten percent commission for the guide per room per night. If the room rate is a hundred fifty thousand rupiah per room per night, I will pay fifteen thousand rupiah commission per room per night. (Lukman)

In reality, there is no common standard for the commission among the entrepreneurs with some entrepreneurs enticing relationships through higher selling commissions. This practice often leads to destructive competition and poor entrepreneurial relations, and negatively affects business development. The commission trend presents entrepreneurs with a difficult choice: whether to satisfy their customers with a reasonable price, or satisfy their business partners with a high rate of commission. Making the first choice can help establish a beneficial relationship with particular customers; however, that choice can mean the termination of the support of business partners.

The trend towards commission-based collaboration stimulated the emergence of the silent enemy. The silent enemy refers to entrepreneurs who use unusual means, such as magic or supernatural power, to help attract buyers and, thus, impact negatively on other entrepreneurs' business performance. Magic is believed to help some entrepreneurs increase their business performance and to help outweigh the competitor's business performance. The silent enemy attracts business partners in mysterious ways, as suggested by an art shop owner in the weaving village:

> As far as I am concerned anyone can be attacked by using magic named the 'quiet village'. When someone is struck by such magic, his or her art shop will always be quiet. No customers come because they cannot see the art shop. The customers don't realise that the art shop is there. If some customers can see the art shop, they don't have a willingness to enter. (Panji)

Magic was believed to help the silent enemy to assist an individual's business as well as affect other entrepreneur's business performance. The existence of the silent enemy may sound irrational and culturally related, yet participants believed that such competitors exist and intensify the destructive business competition in the Lombok tourism industry. Indigenous tourism entrepreneurs can be trapped by these ways of conducting business. Furthermore, the use of magic prevents the entrepreneurs from developing their rational entrepreneurial abilities, such as appropriate marketing strategies that can help establish and develop tourism enterprises.

A range of participants also acknowledged that entrepreneurial culture was impacted by unprofessional business partners. An unprofessional business partner used dishonest approaches to generate business, including breaking formal business contracts. A tour operator who also ran a restaurant in Senggigi expressed the dilemma in the following conversation:

> It has been such an ecosystem that one eats or is eaten in the tariff competition … the hotel gives me contract rate. It is very clear that both sides sign

> the contract. When I accommodate my customers in the hotel, as a part of my package ... the hotel people stole my clients ... The hotel even said, 'Don't join the travel agent, I'll give you the cheaper rate than that of the agent. The next year, those customers didn't return to me because they had a direct contract with the hotel ... be careful with the hotel because our guests are not safe. We should keep them on eyes for 24 hours. Furthermore, if the one who stays there is a tour leader, the group will surely move to the other agent the next day. (Dewinta)

For many entrepreneurs such as Dewinta, unprofessional business partners have affected their short- and long-term business relations. In the short term, the partners dishonestly took over Dewinta's opportunity to generate business, such as selling optional trips to the customers. In the long term, the unprofessional partners intercepted Dewinta's contract with her overseas agents and took over future customers.

Unfortunately, many participants indicated that these unprofessional partners were often organisers of associations they were affiliated with or individuals in position of power. The participants called the organisers *referees who come into play*. The association organisers are supposed to be caretakers of their members and to act in the name of the association. However, they (the organisers) often acted for the benefit of their own enterprises. As Dewinta stated 'I said to them many times ... "Please manage us, don't only manage yourselves. The cake should be shared. It should be shared fairly."' Other examples were government officials who had also established tourism enterprises. They (the officials) often used their political power as a means to compete with other entrepreneurs and win business opportunities. In many cases, the *referees who come into play* developed monopolistic systems in that their businesses were the first to benefit from government tourism policies. An art shop owner in the weaving village revealed that:

> If the local government has a free promotional programme in other regions, this official keeps that information to himself. He never informs us ... he is the head of the industry and trade department; that position means that he is actually a mediator. However, because he also has a business it seems he cannot be fair and objective. He takes everything for himself and leaves nothing for us. (Ramdan)

The government officials, who also run their own tourism enterprises, appear to have a significant conflict of interest in being able to undertake their government duty.

Macro conditions impacting on entrepreneurial culture

In 2000, Indonesia adopted a decentralised governmental system handing autonomy to each region (Rasyid 2002). The purpose of this system is to enable the democratic process, promote the individual's democratic awareness and stimulate economic independence for each region. However, this has resulted in confusion about responsibilities. First, the provincial tourism department is responsible for developing the plans and programmes for tourism development, yet their implementation is reliant on regional tourism departments. Second, all the economic benefit in terms of the tourism sector taxes are retained by the regions and not equitably share with the provinces. While the central government had the right intention to promote the democratic process, in reality it is far from perfect. The operationalising of the scheme has been problematic, and each of the regions and provinces, driven by their own agendas, has developed conflicting tourism development priorities. Indeed, this confusion has resulted in a lack of tourism development around the island.

The political issues may also influence the ability of tourism departments to establish an effective coordination of tourism development with other institutions, NGOs and local people. The participants described how they were never involved in any discussions about tourism development by the tourism agencies. From the participant's perspective, most small tourism enterprises emerged and developed in spite of, or detached from, the government's encouragement. As one participant commented:

> We expect that there is a rigorous network and link between the government and the private sector actors. This, however, has not occurred so far. The private actors go this way and the government goes that way … In developing tourism, our government … has no concept at all. (Derwinta)

The government's lack of communication about the priority of tourism development in Lombok affects the development of entrepreneurial tourism activities. Leo discussed this by stating, 'This creates a great deal of uncertainty for the tourism businesses. I also see that the local government does not take responsibility for this situation …' Knowing the priorities of tourism development (e.g. tourist destinations and infrastructure that will be developed in the short term) can assist the Indigenous entrepreneurs to find appropriate business locations and resources for their products.

The quality of the public service also has an influence on the provision of entrepreneurial activities. Individual officials who hold an important government position have the responsibility to develop tourism strategies and policies but often lack knowledge and experience in tourism development and its related strategic issues and simply develop initiatives for their own self-interest. A surfing organiser in Kuta shared his experience:

> I had to wait to get electric power for more than a year; I still have not got it. My application for 6500 watt electric power has not been realised. Another problem is water. Also, I have to buy tap water from Tanjung Aan. However, water from the tap doesn't work every day … I cannot get water from the ground in this place because it's salty … dealing with the bureaucracy is very difficult. If we want to arrange something, we have to pay …

> I told the electricity official yesterday that this project was not just mine. The project is in collaboration with my Japanese friend. If this project was my own, I would pay whatever you asked … However, I am responsible for my friend and I have to keep his trust in me. (Andika)

In addition, a slow and ineffective bureaucratic process can delay the completion and operation of a new enterprise. Another respondent identified how inadequate government policy formation also resulted in delays and cost overruns. He stated:

> I've got a problem with the customs department. There was no standard procedure about how to export things, what is or is not allowed to be exported. The regulation changes all the time and I have to find them out for myself. No one told me what I should do if I wanted to export wood, or other things … I made a fatal mistake, and I had to pay a high amount of tax … the tax was higher than what I usually paid. (Acelin)

The lack of guidelines, or any formal export procedure, can result in high operational costs, especially for the new entrepreneur. Further, Indigenous entrepreneurs, who are usually supported by only a small amount of capital, have to compete with entrepreneurs having inside information as well as stronger financial backing. Therefore a government policy that is transparent and encourages ethnodevelopment could assist small Indigenous entrepreneurs to develop and expand their businesses successfully.

Inadequate or unfair implementation of legal or business practices by authorities was also a significant factor influencing Indigenous entrepreneurs on Lombok. Weak law enforcement in the tourism industry has increased the number of local people who have established unlicensed enterprises. The unlicensed businesses intensify the competition among tourism entrepreneurs, as they do not bear the costs that legitimate enterprise must pay. While the number of non-licensed enterprises grows day-to-day, the entrepreneurs who operate legitimate businesses suffer financial losses and subsequent frustration, as expressed by a hotelier on Kuta Beach:

> We have problems with government regulation; especially when we have to pay taxes and those who don't … The illegal restaurants, shops and many other enterprises on the beach should pay taxes, but they don't. They sell the same products as we do for cheaper prices because they don't have to pay any tax. They open their business in illegal areas. They are not supposed to be there because that is the beach where the tourists sit and enjoy the environment. When I reported this situation to the government, I was told that those people will be there for a while. But, they've been there for more than four years already … If this condition doesn't change, I may do the same way as those people. In the beginning, there were just a few of them opening business on the beach, but now their numbers have increased. The government

just lets them stay ... The business condition in this area really discourages me. I run my business with an uncertain future. (Leo)

The government's weak law enforcement can lead tourism entrepreneurs into unfair competition, as previously discussed, in which the entrepreneurs tend to focus on short-term business profits and beating the competition. Weak law enforcement encourages unethical business practices such as tax manipulation, bribery and collusion, ultimately creating an environment lacking trust for business in Lombok.

During the 30 years that tourism has been developed on Lombok a number of local, national and international disturbances have significantly affected tourism development. These disturbances include the social unrest on Lombok in 2000 (local level), terrorist attacks in Bali in 2002 and 2005 (national level), and the terrorist attack on New York in 2001 (international level). There have also been other incidences that have impacted the tourism industry, for example Middle East conflicts, natural disasters and epidemics in Southeast Asia, a number of air transportation accidents in Indonesia and increasing media attention on religious fanaticism. Overall, security is an important issue for tourists and the tourism industry. Though Lombok is a small tourist destination in Indonesia, the development of its tourism industry can be affected by the security issues of other regions and countries. Various horrific incidences at the local, national and international level can spark security issues for tourists and, ultimately, affect the entrepreneurial culture of the tourism industry. Table 9.1 shows the key findings that have influenced the entrepreneurship on Lombok region.

Discussion and conclusion

Ethnodevelopment and entrepreneurship is reliant on having an effective entrepreneurial culture that will support and develop small businesses within a society. While the literature on tourism entrepreneurship is well developed, what is lacking is an understanding of the factors influencing and impacting upon the entrepreneurial autochthonous culture of many destinations. This chapter has sought to fill this gap by exploring the results of one research project in five host communities on Lombok, Indonesia. While the results of the study are unique to this research setting there are a number of lessons that other developing countries can observe.

Firstly, entrepreneurial culture, while unique to the context in which it is being experienced, is influenced and impacted upon by a range of micro and macro conditions. Micro conditions involve the immediate set of conditions that tourism entrepreneurs must deal with in their daily activities. These micro conditions are influenced by three main tourism stakeholders: the local communities, other tourism enterprises and tourism authorities. The tourism stakeholders pose a series of threats that challenge and menace the entrepreneur's abilities to cope with their tourism business. In contrast, the macro conditions are influenced by geographical, historical, social and political aspects, as well as the security

Table 9.1 Summary of key findings influencing entrepreneurship on Lombok

Micro conditions	*Macro conditions*
Stereotypes of tourist and locality status	***Decentralised government system***
Negative perceptions of tourists and those working in the sector	Confusion about roles and responsibilities in developing and implementing tourism
Discouraged locals from working in the sector in order to conform to community society values	Local tourism entrepreneurs emerged and developed in spite of government's encouragement
Tourists perceived as wealthy, creating differential tourist pricing	Lack of communication of tourism development priorities on Lombok
Tourists becoming victims of crime or harassment	Positions of power within public sector not linked with qualifications but other factors
Origin of entrepreneur influences their ability to establish and access resources	Self-interested government officials
Destructive competition	Slow and ineffective bureaucratic process
Pursuit of short-term business profits	Lack of transparency in government policy
Commission-based relationships	Inadequate or fair implementation of legal or business practices
'Silent enemy' – unusual means to impact on business performance, i.e. magic or supernatural powers	Weak law enforcement of the tourism industry, i.e. licensed businesses
Unprofessional business partners	***Security issues***
'Referees who come into play', created from unequal power relationships	Local social unrest on Lombok
Street vendors' aggressive selling techniques	National and international terrorist attacks
Lack of encouragement	Other incidents, i.e. natural disasters, conflicts, air transport accidents and media attention on religious fanaticism

issues at the local, national and international level. Despite the different products and services that Indigenous entrepreneurs produce, they all have to deal with the difficulties that the entrepreneurial culture of the tourism industry in Lombok generates. The culture threatens the entrepreneur's abilities to benefit from their tourism businesses, it prevents or stalls sustainable success and it leads to business vulnerability. Nevertheless, the entrepreneurial culture must be overcome if the entrepreneurs are to be successful in their entrepreneurial journey within the tourism industry.

Secondly, previous tourism studies (e.g. Andereck *et al.* 2005; Fredline and Faulkner 2000; Pérez and Nadal 2005) concluded that local people's attitudes towards tourism development varied along a continuum, from those that are highly favourable to development to those that are against development. The findings of this current study extend our understanding of the influence of the local attitudes towards entrepreneurial tourism activities and the influence this has on entrepreneurial culture. For example, on Lombok, the negative stereotyping of tourists stimulated the local negative attitudes towards the 'outsider' (Elias and Scotson 1994). Those who believed in such negative stereotypes forbade their family and community members from learning anything that related to the tourism industry, such as learning to converse in English, and refused to allow them to work in the industry. These attitudes and behaviours stymied the locals' expertise in tourism entrepreneurship, or resulted in what Tosun (2000) defined as 'cultural limitation', and limited the availability of local employees for the tourism industry. The negative stereotyping also stimulated anti-tourist action, which impeded the development of local resources for tourist products and threatened the security of tourism entrepreneurial activities (Saufi *et al.* 2014). Additionally, the culturally bound identification of 'locality' appeared to significantly influence local support for tourism business; as Bennett and Gordon (2007) pointed out, the lack of local support increases business risk and the uncertainties faced by the tourism entrepreneur.

Thirdly, Indigenous entrepreneurs in this study were engaged in commission-based business to attract support. Many participants had to offer high commissions to attract a business partner who could bring them customers; if this rate was not paid the business partner would take the customers to another entrepreneur. In other words, the business partners tended to support those giving the highest commission. Such competition has created business monopolies by those entrepreneurs with strong financial support, while those lacking financial support tended to fail or go bankrupt. Unprofessional behaviours also increased business uncertainty.

An interesting finding of this research, linked with the society's culture, related to the emergence of the 'silent enemy'. The silent enemy refers to the threat of using unusual means, such as magic, to win business competition. The arrival of the silent enemy into the entrepreneurial culture field became a threat to the Indigenous entrepreneur's ability to create products and exploit entrepreneurial opportunities in tourism. Indeed, the silent enemy may sound irrational, but it is contextual and culturally specific to Lombok where the entrepreneurial journey (in the current research) takes place.

Fourthly, the government's role in supporting ethnodevelopment and entrepreneurship should not be underestimated. Normally, government creates the framework, through legislation, rules and regulations, that is needed to be enforced to enable a fair and equitable business environment. The duplicity of and confusion about tourism development within Indonesia impacted upon the entrepreneurial culture evident on Lombok. There was a lack of government protection for legitimate entrepreneurial activities, along with weak enforcement of the laws and regulations relating to the tourism industry. A consequence of this lack of support affected the entrepreneur's independence and ability to create new products and services, as well as a concern for security in the tourism business environment. Furthermore, the lack of law enforcement stimulated the emergence of non-licensed tourism enterprises, and provoked disobedience against business regulation.

Finally, macro conditions beyond the control of the entrepreneur also influence the entrepreneurial culture of tourism business and destinations. However, as shown by the current research, the entrepreneurial culture presents limitations to the success of the entrepreneurial process in the tourism industry. These limitations confirm the earlier findings identified by Tosun (2000) in developing countries, namely that a host community faces limitations at the operational level and within the structural and cultural environment. As a consequence, the host communities on Lombok have been able to deal with a series of problems resulting from limitations at the operational level, such as the lack of protection and weak law enforcement. Such conditions were exacerbated by the structural limitations that have resulted in the lack of tourism infrastructure, the emergence of security issues, the fragmented planning of tourism development and the emergence of unsolved problems.

Entrepreneurial culture presents information about the settings and conditions that a prospective entrepreneur has to deal with when establishing and developing a tourism enterprise. Understanding the entrepreneurial culture enables an entrepreneur to identify an appropriate type of and a strategic location for the tourism enterprise. This understanding also assists the entrepreneur develop relationships with his/her entrepreneurial environment.

The study results can be a reference point for tourism agencies to develop policies that create entrepreneurial opportunities, especially for the Indigenous tourism entrepreneurs. Tourism authorities should promote the benefits of tourism development for the local people, and provide more opportunities for local small-scale tourism to grow rather than encourage larger tourism facilities owned by outside investors (Hampton 2005; Kamsma and Bras 1999). Policies that support small-scale tourism can include appropriate strategies that increase local involvement in tourism and provide more benefits to the local people from tourism. While small-scale tourism requires small capital, which fits the local people's business abilities, this type of business also prevents economic leakage, and helps to better distribute the income among host community members (Dahles 2000). Moreover, such a policy will stimulate the emergence of many Indigenous tourism entrepreneurs delivering authentic products and services that their region offers.

References

Andereck, K. L., Valentine, K. M., Knopf, R. C. and Vogt, C. A. (2005) Residents' perceptions of community tourism impacts. *Annals of Tourism Research* 32(4), 1056–76.

Bennett, J. and Gordon, W. (2007) Social capital and the Indigenous tourism entrepreneur. In J. Buultjes and D. Fuller (eds), *Striving for Sustainability Case Studies in Indigenous Tourism*. Lismore, NSW: Southern Cross University Press, pp. 333–70.

BPS NTB (2012) *Nusa Tenggara Barat in Figures*. Mataram: BPS NTB.

Cole, S. (2006) Information and empowerment: the keys to achieving sustainable tourism. *Journal of Sustainable Tourism* 14, 629–44.

Dahles, H. (2000) Tourism, small enterprises and community development. In G. Richards and D. Hall (eds), *Tourism and Sustainable Community Development*. London: Routledge, pp. 154–69.

de Lima, I. B., Kumble, P. de Almeida, M. G., Chaveiro, E. F., Ferreira, L. C. and Mota, R. D. (2016) Ecotourism community enterprises and ethnodevelopment: modelling the Kalunga empowerment possibilities in the Brazilian savannah. *Brazilian Journal of Science and Technology* 3(1), 1–25.

Elias, N. and Scotson, J. (1994) *The Established and the Outsiders*. London: Sage.

Fallon, F. (2001) Conflict, power and tourism on Lombok. *Current Issues in Tourism* 4(6), 481–502.

Fallon, F. (2003) After the Lombok riots, is sustainable tourism achieved? In C. M. Hall, D. J. Timothy and D. Duval (eds), *Safety and Security in Tourism: Relationships, Management, and Marketing*. Binghamton, NY: Haworth Hospitality Press, pp. 139–58.

Fredline, E. and Faulkner, B. (2000) Host community reactions: a cluster analysis. *Annals of Tourism Research* 27(3), 763–84.

Hampton, M. P. (2005) Heritage, local communities and economic development. *Annals of Tourism Research* 32(3), 735–59.

Harrison, D. and Schipani, S. (2007) Lao tourism and poverty alleviation: community-based tourism and the private sector. *Current Issues in Tourism* 10(2/3), 194–230.

Joseph, C. A. and Kavoori, A. P. (2001) Mediated resistance: tourism and the host community. *Annals of Tourism Research* 28(4), 998–1009.

Kamsma, T. and Bras, K. (2000) Gili trawangan – from desert island to 'marginal' paradise: local participation, small-scale entrepreneurs and outside investors in an Indonesian tourist destination. In G. Richards and D. Hall (eds), *Tourism and Sustainable Community Development*. London: Routledge, pp. 170–84.

Koh, K. Y. (2002) Explaining a community touristscape: an entrepreneurism model. *International Journal of Hospitality and Tourism Administration* 3(2), 29.

Koh, K. Y. (2006) Tourism entrepreneurship: people, place, and process. *Tourism Analysis* 11(2), 115–31.

Kokkranikal, J. and Morrison, A. (2011) Community networks and sustainable livelihoods in tourism: the role of entrepreneurial innovation. *Tourism Planning and Development*, 8(2), 137–56.

McGehee, N. G. and Kline, C. S. (2008) Entrepreneurship and the rural tourism industry: a primer. In G. Moscardo (ed.), *Building Community Capacity for Tourism Development*. Wallingford: CABI International.

Page, S. J., Forer, P. and Lawton, G. R. (1999) Small business development and tourism: terra incognita? *Tourism Management* 20(4), 435–59.

Pearce, P. L. (2008) Understanding how tourism can bring sociocultural benefits to destination communities. In G. Moscardo (ed.), *Building Community Capacity for Tourism Development*. Wallingford: CABI International.

Pérez, E. A. and Nadal, J. R. (2005) Host community perceptions a cluster analysis. *Annals of Tourism Research* 32(4), 925–41.

Rasyid, M. R. (2002) *The Policy of Decentralization in Indonesia*. Paper presented at the GSU Conference. Retrieved from: http://aysps.gsu.edu/isp/2637.html.

Russell, R. and Faulkner, B. (2004) Entrepreneurship, chaos and the tourism area lifecycle. *Annals of Tourism Research* 31(3), 556–79.

Ryan, T., Mottiar, Z. and Quinn, B. (2012) The dynamic role of entrepreneurs in destination development. *Tourism Planning and Development* 9(2), 119–31.

Saufi, A. (2008) An Investigation into the Factors Influencing the Attitudes of Local People Who Live in Remote Villages within Lombok Island Indonesia to Adopt Any Participation in the Tourism Industry. Unpublished dissertation for the degree of Master of Business with Honours (International Tourism and Hospitality Management), Griffith University, Gold Coast, Australia.

Saufi, A., O'Brien, D. and Wilkins, H. (2014) Inhibitor to host community participation in sustainable tourism development in developing countries. *Journal of Sustainable Tourism* 22(5), 801–20.

Schellhorn, M. (2010) Development for whom? Social justice and the business of ecotourism. *Journal of Sustainable Tourism* 18(1), 115–35.

Scheyvens, R. (2002a) Backpacker tourism and third world development. *Annals of Tourism Research* 29(1), 144–64.

Scheyvens, R. (2002b) *Tourism for Development: Empowering Communities*. Harlow: Pearson Education.

Shane, S. and Venkataraman, S. (2000) The promise of entrepreneurship as a field of research. *Academy of Management Review* 25(1), 217–26.

Sharma, P., Chrisman, J. J. and Chua, J. H. (1996) *A Review and Annotated Bibliography of Family Business Studies*. Dordrecht: Kluwer Academic.

Sheldon, P. J. and Abenoja, T. (2001) Resident attitudes in a mature destination: the case of Waikiki. *Tourism Management* 22(5), 435-443.

Simpeh, K. N. (2011) Entrepreneurship theories and empirical research: a summary review of the literature. *European Journal of Business Management* 3(6), 1–9.

Spenceley, A. and Goodwin, H. (2007) Nature-based tourism and poverty alleviation: impacts of private sector and parastatal enterprises in and around Kruger National Park, South Africa. *Current Issues in Tourism* 10(2/3), 255–77.

Storey, D. J. and Greene, F. J. (2010) *Small Business and Entrepreneurship*. Harlow: Pearson Education.

Teye, V., Sirakaya, E. and Sönmez, S. (2002) Residents' attitudes toward tourism development. *Annals of Tourism Research* 29(3), 668–88.

Thompson, C. S. (2004) Host produced rural tourism: Towa's Tokyo antenna shop. *Annals of Tourism Research* 31(3), 580–600.

Timothy, D. J. (1999) Participatory planning: a view of tourism in Indonesia. *Annals of Tourism Research* 26(2), 371–91.

Tomaselli, K. G., Dyll, L. and Francis, M. (2008) 'Self' and 'Other': Auto-Reflexive and Indigenous Ethnography. In N. K. Denzin, Y. S. Linkoln and L. T. Smith (eds), *Handbook of Critical and Indigenous Methodologies*. Thousand Oaks, CA: Sage, pp. 347–72.

Tosun, C. (2000) Limits to community participation in the tourism development process in developing countries. *Tourism Management* 21(6), 613–33.

Tosun, C. (2006) Expected nature of community participation in tourism development. *Tourism Management* 27(3), 493–504.

van Nieuwkoop, M. and Uquillas, J. (2000) *Defining Ethnodevelopment in Operational Terms: Lessons from the Ecuador Indigenous and Afro-Ecuadoran Peoples Development Project*, Latin America and Caribbean Region Sustainable Development Working Paper No. 6. Washington, DC: World Bank.

Wearing, S. and McDonald, M. (2002) The development of community-based tourism: re-thinking the relationship between tour operators and development agents as intermediaries in rural and Isolated area communities. *Journal of Sustainable Tourism* 10(3): 191–206.

Weaver, D. and Lawton, L. (2006) *Tourism Management*. Milton, QLD: Wiley.

Widiani, H. B. T., Rosidi, M., Surenggana, M. M. D. and Putus, L. A. (1997) *Dampak Pengembangan Pariwisata terhadap Kehidupan Sosial di Daerah Nusa Tenggara Barat*. Mataram: Favorit.

10 Community entrepreneurship, female elite and cultural inheritance

Mosuo women's empowerment and the hand-weaving factory

Yang Ningdong and La Mingqing

Introduction[1]

With the implementation of the policy of Pro-poor Tourism (PPT) in China, tourism has been the pillar industry in the ethnic minority areas of West China. During that time, to meet the tourists' need to consume, some ethnic communities began to realise the value of their own traditional culture and transform some cultural elements into tourist commodities by making some adjustments and innovations. Subsequently community entrepreneurship generated by tourism development is emerging in the ethnic minority areas of West China. However, according to our field investigation in recent years, they have been deprived of most of the benefits from community entrepreneurship either by local government or some outside firms so that the ethnic group already been excluded from the range of benefits has become a marginal one in their own homeland. If community entrepreneurship cannot help realise the goal to improve the living standard of the ethnic group, what is the exact significance of developing tourism? If the ethnic group loses the incentive to protect and inherit their culture, what would the attraction of the ethnic community become in the future? Due to these factors it has been a very important and urgent problem to find the resolution to help the ethnic group regain the power of self-determination and self-development. In other words, how can we empower them more to help change their position from a marginal one to a central one during tourism development?

The 'Mosuo People', a small ethnic group situated in the Southwest of China, is famous for its old tradition of walking marriage and female-dominated folk customs. Their homeland at Lugu Lake has become a famous tourist destination and their hand-woven fabrics are popular in the tourist market. Inspired by this, a local Mosuo woman, A Qi Du Zhi Ma ('A Qi' will be used in the chapter), set up a Mosuo hand-weaving factory to produce some traditional textiles inherited from their ancestors. Under her leadership and with the help of the local government and some third-party organisations, the factory became a famous ethnic tourism enterprise in the region and helped the local residents obtain much economic benefit. Meanwhile, community entrepreneurship promoted individual development and strengthened their collective harmony. This chapter will critically review both the process of empowerment provided by community entrepreneurship to find the reference value for other potential community entrepreneurship in the ethnic minority areas.

Literature review

The research on empowerment has been addressed by various scientific approaches, with the basic goal of understanding how the power of the poor is enhanced and their own benefit is refunded. Its roots go back to the tradition of social work in Western countries and to develop the practical support and action from the view of social maintenance, the contribution of women and citizen rights as well as the gestation of grassroots organisations in the 1960s. The academic research and practical exploration of empowerment theory has emerged since the 1980s.

In previous research, the notion of 'empowerment' has multiple meanings due to the various views of different scholars. However, there is a common idea that it is to assist the disadvantaged group, including its members, to obtain the benefits that they should get. Thus it can create a just society to offer an opportunity to access resources through action, social policy and planning (Lee 1994). With the development of cross-disciplinary fields, empowerment theory has been applied in the field of tourism research. The earliest research on empowerment in tourism proposed the importance of giving power to the community through tourism development (Akamal 1996). To realise the goal, an analytical framework with four dimensions – political, economic, psychological and social – has been constructed (Scheyvens 1999). Finally, the conception, theory and research methods of empowerment in tourism have been explored thoroughly (Sofield 2003).

The typical characteristics and methodology of the case

In the Southwest of China, there is a special ethnic group called the 'Mosuo People'. With the development of tourism there in recent years, a local Mosuo woman named A Qi Du Zhi Ma ('A Qi') has been living in Wa La Bi village, a typical ethnic community comprising two main minority groups: the 'Mosuo' and the 'Yi'. Wa La Bi village is situated in the northwest of Ning Lang County in Yunnan province, at a distance of about 20km from Lugu Lake and 100km from the ancient town of Lijiang, one of the most famous UNESCO World Heritage Sites.

There are 747 households and a population of 3,862 in this community, among whom there are 1,416 Yi people, 1,092 Mosuo people, 442 Pumi people and 912 other minority peoples. Before the development of tourism, the local residents made a living from farming, planting and animal husbandry. Similar to other ethnic communities in China, they were generally very poor. To earn more money for children's tuition and for health expenses, some residents were forced to leave their hometown and went to big cities nearby as cheap migrant workers. Thus their power of managing and developing the community was lost and the traditional social structure of the maternal clan culture also gradually collapsed. In a sense, with the appearance of the hand-weaving factory, the problems described above had been resolved. Based on it, we made a field investigation from July to August 2014. Our research is qualitative and the research methods mainly focus on field observation, literature analysis and in-depth interviews.

Community entrepreneurship, the female elite and tourism development

As for tourism development, entrepreneurship is a series of actions for taking risk and engaging in the operation and organisation of setting up a new enterprise. The key word is 'action' and the subject of the action is 'entrepreneur' (Shaw 2004). For ethnic entrepreneurs, their entrepreneurship represents their own unique motivation, characteristics and organisational behaviour (Fuller-Love *et al.* 2006). In A Qi's case, the 'action' of the 'entrepreneur' was mainly embodied in the identification of the tourist market and the design of cultural products.

For one thing, A Qi was the first person in the community to see the emerging opportunity for new ideas reusing traditional hand-weaving skills. With the development of tourism around Lugu Lake and the ancient town of Lijiang in the 1990s, some backpackers came to A Qi's village and were attracted by the scarves in her home. When the backpackers left the village, they asked to buy several of her scarves. To satisfy them, she sold them and earned her first income. Inspired by that, she borrowed US$11 from her neighbour and bought some raw materials with it to weave more scarves. In 2006, when she had accumulated US$740, she set up a hand-weaving factory with the support of local government. Later, about 900 Mosuo women from the villages nearby gathered around her so that a special hand-weaving industry owned and operated by the Mosuo people took shape. A Qi's community became an ethnic cultural site sponsored by the local government.

However, it was not easy for A Qi and her partners with their poor educational background to find a balance between the display and use of ethnic culture and meeting market demands. On the one hand, for the Mosuo women, they had to learn the weaving skills of the older generation but adapt the products for the market, not merely for use in the village. For example, the traditional Mosuo handbag appeared very large without being layered inside and was made from linen in a single dark colour. On the other hand, there were tourist consumer preferences. In particular, women from the big cities were attracted to the fashionable, unique and artistic products. How to balance the two traditional and modern aspects? A Qi asked her son, Ni Ma, who had majored in economics and management during his college years and who worked in Kunming, the provincial capital of Yunnan, to help her. Ni Ma decided to return to the community to bring some new ideas to the group of Mosuo women. These included creative product design, fashionable product packaging and product promotion through the internet.

Figure 10.1 A Qi's family workshop.
Source: Picture taken during the study in July 2014.

Empowerment: the fulfilment of inclusion and self-determination

Empowerment theory is constructed from such conceptions as power, powerlessness, empowerment and disempowerment. For these conceptions, power is the key notion that means the existing or potential ability to compete and obtain a certain competitive resource (Sofield 2003). Relatively speaking, disempowerment means that some group members in the society have been deprived of power so that they lack the ability to change their own lives. Consequently, their lack of self-respect and confidence will be internalised and integrated into the process of self-development to form a sense of powerlessness (Parsons 1989). To solve this problem, the conception of 'empowerment' has been addressed to strengthen personal power and individual cognition towards power. Meanwhile, it can reduce the sense of powerlessness from the disadvantaged group by way of external intervention and assistance. This concept points to the social action with which power will be obtained and through which the society will be altered (Zimmerman 1990). Therefore empowerment may be regarded as an effective path that can help the poor participate in the development of their own community.

Figure 10.2 A Qi demonstrating some manual weaving skills to members of the community.

Source: Picture taken during the study in July 2014.

Economic empowerment: the improvement in the standard of living through handicraft production

As most of the regions which Mosuo people inhabit are mountainous, transportation and infrastructure are not available to develop an industrial economy. The local residents have been extremely poor for many years though they still keep some of their traditions. However, with the popularity of cotton and other raw materials for clothing and other cloth products, hand-weaving had been in decline and many Mosuo women no longer wove for their families. In the end, they had no strong means of survival which limited their self-development. It seemed that they could not find effective ways to change their lives and were excluded from the mainstream of social development. But with increasing numbers of tourists appearing in the region, some commercial opportunities were recognised by a few ethnic members with smart ideas and an open mind. A Qi was one of them. Compared with other Mosuo women, A Qi had acquired a higher level of education though she had only graduated from a local junior middle school, but she had the ability to identify and grasp market opportunities in advance. In her spare time, she chose to learn some weaving techniques from her mother and other old women in the community. Yet her goods did not sell well so she decided to go to Lijiang where a large numbers of tourists gathered in order to promote her textiles.

At first she adopted the mode of a family workshop. She and her family, including her daughters and her sisters, collaborated and produced some textiles by hand. To avoid the risk of overstocking, she let her family members complete a small batch of goods in advance and then it was her duty to sell these products. After her goods were sold, she used the earnings to purchase some new raw materials to continue the production. By this cyclical method, her goods were in great demand so that she and her family could not complete the number of orders from tourists in time. Hence she invited her neighbours and other women in this community, even other ethnic groups such as the Yi minority and Pu Mi, to participate in this production. A Qi would pay them for their labour, with members able to obtain a salary from US$74 to US$444 every month. This was a large income for them and their family. Their children could go to school and their parents could see a doctor with this extra income. They recognised the value of their handicraft and moved the process from being a cultural resource to cultural capital.

From the perspective of resource utilisation, Mosuo ethnic handicraft is a kind of cultural resource with a low cost and a high benefit. How should they change this cultural resource into cultural capital to empower the local residents and derive more economic benefit? According to A Qi's example, we argued that the cultural identity of ethnic entrepreneur, the organisational behaviour of the ethnic community and the cultural institution of the ethnic group are the main factors for the fulfilment of economic empowerment for an ethnic minority group.

Compared with other entrepreneurs outside, those entrepreneurs with a background in their own ethnic identity could stress the ethnic characteristics of their cultural products. It is both a strong attraction for the tourist market and an authentic resource of social trust. A Qi could therefore be regarded as a typical ethnic entrepreneur and a member of a 'female elite'. According to the theory of social stratification, the female elite comprise those who are the core force and the biggest beneficiaries of their own knowledge, technique, ability and bravery. A Qi was good at using her personal ethnic image and collective culture to earn money for her family and the rest of the members of the Mosuo group. Whether it was her enthusiasm for the traditional culture or her eagerness for economic benefit, when A Qi did some weavings, she always insisted on using traditional skills and the productive procedure. That is, the 'doing' is always 'by hand', not 'by machine'.

With the foundation and enlargement of A Qi's factory, she was elected as the Communist Party leader of this community for her contributions to the residents. Thus it was more convenient and powerful for her to call on more women to join in the factory. She often combined the affairs in this factory with the management of this community. In 2010, she organised a textile commission to manage any affairs about hand-weaving. This institution was in charge of many affairs related to production, promotion, investment, employment and so on. If they encountered unfair competition, they would seek assistance from this organisation which would represent them in negotiations with outsiders, such as the local government, external firms and retailers in Lijiang. This organisation helped them obtain the benefits of their labour and prevented profits from leaking out of the community. As a result, this organisational behaviour ensured the stability of human resources for the factory. Meanwhile, this phenomenon of participation by all the members in this community expressed the origins, purity, harmony and stability of their traditional culture. It was also another important component for tourists to strengthen their cultural trust in an ethnic minority group.

In addition, there is an old cultural tradition called 'the House System' which is a result of another tradition called 'Walking Marriage'. As marriage does not exist among the Mosuo the responsibility of leading an extended family of over ten people has been taken up by the oldest and most capable woman among them, referred to as 'Grandmother'. In the same way, when A Qi worked out the factory rules, including the principle of benefit distribution, she still followed the organisational arrangement on which the family was based and did her best to involve everyone in the community and to ensure every member obtained some earnings for weaving.

Cultural empowerment: the protection and inheritance of culture through knowledge

Since A Qi's textiles became more and more popular in the tourist market, some other firms in Lijiang began to copy her commodities without any cost. Compared with A Qi most of those firms produced their textiles by machine not by hand. Hence more goods and lower costs could be obtained in those firms, while A Qi's textiles were excluded from the tourist market. According to A Qi she could not afford to buy or rent shops to sell her textiles in Lijiang as the price there was very high so she had to ask other shopkeepers in Lijiang to help her sell her goods. Every time she went into the shops, her textiles were picked out as having many flaws such as the disunity of length and width for each scarf, the out-of-date style of their weavings as well as the rough techniques. For these reasons these shopkeepers would lower the price of her products deliberately so that there was little profit. 'I am very worried about it and I could not sleep well for a long time …', A Qi recalled and appeared very sad when we interviewed her. 'Later I asked for my son, Ni Ma, who majored in economics and management when he studied in college. He suggested that I apply for a trademark in my name immediately. In 2008 the trademark of 'A Qi Du Zhi Ma' had been approved by the local department with the help of all levels of government, including the Ethnic Affairs Commission, the Women's Federation and other institutions. In 2012, they created twelve totem patterns of the Mosuo and registered the copyright. Finally, not only her own brand of textile commodities was established but also she could adapt to the changeable commercial environment. In the process of competing with other firms A Qi and her son recognised the important value of their ethnic culture and knew how to protect their intellectual property with a more rational mind.

Further, they recognised the importance of innovation and creation. In the light of the suggestion from those shopkeepers in Lijiang, A Qi's son investigated in particular the whole market of ethnic textiles in Lijiang and Lugu Lake to find what style and which patterns were most popular with tourists. He learned some aesthetic knowledge and artistic design from experts in Kunming. To obtain more consumer information from women in the large cities, A Qi's son brought his mother to visit makeup counters to observe how the cosmetic products were packed in a fashionable way. By learning from them he had some new ideas for their weaving products. For example, he decided to sell their products by matching them with popular dresses, jewellery and perfumes to improve their attractiveness. Next, influenced by her son, A Qi planned to segment the market for her products according to multiple female preferences by adding other cultural factors such as nostalgia, romanticism and artistry.

Therefore, as a member of the female elite in the ethnic community, A Qi and her family could utilise and develop innovations in their traditional culture. In the end, cultural empowerment was achieved by way of the protection of cultural values and the reproduction of regional knowledge; meanwhile Mosuo traditional culture has been inherited creatively.

Social empowerment: the recovery of community order by collaboration

In some cases, community entrepreneurship can bring the recovery of community order by offering stable and profitable employment opportunities for all members of the ethnic group. Before A Qi set up her hand-weaving factory, there was almost no commercial employment for the local residents to make extra money. Many Mosuo women were forced to leave their community for the large cities nearby to make a living and only the old and the children stayed in their homeland. The result of this was the collapse of the matriarchal clan culture. In the community of Mosuo people, female members had occupied the most important role in their family. The females were responsible for the operation and management of their extended family. However, the social structure and culture of this community were being undermined as more and more women left to earn money. Now this condition has been changed as A Qi's factory attracted many Mosuo women to return home. With the return of the women to this community, the traditional cultural core of Mosuo began to recover. Furthermore, their social structure was consolidated because more Mosuo women were making more money than before for their family. The meaning of their social role for the whole family and community was increased. Thus community order recovered and its cultural roots were revived through collaboration.

As A Qi's factory became more and more famous in the region, the local government gave more attention to it. Before the foundation of the factory, A Qi accumulated some of her social capital, such as a good reputation and interpersonal relationships brought by her excellent weaving skills. For example, she was praised by the Women's Federation of Ninglang County many times and was awarded the title of 'Female Master of Yunnan Province'. Next, she was given the honour of 'The Handicraft Successor in Lijiang City' in 2005 and 'The Inheritor of the Intangible Cultural Heritage of Yunnan Province' in 2006. After the establishment of the factory, she was invited to travel to display the traditional handicraft of the Mosuo. At the end of 2006, she went to Cambodia to attend the conference on 'Talents and Network Information Exchange'. In 2007, she was invited to display her traditional textiles in the 'Chinese Countryside Art Fair' in Beijing. With her fame growing rapidly, she developed multiple relationships with various parties, including government departments, business circles and some third-party organisations. During her entrepreneurship, she did her best to bring external resources and information into the community.

In 2011, her factory was supported as an innovative and public welfare project by the combination of the United Nations Development Programme, the State Ethnic Affairs Commission of China and the Ministry of Commerce of China. This event was reported by China Central Television, the top agency of Chinese news reporting. Next an Enactus team made up of students from the Southwest University for Nationalities in China joined in the protection and inheritance of Mosuo culture by teaching the ethnic group to design their products, which helped A Qi's weaving products to gain more market competitiveness. Although A Qi did not act directly to recover the community order, her work for this factory and her reputation among the Mosuo created opportunities to help in this process and optimise the results of community reconstruction.

Political empowerment: the enhancement of discourse by institution

As A Qi made many contributions to community development, she was elected the head of Wa La Bi village in 2010. To serve the factory better, she organised a special institution, the weaving committee for tourists. The weaving committee was a branch of the village committee. It was made up of several capable and articulate villagers, who were elected and approved by all the members of the Mosuo community. The duty of this committee was to negotiate some subjects of primary concern in protecting the interests of the villagers

For example, before joining the factory, the villagers in this community were very shy and timid because they seldom went out to the world outside. But since becoming members of A Qi's factory, some of them had several opportunities to visit such cities as Lijiang, Kunming and Hangzhou to learn new weaving techniques. After returning to their community, they recognised the importance of training other members. So they worked out a plan of how to apply for financial support from the local government to hold training courses for the villagers. Under the leadership of the weaving committee, they learned to negotiate with the government departments in a flexible and rational way. Finally they succeeded in getting support from the local government to help improve their design levels with the guidance of some experts invited by the local government.

In addition, the community was situated at the central site of two provinces between Yunnan and Sichuan in historical terms. There were historical transactions in the exchange of tea and horses. The weaving committee suggested that the head of the town create a cultural zone to display traditional culture besides hand-weaving skills, which would help tourists learn more about the cultural background of the Mosuo, especially the understanding of the traditional patterns and styles in the textiles. Finally, following their efforts, their ideas were adopted to build a public museum to display traditional Mosuo culture. Moreover, the local government funded them to add some new equipment including a loom, a sewing machine and a winding machine to the museum at the request of the Mosuo women.

With the establishment of the weaving committee, it became a platform for the Mosuo to express their opinions and ideas. They could realise political empowerment by improving their level of participation and their consciousness.

Psychological empowerment: the attainment of cultural consciousness through entrepreneurship

With the support of the local government and other organisations, A Qi's hand-weaving factory brought the Mosuo much cultural confidence, especially in the appreciation and affection shown by the tourists. It made A Qi and other Mosuo women recognise the value of their own culture, which encouraged their enthusiasm and collective memory on Mosuo culture. It also demonstrated that these women who were skilled in knitting and weaving could earn more money than others who were not in the factory. Because the quality of the handicrafts had a close relationship to the amount of money that could be earned, the Mosuo women's focus has been placed on improving their weaving skills in their spare time. At the same time, other groups like Yi women, Pu Mi women and even Han women in the nearby villages also came to A Qi's factory to learn from Mosuo women how to weave textiles. With more 'gazes' from 'the third party', Mosuo women became proud of their traditional handicraft and were even willing to explore the deep meanings of the patterns embroidered on these textiles actively for tourists. In addition, under the leadership of A Qi they are also trying to recover other cultural elements such as traditional dancing and songs, and the coming-of-age ceremony of Mosuo children.

Community entrepreneurship helped them construct their own cultural consciousness including cultural confidence, cultural self-esteem and even cultural tolerance as well as self-development. A Qi and her members no longer rejected those factories whose goods were produced by machine because they believed their manual handicraft was a rare cultural resource and should have a special place in the tourist market today.

Results

The effective role of a female elite has been the important impulse given towards a community empowerment in the process of ethnic development. A number of tourists created a large market space and many new entrepreneurial opportunities for ethnic entrepreneurs since the rapid development of ethnic tourism in the 1990s in China. Tourism development encouraged ethnic entrepreneurs to learn how to distinguish and utilise the opportunities before them and transform themselves into suppliers of tourist commodities. In the process of entrepreneurship, the entrepreneur's personal level of technique, reputation, brand effect and social competence are key factors for the fulfilment of empowerment. Meanwhile, the process of entrepreneurship also turned an ordinary ethnic woman into a member of the female elite in the community and she played a very important role in this process. When starting the process of her entrepreneurship she had the courage to break conventions and provide leadership to the other women in this community to continue this action. As a member of the female elite in the process of tourism development, she had a substantial following and political resource to formulate and carry forward planning and organisational capacity. Based on this, she had the strong desire and motivation to encourage collaboration between herself and her villagers. Finally she inherited and protected a traditional cultural resource with other members of the community.

On the other hand, the systematisation of the community members is another effective approach for community empowerment in the process of ethnodevelopment. How to organise the community members effectively was one of the most important approaches in the process of empowerment. A Qi's case suggests that if the members of the community had common cultural capital then this was a precondition to develop the systematisation of ethnic members. On the basis of their common hand-weaving skill, A Qi could call other members of the community together to develop their entrepreneurship. After A Qi and her members established the weaving committee, the process of the systematisation of ethnic members began to be achieved. This committee was a regional institution beyond the family and helped in the realisation of the organisation of community participation. In a sense, the effective organisation of community residents would enhance the beneficial abilities of the community and improve the opportunities to realise profit. Moreover, it could strengthen the discourse, selective power and rights of control in the engagement with external stakeholders. Thus it could be ensured that the benefits brought by tourism development would remain in this community.

Finally, it could also regulate the community order and enhance social trust to generate social capital, including cultural confidence and cultural consciousness to protect and preserve the traditional culture. However, in A Qi's case there are still some problems to address. As A Qi is just the representative of a small number of Mosuo women her contribution is not yet generalisable to the wider culture and society. So the next stage of research is to investigate how to develop a sustainable and institutionalised approach to ensure the fulfilment of empowerment more generally and ensure that the work of people like A Qi can be carried on for the benefit of future generations.

Note

1. This research is funded by the Planning Project of the Ministry of Education, China in 2016: Industrial transformation, social stratification and community reconstruction – based on the empirical study of ethnic tourism communities in West China (Project Number: 16XJAZH004).

References

Akamal, J. (1996) Western environmental values and nature-based tourism in Kenya. *Tourism Management* 17(8), 567–74.

Fuller-Love, N., Lim, L. and Akehurst, G. (2006) Guest editorial: female and ethnic minority entrepreneurship. *Entrepreneurship Management* 10(2), 429–39.

Lee, J. A. B. (1994) *The Empowerment Approach to Social Work Practice: Building the Beloved Community*. New York: Columbia University Press.

Parsons, R. (1989) Empowerment for rude alternatives for low income minority girls. In A. Lee (ed.), *A Group Work Approach: In Group Work with the Poor and Oppressed*. New York: Haworth Press.

Scheyvens, R. (1999) Ecotourism and the empowerment of local communities. *Tourism Management* 20(2), 245–9.

Shaw, G. (2004) Entrepreneurial cultures and small business enterprises in tourism. In M. C. Hall and A. M. Williams (eds), *A Companion to Tourism*. Oxford: Blackwell.

Sofield, T. H. B. (2003) *Empowerment for Sustainable Tourism Development*. Amsterdam: Pergamon Press.

Zimmerman, M. A. (1990) Taking aim on empowerment research: on the distinction between psychological and individual conceptions. *American Journal of Community Psychology* 18(5), 169–77.

11 Sámi indigenous tourism empowerment in the Nordic countries through labelling systems

Strengthening ethnic enterprises and activities

Cecilia de Bernardi, Outi Kugapi and Monika Lüthje

Introduction

Tourism can have both positive and negative outcomes for indigenous Sámi communities. Indigenous tourism has been described in many studies as having negative effects for the local communities: for instance, it can exploit the natural and cultural resources and exclude the locals from the decision-making process in every area. Community-based tourism could be a solution to this kind of dilemma. The main issue is to find a positive balance between tourism and local communities, for example by introducing a label. By label we mean a set of predetermined criteria to which companies decide to adhere to gain visibility. A labelling system could empower indigenous communities, give more grounds for empowerment and benefit locals economically. It can also make the tourists, as well as the indigenous populations themselves, aware of the local culture and heritage by learning from each other. Furthermore, both parties can also learn about nature and how to respect it and not exploit it. This chapter is going to discuss different aspects of adopting labelling systems to indigenous tourism companies and other businesses and activities. With the help of labelling, tourists have the possibility to consciously choose to visit certified enterprises, which would provide them, not only with meaningful tourism experiences, but also with a story of Sámi culture told by the Sámi themselves.

The Sámi are the only indigenous population of Europe. The territory, collectively called Sápmi, is located through northern Norway, Sweden, Finland and Russia. It is not easy to estimate the numbers of the Sámi population, but it is estimated to be about 50,000, all countries included (Samer.se, n.d. (a)). The Sámi speak nine different languages. Reindeer herding is one of the main sources of sustenance, but a greater part of the Sámi population have conventional jobs (Josefsen 2007), such as tourism. In Sápmi, the main tourist attraction is nature and nature-based activities (Regional Council of Lapland 2015). According to Viken and Müller (2006), the indigenous culture is often only a minor attraction, such as for example visiting museums or taking part in small activities organised by indigenous people, not the main reason to visit Lapland. Sápmi, as an area, has adopted tourism as one of the main livelihoods, but the actual Sámi culture has not been at the centre of tourism (Viken and Müller 2006).

The Sámi have also started to create and manage tourism companies to integrate tourism with reindeer herding or other traditional livelihoods (Müller and Pettersson 2006). The activities comprising Sámi tourism can be described under the definition 'indigenous tourism'. Smith (1996) has implemented four different categories to help define the term: *habitat* (geographical settings), *heritage* (traditions), *history* (acculturation, assimilation) and *handicrafts* (tangible, marketable products), widely known as the four *H*s in indigenous tourism. They 'describe the indigenous tourism phenomenon, as a culture-bounded visitor experience' (Smith 1996: 287). These categories can help the local populations or indigenous communities to choose which way they want to participate in the tourism business and for researchers to understand indigenous tourism in all aspects (Smith 1996).

According to Hinch and Butler (1996), tourism in indigenous areas is defined as a type of tourism where members of indigenous communities participate in tourism as organisers, controlling activities held in the area, or indigenous culture is one of the pull factors in tourism in the area. There are many ways of controlling tourism in the area, and of how indigenous communities can accommodate it (Hinch and Butler 1996). Hinch and Butler (1996) also say that, for example, in certain areas indigenous culture can be visible, but actually the indigenous community has not been part of the planning, which means that it does not have control of tourism in that particular area. Nevertheless, there are tourist attractions that are moderated and operated by indigenous communities (Hinch and Butler 1996). The Sámi populations have had issues with control over tourism related to Sámi culture. For instance, symbols related to Sámi culture and customs have been used in the non-Sámi tourism industry in Norway, Sweden and Finland for many years (Müller and Pettersson 2001; Olsen 2006; Saarinen 1999). Despite the differences in the countries' tourism development related to the Sámi, in all of them the Sámi have felt irritation towards tourism. However, the Sámi have also seen it as a positive force from both a cultural and an economic point of view (Müller and Huuva 2009; Pettersson and Viken 2007; Tuulentie 2006; Viken 2006).

The Sámi have also been struggling politically. As many other indigenous populations, the Sámi have been fighting to achieve self-determination, to have more political power over territorial issues, identity issues and linguistic issues (Josefsen 2007). This has resulted in the creation of Sámi parliaments and of different Sámi-related associations in the Nordic countries, which have political power over Sámi issues (Josefsen 2007). Norway is the only country in Sápmi, which has signed the ILO-169 convention for indigenous populations (Josefsen 2007), while Sámi representatives and politicians in Sweden and Finland still fight for a signature (e.g. Sedlacek *et al.* 2014; Yle Uutiset 2015). In the context of this chapter, we propose some possible solutions, which could help the Sámi in supporting their conventional livelihood with tourism, while at the same time giving them more control over their cultural heritage.

This chapter makes a contribution to the debate relating different forms of tourism to the commoditisation of culture and empowerment of local populations. The perspective of labelling has not been examined before, to our knowledge, as a possible solution to different kinds of problems that tourism may bring, so we suggest a new way that would positively associate tourism and empowerment.

In the following sections, we will be giving an overview of the concept of ethnodevelopment to then connect it with labelling as a way to achieve empowerment in the context of Sámi tourism. Labelling is meant here as the process of adopting a set of principles that distinguish the certified companies from other companies in terms of environmental and cultural sustainability. The practical examples of a label created in the context of Sámi tourism activities and in connection with souvenirs and Sámi handicrafts will be illustrated and problematised. These examples will serve as the basis for a discussion concerning the link between ethnodevelopment in tourism, labels and empowerment. There are positive and negative sides to this connection that will be considered. The conclusion of this chapter will include recommendations for future research and for application of the labels as a practical means of ethnodevelopment.

Perspectives on ethnodevelopment and empowerment

Development can be defined as a process in which there is a growth or a change. Furthermore, development means also advancement (Cambridge English Dictionary, n.d. (a)). Stavenhagen (1986) argues for the inclusion of ethnicity in the research and debates concerning development and explains how usually nations develop based on homogeneity regarding ethnicity, culture and language. Ethnodevelopment is a reaction to this kind of nation-building ideology (Stavenhagen 1986). De Lima *et al.* (2016: 5) illustrate two approaches by Stavenhagen (1986) on the definition of ethnodevelopment: one is about an ethnic group's economic development and the other is related to the development of the ethnicity of a group. However, they also mention that these two approaches do not exclude each other (Little 2002, as mentioned in de Lima *et al.* 2016: 5). Ethnodevelopment is also defined as a way for indigenous populations to contrast appropriation and commodification of their assets both related to culture and to the environment (de Lima *et al.* 2016).

According to Chernela, ethnodevelopment is a rather new term and it has also become part of the discourse on development in the context of UNESCO (Chernela 2012). Ethnodevelopment is defined by Stavenhagen (1986) as 'the development of ethnic groups within the framework of the larger society, which may become a major issue in the development thinking, both theoretically and practically.' Chernela (2012) explains how ethnodevelopment now refers to policies and processes related to development that deal with indigenous populations. Possibly, control should be in the hands of the indigenous populations, as Hinch and Butler (1996) also argue. Davis and Partridge (1999: 2) maintain that programmes related to development are based on the 'cultural strengths of the indigenous populations or entail their active participation'.

De Lima *et al.* (2016) talk about tourism and ethnodevelopment in Brazil and mention that the Kalunga population should find ways to self-finance themselves and become economically independent. In relation to this goal, de Lima *et al.* (2016) suggest the notion of ethnic entrepreneurship, which is meant to provide long-term development for the community and continuous generation of income. De Lima *et al.* (2016) review the common definitions of ethnic entrepreneurship and mention how they refer to the connections created by immigrants with a common origin. The definitions presented by de Lima *et al.* (2016) include some form of bonding. In relation to indigenous populations, these connections and bonds are given by different elements such as the environment, religion, artefacts, territory and identity, among many others (de Lima *et al.* 2016). As previously mentioned, de Lima *et al.* (2016) define ethnodevelopment as a way for indigenous populations to exercise control over their assets. In this kind of definition, the principle of sustainability is also included as a way to strengthen the indigenous populations.

Tourism and empowerment have been connected in several articles, especially pertaining to ecotourism or community-based ecotourism ventures (e.g. de Lima *et al.* 2016; Scheyvens, 1999; Wallace and Pierce 1996). The goal of empowerment through tourism has been described as having both positive and negative outcomes for the local and indigenous populations. Wallace and Pierce (1996), for example, argued that ecotourism ventures brought some benefits, but that possibilities for career advancements and training should be offered to prevent local populations from overexploiting the area with activities such as fishing and farming. As previously mentioned, de Lima *et al.* (2016) see empowerment in the context of tourism as the result of entrepreneurship, financial aids and partnerships, which would ultimately result, in one way among others, in alternative sources of income. Empowerment is also seen as a means to exert more control over tourism development (Scheyvens 1999).

Empowerment is one of the aspects of ethnodevelopment and both are related to obtaining more diversified income and with sustainable ways to stop commoditisation. Cultural experience labelling is considered a viable way to achieve all or some of the goals for the Sámi populations in the context of tourism. This also has the potential to be applied to other indigenous populations across the world.

Labelling and certifications, what are they exactly?

Labelling in itself is the act of giving something a label (Cambridge English Dictionary, n.d. (c)), but environmental and cultural labels are not so simple. The descriptions of environmental labels are also called certifications, and in this context both will be used without distinction. D'Souza *et al.* (2007) talk about environmental labelling and the understanding that the population has of them. They explain how there are different categories of environmental labels – for example there are the ones that are sponsored by the government (D'Souza *et al.* 2007).

In addition, the authors describe three kinds of labelling. The first type deals with environmental labelling schemes involving third parties. In this first type, a set of criteria is pre-defined, and when they are met, the company receives a seal to show they have done so. The second type refers to recyclable wares and similar. The third kind is similar to the first, but this time there is an independent third-party company checking that the criteria are met (D'Souza *et al.* 2007). The European Union has also created a common label to provide for the member states' information about the environmental superiority of products; the label is a third-party scheme and voluntary (Karl and Orwat 1999). Mainly, it is concerned with issues of pollution and waste (Karl and Orwat 1999).

Related to tourism, environmental labels have been considered beneficial for hotels since it signals to the tourists that there is an environmental commitment in place (Blackman *et al.* 2014; Peiro-Signes *et al.* 2014). Environmental certifications are also perceived by hotel managers as a solution to possible 'greenwashing' (Geerts 2014). 'Greenwashing' is defined as the fact that people are made to believe that a company is working for environmental protection when it does not actually do very much in that direction (Cambridge English Dictionary, n.d. (b)).

For what concerns cultural or ethnic labels, they are not only connected to tourism. Environmental labels are also called certifications and they have different formats, but they only exist in their context. Ethnic labelling has been used to describe belonging to an ethnic group, for example in the context of Sámi Norwegian adolescents (Kvernmo and Heyerdahl 1996). However, we have not been able to find any published connection between ethnic labelling and tourism. Cultural labelling, on the other hand, is related to the intrinsic identity of a destination, which is much deeper than its services and events. Cultural labelling has been described as an integration of 'a given atmosphere, style and identity, based on a form of cultural and historical consistency that underscores the value and attractiveness of the place' in the tourist destination (Corneloup *et al.* 2016: 59). Outside of tourism, cultural labelling has been connected with 'othering' (Heikkilä 2005) and seems to hold a negative connotation (Dubois and Laborier 2003; Wood 2016).

To avoid possible misunderstanding concerning labelling, this chapter will concentrate on cultural experiences which are considered the label's main focus. They will be discussed next with a few examples.

Sápmi Experience

Related to the labelling of cultural experiences, the Sápmi Experience label was created in Sweden and is based on another label called Nature's Best. The label is related to cultural protection and ecotourism principles (Nature's Best, n.d.). It is also the focus of the current section of this chapter and about how a label concerning Sámi ecotourism was developed in Sweden.

Lordkipanidze *et al.* (2005) talk about the Swedish label 'Nature's Best' for tourist activities. It was developed by the Swedish Ecotourism Association

Figure 11.1 The Sápmi Experience label logo.

together with the Swedish Travel and Tourism Council. The main goal of this label is to make ecotourism activities more environmentally friendly to contribute to conservation and viability. The criteria of Nature's Best are also the basis for a cultural and environmental label called Sápmi Experience created by the NGO VisitSápmi. The scope of VisitSápmi is to promote the sustainable development of Sámi tourism. This also has the goal of strengthening Sámi culture (VisitSápmi, n.d. (a)[1]). The Sápmi Experience label has a symbol that the approved companies can show, as previously explained concerning the different kinds of labelling. The symbol shows the tourist that Sámi culture is being ethically presented at the certified destination. The goals of the label are to construct Sápmi in Sweden, Finland, Norway and Russia as a culturally and environmentally sustainable tourism destination. The point is to contrast the commoditisation of the Sámi culture in the context of tourism, and to promote cooperation between different companies (VisitSápmi, n.d. (c)). The criteria of the Sápmi Experience label are of three kinds, which are ethical criteria, service criteria and sustainability criteria. The first set of criteria is meant to support the Sámi culture and to be able to ethically communicate it to the world. The second set is about working with tourism in a professional way and to represent and market it correctly. The third set of criteria is about preventing negative impacts on the environment of Sápmi (VisitSápmi, n.d. (b)).

Currently, the label is not functioning. After the money and the project that drove its development and implementation ended the two main actors behind it left the supervision of the label. At that point, the label was given new leadership, but it virtually stopped operating (personal communication, 2016). The Sápmi Experience label is also featured in the latest edition of the Lonely Planet guide to Sweden (Ohlsen *et al.* 2015).

Figure 11.2 The Sámi Duodji label logo.

Sámi Duodji

The well-known handicraft trademark in Sápmi is Sámi Duodji. According to Lehtola (2006), the history of Sámi Duodji organisations varies in every country, for example in Finland it was established in 1975 with another name. The actual trademark was established in 1980 in Sweden, Norway and Finland and in 1996 in Russia, and it is the same in every country (Lehtola 2006). The juridical owner of the trademark is the Saami Council, but the right to give the licence and decide which craft producers are allowed to use the label is under different associations in each country (Sámi Duodji in Finland, Same Ätnam in Sweden, Sámiid Duodji in Norway and Cepes Sami in Russia) (Lehtola 2006).

The aims of the trademark are to show the buyer that the producer is Sámi, to protect the quality of the trademark and to show to the public that Sámi handicraft production is a living culture (Saami Council, n.d.). There are strict rules on who is allowed to use the label: one has to be Sámi and has to have either an education or excellent experience in handicrafts (Saami Council, n.d.). The products need to represent traditional handicrafts, or new products that are made using traditional methods (Saami Council, n.d.). Products that are not made for traditional use and are marked as a souvenir are not allowed to use the trademark (Saami Council, n.d.). The latter is the actual basis for Sámi handicrafts: the products have always been made for use (Ylimartimo 1999), not to put on shelves as souvenirs. When visiting a Sámi Duodji shop this fact is visible. The shop sells, for example, scarves, knives, wooden cups (*guksi*), jewellery, leather bags and other products made from leather – everything is made to have an actual use in everyday life, even though they may act as a souvenir for tourists. Although the price for Sámi Duodji products is quite high, there are still tourists who are willing to spend money to buy quality authentic and locally made products.

Current challenges and opportunities of Sámi labels in tourism

When establishing a label and then selling cultural products according to its criteria, the procedure can have a multidimensional effect on communities. In this part of the chapter, we focus on these different dimensions of the labels Sámi Duodji and Sápmi Experience. We discuss the possible implications of the labels for the tourists visiting Sápmi and their possible role in attracting potential visitors. Finally, we consider the more ethical aspects of the labels.

Products with the Sámi Duodji label can represent souvenirs for many tourists. Graburn (2005) and Edelheim (2015) mention that souvenirs themselves have always been artefacts and memoirs from holidays and events, as well as reminders of different situations. Every souvenir has a different meaning to the owner: it can be a reminder of some person or even act as a piece of art in the home. The souvenir can also be a status symbol, to show others where you have been, how you relate to life and what kind of experiences you have gained (Graburn 2005; Edelheim 2015: 215). However, is a product bought from a souvenir shop or a service bought from a tourist company actually giving empowerment to the locals? Is it a status symbol for the community member?

Often souvenirs sold at shops are cheaply made, mass-produced artefacts (Kugapi 2014; Lüthje 1995). Hitchcock argues that imported goods exploit the local culture without giving the advantage to the locals (Hitchcock, 2005). This has been visible, for example, in the Finnish souvenir market for decades (e.g. Kugapi 2014; Lüthje 1995). In addition, according to Hitchcock, the seller is responsible for the authenticity of the product. Often the buyer believes that the seller has direct contact with the producer and the culture, but most of the time this is not true (Hitchcock 2005). Furthermore, tourism companies are responsible for the images they give about the indigenous communities, but, as our experiences show, the information given to tourists is often biased, based on the fact that guides are not necessarily from the area. Luckily, the label Sápmi Experience, for example, guarantees that the information is correct, and that guides will in fact have the knowledge required about indigenous culture.

As already discussed, the souvenir industry can damage local communities by giving false images and impressions of the culture itself (Timothy 2012). Johan Edelheim also takes up this issue in his book: the inauthentic souvenir shop steals the tourist's right to re-live the experience by not selling unique products (Edelheim 2015: 222). After the holiday, a tourist may not even remember where the product was bought, because the mass-produced imported souvenirs all look the same in every corner of the world. Pietikäinen and Kelly-Holmes initiate a discussion about how labels for souvenirs function as an advertisement for the place as well as differentiate the location from others (Pietikäinen and Kelly-Holmes 2011), which can also empower the locals by offering opportunities for earning extra income. Many museums in Sápmi have their lobby shops, where they sell handmade products made by local producers – the names of the craftspeople are visible for the tourists. When buying a product with a label, especially when seeing a craftsperson's name on the label, the buyer does not only get satisfaction from the product, but also may feel pleasure because s/he has given economic support to the local craftsperson. In recent years, handicrafts have been seen as a solution to combat migration, the loss of business investments and services (Dlaske 2014), and have now started to become visible in shops. Furthermore, when visiting a place with the Sápmi Experience label (if the tourists are informed what the Sápmi Experience label stands for), tourists can trust that the product is authentic and that the economic input brought to the company remains in the area.

Currently, the Sámi Council is conducting research into the potential need for establishing another trademark alongside Sámi Duodji, which would be offered to people who are Sámi themselves, but not making handicrafts under the Sámi Duodji trademark (Torikka 2016). The products could be more artistic and not based on traditional patterns, but still the products would be made by locals, members of the indigenous community and the new trademark would show the authenticity of the product (Torikka 2016). Often the Sámi Duodji label has served as a good stepping-stone for the craftsperson's own career. However, if the craftsperson's wish is to be more creative and use modern styles alongside the traditional ones, the only solution has been to establish and manage a new trademark (Dlaske 2014). The good thing is that there is a space and need for both. Products made under the traditional Sámi Duodji label will show the traditions and history of the Sámi people, and the others – the own labels of craftspeople – show that it is not a dead culture; instead, it is a living culture. The idea of the new trademark is actually to show tourists that there are other options to imported products, and – little by little – make the imported goods less visible in souvenir shops (Torikka 2016). Nowadays, tourists are more culturally aware and are willing to spend more money if the product or service is actually made or provided locally. If there is no label, how can the tourist actually know the locality of the handicraft or service? Therefore, to make tourists more aware and to prove authenticity, there is a need for different labels.

Some challenges in the labelling process are, of course, that those who cannot or will not participate in the label risk being excluded. The exclusion can be related, for example, to the definition of a member of the Sámi community, which varies slightly in every country, but which is, in all cases, based on language or on provable family ties to the Sámi community (Samediggi, n.d.; Samer.se, n.d. (b)). This excludes those who consider themselves Sámi but who have lost the language and cannot prove their belonging. However, the label should be developed to be as inclusive as possible. It is important that the Sámi benefit from the label but it is also important to promote cooperation. The label should be designed, then, to include all parties that can respect and promote Sámi culture and the environment, but with particular attention to the fact that the certified companies are locally owned and operated. This is to make sure that the tourism income remains in the areas where the Sámi live and operate. All these actions are needed in order to ensure sustainable tourism in indigenous areas. The Sápmi Experience label does not, in fact, explicitly mention that the certified companies need to be run by members of the Sámi community, but only that Sámi culture should be respected (VisitSápmi, n.d. (b)). This discussion is not meant to suggest that all members of the Sámi population should be part of the labelling project. For example, reindeer herding is the only source of income for many of the Sámi population and it does not need to be integrated if not needed or wanted. On the other hand, as previously mentioned, the labelling process should be as inclusive as possible for those who want to participate, since the Sámi are the rightful owners of their culture, and it can be a concern for them how it is labelled.

Conclusion

In the previous sections of this chapter, we have considered the concept of ethnodevelopment, and how labelling in the context of tourism can be a way for the Sámi to achieve control over the use of their cultural symbols in tourism and engage in an alternative livelihood, while at the same time applying sustainable practices to the development of their tourist enterprises.

The discussion on ethnodevelopment has shown how it is a concept related to ethnicity, culture and empowerment. More closely, ethnodevelopment is related to cultural development and contrasts with commodification. Ethnodevelopment should also translate into self-financing for indigenous populations. Labels can provide the tools for creating tourist activities that are based on the principles of sustainable development, for instance by adopting a label that is similar to the previously described Swedish Nature's Best. These principles would also ensure that the Sámi culture is represented in a respectful way, making it a source of pride while at the same time avoiding commoditisation.

Labels have the potential to create a favourable situation for the Sámi and other indigenous populations. The product (either tourist or handicraft) receives a label and therefore it gains a certain uniqueness. This uniqueness can be a way for tourists to be more willing to purchase the product and the extra income – that derives from the sale of tourism products – is one step towards alternative livelihoods and a source of empowerment for the indigenous populations adopting the label. At the same time, the label can also be a way for the tourists to know that their purchases are supporting the indigenous population they are visiting. This could make the standard souvenirs less attractive. Most of all, the labelling process, as one side of ethnodevelopment, would make people more aware of the only indigenous population in the EU. The source of empowerment, then, is both related to control over one's culture and income and to cultural preservation.

This chapter has suggested a new path to ethnodevelopment through economic stability and cultural preservation as empowerment tools. At this stage, this discussion is meant as a suggestion for further research. The only existing label of this kind, Sápmi Experience, should be further developed and spread to other countries in Sápmi. It would then be possible to start measuring its wider effects. Sápmi Experience is featured in the Lonely Planet Sweden guide so further research can be conducted into its potential effects on Sámi perception of their own culture and on the tourists' perception of Sámi culture, among others. Also, the development of the new trademark alongside the Sámi Duodji – the labelling process, impacts on craftspeople and the concrete effects of the labels, among others – will definitely be worth researching.

Note

1. The website VisitSápmi has not renewed its certificate so some operating systems may block it as unsafe but by adding a security exception it is possible to access the content.

References

Blackman, A., Naranjo, M. A., Robalino, J., Alpízar, F. and Rivera, J. (2014) Does tourism eco-certification pay? Costa Rica's blue flag program. *World Development* 58, 41–52.

Cambridge English Dictionary (n.d. (a)), *Development Meaning*. Available online: http://dictionary.cambridge.org/dictionary/english/development (accessed 11 August 2016).

Cambridge English Dictionary (n.d. (b)) *Greenwash Meaning*. Available online: http://dictionary.cambridge.org/dictionary/english/greenwash (accessed 3 September 2016).

Cambridge English Dictionary (n.d. (c)) *Labelling Meaning*. Available online: http://dictionary.cambridge.org/dictionary/english/labelling (accessed 3 September 2016).

Chernela, J. M. (2012) Indigenous rights and ethno-development: the life of an Indigenous organization in the Rio Negro of Brazil. *Tipití Journal of the Society for the Anthropology of Lowland South America* 9(2), 92–120.

Corneloup, J., Bourdeau, P. and Mao, P. (2016) Culture, a factor for recreation emergence and creativity. In J. C. Dissart and J. Dehez (eds), *Tourism, Recreation and Regional Development: Perspectives from France and Abroad*. New York: Routledge, pp. 47–60.

D'Souza, C., Taghian, M., Lamb, P. and Peretiatko, R. (2007) Green decisions: demographics and consumer understanding of environmental labels. *International Journal of Consumer Studies* 31(4), 371–6.

Davis, S. and Partridge, W. (1999) Promoting the development of Indigenous peoples in Latin America. *Finance and Development* 31(31), 38–40.

de Lima, I. B., Kumble, P. A., de Almeida, M. G., Chaveiro, E. F., Ferreira, L. C. G. and Mota, R. D. (2016) Ecotourism community enterprises and ethnodevelopment: modelling the Kalunga empowerment possibilities in the Brazilian savannah. *Brazilian Journal of Science and Technology* 3(1), 1–25.

Dlaske, K. (2014) Semiotics of pride and profit: interrogating commodification in Indigenous handicraft production. *Social Semiotics* 24(5), 582–98.

Dubois, V. and Laborier, P. (2003) The 'social' in the institutionalisation of local cultural policies in France and Germany. *International Journal of Cultural Policy* 9(2), 195–206.

Edelheim, J. R. (2015) *Tourist Attractions. From Object to Narrative*. Bristol: Channel View Publications.

Geerts, W. (2014) Environmental certification schemes: hotel managers' views and perceptions. *International Journal of Hospitality Management* 39, 87–96.

Graburn, N. H. H. (2005) Foreword. In M. Hitchcock and K. Teague (eds), *Souvenirs: The Material Culture of Tourism*. Aldershot: Ashgate, pp. xii–xvii.

Heikkilä, E. (2005) Mobile vulnerabilities: perspectives on the vulnerabilities of immigrants in the Finnish labour market. *Population, Space and Place* 11(6), 485–97.

Hinch, T. and Butler, R. (1996) Indigenous tourism: a common ground for discussion. In R. Butler and T. Hinch (eds), *Tourism and Indigenous Peoples*. London: International Thomson, pp. 3–19.

Hitchcock, M. (2005, Introduction. In M. Hitchcock and K. Teague (eds), *Souvenirs: The Material Culture of Tourism*. Aldershot: Ashgate, pp. 1–17.

Josefsen, E. (2007) The Saami and the national parliaments. Channels for political influence. *Gáldu Čála. Journal of Indigenous Peoples Rights* 2. Available online: http://www.galdu.org/govat/doc/national_parlaments.pdf.

Karl, H. and Orwat, C. (1999) Environmental labelling in Europe: European and national tasks. *Environmental Policy and Governance* 9(5), 212–20.

Kugapi, O. (2014) Se on sydämen asia se saamenkäsityö. Matkailun vaikutukset saamelaiseen käsityökulttuuriin ja kulttuuri-identiteettiin, Master's thesis, University of Lapland, Rovaniemi.

Kvernmo, S. E. and Heyerdahl, S. (1996) Ethnic identity in aboriginal Sami adolescents: the impact of the family and the ethnic community context. *Journal of Adolescence* 19(5), 453–63.

Lehtola, J. (2006) *30 vuotta käsityö sydämellä. Sámi Duodji ry. 1975–2005*. Inari: Kustannus-Puntsi.

Lordkipanidze, M., Brezet, H., and Backman, M. (2005) The entrepreneurship factor in sustainable tourism development, *Journal of Cleaner Production* 13(8), 787–98.

Lüthje, M. (1995) *Matkailun vaikutukset saamelaisalueella: näkökulmana alueen kantokyky ja saamelainen kulttuuri*. University of Helsinki, EKT-serie 973.

Müller, D. K. and Huuva, S. K. (2009) Limits to Sami tourism development: the case of Jokkmokk, Sweden. *Journal of Ecotourism* 8(2), 115–27.

Müller, D. K. and Pettersson, R. (2001) Access to Sami Tourism in Northern Sweden. *Scandinavian Journal of Hospitality and Tourism* 1(1), 5–18.

Müller, D. K. and Pettersson, R. (2006) Sámi Heritage at the Winter Festival in Jokkmokk, Sweden. *Scandinavian Journal of Hospitality and Tourism* 6(1), 54–69.

Nature's Best (n.d.) *Six Basic Principles*. Available online: http://www.naturesbestsweden.com/nb/grundprinciper.asp (accessed 3 September 2016).

Ohlsen, B., Kaminski, A. and Quintero, J. (2015) *Sweden*, 6th edn. Victoria: Footscray.

Olsen, K. (2006) Making differences in a changing world: the Norwegian Sámi in the tourist industry. *Scandinavian Journal of Hospitality and Tourism* 6(1), 37–53.

Peiro-Signes, A., Segarra-Ona, M.-d.-V., Verma, R., Mondejar-Jimenez, J. and Vargas-Vargas, M. (2014) The impact of environmental certification on hotel guest ratings. *Cornell Hospitality Quarterly* 55(1), 40–51.

Pettersson, R. and Viken, A. (2007) Sami perspectives on Indigenous tourism in Northern Europe: commerce or cultural development? In R. Butler and T. Hinch (eds), *Tourism and Indigenous Peoples: Issues and Implications*. Oxford: Elsevier, pp. 176–87.

Pietikäinen, S. and Kelly-Holmes, H. (2011) The local political economy of languages in a Sámi tourism destination: authenticity and mobility in the labelling of souvenirs. *Journal of Sociolinguistics* 15(3), 323–46.

Regional Council of Lapland (2015) *Lapin matkailustrategia 2015–2018* (*Tourism strategy of Lapland*). Available online: http://www.lappi.fi/lapinliitto/c/document_library/get_file?folderId=2265071andname=DLFE-25498.pdf.

Saami Council (n.d.) The Sámi Duodji certificate. Available online: http://www.saamicouncil.net/en/organization/ossodagat/kulturossodat/sami-duodji-certificate/ (accesed 20 August 2016).

Saarinen, J. (1999) Representation of indigeneity: Sámi culture in the discourses of tourism. in J. N. Brown and P. M. Sant (eds), *Indigeneity: Construction and Re/Presentation*. New York: Nova Science, pp. 231–49.

Samediggi (n.d.) *Saamelaiskäräjät – The Sámi*. Available online: http://www.samediggi.fi/index.php?option=com_contentandtask=blogcategoryandid=105andItemid=167andlang=english (accessed 3 September 2016).

Samer.se (n.d. (a)) *Samerna i siffror*. Available online: 3 September 2016: http://www.samer.se/1536 (accessed 3 September 2016).

Samer.se (n.d. (b)) *Who Is a Sami?* Available online: http://samer.se/453 (accessed 3 September 2016).

Scheyvens, R. (1999) Ecotourism and the empowerment of local communities. *Tourism Management* 20(2), 245–90.

Sedlacek, P., Festin Stenlund, C. and Westerberg, A. (2014) Ratificera ILO 169. *Västerbottens-Kuriren*. Available online: http://www.vk.se/1139232/ratificera-ilo-169 (accessed 3 September 2016).

Smith, V. (1996) Indigenous tourism: the four Hs. In R. Butler and T. Hinch (eds), *Tourism and Indigenous Peoples*. London: Thomson International, pp. 283–307.

Stavenhagen, R. (1986) Ethnodevelopment: a neglected dimension in development thinking. In R. J. Apthorpe and A. Kráhl (eds), *Development Studies: Critique and Renewal*. Leiden: E. J. Brill, pp. 71–94.

Timothy, D. J. (2012) Destination communities and responsible tourism. In D. Leslie (ed.), *Responsible Tourism: Concepts, Theory and Practice*. Wallingford: CABI, pp. 72–81.

Torikka, X. (2016) *Apuneuvoja saamelaistuotteista kiinnostuneille turisteille – Tulevaisuudessa kaksi erillistä tavaramerkkiä*. Yle. Available online: http://yle.fi/uutiset/apuneuvoja_saamelaistuotteista_kiinnostuneille_turisteille__tulevaisuudessa_kaksi_erillista_tavaramerkkia/9122732 (accessed 30 August 2016).

Tuulentie, S. (2006) The dialectic of identities in the field of tourism. The discourses of the indigenous Sámi in defining their own and the tourists' identities. *Scandinavian Journal of Hospitality and Tourism* 6(1), 25–36.

Viken, A. (2006) Tourism and Sámi identity – an analysis of the tourism-identity nexus in a Sámi community. *Scandinavian Journal of Hospitality and Tourism* 6(1), 7–24.

Viken, A. and Müller, D. (2006), Introduction: tourism and the Sámi. *Scandinavian Journal of Hospitality and Tourism* 6(1), 1–6.

VisitSápmi (n.d. (a)) *Information om Samisk turism och kultur*. Available online: https://www.visitsapmi.org/om-oss.html (accessed 3 September 2016).

VisitSápmi (n.d. (b)) Kriterierna. Available online: https://www.visitsapmi.org/kriterierna.html (accessed 3 September 2016).

VisitSápmi (n.d. (c)) *Visitsápmi information om Samiska Upplevelser som är ekoturism*. Available online: https://www.visitsapmi.org/s-pmi-experience.html (accessed 3 September 2016)

Wallace, G. N. and Pierce, S. M. (1996) An evaluation of ecotourism in Amazonas, Brazil. *Annals of Tourism Research* 23(4), 843–73.

Wood, G. (2016) Beyond colonialism: continuity, change and the modern development project. *Canadian Journal of Development Studies/Revue Canadienne d'études du Développement*, pp. 1–19.

Yle Uutiset (2015) *Sámi Activists Speak Out at Independence Ball*. Available online: http://yle.fi/uutiset/sami_activists_speak_out_at_independence_ball/8510683 (accessed 3 September 2016).

Ylimartimo, S. (1999) Selviämispeliä, statusta ja silmäniloa. in K.-R. Helminen and S. Miettinen (eds), *Käsityöläisen kirja*, Meri-Lappi Institute Proceedings No. 2. Kemi, pp. 6–15.

Part III

Empowerment Approaches in Ethnic Tourism

Issues of Authenticity, Cultural Commodification and Gender

12 Exotic tourists, ethnic hosts

A critical approach to tourism and ethnodevelopment

Tuhina Ganguly and Mike Grimshaw

Introduction

This chapter situates itself within scholarly studies on the commodification of the Other in ethnic tourism. Where ethnic minorities are marketed by governments and the tourism industry specifically for their exotic appeal, issues are bound to arise around cultural consumption and asymmetrical relations in host–guest interactions. Based on the first author's auto-ethnographic record of a trip to Cuzco and Machu Picchu in Peru, this chapter focuses on ethnodevelopment in the context of the Quechua-speaking indigenous people. However, previous studies on commodification of the Other have been primarily contextualised within the binary of white, Western tourists and exotic, non-white hosts. This represents a glaring gap in existing tourism studies since middle-class tourists from 'exotic' countries like India are increasingly travelling to far-off destinations due to their enhanced consumption power. This chapter addresses the gap in existing literature by examining the engagements between the first author, an Indian outbound tourist to Peru, and the indigenous hosts. It shows that commodification of the ethnic hosts is perpetrated by both Western and non-Western tourists (the first author) even as the latter is treated as the 'exotic Other' by her Western fellow-tourists. Drawing on some insights from postcolonial theory, this chapter makes a case for tourism studies to undertake a detailed examination of the dynamics between tourists and hosts, particularly indigenous women, where such interactions are clearly transgressing the white tourist/non-white host binary. These new developments have important ramifications for determining host agency and self-determination, and for addressing cultural consumption within changing tourism scenarios.

Modern tourism is often characterised by the desire for the Other – to see, experience and encounter other peoples and places. The high level of tourist traffic from developed to developing countries is testament to the historical, socio-political and economic asymmetries within which modern, mass tourism necessarily operates – and indeed thrives. Academic literature on ethnic tourism has discussed the production and projection of entire groups of people and their lifestyles as grist to the tourist mill. Thus, in *Hosts and Guests*, Smith defined ethnic tourism as tourism, 'marketed to the public in terms of the "quaint" customs of indigenous and often exotic peoples' (Smith 1977: 2). The entry on 'Ethnic Tourism' in the *Encyclopedia of Tourism* describes ethnic tourism 'as a form of tourism in which the prime motivation of the tourist involves a desire to experience and interact with exotic ethnic peoples' (Oakes 2000: 204). In ethnic tourism, the exotic hosts 'themselves are the primary, or at least a significant, attraction. In ethnic tourism, the "native" is not simply "there" to provide services; he is an integral part of the exotic spectacle, an actor whose "quaint" behaviour, dress and artefacts are themselves significant attractants' (van den Berghe 1980: 377).

It is, therefore, not uncommon to see the promotion of certain ethnic or indigenous groups by governments and the tourism industry as international tourist attractions. For example, the Tuva minority group in China is an important 'must-see' for tourists going to the Kanas Scenic Area (Yang *et al.* 2013); the Maasai of Kenya have long been an object of tourist fascination (Bruner 2005); the Maori people are a central feature of New Zealand's tourism campaigns (Amoamo 2007); and, as concerns this chapter, in Peru, the Quechua-speaking *indígenas* are marketed as symbols of ancient heritage to tourists (Knight and Cottrell 2016).

Given the marketing of certain groups of people as tourist attractions, there emerge issues of commodification of the Other which need to be examined in terms of its ramifications for ethnodevelopment through tourism. Is ethnodevelopment truly possible in the face of asymmetrical relations between hosts and tourists? We must also be cognisant of the asymmetrical relations between governments and tourism agencies and those people marketed as a tourist attraction. Further, in studies of ethnic tourism, the tourist primarily refers to the white, Western (male) tourist. The host–guest binary undergirding ethnic tourism is thus the binary of non-white, exotic hosts and white, Western tourists. Retrospectively analysing the travel of the first author, an Indian middle-class woman, to Cuzco, Peru, this chapter aims to complicate precisely such a binary by focusing on outbound tourist(s) from non-Western countries engaging in ethnic tourism in other exotic tourist destinations. Admittedly, an auto-ethnographic approach means that the contextual range of this chapter is limited. Looking back at Ganguly's trip, however, we believe that some questions and issues arising out of it can be asked in the context of other works as well concerning postcolonial tourists to other countries. This chapter seeks to address the gap in current tourism studies literature regarding the minimal work on outbound tourists from developing countries to other countries. We ask, what are the ramifications of an expanding global middle class on ethnodevelopment? If the tourist is herself from a developing country, does this make her more reflexive about her touristic encounter with the ethnic host? Or are exotic tourists themselves objectified by fellow-tourists while also guilty of commodifying the ethnic host?

These questions and issues run through the length and breadth of this chapter. We will begin with an overview of auto-ethnography as a well-recognised method in anthropology. This section will also situate the first author Ganguly within the Indian middle classes to provide a background to her travels to Peru. The second section will look at the broader issues of commodification in ethnic tourism and their impact on ethnodevelopment. Thereafter, we will discuss tourism and ethnodevelopment in the specific context of Cuzco. With this discussion in mind, the next section will discuss Ganguly's travel experience. The following section will analyse and critique her touristic consumption of the indigenous women of Peru. Lastly, the conclusion will sum up the main arguments and also offer some suggestions for future research. In examining the issues briefly outlined here, we seek to contribute to the overall concerns of this book, namely the ways in which tourism advances or limits ethnic development.

Auto-ethnography as method

Auto-ethnography emerged with the postmodern, 'self-reflexive turn' in anthropology in the 1980s. Countering the trend to simply observe, report and analyse the research subjects, the postmodern turn appreciated the complex nature of the anthropological subject matter (Ellis *et al.* 2011). Seminal texts such as Clifford and Marcus's *Writing Culture: The Poetics and Politics of Ethnography* (1986), Crapanzano's *Tuhami: Portrait of a Moroccan* (1980) and Rabinow's *Reflections on Fieldwork in Morocco* (1977) challenged the objectivist and universalist cannon in order to portray the complex, particularist nature of the subject at hand. Central to this was the recognition that the anthropologist was not simply an observer but a participant in the research such that his/her very presence changed the nature of interactions in the field. Auto-ethnography required the researcher to critically reflect on their own experiences, emotions and actions in the field, which in turn reflected on the researcher's socio-political and economic location vis-à-vis that of the research participants.

However, it is not as if earlier anthropologists had been unmindful of their experiences and emotions in the field. Malinowski's personal diaries in which he recorded his perceptions of and frustrations with the Trobrianders is a case in point. Yet, Malinowski's final monograph was a sanitised, 'objective' portrait of the Trobriand people, containing little of the personal contents that his diary was privy to. In contrast, auto-ethnography necessitated situating the ethnographer – prejudices, warts and all – in the final text such that the researcher too would be subject to scrutiny by himself/herself and the audience. Thus, citing Ellis and Bochner (2000), Ellis *et al.* argue that auto-ethnography sought to produce, 'meaningful, accessible, and evocative research grounded in personal experience, research that would sensitise readers to issues of identity politics, to experiences shrouded in silence, and to forms of representation that deepen our capacity to empathise with people who are different from us' (2011: 274).

Auto-ethnography has not been without its critiques. Critics have pointed out that it could lead to 'navel gazing' on the part of the researcher (Jarvie 1988). More recently, Anderson has argued that the auto-ethnographic approach is limited insofar as not all our research at all times is 'intertwined with our personal lives' (2006: 390). Moreover, he argues, 'Sociological inquiry must not be solely directed toward our own biographical involvements' (ibid.). Nonetheless as Erik Cohen points out in his auto-ethnographic essay on the 2011 Bangkok floods, auto-ethnography as a research method is contentious but not without merit (2012). He writes, 'there are situations outside the research context which may call for auto-ethnography, particularly those in which a researcher is caught serendipitously in a dramatic event, which he/she is able to enlighten in an auto-ethnographic essay, though he/she had not studied it systematically' (Cohen 2012: 317). Although Ganguly did not get caught in a dramatic event, nor was it serendipitous in that she deliberately chose to travel to Peru, yet, given the rather limited work on postcolonial or Third World outbound tourists, we believe this auto-ethnographic study has the potential to ask questions that can be taken up more systematically in future studies. Her self-experience as a visitor to Peru and critical examination of touristic encounters between herself, the hosts and fellow-tourists serves to highlight issues of ethnic commodification sustained by exotic otherness in the context of indigenous Peruvians and outbound tourists from developing countries, a context which still suffers from a lack of substantial academic examination despite the fact that tourism 'is the new must-have consumer product not only in the developed world, but increasingly among those with the means to buy it in the developing world' (Page 2011: 340).

India is predicted to account for 50 million outbound tourists by 2020 (UNWTO). The number of Indian outbound tourists increased from 1.94 million in 1991 to 14.92 million in 2012 (Government of India 2012). The most favoured destinations for Indian tourists in 2011, according to the India tourism statistics report, were 'Saudi Arabia, Thailand, Singapore, Kuwait and Malaysia. While in 2010, the top 5 destination countries were Singapore, Kuwait, Thailand, Malaysia and USA' (81). Compared to the high number of Indian outbound tourists received by some of the top five destinations in 2011 like Saudi Arabia (1,501,308), Thailand (891,748) and Singapore (868,991), Peru received only 3,471 (ibid.). Although not a major tourist destination for Indian outbound tourists, Indian arrivals in Peru have demonstrated a '12 percent year-on-year growth' (Peruthisweek.com 2014). Considering the long distance and high cost of travelling to Peru, this is not an insignificant figure, for it points to the consumerist aspirations of those Indian tourists who can afford to and are willing to travel as far as Peru.

In 2011, out of the 3,471 Indian outbound tourists to Peru, Ganguly was one. She went to Lima to participate in an academic social sciences workshop from 19 to 29 April. Once the workshop was over, she travelled to Cuzco to visit Machu Picchu. The Cuzco and Machu Picchu trips were self-sponsored. Ganguly is an upper-caste, middle-class, urban woman from Delhi. Born to highly educated parents, both service class professionals, she completed her MA and MPhil in Sociology from Delhi University. The fact that she could pursue higher education was largely owing to her middle-class background, giving her access to the economic, social and cultural resources necessary for making it to university for postgraduate degrees. A 2014 report by the British Council, *Understanding India: The Future of Higher Education and Opportunities for International Cooperation* points out the middle-class character of higher education stating that, 'Higher education in India is undergoing considerable change … India's young population has a huge appetite for education and as the growth in the size of the middle classes escalates, millions are increasingly able to pay for it' (2014: 8). The postgraduate population of India, within which we must situate Ganguly, represents a small albeit highly visible and mobile section of the total population, with the resources to participate in the 'world culture' (Hannerz 1990) of consumerism including touristic consumption. Certainly, in the years to come, the number of middle-class outbound tourists from developing countries will form a significant percentage of tourists engaging in practices of ethnic tourism, presenting a rich avenue for further research.

Ethnic commodification in tourism

In the next section, we will specifically look at tourism in Cuzco, pointing to the emergence and limits of ethnodevelopment in the Andean context. However, before that, it is worthwhile to consider more broadly the issue of commodification in ethnic tourism and its impact on ethnodevelopment.

The commodification of particular peoples and cultures has been an area of focus in several studies concerning ethnic tourism, as also tourism in general (Ateljevic and Doorne 2003; MacCannell 1973; Mbaiwa 2011). Cohen states: 'Commodification of culture has been used to describe a process by which things come to be evaluated primarily in terms of their exchange value, in a context of trade, thereby becoming goods' (1988); or as Mbaiwa states: 'In tourism, the packaging of cultural activities and artefacts for the tourist market is known as the commodification of culture' (2011: 292). In other words, aspects of indigenous culture are showcased, reinvented and often modified for the gratification of tourists, forming an important part of the latter's total touristic experience. The commodification and consumption of peoples and their cultural practices is inextricably linked with the issue of authenticity, for touristic consumption of people and their cultural practices are said to lead to the production of 'fake' practices or the reinvention of practices for the sole purpose of their presentation to tourists (MacCannell 1973; Picard 1997). Proponents of the cultural erosion argument argue that 'While tourism may promote a renewed interest in traditional arts and social practices among local craftsmen and others, tourist purchases are fuelled by a desire to possess a mark, rather than any genuine interest in local cultural traditions or beliefs' (Shepherd 2002: 185). Thus touristic commodification of cultures and ethnicity is argued to both thrive on and lead to a distancing from the 'original' source of meaning for the locals.

However, more recent studies have challenged this view on the grounds that not only can tourism provide the means of social and economic empowerment to the host communities but also that culture is not static, and therefore trying to discern what qualifies as authentic cultural practices is a futile exercise (Cole 2007; Ryan 2005; Shepherd 2002; Stronza 2001). In this view, the preservation and reinvention of certain cultural practices for the benefit of tourists is also seen as making a positive contribution to the hosts' sense of self-worth and strengthening their ethnic identity, giving them greater agency vis-à-vis majority groups in their own country. Thus indigenous and/or ethnic tourism 'is increasingly viewed not simply as a force for the creation of a stereotypical image of a marginalised people, but a means by which those peoples aspire to economic and political power for self-advancement and as a place of dialogue between and within differing world views' (Ryan 2005: 4). As we shall discuss in the next section, tourism in and around Cuzco has led to improvements in the economic and social conditions of indigenous hosts in some regions. In other countries too, such as Ecuador, community-based ethnic tourism has led to significant improvements in the lifestyle and aspirational ideals of hosts (Ruiz-Ballesteros and Hernández-Ramírez 2010). Similar findings are noted in the case of two villages in Ngadha in Indonesia where hosts have economically benefited from tourism as well as fostered a strong sense of ethnic identity in presenting themselves as a coherent ethnic group to tourists (Cole 2007). In both the Ecuadorian and Indonesian cases, the transformation of cultural practices and traditions into tourist objects has in fact led to greater ethnic cohesion and self-worth among the host communities. These case studies make a clear case in favour of understanding the positive impact that tourism may have on ethnic development.

Having said that, more often than not, as also discussed in this chapter, it is the economically and socially marginalised people of a country and their cultural practices which are offered to tourists as 'ethnic objects' (Cohen 1989; Oakes 1998; Yang and Wall 2009). Not only in developing countries but also in developed countries such as Canada (Cassel and Maureira 2015), it is the most marginalised people of those countries who have historically been discriminated against that serve as hosts in the context of ethnic tourism. In the face of poverty and very limited social capital, tourism often provides them with the only means of improving their condition. Yet, clearly, ethnic tourism thrives on this already established inequality, for without the existence of the most marginalised there would be no ethnic tourism. Therefore, instead of approaching ethnic tourism and ethnodevelopment simply through a 'negative' versus 'positive' impact of tourism approach, it is necessary to situate the ethnic hosts vis-à-vis the tourists in order to understand the former's relational position in the wider tourism market. The following sections aim to locate the Peruvian indigenous hosts vis-à-vis the first author and analyse the implications of their interactions.

Cuzco, tourism and ethnodevelopment

The Andean city of Cuzco has emerged as one of the top tourist destinations in Peru. Situated at an altitude of 3,400 metres above sea level in the beautiful Andean mountain range, it is a major international tourist spot, a UNESCO World Heritage Site and a space of national heritage. As van den Berghe and Ochoa (2000) rightly argue, Cuzco has emerged as the face of a romanticised, mythicised 'lost' civilisation – the Tawantinsuyu popularly known as the 'Incas'. The city of Cuzco is testament to the Inca Past and subsequently the Spanish Conquest. The contestations between the Incas and the Spanish are more than evident in the architecture of the city where Spanish constructions are clearly superimposed over Inca masonry in the same monument such as in Qoricancha – the Inca temple of the sun and a convent of Santo Domingo for the Spanish conquistadores. The various monuments in Cuzco reflecting *incanismo*, that is pride in the Inca past (ibid.) make the city a popular draw for tourists who wish to explore the pre-Colombian history of Peru.

Cuzco entered the international tourist map, most importantly, because of its location as the 'gateway' to Machu Picchu, one of the most famous Inca sites popularised by the 'discovery' of Machu Picchu by a Yale University expedition in 1911 led by Hiram Bingham. Better air and rail connectivity to Cuzco, and better means of transport between Cuzco and Machu Picchu since the 1960s, has led to burgeoning tourist numbers to Cuzco (van den Berghe and Ochoa 2000). Along with the Inca ruins, tourism in Cuzco and the surrounding areas involves one more attraction, that is the *indígenas* who are monolingual speakers of Quechua.

The *indígenas* are everywhere in Cuzco and in the surrounding tourist sites such as Sacsayhuaman, Pisac and Chinchero. Some of the indigenous women dress in colourful clothes to pose for tourists. For instance, in the Pisac handicrafts market, tourists inevitably encounter the indigenous women, the *sacamefotos*, literally 'take-my-photo women' (Ypeij 2012: 18). These women, usually from the surrounding areas, are 'colourfully dressed … often with children by their sides, small goats in their arms, or llamas on the end of their ropes. These sacamefotos approach tourists and invite them to take their pictures in return for tips' (Ypeij 2012: 22). Similarly, in the village of Chinchero, indigenous women demonstrate traditional ways of weaving and dyeing to groups of tourists in small weaving centres. The indigenous men and women constitute modern representations of the performance of seemingly 'authentic' *incanismo* for tourists looking for 'exotic experiences – something to write home about' (van den Berghe 1980: 379).

Some of the earlier studies on ethnic tourism in Peru point to the economic and political asymmetries between the *indígenas* and international tourists. As van den Berghe (1980) argues, tourists to Cuzco are privileged consumers for whom the indigenous host 'is so poor and so downtrodden under centuries of mestizo domination, that he can be gawked at for little cost and with little overt opposition. He is, in short, authentic: a bona fide downtrodden Third World peasant in colourful costume. What more can the tourist ask for?' (385). Despite his critique of touristic commodification of the *indígenas*, van den Berghe (ibid.) points out that the indigenous hosts are not necessarily hapless victims. Rather, they seek to make the most of the tourist encounter by manipulating tourists to pay more for their wares than the local rate.

Recent studies have focused on the economic and social benefits accruing to the indigenous people through tourism. These studies have looked at the ways in which tourism has contributed to better economic conditions, changes in gender norms and greater self-worth for the *indígenas*. In the case of the *sacamefotos*, Ypeij (2012) notes that although the women posing for tourists earn only a few sols a day (one or two US dollars), this meagre income is crucial to their families' survival and everyday needs. On a similar note, Simon (2009) points out that the tourism industry is crucial to the lives of indigenous people facing a shortage of good agricultural land. In such situations, producing commodities for tourists and indeed commodifying themselves as tourist souvenirs appear as a viable alternative to many. Improvement in economic conditions is especially visible in community-based tourism where 'Rural communities located along major tourism corridors (e.g., between Cuzco and Machu Picchu) have become a focal point of tourism-based poverty alleviation efforts, with myriad institutions from the public, private, and voluntary sectors working with community tourism associations to encourage increased local involvement in tourism enterprise and entrepreneurship' (Knight and Cottrell 2016: 33). In his study of indigenous communities in four villages within an hour and a half's drive from Cuzco, Knight (n.d.) reports that community-based tourism initiatives and government funding through tourism taxes and visitor fees have led to improvement of local infrastructure including building clinics, libraries, soccer fields and bathrooms.

In addition to better economic conditions, scholars have pointed out the ways in which participating in the tourism industry has augmented the *indígenas*' self-worth, especially in the case of women. For example, Babb (2012) argues that the demonstration and marketing of native Indian-ness by indigenous women can become a form of cultural capital, giving them greater social standing within their community and families. Women weavers of Chinchero, according to Ypeij (2012), have emerged as chief economic generators for their families and may even earn more than their husbands. Their husbands, in turn, have started participating more actively in household chores. Thus tourism has helped in redefining gender norms among some indigenous communities in and around Cuzco.

These studies clearly show the positive impact of tourism on ethnic communities. However, the studies are also emphatic in pointing to the continuing commodification of the indigenous people. As Babb (2012), van den Berghe (1980) and Ypeij (2012) indicate, it is precisely the objectification of 'authentic' traditionalism in the figure of the indigenous woman that sells in the tourism market. Although the *indígenas* have reinvented their traditions for touristic consumption and have some agency to negotiate with tourists, the fact remains that they are still exotic commodities in the global tourism landscape underscored by economic and political asymmetries. With people from developing countries such as India entering the ranks of the expanding global middle class, what, if any, new developments are taking place as regards the interactions between hosts and tourists? It is this question we turn to address in the following sections.

Recounting the trip to Cuzco

In 2011 when Ganguly travelled to Peru, buying into the tourism discourse of the magical allure of Machu Picchu, she decided that her trip to Peru would be incomplete without a visit to the World Heritage Sites of Machu Picchu and Cuzco. Although quite ignorant of the indigenous Quechua people, browsing through the internet, she had seen photographs of Quechua women in their bright regalia with llamas. These images stayed with her as she prepared for her trip to

Cuzco. She booked a tour package with a tourist agent in her hotel in Lima who arranged her flight to and accommodation in Cuzco and the much awaited connecting trip to Machu Picchu. Ganguly's itinerary represented a fairly typical tourist route involving: *Day 1:* A city tour of Cuzco and 'the nearby ruins' of Sacsayhuaman, Kenko, Puca Pucara and Tambomachay. *Day 2:* Tour of the Sacred Valley including a visit to Pisac market and a trip to a weaving centre in Chinchero. *Day 3:* Cuzco – Aguas Calientes – Machu Picchu – Cuzco

Ganguly was the only Indian tourist among her fellow tourists who were comprised mainly of Europeans and Japanese. They were taken to the different tourist spots noted above in a large bus. There was a different tour guide each day who was fluent in English and Spanish and appeared to know Quechua as well although, as Ypeij (2012) points out, often tour guides claim to be fluent in Quechua when in reality they know only a smattering of Quechua words. None of the tour guides were indigenous people indicating the hierarchical and tense relations between the indigenous people and the urban mestizo population of Cuzco which often fills in the role of tour guide, a position that requires a certain level of education necessary to be able to converse with the tourists in English and other languages.

The *Day 1* tour involved a trip to Sacsayhuaman, another UNESCO World Heritage Site, among other places. A fortified citadel, Sacsayhuaman was the first stop, a sprawling, impressive site. The well maintained surroundings give it a sense of peace and quiet which is one of the attractions that Western, middle-class tourists often seek to experience in the non-Western Other. For urbanites, non-urban environments are themselves Other. Furthermore, the fact that the site is well-maintained is evidence that it is a constructed experience for the benefit of tourists who wish to believe they are undertaking an authentic and original experience. Going there late in the afternoon, apart from their tour group and some other tourists, the only other people there were two indigenous women with their grazing llamas and alpacas. The indigenous women were not in the bright, traditional costumes that are worn by those who pose for tourists. But when Ganguly approached the tour guide asking if she could photograph one of them, the guide went and spoke to one of the indigenous women who in turn posed for a photograph in exchange for one sol. Ganguly photographed her with the llamas and alpacas as proof of her encounter with the local culture, to show others at home and remind herself of her trip (Figure 12.1). Given the backdrop of the setting, the indigenous women seemed almost a 'natural' part of this well preserved past, and unwittingly but unreflexively Ganguly turned their llamas and alpacas into the perfect accessory to her touristic consumption of this highly exoticised experience. In this way, she framed the 'real' in her photographic image, for 'the photograph becomes our capturing of the presence of the real' (Grimshaw 2008: 33).

On *Day 2*, the tour of the sacred valley included a trip to the large indigenous market in Pisac, a huge tourist attraction (Figure 12.2). Tourists ambled along the market, looking at the handicrafts, haggling over prices and taking photographs. Much of the wares on sale were clearly aimed at tourists – rucksacks, alpaca wool scarves and sweaters, jewellery and assorted souvenirs.

Figure 12.1 Outside Sacsayhuaman.
Photo courtesy Tuhina Ganguly.

Figure 12.2 At the entrance of the Pisac market.
Photo courtesy Tuhina Ganguly.

However, one of the main tourist attractions of the Pisac market is the *sacamefotos*. The *sacamefotos* were at the entrance of the Pisac market, their colourful attire in tune with the colourful Pisac market. Where the indigenous women at Sacsayhuaman had seemed to be a 'natural' part of the Inca ruins, the indigenous women at Pisac along with the market seem to offer a heightened, visually sensuous experience of indigenous culture. Ganguly 'captured' one of the indigenous women with her child just as she turned to speak to a little boy (Figure 12.3). The photograph at the time seemed more authentic because the woman had been 'caught' in an off-guard moment rather than the usual pose struck for the camera. It was only much later that the author realised the ways in which she had Othered the host – Ganguly photographed the indigenous woman even as she looked elsewhere, thus in that moment depriving her of the chance to gaze back at the tourist-photographer. But further to this, given the existing exchange economy of the posed photo for money that exists in this tourist-experience context, by taking the photo without consent, Ganguly also potentially denied the subject of the photo her exchange-income. In doing so Ganguly, unwittingly, not only denied the woman income, she also shifted the nature of the encounter to a point whereby the indigenous woman was no longer even a participating subject but rather became an object to be captured.

Figure 12.3 Photographing the indigenous woman at Pisac
Photo courtesy Tuhina Ganguly.

On the way back to Cuzco, at the end of the tour of the Sacred Valley, the bus stopped at a weaving centre in Chinchero where indigenous women demonstrated their weaving skills and techniques. The two women sat on low benches surrounded with spools of thread and an assortment of dried herbs and colours. The tourists sat around the two women while they explained the processes of dyeing wool and weaving techniques with the tour guide translating their explanations for us. Their weavings in the form of mats and garments with elaborate patterns hung on the walls and clothes lines. The indigenous women's demonstrations were meant to show how they continued to use traditional ways of dyeing and weaving, a discursive practice that, again, fits in well with the wider tourism discourse of *incanismo*.

At the time of taking the photographs, Ganguly's sole purpose was to have some souvenirs of her encounter with the indigenous women because, as probably to others on the trip, they appeared exotic. Notwithstanding the problematic nature of labelling anything or anyone 'exotic', what surprises us now is that Ganguly failed to recognise the irony in her act of photographing them – the 'exotic' tourist photographing the 'exotic' locals! Ganguly's own supposedly exotic character had been emphasised repeatedly during the trips through Cuzco and surrounding areas. More than once, fellow male tourists had wanted to photograph her, giving compliments on her exotic appearance. For them, presumably, she was as exotic as the indigenous Quechua women, or at least represented one end of the exotic spectrum. While they reified Ganguly's Otherness – a historically created differentiation based on political and socio-economic asymmetries implicated with colonialism and Orientalism – Ganguly simultaneously differentiated the indigenous women from herself by capturing them in photographic images as markers of her encounter with them. How should we, then, understand this complex social situation exemplified by the tourist practices of gazing at the exoticised Other that lies at the heart of ethnic tourism? What are the ramifications for ethnodevelopment in the context of exotic tourists and ethnic hosts?

The politics of location and ethnodevelopment

Ganguly's position vis-à-vis the indigenous people in Cuzco can be best understood in terms of what Adrienne Rich called 'the politics of location' which 'emerged in the early 1980s as a particularly North American feminist articulation of difference and even more specifically as a method of interrogating and deconstructing the position, identity, and a privilege of whiteness' (Kaplan 1996: 162). The politics of location underscored the problems of racism and homophobia that were apparent in the US women's movement such that it became imperative to move away from 'assertions of similarity and homogeneity' based on the assumption that all women are in the same position because of their gender to 'examinations of difference' based on the material implications of differences in class, race and sexuality, among other things (ibid.). Mainstream, white feminists were thus compelled to unravel the privileges of their socio-political and economic location vis-à-vis the socio-political and economic location of historically unprivileged women, highlighting the politics of location.

Using 'politics of location' in tourism studies is particularly useful in situating middle-class outbound tourists from so-called developing countries within the tourism network by highlighting the complicated situatedness of the tourist–host interactions. The urban, middle-class population from India wilfully participates in the consumption-oriented discourse of international tourism that is still primarily framed by Western, capitalist desires and a Western, capitalist gaze. In fact consuming international destinations is an aspirational ideal, a status marker, for the growing ranks of the Indian middle class. Given this scenario it becomes vital to situate the Indian middle-class tourists in terms of their socio-economic location vis-à-vis that of the indigenous hosts in other countries. Clearly, Ganguly's socio-economic location placed her in a far more privileged position than the indigenous women who were being toured, leading to the construction of contentious Otherness.

While no longer in the throes of colonialism, the postcolonial Indian middle class finds itself embedded in international socio-political asymmetries where the white, Western world continues to hold economic and political dominance. In the context of global tourism, the Indian middle-class tourist tries to find an Other to counter its own Otherness vis-à-vis the white, Western tourists. Caught in the global network of tourism and the flows of asymmetrical relations, the indigenous people from Peru served the function of the Other against which the postcolonial Westernised, globalised tourist (Ganguly) could declare her own 'modernity'. In short, her gaze of the indigenous Peruvian was in its effect and undertaking no different in intent than that of any Western tourist, white or otherwise. That is, her gaze was undertaken in the same tourist performance and exchange as her fellow non-Indian tourists.

In her work, postcolonial critic Gayatri Chakravorty Spivak (1999) has addressed the figure of the native as the site of cultural resources for the colonialist, on and against which the latter articulates his (and occasionally her) subjectivity marked by radical difference and superiority. The native himself, and more so herself, is expelled from the 'name of Man' (Spivak 1999: 6), as his or her identity is denied the possibility of articulate subjectivity. Appropriating the colonialist position against the native Other, in this instance Ganguly's act of photographing the indigenous women is performative of her own superior subjectivity, etched against the 'still marginalised' poor women' of Peru. Furthermore, while tourism may have granted greater avenues for self-determination to indigenous women, it must be noted that throughout the tour, indigenous women had little or no voice within touristic encounters.

Mestizo tour guides decide how much tourists should pay the indigenous women and the latter have hardly any say in what they receive from tourists. The language barrier also makes it difficult for tourists to engage with the women, and these encounters, as Ganguly observed, remain fleeting and momentary. In her examination of the figure of the native woman, Spivak goes on to argue that 'the typecast of the foreclosed native informant today is the poorest woman of the South' (1999: 6). Spivak's point is crucial to understanding the politics of location in a global world. As the constitution of the global middle class expands to incorporate people from the developing world, the marginalised women of the global South serve as the source of value, not only for the First World, but also for the aspirational, privileged segments of the Third World. Thus, in Cuzco, Ganguly's negotiation with her location vis-à-vis the white, Western male tourists found an object of Othering in the form of the indigenous women who seemed less modern insofar as they were indigenous and performed 'timeless' practices of indigenous weaving and craftsmanship. The *indígenas* are, therefore, subjected to double commodification – by the Western tourists and by the postcolonial tourists trying to negotiate their position vis-à-vis more privileged First World tourists.

We argue that in the face of such global political asymmetries, the expansion of the global middle class further marginalises the poorest of the poor in the Global South (Brosius 2012; Chatterjee 2004). As Brosius notes, 'The lower middle class, the rural and urban poor, in many ways, are at the receiving end of globalization and urbanization' (2012: xiv). The *indígenas* provide very important services in the tourism industry. Yet, and despite the improvement in the economic conditions of some indigenous people and a few communities, they remain a part of the global 'precariat', that is a class of people with precarious existence (Standing 2011).

Conclusion

In the discussion above, we have tried to show the complex nature of tourist encounters in a world with a rapidly expanding global middle class. Whereas traditionally the tourist referred to the white, Western male, in this chapter we have argued that there is a need to shift our attention to tourists from developing and/or postcolonial nations. We have argued that middle-class people from India are increasingly engaging in consumption practices, including touristic consumption, forming a significant proportion of global outbound tourists. In such a scenario, tourism studies would benefit from examining the impact of the changing dynamics of the tourist population on the hosts in other countries. It also behoves us to ask if any significant changes can be seen in the touristic encounter between non-white hosts and non-white tourists and what impact this has on ethnodevelopment.

Analysing Ganguly's experiences we argued that the fact that the tourist belongs to a developing country, like the indigenous host, does not necessarily mitigate or lessen the power imbalances between the ethnic host and the exotic tourist. Rather, for the middle-class, Westernised tourist from the global South, as for the white Western tourists, the indigenous people symbolise the exotic Other over and against whom the tourists assert their own (perceived) superiority. In fact, the consumption of the indigenous host is all the more important to the exotic tourist, for it becomes a means of performing her superior identity in negotiating her location vis-à-vis that of white, Western fellow-tourists. Thus, unfortunately, the encounter between ethnic hosts and ethnic tourists is unlikely to stop contributing to the marginalisation of the former.

For more egalitarian tourism practices which would empower the Quechua-speaking hosts, we believe that there should be more emphasis on community-driven tourism projects, as have been undertaken in some parts around Cuzco (Knight and Cottrell 2016). This would ensure more active participation by the hosts, especially the indigenous women. It would also demand more commitment from tourists in terms of the amount of time they spend with the hosts, leading to greater appreciation of the hosts and their cultural practices. Currently, as Ganguly noticed, coherent organisation on the part of indigenous communities is limited with private tour companies/agents likely to end up with the bulk of the revenue. In this regard, government-initiated community projects where the bulk of the revenue is ploughed back into the community would be helpful to ethnodevelopment. Community-based tourism projects should be granted more incentives by the government, and privately run tourism agencies and companies should be charged a higher levy which should be used to develop better infrastructure for the *indígenas*.

Furthermore, we suggest a longer, more sustained study be done, looking at the motivations and experiences of Indian tourists to Peru as well as other countries offering ethnic tourism. A question to be asked, if not answered, here is whether Ganguly would undertake the same gaze and effects if she encountered the poor, indigenous populations collectively labelled the *Adivasi* in South Asia? Thus we also suggest doing a comparative analysis of Indian tourist encounters with the *Adivasis* in South Asia. Comparing the two situations will inform us of the extent to which indigenous people are commodified (or not) by ethnic tourists across locations. We believe that such studies would be instrumental in the coming days to better understand the predicament of ethnic hosts within complex tourism exchanges brought about by a rapidly expanding global middle class.

References

Amoamo, M. (2007) Māori tourism: image and identity – a postcolonial perspective. *Annals of Leisure Research* 10(3–4), 454–74.

Anderson, L. (2006) Analytic autoethnography, *Journal of Contemporary Ethnography* 35(4), 373–95.

Ateljevic, I. and Doorne, S. (2003) Culture, economy and tourism commodities: social relations of production and consumption. *Tourist Studies* 3(2), 123–41.

Babb, F. E. (2012) Theorizing gender, race, and cultural tourism in Latin America: a view from Peru and Mexico. *Latin American Perspectives* 39(6), 36–50.

British Council (2014) *Understanding India: The Future of Higher Education and Opportunities for International Cooperation*. Available at: http://www.britishcouncil.org/sites/britishcouncil.uk2/files/understanding_india_report.pdf (accessed 10 July 2015)

Brosius, C. (2012) *India's Middle Class: New Forms of Urban Leisure, Consumption and Prosperity*. London and New York: Routledge.

Bruner, E. M. (2005) *Culture on Tour: Ethnographies of Travel*. Chicago: University of Chicago Press.

Cassel, S. H. and Maureira, T. M. (2015) Performing identity and culture in indigenous tourism – a study of indigenous communities in Quebec, Canada. *Journal of Tourism and Cultural Change* 30(12), 1–14.

Chatterjee, P. (2004) *The Politics of the Governed: Reflections on Popular Politics in Most of the World*. New York: Columbia University Press.

Clifford, J. and Marcus, G. E. (eds) (1986) *Writing Culture: The Poetics and Politics of Ethnography*. Berkeley, CA: University of California Press.

Cohen, E. (1988) Authenticity and commoditization in tourism. *Annals of Tourism Research* 15, 371–86.

Cohen, E. (1989) 'Primitive and remote': hill tribe trekking in Thailand. *Annals of Tourism Research* 16, 30–61.

Cohen, E. (2012) Flooded: an auto-ethnography of the 2011 Bangkok flood. *Austrian Journal of South-East Asian Studies/Österreichische Zeitschrift für Südostasienwissenschaften* 5(2), 316–34.

Cole, S. (2007) Beyond authenticty and commodification. *Annals of Tourism Research* 3(4): 943–60.

Crapanzano, V. (1980) *Tuhami: Portrait of a Moroccan*. Chicago: University of Chicago Press.

Ellis, C. and Bochner, A. P. (2000) Autoethnography, personal narrative, reflexivity. In N. K. Denzin and Y. S. Lincoln (eds), *Handbook of Qualitative Research*, 2nd edn. Thousand Oaks, CA: Sage, pp. 733–68.

Ellis, C., Adams, T. E. and Bochner, A. P. (2011) Autoethnography: an overview. *Historical Social Research/Historische Sozialforschung* 36(4), 273–90.

Government of India (2012) *India Tourism Statistics 2012*. Available at: http://tourism.gov.in/writereaddata/CMSPagePicture/file/marketresearch/publications/India%20Tourism%20Statics%282012%29%20new.pdf (accessed 5 July 2015).

Grimshaw, M. (2008) *Bibles and Baedekers: Tourism, Travel, Exile and God*. London and Oakville, CT: Equinox.

Hannerz, U. (1990) Cosmopolitans and locals in world culture. *Theory, Culture and Society* (7), 237–51.

Jarvie, I. (1988) Comment on Sangren's rhetoric and the authority of ethnography. *Current Anthropology* 29, 427–9.

Kaplan, C. (1996) *Questions of Travel: Postmodern Discourses of Displacement*. Durham, NC and London: Duke University Press.

Knight, D. (n.d.) *Poverty Alleviation Through Tourism? Community Perceptions of Intrepid Travel in Peru's Sacred Valley*. Available online: http://www.intrepidtravel.com/http_cdnintrepidtravelcom/sites/default/files/1.%20Peru%20Research%20Summary,%20David%20W%20Knight.pdf (accessed 20 September 2016).

Knight, D. and Cottrell, S. (2016) Evaluating tourism-linked empowerment in Cuzco, Peru. *Annals of Tourism Research* (56), 32–47.

MacCannell, D. (1973) *The Tourist: A New Theory of the Leisure Class*. Berkeley, CA: University of California Press.

Mbaiwa, J. E. (2011) Cultural commodification and tourism: the Goo-Moremi community, Central Botswana. *Tijdschrift voor economische en sociale geografie* 102, 290–301.

Oakes, T. (1998) *Tourism and Modernity in China*. London: Routledge.

Oakes, T. (2000) Ethnic tourism. In J. Jafari (ed.), *Encyclopedia of Tourism*. London: Routeledge, pp. 204–6.

Page, S. J. (2011) *Tourism Management: An Introduction*, 4th edn. Abingdon and New York: Routledge.

Peruthisweek (2014) *Peru-India Free Trade Agreement Could Raise Trade to US$2 Billion.* Available at: http://www.peruthisweek.com/news-peru-india-free-trade-agreement-could-raise-trade-to-us2-billion-103122 (accessed 5 July 2015).

Picard, M. (1997) Cultural tourism, nation-building, and regional culture: the making of a Balinese identity. In M. Picard and R. Wood (eds), *Tourism Ethnicity and the State in Asian and Pacific Societies*. Honolulu, HI: University of Hawaii Press, pp. 181–214.

Rabinow, P. (1978) *Reflections on Fieldwork in Morocco*. Berkeley, CA: University of California Press.

Ruiz-Ballesteros, E. and Hernández-Ramírez, M. (2010) Tourism that empowers? Commodification and appropriation in Ecuador's Turismo Comunitario. *Critique of Anthropology* 30(2), 201–29.

Ryan, C. (2005) Introduction: tourist-host nexus: research considerations. In C. Ryan and M. Aicken (eds), *Indigenous Tourism: The Commodification and Management of Culture*. Abingdon and New York: Routledge, pp. 1–14.

Shepherd, R. (2002) Commodification, culture and tourism, *Tourist Studies* 2(2), 183–201.

Simon, B. (2009) Sacamefotos and tejedoras: frontstage performance and backstage meaning in a Peruvian context. In M. Baud and A. Ypiej (eds), *Cultural Tourism in Latin America: The Politics of Space and Imagery*. Leiden: Brill, pp. 117–40.

Smith, V. L. (ed.) (1977) *Hosts and Guests: The Anthropology of Tourism*. Philadelphia: University of Pennsylvania Press.

Spivak, G. C. (1999) *A Critique of Postcolonial Reason: Toward a History of the Vanishing Present*. Cambridge, MA and London: Harvard University Press.

Standing, G. (2011) *The Precariat: The New Dangerous Class*. London: Bloomsbury Academic.

Stronza, A. (2001) Anthropology of tourism: forging new ground for ecotourism and other alternatives. *Annual Review of Anthropology* 30, 261–83.

Van den Berghe, P. (1980) Tourism as ethnic relations: a case study of Cuzco, Peru. *Ethnic and Racial Studies* 3(4), 375–93

Van den Berghe, P. and Ochoa, J. F. (2000) Tourism and nativistic ideology in Cuzco, Peru. *Annals of Tourism Research* 27(1), 7–26.

Yang, L. and Wall, G. (2009) Ethnic tourism: a framework and an application. *Tourism Management* 30(4), 559–70.

Yang, J., Ryan, C. and Zhang, L. (2013) Ethnic minority tourism in China – Han perspectives of Tuva figures in a landscape. *Tourism Management* 36, 45–56.

Ypeij, A. (2012) The intersection of gender and ethnic identities in the Cuzco–Machu Pichu tourism industry: sacamefotos, tour guides and women weavers. *Latin American Perspectives* 39(6), 17–35.

13 The legacy of black people and dialectic inclusion-exclusion in the building of the cultural heritage of a tourist destination in Vale do Paraíba

Clarissa Gagliardi and Rosana Bignami

Introduction

The term 'ethnicity' has become increasingly popular in hybrid cultures, mostly observed in countries formed by an intense and prolonged colonisation period such as Brazil, where historic construction occurred through racial, linguistic, religious and cultural blends. Ethnic studies have contributed in great part to the understanding of hegemonic processes which constitute the base of their respective identity building. Brazil is a nation-state which was formed deeply rooted in more than three hundred years of Portuguese colonialism with an intense ethnic miscegenation of Europeans, Africans and Indians, while envisaging its own decolonisation process to become a nation-state, and creating its own institutional foundations and new perceptions that could support a multi-ethnic country. The chapter discusses the importance of the black legacy related to the period of slavery as a key element of ethnodevelopment in the process of building the Paraíba Valley as a tourist destination. Critical for this analysis is to identify how the 'black population' has been positioned within Brazilian history and which elements constituted advances or drawbacks in terms of 'ethnic development' (ethnodevelopment). The leading question is whether tourism in Vale do Paraíba has contributed to culturally recognise the African-Brazilian human element by promoting inclusion and empowerment, or whether tourism has only been the continuation of practices that marginalise and undermine an ethnic group, reproducing the equivocal attitudes noted in the construction of a nation. Are the collective memories and symbolic elements of an African-Brazilian legacy and of its rich contribution to the formation of a country being used to subsidise the cultural tourism products in Vale do Paraíba and giving justice to this ethnic group? How can African-Brazilian human and cultural assets contribute to strengthen Vale do Paraíba as a tourism destination?

Critical glimpses will help to read the history by contextualising the formation of a society permeated by injustices against black and Indigenous groups, particularly by the colonisers and by an emergent rural oligarchy, clothed as an 'aristocracy of a coffee economy'. Therefore the social and racial struggles in Vale do Paraíba – power issues of a polarised society of blacks and whites, that is unprivileged (descendants of African slaves) and privileged (white coffee elite) ethnic groups – situate the discussion within the realms of an ethnodevelopment perspective as conceptually proposed by the seminal work of Rodolfo Stavenhagen.

Ethnicity, identity and social and racial imbalances are the focus of this desk research, based on a literature review and document analyses, combined with the findings and observations of the authors during their Master's degree research and dissertation. Methodologically the text is highly descriptive and qualitatively oriented.

Thus this chapter analyses to what extent the neglect of black history related to the slave period in the Vale do Paraíba (Paraíba Valley), a Brazilian coffee-producing region during the nineteenth century, has hindered the recognition of this territory as a historic place as well as its consolidation as a tourist destination shared between different social segments, despite having a wealth of natural and cultural attractions. It is possible to affirm that the selective use of memories by market agents and tourism planning produces harmful effects on the performance of the sector itself. This seems to be a fundamental condition for the community to recognise its role as a protagonist actor and to become the manager of its own development with the insertion of the population in the processes of tourism development, as well as the identity retrieval of its populations. The chapter inserts the touristic use of cultural elements representative of the Afro-descendant community in the discussion about ethnodevelopment and its capacity to emancipate economically and politically populations once prevented from carrying out their own development paths.

A Brazilian history of ethnic and social struggles: an economy of colonised and colonisers.

Silvio Romero (1851–1914) – a well-known Brazilian intellectual, writer and essayist and one of the precursors of such a national ideology, advocated in his writings that slavery and the African presence played a central role in the formation of Brazil's society, culture and economy '[...] on the creation of what he called "the Brazilian soul" of racial groups long since extinct' (Smith 1997: 729). Ethnicity – particularly related to black slavery – has permeated the whole of Brazilian history (Sansone 2003; Tosta 2016). Notwithstanding, during the Second Empire (Dom Pedro II), the end of the slave trade in 1850 created a crisis due to a shortage of 'black labour', and this crisis prolonged illegal slavery as part of a national reality until 1888, when *Lei Áurea* (the Golden Act) was finally promulgated (Rodriguez 2015), and in the following year Brazil proclaimed its status as a Republic in 1889.

By pursuing a Brazilian identity consolidation, institutional and cultural movements sought to constitute the base for the creation of the Brazilian people by accounting for the culture of the native Indian, the African black and the European white, through a project of hybrid composition that some authors have referred to as the 'myth of the three races' (Tosta 2016; Dutra 2007; Sansone 2003; Freyre 1933). The conceptual and ideological basis of an ethnic-mixed nation has been also drawn from Romero's views that the 'elevation' of the 'lower races' (indigenous and black people) would be the only way to obtain a Brazilian race, 'more pure' and 'more white', in which the amalgamation of races (or miscegenation) would occur as a natural element of human evolution. The idea of miscegenation as 'whitening' of the Brazilian people has oriented to a large extent the political, historical and social movements consolidating the myth of three races. The ideological processes of miscegenation in Brazil conceptualised each of the races as watertight categories: *to the white race*, superiority and intelligence; *to the indigenous race*, indolence, inertia and ineptitude; *to the black race*, inferiority, nonchalance, infidelity and betrayal (Bignami 2010; Cunha 2006; Prado 1931), and Skidmore (1974) corroborates the historical view that 'all aspects of society have been contaminated by ideas of white superiority and black inferiority. Consequently, many African descendants have accepted the imposition of ideological settings of 'whitening' and of a 'racial democracy' (Andrews 1991: 212); the whitening ideology persisted fiercely in Brazil from 1889 to 1914, 'assuming the continued arrival of European immigrants in the country, racial mixture would gradually 'breed out' African and Indian racial characteristics and produce the eventual 'whitening' (*branqueamento*) of Brazil' (p. 136). Such semantic and symbolic categories, in turn, clarify, for instance, what substantiates choices which lead to the devaluation of the black populations, the absence of public policies for the Indigenous populations, and the affirmative policies that try to account for the social inequality related to ethnic groups, among others.

In this respect, therefore, it may be affirmed that the 'myth of three races' acts on a symbolic level as a discursive space that tries to account for a social issue yet to be consolidated, the [social] Brazilian miscegenation. It is relevant to detect in such symbolic systems which signs remain and which are relegated or have disappeared in the struggle for identity. Such ideological and symbolic struggles in the arena of national identity under the prism of identity theories (Castells 1999; Hall 2006; Holanda 1995; Matta 1983; Ortiz 1985) explain how difficult it is for the Brazilian people to identify themselves as mixed-race (*mestiço*) people. It explains, in a certain way, the sense of 'not belonging' to a respective territory and the non-recognition of own culture or identity. Ultimately, the belief in the myth of three races is an element inherently part of the Brazilian identity, which, by the way, symbolically affects political practices and struggles for power (Bourdieu 1996).

Hall (2006: 8) stresses the importance of 'aspects of our identities that arise from our 'belonging' to ethnic, racial, linguistic, religious and, above all, national cultures', which, in the process of the Brazilian identity building, constitute a symbolic struggle between the three races or ethnicities constituent of the Brazilian people. When becoming 'more Brazilian', one was no longer 'black', 'indigenous' or 'white', suffering a process of hybrid replacement formed by an idealised imaginary construction, in which the miscegenation of races replaces each of the cultures (indigenous, black and white), in order to build the Brazilian identity. It is worth stating that such a new identity – or the identity of the Brazilian people – does not recognise entirely the black and indigenous culture or, when they do, usually they situate it in a lower position which clearly resembles a form of social stratification. With regard to the indigenous matrix and identity formation of Brazilians, this has not been examined in this chapter, even though ethnodevelopment issues are associated with the promotion of mechanisms of the development of indigenous people.[1] The objective of this chapter is rather the investigation of the dispersed ethnic black groups – Afro-descendants of slaved ancestors – and ethnodevelopment outcomes on Paraíba Valley as a heritage and cultural tourism destination. In Brazil, even having been a country in which the black presence is striking not only in historical and cultural terms, 53.6 per cent of the population has declared itself black in 2014, according to the Brazilian Institute of Geography and Statistics (IBGE). The use of a cultural heritage representative of Africans and their descendants is minimal.

Coffee, black people and the elite of Vale do Paraíba: memoirs and symbolic subsidies for a cultural tourist product

The region of Vale do Paraíba was formed around 1611, in the course of the transportation to the gold fields and subsistence production to supply villages. From 1630 to 1775, the region of Vale do Paraíba experienced the 'cycle of subsistence economy', at the time based in small properties with little use of slave labour. The second period was called the 'cycle of the mills', from 1775 to 1800 and the beginning of the nineteenth century, but it was undoubtedly the coffee culture that defined the region's profile, with the massive entry of African slaves.

In this region, the settlement of Bananal distinguished itself, where coffee crops were cultivated from the late eighteenth century; then starting around 1835 it entered its most productive phase which extended until the 1870s. As of the mid-nineteenth century, the town's wealth was booming as Bananal was the largest coffee producer in the province of São Paulo in 1854, largely contributing to the Imperial State finances with local farmers holding vast deposits at London banks and with preferences for loans. In 1864, it was already considered the largest town in the province of São Paulo, even greater than the capital itself, and also constituted an important political and administrative centre, where important positions were occupied by land and slave owners.

Galvão (1986) analysed the transition from the Brazil Colony to an independent country, in which the creation of a formal framework of institutions for the election of representatives enabled a rural aristocracy to enter the political system. There was no change in the effective power system, just an adjustment with the creation of formal frameworks (Galvão 1986: 44). There was such wealth generated in this region that, of the few travellers who went from Brazil to Europe, many belonged to the coffee elite of the Valley, travelling for academic education. Thus a new aristocracy in Vale do Paraíba established itself as a regional political power increasing even more the social distance between them and an ethnic black population.

The historical records show that Resgate Farm in this region was owned by a pioneer coffee-growing family. Its Portuguese-designed house dates back to the early nineteenth century, with neoclassical design. The array of rooms, furniture and silverware and the ostentatious layout and arrangements of domestic spaces – influenced by a European way of living – can be regarded as one of the visible aspects of a highly stratified society at Resgate governed by a polarised system composed of recently emerged powerful landlords on the one hand and the 'lower black citizen class' on the other (Castro and Schnoor 1995: 48–54). Resgate Farm is still very well preserved and it has been a heritage site and an appealing attraction for visitors interested in an Afro-Brazilian legacy ruled by a system based on a coffee production economy.

In Vale do Paraíba, farmers were agents of a huge landscape change with coffee plantations, with negative environmental impacts in reducing soil productivity. There was a gradual decline in coffee production, along with the negligence of landowners who continued to show off their wealth and opulent status without planning for future development and economy. This stood in contrast to the life of poverty of the black population leading tragically to regular harvest failures affecting the regional economy and lifestyle of the coffee oligarchy. This phenomenon was observed in many coffee plantations in São Paulo (Tosta and Coutinho 2016). The maintenance of the spaces of social representation created by such an elite became incompatible with the situation of the Valley in the second half of the nineteenth century. As explained by Schnoor (1995), Vale do Paraíba slaves, besides working on the coffee plantations, were also 'indoor' domestic slaves to serve the emergent rural oligarchy, featuring a sort of 'aristocratic ideal of modernity'.

The existence of *Quilombola* (*Quilombo*) communities – an escaped slave hinterland settlement (Covin 1999: 91), in the region, combined with the lack of organisation and mobilisation of the black community in the history of the Vale do Paraíba, are aspects which, aside from contributing to the invisibility of the black individuals at the site, have served as barriers to the formation of an ethnic human resource for development; more precisely, an embryonic ethnodevelopment framed by the following elements: (1) the economic development of an ethnic group (of black people); (2) the ethnic development of a social group – two aspects that are of course not mutually exclusive (Little 2002: 39). That is, the maintenance of cultural diversity with progressive economic development of the black people in the Historic Valley depends, to a certain extent, on the maintenance of respective memory spaces, as a way to make them part of the physical, symbolic, territorial and political landscape of that region.

Local social bases are also needed to build new development alternatives fostered by an ethnic community. It is possible to assert that, independently from the advances in the organisation of the black movement in the country, it is at a local level that ethnic power and human resources should be articulated to form the human and social ethnic capital essential to construct an ethnodevelopment model for group emancipation, empowerment and self-determination. The wealth and prosperity of Vale do Paraíba has been researched by economists and historians who have found undisputed data about the constitution of such wealth based on the slave trade and not exclusively on coffee production, although it is a myth constituted not only in the region of Vale do Paraíba, but also in the western region of the state of São Paulo (Motta 1999; Faria 1995).

Faria (1995) lists some activities that explain the considerable increase in some of the fortunes: weddings with dowries, inheritances, participation in commercial ventures and, above all, interest loans, in a chain of indebtedness between merchants and producers, which highly favoured capital accrual. But the most perverse modality which seems to have contributed to the growth in fortunes was the slave trade. Even after the abolition of the Atlantic slave trade, there are records of a large shipment of black Africans which was landed in *Angra dos Reis*, with the involvement of Manoel de Aguiar Vallim and Joaquim de Souza Breves, two eminent Bananal[2] farmers. According to Faria (1995) this event can be considered a 'clue' to another very profitable activity. So-called farmer-capitalists, the noble barons, by promoting usury in moments of crisis, deepened inequality, concentrated wealth and multiplied respective fortunes.

Motta (1999), in a thorough study of the ownership of captives and slave families in Bananal in the early nineteenth century, presents data demonstrating calculations to achieve an ideal composition of breeding stock by considering the sex and age group of slaves in order to ensure the best figures, despite derailing the stability of slave families in several instances, since respective members held different values depending on utility and, therefore, could be separated at any given time; at other times matrimonial bonds were prevented, given the scarcity of slave women. The data presented by Motta (1999) in his study corroborate the fact that the wealth of Bananal had not only been built on coffee plantations, but above all at the expense of a black town.

The decline started from 1870, although there are records of coffee crops until the early twentieth century. The predatory nature of respective cultivation in the region of Vale do Paraíba exhausted the soil and, with the difficulty in acquiring slave labour after 1850 due to slave trade disruption, this led to the collapse of the coffee economy sustained by slaves. Such a process constitutes the dismantling of the Second Reign foundation, based on the slave system. Culminating with the abolition of slavery and with the competition in coffee in the western region of the state of São Paulo, mid Vale do Paraíba witnessed the abandonment of coffee cultivation, with consequent depletion of the population. During the apogee of the coffee era, urban life expanded (Tosta and Coutinho 2016; Araujo 2010). After the decline in coffee, cattle farming started to expand in Bananal, especially dairy cattle, setting itself as an important current economic activity; this together with cotton cultivation, aside from tourist activities, became the major sources of income and revenue in the town.[3] Since 1990 tourism has become one more option for employment and income in Bananal and the so-called Historic Valley, mainly in the ecotourism sector, due to the natural attractions in a hilly area, and especially in the historical-cultural segment, offering a huge cultural collection inherited from the coffee period.

Social relations established by the local elite constitute symbolic capital (Bourdieu 1996), which happens to be converted into a resource of domination. What may be questioned here is to what extent tourism which focuses exclusively on this elite and its memoirs as a historical attraction in the region is contributing to the perpetuation of such domination given the possible interpretations a tourist may develop when visiting the site. The memoirs of black slaves, such as the *senzalas* (slave accommodation), which sheltered crop slaves (not indoor slaves), are part of a tourism attraction, as are the elite's farm houses. The use of such symbolic capital (Bourdieu 1996) during tourist programmes may also be questioned, leading to the identification of this group, which constituted the coffee elite, as hegemonic agents of this social space, thus maintaining historical social inequalities.

In this sense, a tourism programme which maintains the dominant relationships of the past is opposed to the founding premises of ethnodevelopment [ethnic emancipation], if one considers the understanding of the region's historical roots which had the black person as its foundation. An insertion of this neglected former slave population into the processes of tourist development seems to be a fundamental condition so that the community becomes effectively the manager of its own development, retains authority over its territory and resources, and makes a conscious use of its memoirs. If ethnodevelopment is also guided by environmental concerns underpinned by ethnic and social aspects, then one must contemplate such sustainability according to its multiple dimensions, including cultural ones, in conserving nature and culture as human-related assets, so that ethical standards are established in order that tourism will be developed and maintained in the future. Such symbolic re-appropriation can contribute to revive characters, traditions, costumes, habits, places and other cultural elements which have been 'hidden' in the silence of local narratives on the struggles between the 'dominated' and the 'dominant'. These aspects are fundamental to serve as a driver for a cultural and symbolic ethnic inclusion which can be presented to the tourist visitors and their learning experiences about the African-Brazilian legacy in Vale do Paraíba.

Stories, identity and memoirs about coffee at the bottom of local tourism

Historical-cultural tourism in Bananal and neighbouring cities of the same size rests mainly on attractions related to the coffee period. Former coffee farms converted for tourist use as visitation or hosting sites, urban neoclassical architecture, graveyards, furniture and instruments of torture from the slavery period are examples of the attractions sought after by visitors interested in history and culture. Apart from the travel agencies in Rio de Janeiro and São Paulo that organise visits to the Vale do Paraíba, there is also a flow of visitors from nearby urban centres, attracted to the material heritage which represents the coffee elite. The basic tourism programme of Bananal, for example, is to visit farms by means of guided tours or stay at an old coffee farm transformed into a hotel, spending a weekend of leisure activities offered by the hotel, visiting the urban nucleus, enjoying neoclassical facades, purchasing handicrafts and visiting natural attractions. In the Rio de Janeiro portion, where the farm management is articulated for more time by the association between traders and owners of buildings of historical value, in addition to offering lodgings, recreation and regional cooking, efforts are made to take visitors back into the nineteenth century by means of theatrical productions that remind them of the social practices of the time, not forgetting the place occupied by the slaves.

Given the context, tourism constitutes a very welcome economic activity, once it has become an employment and income option, based on the maintenance of cultural heritage, at the same time keeping a political dimension, since it is a resource for reinterpretations of the past, contributing to the 'formation of a historic culture about slavery among the general public' (Reis 2014: 8). However, there is a certain elite coffee hegemony in narratives about the local history which is enhanced by tourism.[4] A few issues arise on what usually excites the visitor's imagination at the moment of planning their programmes of interest, often not caring about the scientific or historiographical accuracy of the information reproduced (Gagliardi 2012; Reis 2014). In addition, they do not offer a critical reading of the space so that the historical culture of slavery would in fact be enriched. Public tourism policies, in turn, have not given priority to actions in order to reconsider elements of local identity, preferring specific and disarticulated interventions of a regional project of tourist development where such an issue could also constitute a distinguishing element in relation to other competing tourist regions. On the other hand, black populations have not attained or do not even recognise their role as fundamental social actors in ethnodevelopment. Therefore an attractive fetish type is created, to the extent that it does not exceed the aesthetic dimension, the level of visuality,[5] to promote new interpretations regarding the participation of black people in that society.

It is worth noting that the reframing of history, as a symbolic asset, reiterates the relationship of dominated/dominant, in which 'to exist' is to be legitimately recognised as 'different'. On the other hand, one must be reminded that the building of the Brazilian identity occurred through political, historical and social processes that, ideologically trying to consider an ethnic diversity (indigenous, black and white people) to establish the Brazilian identity, has done it in discursive terms, creating a national myth, the myth of the three races. Yet, it is necessary to incorporate meanings and elements associated with indigenous and black ethnic groups to do justice to a national miscegenation in response to blacks being positioned as 'disqualified' and being objects of deprecation, as opposed to the exaltation or elevation of meanings related to white ethnicity (Bignami 2010).

With the project of building the national identity, from a colony to a nation-state, in a period that also coincides with the end of slavery, it was necessary to account for what, at the time, took on the character of an ideological conflict, a struggle for power, in which

> the white person was expected to play the role of the civilising element; to the indigenous person, it was made necessary to restore his original dignity,

> by helping him to climb the steps of civilisation; to the black person, finally, the role of detraction was left, once he was considered a preventing factor to the nation's progress. (Schwarcz 1993: 112)

In fact, the fetish-type[6] tourist attraction consists of lending visibility to the symbolic space representing the dominant person, that is the farm owner, the coffee elite, while the symbolic space representing the dominated person is devoid of signs or acquires poor re-signification, distant from the plurality of black identity. In this respect the dominated people do not have any choice but to accept the dominant definition about their identity or the 'search for assimilation which assumes a type of work that makes disappear all signs meant to remember the stigma [...] and that intends to propose, by means of strategies of deception or hoax, the self-image as the least far possible to the legitimate identity' (Bourdieu 1996: 124). That is why, in historical narratives produced during visits to coffee farms, it is common to hear, for example, that slaves were faithful and grateful to their masters or that farmers maintained a cordial and equal relationship with the slaves. Such certainly are re-signification processes which hide the actual relationship between masters and slaves, often violent and charged with denial of the identities of black people.

Memoirs of some of the residents about slavery still pulsate, as in the case of a black resident, a bar owner in the town centre, that upon seeing the picture of a musical band comprising slaves,[7] reacted by wondering how such musicians could sing and play if they were awfully beaten. On this same occasion, the local resident, born on a farm in Bananal, remembered conversations held with his father, born in 1901, about slaves that were buried in their own farms, without anyone knowing how many they were and or cause of their deaths, compared to the cemeteries in the town, where only 'important and eminent people, people of money, farm owners, practically owners of the cemetery' were buried. In the farm where his parents were born no slave quarters were left, only the main house. His opinion about tourism: 'They say it brings money into the town, but I don't see anything, to me it doesn't change anything.'

For a young historian and resident of Bananal, it is considered a 'dead town' which they tried to rebuild and reframe by means of tourism but in a very superficial way in the face of the importance it had enjoyed in the past. On the other hand, the self-employed worker believes that local history is disguised and regrets that Bananal does not have historical documents, 'there are no files, there's nothing else here ...' A retired black man who was interviewed reported that his sister does not visit him because she says that Bananal history 'is very oppressive, it is a place of much suffering'.[8]

A slave descendent who still lives in Bananal relates that the relationship of her family with the town was very distant, they left the farm where her parents worked very little during the year, sometimes only to attend religious events. She did not study during her infancy, current tourist sites are not part of her memoirs and her perception of when slavery ended is very vague, which suggests how much the black people stayed at their work sites, even after abolition. Her testimony reveals that her population is currently just as far apart from urban life as it was during the nineteenth century. Memories of this person interviewed refer to the *jongo*[9] and other farms where her parents and friends worked and where the black people gathered,[10] cultural aspects absent from the city but which today is presented to the tourist.

According to such extracts from collected testimonials, the need to revise local history can be observed, so that historical tourism does not deepen conflicts by means of the touristic elements that it has introduced to the market. On the contrary, it is possible to think that tourism may offer new interpretations of local history instead of reinforcing the official story in which the elite is the primary agent. Therefore tourism is based on the attractions that are attached to the elite and the interpretations offered do not provide access to the black person's role in the social, cultural and economic development of the town; a great opportunity has been missed to include symbolically a whole class of people dismissed and excluded from its own territory and memoirs.

Accordingly, it was sought to analyse to what extent these tensions which arise from this friction between tourism and local history has hampered the consolidation of tourism development. In early 2000, for example, some training courses for young tourism guides did not enjoy much success, as those who had undergone the training process did not identify themselves with the history that they had to reproduce to the visitors. One of the students and a descendant of one of the largest coffee farmers of Bananal reported that most of the younger people do not like the history of the town 'because they even become tired with so much aristocracy, so far apart from the reality we live'. He, as someone who came to know the town's history during a course for training guides, considered that more accurate local historical data should be accessed and deployed before being transmitted, 'because Bananal is a representative town, but one does not know to what extent the story is true or if it was created by a nostalgic person'.[11]

In addition to the collection of statements, since early 2000 the tourist development of the region has been noticed and, despite the available resources,[12] some cities of the Historic Valley still lack a 'reconciliation' with the past. If such tensions are more pronounced in cities such as Bananal, which were more powerful during the golden coffee period, neighbouring towns that try to project themselves with the same profile of activities, such as the nearby São José do Barreiro, have also revealed some discomfort among residents who question, aside from the absence of black people as agents of local histories, the lack of indigenous memory[13] of the occupants of such regions long before the cultivation of coffee.[14]

Final considerations

It is possible to observe through the theoretical lens of Walter Benjamin that the past can pose a unique experience to the extent that the town lacks reconciliation with its historically underprivileged subjects; such inequalities still persist. The search for an unjust and segregating history as the pillar of tourism and its respective products, presenting itself as a new means of employment and source of income, builds such an option on an extremely fragile basis. Only with the participation and valuing of multiple local identities, inspired by concepts and proposals of ethnodevelopment, placing communities as effective managers of their own development, will it be possible to bring significant changes to the population, and also strategically to offer a differentiated tourist product, due to the valuable historical and cultural heritage of Vale do Paraíba.

The fact that coffee acts as a sanitiser of the fortunes built from such brutal human relationships does not prevent this past still having a pulse and relevance, in the relations that the population creates with its history and with which it inevitably has to deal, when it comes to recovering it by means of tourism. While constituting an activity that appropriates to itself the town's historical reminiscences, tourism can appear to be distancing part of the population that currently still tries to 'recover' its symbolic capital, yet it does not identify itself with the cultural heritage and adopts a posture of indifference and neglect. However, it can help to give back to the population a heritage which is theirs by right. Those who really vanished from the town were the elite with their respective income; the others who remained, the slaves and their descendants, remained to live in poverty.

Currently it may be said that, although black people are present in the Historic Valley, therein there is no ethnodevelopment, and in order to build its bases and with tourism taking part in the process, it seems fundamental to blend development with the recognition of cultural diversity, building an economic alternative, examining the needs of the black community and their descendants, at socio-economic, political and symbolic levels, rewriting the story currently told to visitors.

Notes

1. In this regard, see the collection of texts published in the work entitled *Etnodesenvolvimento e Políticas Públicas: bases para uma nova política indigenista* (Souza Lima and Barroso-Hoffmann 2002).
2. For further details on the case, see A. Martha (1995) *O Caso do Bracuhy*, cited in Castro and Schnoor (1975).
3. According to IBGE (http://cidades.ibge.gov.br/v3/cidades/municipio/3504909), coffee farming has been replaced by cotton and dairy cattle, which are still important sources of income. However, the service sector has greater weight in the city's economy (including the tourism sector, which in turn includes activities such as those we observe in our field activities, such as artisanal products in string, jams, *cachaças*), followed by the industrial sector and agriculture.
4. In this sense, the work *Casa-Grande e Senzala* by Gilberto Freyre, first published in 1933, illustrates in detail life at the coffee farms under the slavery system and corroborates, even decades after the end of slavery, the consolidation of the myth of the 'good lord of the farm' and the 'kind slave'. Such myths continue currently, even in narratives reproduced by tourist guides when explaining life at such farms. The *casa-grande* was the space occupied by the white elite coffee-growing property owners; the *senzala* was the space occupied by black slaves, coffee plantation workers and slaves serving at the *casa-grande* (or main house of the farm, the big house).
5. Notions of *visuality* and *visibility* explored by Ferrara from the proposal of Calvino on the pedagogy of the imagination were pertinent when considering the potentiality

brought by tourism in its process of making images and places public. This author proposes reflective elaborations of visual data in place of just expending a concrete and physical-visual datum. *Visuality* corresponds to the record of a physical and referential datum; *visibility*, on the contrary, is part of a visual representation in order to generate a complex perceptive process, clearly marked as an experience generator of continuous, individual and social knowledge (Ferrara 2002: 74).

6. The term 'fetish-type' refers to a type of attraction that reduces to the visual; something that refers to the idea of artifice, appearance, superficiality; that which attracts only by its visuality and not by the meaning underlying its physical/aesthetic dimension.
7. A photo presented to the interviewee depicted a band of musicians owned by a coffee producer of Bananal, composed of slaves and specialising in European operas. The interview was held in 2006, when the interviewee was 64 years old.
8. At the time of the interview, the historian was 28 years old, the self-employed worker 42 and the retired person 61. The interviews were held in 2006.
9. *Jongo* is an Afro-Brazilian form of expression which integrates drums, collective dancing and magical practices, having come together among slaves working in coffee and sugar cane crops in the Brazilian Southeast, mainly in Vale do Paraíba (IPHAN – National Institute of Historic and Artistic Heritage publication (2005) *Jongo, patrimônio imaterial brasileiro*).
10. The interviewee is 75 years old and gave her testimony to the authors in 2016.
11. The interviewee was 23 years old at the time of interview in 2005, referring to a training course for tourism guides which provided basic ideas on the historic and natural heritage of Bananal. Months after the interview several of the guides on this course had already abandoned their function to pursue other professional activities.
12. Out of five cities surveyed, two are considered Tourist Resorts (Bananal since 1980 and São José do Barreiro since 1998); such a title enables the resorts to receive resources resulting from taxes collected and passed on by the state government, which are a considerable drain on municipal budgets. For further details on such resources, consult DADE (Department of Support to the Development of Tourist Resources and Resort Improvement Fund of São Paulo State), at http://www.turismo.sp.gov.br/publico/noticia_tour.php?cod_menu=54.
13. The *Puris* Indians were the first inhabitants of Vale do Paraíba, with records of their presence in the sixteenth century.
14. Such questioning arose among local inhabitants when a participative workshop was held in 2015 for the elaboration of a tourist diagnosis which subsidised the Municipal Plan of Tourist Development of São José do Barreiro, in which the authors took part between 2015 and 2016.

References

Andrews, G. R. (1991) *Blacks and Whites in São Paulo, Brazil – 1888–1988*. Madison, WI: University of Wisconsin Press.

Araujo, A. L. (2010) *Public Memory of Slavery*. Amherst, NY: Cambria Press.

Bakhtin M. (1999) *A cultura popular na Idade Média e no Renascimento: o contexto de François Rabelais*. São Paulo: Hucitec.

Benjamin W. (1994) *Obras Escolhidas: magia e técnica, arte e política*. São Paulo: Ed. Brasiliense.

Bignami, G. R. (2010) *Identidade Brasileira e condição do negro em Viva o Povo Brasileiro*. PhD thesis. São Paulo: UPM.

Bourdieu P. (1989) *O Poder Simbólico*. Lisbon: Difel.

Bourdieu P. (1996) *Razões práticas: sobre a teoria da ação*. São Paulo/Campinas: Papirus.

Carrilho, M. J. (2006) Fazendas de café oitocentistas no Vale do Paraíba. *Anais do museu paulista* 14(1), 59–80. Available online at: http://dx.doi.org/10.1590/S0101-47142006000100003.

Castells, M. (1999) *Information Technology, Globalization and Social Development*, United Nations Research Institute for Social Development, Discussion Paper No. 114 (September). Geneva, Switzerland. Available online at: https://pdfs.semanticscholar.org/73e7/bf77de764f648560da3ed13038c9923f27f8.pdf.

Castro, H. M. M. and Schnoor, E. (1995) *Resgate: uma janela para o oitocentos*. Rio de Janeiro: Topbooks.

Covin, D. (1999) Learning from Brazils unified black movement: whither goeth black nationalism? In G.A. Persons (ed.), *Race and Ethnicity in Comparative Perspective*. New Brunswick, NJ: Transaction Publishers.

Cunha, E. L. (2006) *Estampas do imaginário. Literatura, história e identidade cultural*. São Paulo: Humanitas.

Dutra, E. de F. (2007) The mirror of history and images of the nation: the invention of a national identity in Brazil and its contrasts with similar enterprises in Mexico and Argentina. In S. Berger (ed.), *Writing the Nation: A Global Perspective*. New York: Palgrave Macmillan.

Faria, S. C. (1995) Fortuna e família em Bananal no século XIX. In H. M. M. Castro and E. Schnoor (eds), *Resgate: uma janela para o oitocentos*. Rio de Janeiro: Topbooks.

Ferrara, L. A. (2002) Os lugares improváveis. In E. Yázigi (ed.), *Turismo e paisagem*. São Paulo: Editora Contexto, pp. 65–82.

Freyre, G. (1933) *Casa-Grande e Senzala*, 1st edn. Rio de Janeiro: Ed. Record (1992).

Gagliardi, C. M. R. (2012) *As Cidades do Meu Tempo: turismo, história e patrimônio em Bananal*. São Paulo: FAPESP/Annablume.

Galvão, W. N. (1986) *As formas do falso*. São Paulo: Perspectiva.

Hall, S. (2006) *A identidade cultural na pós-modernidade*, 11th edn. Rio de Janeiro: DP&A.

Heise, T. S. (2012) *Remaking Brazil: Contested National Identities in Contemporary Brazilian Cinema*. Cardiff: University of Wales Press.

Holanda, S. B. (1995) *Raízes do Brasil*. 26 edn. São Paulo: Companhia das Letras.

Ickes, S. (2013) *African-Brazilian Culture and Regional Identity in Bahia, Brazil*. Gainesville, FL: University Press of Florida.

Little, P. E. (2002) Etnodesenvolvimento local: autonomia cultural na era do neoliberalismo global. *Revista Tellus* 2(3): 33–52.

Matta, da R. (1983) Dona Flor e seus dois maridos: um romance relacional. In *Tempo Brasileiro* 74: J. Amado, 70 KM, 3–33.

Motta, J. F. (1999) *Corpos escravos, vontades livres: posse de cativos e família escrava em Bananal (1801–1829)*. São Paulo: FAPESP/Annablume.

Nanda, S. and Warms, R. L. (2010) *Cultural Anthropology*. Belmont, CA: Wadsworth.

Ortiz, R. (1985) *Cultura brasileira e identidade nacional*. São Paulo: Brasilience.

Prado, P. (1931) *Retrato do Brasil*. Rio de Janeiro: F. Briguiet

Reis, C. (2014) *Memórias, histórias e a construção de narrativas sobre a escravidão no Vale do Paraíba*. In Annals of the 6th Regional Meeting on History by ANPUH Saberes e práticas científicas. Rio de Janeiro. Available at: http://www.encontro2014.rj.anpuh.org/resources/anais/28/1399986568_ARQUIVO_TextocompletoANPUH2014-CarolineReis.pdf.

Rodriguez, J. P. (2015) *Encyclopedia of Emancipation and Abolition in the Transatlantic World*, Vols 1–3. London and New York: Routledge.

Sansone, L. (2003) *Blackness Without Ethnicity: Constructing Race in Brazil*. New York: Palgrave Macmillan.

Schwarcz, L. M. (1993) *O Espetáculo das Raças – cientistas, instituições e questão racial no Brasil 1870–1930*. São Paulo: Companhia das Letras.

Skidmore, T. (1974) *Black into White: Race and Nationality in Brazilian Thought*. New York: Oxford University Press.

Smith, V. (ed.) (1997) *Encyclopedia of Latin American Literature*. Chicago: Fitzroy Dearborn Publishers.

Souza Lima, A. C. de and Barroso-Hoffmann, M. (2002) *Etnodesenvolvimento e políticas públicas; Estado e povos indígenas; e Além da tutela: bases para uma nova política indigenista*. Rio de Janeiro: Contra Capa Livraria.

Stavanhagen, R. (1996) *Ethnic Conflicts and the Nation-state*. New York: Palgrave Macmillan.

Tosta, A. L. de A. (2016) *Confluence Narratives: Ethnicity, History and Nation-making in the Americas*. London: Bucknell University Press.

Tosta, A. L. de A. and Coutinho, E. F. (2016) *Brazil – Description and Travel*, Latin America in Focus Series. Santa Barbara, CA: ABC-CLIO.

14 Tourism in the Fond Gens Libre Indigenous community in Saint Lucia

Examining impacts and empowerment

Lorraine Nicholas and Brijesh Thapa

Introduction

Globally, over the past decade, the need to empower community residents in the tourism development process has been acknowledged in developing countries with numerous national organisations incorporating community-based tourism (Cahyanto *et al.* 2013; Moswete *et al.* 2009; Scheyvens 2000). Several studies have endorsed this realism that there are tremendous economic, social and environmental benefits to be derived, especially in remote yet historically significant communities (Buckley *et al.* 2003; Lima and Weiler 2015; de Lima and Kumble 2015; Moswete and Thapa 2016; Parker and Thapa 2012; Singh *et al.* 2003). Such communities tend to be coterminous to parks and protected areas where tourism is a major economic driver of the local economy. However, while such communities have been the traditional stewards of protected areas, they have been largely marginalised and excluded from their development (Drumm and Moore 2005; Moswete and Thapa 2016).

Notwithstanding, destinations in the developing world, particularly those pursuing tourism as a key economic driver, are increasingly valuing the pivotal role of local communities in sustaining protected areas, and have established strategies to include locals in the management and development process (Kala and Maikhuri 2011; Moswete *et al.* 2009; Nicholas *et al.* 2009; Nyaupane and Thapa 2004). Such strategies include inclusion and empowerment through building and enhancing the capacity of individuals and groups to enable them to support various elements of community development (Aref and Redzuan 2009; Blackwell and Colmenar 2000; Dhakal and Thapa 2015; Parker and Thapa 2011). Concomitantly, increasing interest by tourists in learning about and experiencing different cultures has also served as leverage for the involvement of local communities in protected area management (Eagles *et al.* 2002). Furthermore, sites enjoying global significance such as UNESCO World Heritage Sites have an obligation to ensure the sustainability of the natural and cultural resources (Nicholas 2007; Thapa 2007). Hence, there is a need to involve community residents in the management, which can promote respect and the importance of protecting the World Heritage Site, as well as the need to integrate tourism into the local economy (Wager 1995).

While the concepts of involvement, empowerment, inclusion and ethnodevelopment within the nexus of conservation, tourism and sustainability have been promoted globally, the reality is that such terms and action plans only surfaced in the Eastern Caribbean in recent decades. The small island developing states of the Eastern Caribbean are among the most tourism-dependent regions and is largely demand-driven with little focus on the host communities (Nicholas *et al.* 2009). Moreover, the benefits have not been widespread among communities due to the nature of enclave tourism development in various island destinations (Zappino 2005). Consequently, the lack of involvement and accrual of tourism benefits has been an impediment for development, especially among the few remaining indigenous communities. The need for further inclusion and empowerment of indigenous groups is evident given tourism's renewed role in the transformation of their natural and cultural landscapes and human resources (Nicholas and Thapa 2006). Considering these issues, this chapter explores the Fond Gens Libre indigenous community which is strategically situated at the foot of one of Saint Lucia's iconic twin mountains – the Pitons.

Site context

Fond Gens Libre is a small, remote, rural community situated in the southwest region of the Caribbean island of Saint Lucia,[1] near the town of Soufrière. Literally translated from the local Creole language as 'valley of the free people', Fond Gens Libre is an old settlement dating back to the 1700s and is known to be home to the descendants of the Brigands (run-away slaves). During the slave rebellion of 1748, the Brigands capitalised on the remoteness of the area as a safe haven, and it is believed that a few descendants still live in the community (Humes 2008). Based on the 2010 census, a population of 164 residents and 55 households were reported in the community (Central Statistics Office 2011).

Fond Gens Libre is located within the Pitons Management Area (PMA) which was inscribed as a UNESCO World Heritage Site in 2004. The PMA (2,909ha) is one of the five sites[2] in the Caribbean that is categorised as a *natural* site. A component of the PMA is the 'Pitons' that comprise two volcanic mountains – Gros Piton (771m) and Petit Piton (743m), rising from the sea, alongside each other, linked by the Piton Mitan ridge (Nicholas and Thapa 2013). The Pitons are comprised of lush green vegetation with some areas of natural, undisturbed forest, preserved by the steepness of the land. At least 148 species of plants have been recorded on Gros Piton, and 97 on Petit Piton and the ridge; many are endemic. The Pitons are also home to 27 bird species (5 endemic) and numerous indigenous rodents, reptiles and amphibians (UNESCO 2011).

The Pitons are arguably Saint Lucia's most iconic landmarks and dominate the landscape. The inscription of the PMA as a World Heritage Site justifies the attractiveness of the area, particularly as it relates to tourism development. These mountains are unique to Saint Lucia's scenic beauty, and have traditionally been used in tourism promotional materials such as brochures, posters, guidebooks and so on. Additionally, the site is a volcanic complex with a geothermal field comprised of sulphurous fumaroles and hot springs which make it a major visitor attraction. In fact, the two most visited attractions are the Pitons and the sulphur springs with 200,000 visitors annually (Nicholas and Thapa 2010).

Fond Gens Libre is strategically located at the base of Gros Piton which makes it imperative for visitors to walk through the community to access walkways and paths. A major attraction to the community is the Gros Piton Nature Trail that was originally co-managed by the Forestry Department and the descendants of the Brigands (CANARI 2009a). The Gros Piton Nature Trail is a unique attraction endowed with a blend of the natural, cultural and historical resources that have catalysed the development of tourism in the community. In addition to the tours and group hikes, a visitor and interpretive centre is located in the community to educate domestic and international visitors about cultural and natural resources (Nicholas and Thapa 2006).

Recent changes in the evolution of the community, primarily attributed to tourism development, have been noted. Once regarded as unheard of, isolated and pastoral, however, the introduction of tourism has transformed the ecological, economic and socio-cultural milieu of the community (CANARI 2009a; Nicholas and Thapa 2006). Based on these developments, the purpose of this study is to delineate the impacts of tourism in Fond Gens Libre. Specifically, this study provides a comparative analysis of the community pre- and post-tourism development, and examines the role of tourism in shaping the socio-cultural, economic and environmental landscape. This study utilised information gathered via primary and secondary sources. Primary data was based on informal interviews with an office administrator and several community residents that comprised of free-flowing open discussions about the impact of tourism on their lives and community. Secondary sources included academic journals, unpublished reports and associated government documents. A case study approach was employed for this study to provide a more in-depth perspective via discussions with local residents. Future research will be able to build on this case study via empirical analysis or a mixed methodology approach.

Tourism – early beginnings

Sustainable community development is particularly challenging in protected areas located in high-altitude environments due to a lack of infrastructure. In addition, communities situated in higher elevations have less access to development programmes and capacity-building initiatives, even though these services are seemingly in greater demand in these areas (Mehta and Kellert 1998; Parker and Thapa 2012). This issue was evident in Fond Gens Libre: prior to the 1990s, the community was not known to the majority of the Saint Lucian populace, much less to the outside world. Back then, the major sources of livelihood included activities such as pig-rearing, charcoal production and sand-mining, all of which were environmentally destructive. Small-scale agriculture was also largely confined to small hill-farms (CANARI 2009b). In the early 1990s, Saint Lucia was a beneficiary of the United States Agency for International Development

(USAID)-funded project Environmental and Coastal Resources (ENCORE). The project was designed to promote partnerships between the government, private sector and local communities with respect to sustainable use of natural resources. Additionally, the project also emphasised environmental awareness capacity-building and institutional development based on the causes and impacts of degradation in the region (CANARI 2009a).

Furthermore, since tourism can promote and accrue several vital national objectives such as economic growth and development, improved welfare and equity, empowerment of local people, conservation of natural resources and diversification of the tourism product (Ashley and Garland 1994), a programme was focused on the assessment of nature and heritage tourism in the west coast of Saint Lucia. Also, given that tourism could be used as a mechanism to enable local communities to coexist with protected areas, the programme identified the potential for the Pitons to be a catalyst for nature-based tourism activities (Larson *et al.* 1998).

Based on this potential, the implementation was led by the Forestry Department, Saint Lucia National Trust and the Soufrière Regional Foundation. A major outcome of this partnership was the formulation of a community-based organisation named Gros Pitons Tour Guiding Association (GPTGA). Since a key objective was to empower the local community to engage in conservation and management of the area, the implementing team worked with the residents, especially to develop and upgrade the Gros Piton trail. The project also conducted an inventory of the flora and fauna, the erection of interpretive signs, the construction of an interpretation centre with amenities, the training of guides, the production of information brochures and the establishment of a multi-stakeholder management committee (Larson *et al.* 1998).

The multi-stakeholder management committee was mandated to facilitate the capacity of GPTGA to develop and manage tourism activities in the area. However, this committee did not fulfil the mandate due to the changes in membership. Also, some agencies, particularly the Forestry Department, lacked resources to successfully execute the mandate. Consequently, GPTGA became inactive as they lacked the human, technical and financial resources required to sustain the initiative when assistance from the project ceased (CANARI 2009a, 2009b).

Tourism – growth and development

The dormancy of the GPTGA, largely due to their inability to autonomously manage tourism in the community. created a gap, which enabled a private individual to take over the touring business under the name of Gros Piton Tours (GPT). The founder, who claims to have family roots in the community, registered GPT as a private company in 2003 as J. Haynes' Gros Pitons Tours BN. GPT offers visitors to the community an opportunity to hike the Gros Piton. Visitors who wish to climb the Pitons are required to walk from one end of the community to the other end where the base of Gros Piton is located. Hikers are

Table 14.1 Number of hikers (2006–10)

*Year**	*Number of hikers*
2006	4,266
2007	4,719
2008	5,584
2009	5,320
2010	6,241

* Data only available up to 2010.
Source: GPT Administrative Office.

accompanied by a local guide and the duration of the hike takes about four hours for the round-trip. The hike has been described as very adventurous and intriguing. The trail, though challenging, is rewarded by breathtaking views and the sampling of fruits such as mangoes. The rich volcanic soil produces magnificent tropical vegetation including dry coastal forest, cloud forest and woodland. There are also several caves along the way which were traditionally used as hideouts and camps by the Brigands who had escaped.

Today, GPT is being managed by the Soufrière Regional Development Foundation (SRDF). The SRDF was established in 1991 as a non-profit organisation established by the people of Soufriere to promote, encourage, support, facilitate and coordinate local development initiatives in the region. A primary goal of the Foundation is the promotion of coordinated socio-economic development for the region and the creation of socially acceptable, environmentally friendly and economically beneficial tourism-related infrastructure and amenities. The SRDF is best known for its development of the Sulphur Springs Park, construction of the jetties and waterfront, and the development of an inventory of the community's heritage assets. Tourists are charged US$35 for a guided hike while and locals pay EC$16.5 (US$6.00). Approximately 5,000 hikers climb Gros Piton annually. Table 14.1 illustrates that there has been an increase in visitor numbers over the years.

Socio-cultural impacts

Fond Gens Libre has traditionally encountered a relatively high level of poverty along with limited opportunities for improvement in the residents' livelihoods. Illiteracy levels have been high largely due to the inability to attend a school because of many factors such as lack of financial resources and poor infrastructure (e.g. road conditions, dwellings, utilities). Residents rarely ventured out of the community unless for shopping and likewise had minimal contact with outsiders. The community has experienced substantial migration of residents to urban areas in search of a better life. Overall, the community has been denied access to essential services and infrastructure largely due to the remoteness of the area.

The emergence of tourism in Fond Gens Libre has resulted in extensive exposure of the community, making it better known not only at the national level, but also regionally and internationally. Visitation over the past two decades have also stimulated an increased sense of pride and identity among community residents. Once ashamed to be from the 'valley of the free people', residents now are very proud to be 'custodians' of the Pitons, Saint Lucia's iconic landmarks. The development of tourism has also helped to alleviate the problem of rural–urban drift. With increased livelihood opportunities, residents, now empowered through tourism development, no longer feel compelled to relocate to the city or travel miles to work in the town of Soufrière. Consequently, this has had positive implications for family cohesion. Owing to the training provided by GPT, the capacity of some residents has been built with skills and knowledge acquired in areas such as communications and conservation. Additionally, every household is now equipped with electricity and flushing toilets resulting from infrastructure upgrades initiated by the GPT to support tourism development in the community.

Women are perceived to have equal opportunities as men as it relates to employment as tour guides. This serves to empower women in the community, who traditionally stayed home to care for the needs of the household. However, climbing almost 3,000 feet at least once daily does not appeal much to females. In addition to gender, there appears to be little discrimination based on age. Given the strenuous nature of the employment, one might expect it to be limited to the young. However, reflective of the general employment age, the tour guides' ages range from 19 to 55 years old. Since 2006, the population of the community has increased by 38 per cent and the number of households has also doubled.

A decade ago, under the management of Haynes' Gros Pitons Tours BN, GPT employed 23 tour guides all of whom resided within the community. The operations were administered from a small office situated near the base of Gros Piton, managed by one Administrative Officer who was also a resident of the Fond Gens Libre community. GPT was the principal employer in the Fond Gens Libre community. While the tour guides were trained to communicate and interact with visitors to the site, their training was primarily focused on basic skills to improve their command of the English language given that their main language spoken in the community is Kwéyòl. GPT has also contributed to improvements in the infrastructure in the community. This includes the construction of a paved walkway with proper drainage and lighting (CANARI 2009b). Additionally, the community did not have a full-fledged food and beverage facility such as a restaurant. However, GPT offered packages to visitors which were inclusive of a meal and the tour. Under this arrangement, the catering was operated by a resident of the community. However, upon return from their hike, climbers could also purchase drinks (i.e. water, soda, beer) from a woman who sold items from an ice-box cooler. There was also a small community shop at the entrance.

Today, fuelled by increased business at the GPT, the number of employees has almost doubled. There are 42 tour guides, 25 of whom are male and 16 female.[3] Almost all (90 per cent) the employees live in Fond Gens Libre. Tour guides are trained on a regular basis. Their training involves building their capacity in several areas including interpretation and customer service. The site and by extension the community infrastructure has also been significantly improved. This includes two small food establishments that serve visitors.

Notwithstanding these benefits, while equity is underscored as a fundamental tenet of the social dimension of sustainability, under the previous management arrangement, there was an apparent inequitable distribution of benefits from tourism development in the community. Given that the owner of GPT enjoyed all the profits, there was a lack of profit-sharing in the community. Only a minority – the employees of GPT and the vendor of drinks (and the community shopkeeper to some extent) – benefited directly. The majority of the community was not involved in tourism. Moreover, the community residents were not involved in any decision-making related to tourism development. As such, the development of the community did not necessarily reflect the aspirations of its residents. There appeared to be a subtle trade-off for the right to partake in decision-making as a collective unit for personal employment opportunities. The fact that all decision-making and management was entrusted to the care of a single individual who was not accountable to the community undermined the sustainability of tourism as well as the development of the community.

Originally, the GPT operated under a one-year tripartite agreement with the GPTGA and the Forestry Department. The company collaborated with and received support from the department from time to time. However, there was no formal arrangement between the two organisations and the GPT did not pay for the use of the Pitons for visitor tours. Additionally, the government of Saint Lucia received no share of the revenues collected by the GPT (CANARI 2009a). With the GPT currently being managed by the SRDF, there appears to be greater transparency and increased accountability. There is also a board of directors that oversees the operations of the SRDF.

Economic impacts

The expansion of the economic fabric of the Fond Gens Libre community, which is arguably directly attributed to increased tourism, is noteworthy. From 2000 to 2006, there has been an increase in employment creation in Fond Gens Libre, as the total number of employees doubled to 26 tour guides, two office administrators, two janitors and four trail maintenance workers. Ten years later, the number of employees has further doubled.

Bank accounts have been established for all employees to facilitate the direct deposit of salaries. This has served to enhance the residents' propensity to save. Overall the economic status of residents has improved, which enables ownership of their homes. Despite these economic benefits, under the previous management structure, residents lamented the lack of financial transparency, as information on revenue or financial accounts was not shared. The revenue collected was used to pay the guides and the residual income was retained by the owner of GPT. Thus, it was a challenge to assess whether guides were getting a fair share of the profits accrued. However, it was possible to estimate the revenues earned based on data related to the number of hikes and the fees. For example, if the total number of hikes in 2010 was 6,201 (foreigners) at US$30 per person and 40 locals at US$5.50 per person, the total revenue can be approximated at US$186,250 (EC$

500,000). This is a significant amount of revenue by local standards, especially since GPT did not pay for the use of the Pitons.

Under the new management structure, the use of the profits is more transparent. In addition to workers who claim to be better paid, they are also encouraged by the visible reinvestment of the profits in the community. The site has and is currently undergoing significant infrastructure improvements. The SRDF has recently leased a property (larger than the current office) from a resident in the community which will now serve as the secretariat for the GPT. Washroom facilities have been enhanced. The actual trail has also been improved to enhance visitor safety, following some unfortunate incidents. There are also plans to establish soon an additional official access point to the hike Gros Piton which will be from the Anse l'vrogne beach adjacent to Fond Gens Libre.

Environmental impacts

GPT has provided the opportunity for some community residents to replace environmentally destructive practices to sustain their livelihood such as sand-mining and deforestation (for example, charcoal production) with a more ecologically friendly source of livelihood. Tour guides have also benefited from training and education about the potential environmental impacts on the community, as well as the implications for environmental conservation and their livelihoods. Additional efforts have also been geared towards the maintenance of the greenery and naturalness of the community. Apart from a narrow paved walkway and some houses (most of them made from wood), the community is rich with plants, flowers and a variety of fruit trees including gooseberries, mangoes, orange, grapefruit, tamarind and breadfruit. For the most part, the community has maintained its natural appearance with minimal destruction since the establishment of GPT.

Discussion

The community residents of Fond Gens Libre have to varying degrees been empowered through the development of tourism in this community. They have experienced numerous benefits such as enhancement in their socio-economic status, increase in educational levels, improved infrastructure, cross-cultural exchanges, increased sense of pride, and greater unity and cooperation among residents. Their resilience and self-determination rooted in their ancestral heritage have augured well for the successful development of tourism in the community. Notwithstanding the social, economic and ecological benefits of tourism development, the community has yet to unlock the full potential to be derived from its proximity to the Pitons. Previously, several issues that relate principally to the management structure of tourism activity in the community threatened the sustainability of tourism and the development of the community. However, this has been partly addressed with the introduction of a recalibrated management structure that enhances transparency.

Nevertheless, there is still a need for increased empowerment by fostering the involvement of a greater proportion of community residents in the decision-making roles to promote and develop the community that better reflects the aspirations and desires of all residents. For example, a community resident could be a member of the board of directors of the SRDF. The absence of a decentralised decision-making system, coupled with a minority of residents benefiting directly from tourism, may galvanise conflict and ultimately lead to resentment towards visitors. In fact, currently, a prevailing sentiment is that the SRDF makes millions from GPT and the community does not receive a fair share of the profits. The dream of the community residents is one day to autonomously take charge of the management of the GPT.

Community participation and nature-based tourism vary in both character and extent. The role played by a community depends on several factors such as its culture, organisational capacity, quality of natural and cultural resources, tourism demand, training opportunities, funding availability, public and private sector interest and the presence of strong leadership and experience (Drumm and Moore 2005). Decentralisation of natural resource management has been successfully employed as a useful tool to foster the equitable distribution of benefits to residents and equal access to decision-making roles (Agrawal and Gupta 2005; Moswete and Thapa 2016; Parker and Thapa 2011, 2012; Persha *et al.* 2011). Additionally, communities will benefit more if they have the right to manage their resource and have a say and a share of the revenue in the tourism development process (Ashley and Garlan 1994; Moswete *et al.* 2009).

The current management structure of tourism in Fond Gens Libre, while improved, should still be modified to enable the community to profit more from the revenues earned. For example, a representative management committee should be established and empowered within the community, with assistance from agencies outside the community such as the Ministries of Social Transformation, Education, Tourism and Agriculture, and the SRDF. Alternatively, the Fond Gens Libre Development Committee should be strengthened and reinvigorated. In addition, adaptive co-management can be explored as a modality for a governance structure that involves multiple heterogeneous actors who engage in shared decision-making and work together to solve problems (Plummer and Fennell 2009). Such a management structure promotes transparency and accountability while enhancing benefits to the community.

Furthermore, once the community has been empowered through inclusion via the establishment of the suggested community groups, it is proposed that a Foundation (similar to the SRDF but on a smaller scale) be created. Figure 14.1 illustrates the proposed business model. It is envisaged that the establishment of a Fond Gens Libre (FGL) Community Development Foundation (FCDF) tasked with the responsibility of managing the Gros Piton Trail would result in greater direct benefits to residents and ultimately improve their standard of living.

The potential for other complementary revenue-generating enterprises also exists. These include: ecolodge homestays, a full-service restaurant specialising in local cuisine and a gift shop with merchandise related to the Pitons. The tourist

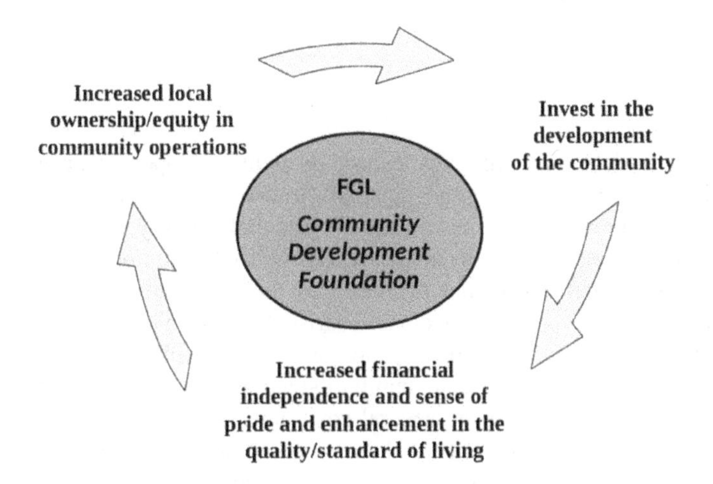

Figure 14.1 Proposed community business model.

experience can be enhanced with the performance of activities developed in accordance with the local heritage. These enterprises have significant income-earning potential for residents while enhancing the visitor experience. Moreover, a wider cross-section of the populace could be involved in tourism activities.

The training programmes should also be extended to all residents to ensure that a significant proportion of the local populace is knowledgeable about conservation and its benefits. The exclusion of community residents from conservation activities may lead to social conflict and non-conformity to conservation-related regulations (Robbins *et al.* 2006; Romero and Andrade 2004). Hence, the involvement and capacity of local residents should be enhanced to make informed decisions that relate to the management of resources. Advocates of the decentralised conservation management model also argue that the involvement of the majority of the populace will result in better protection of natural resources by reducing non-sustainable practices (Parker and Thapa 2012; Ribot 2002). Furthermore, if local community residents are involved and accrue benefits from tourism they will become efficient guardians of their natural and cultural resources (Kala and Maikhuri 2011; Moswete and Thapa 2016).

The inscription of the PMA World Heritage Site in 2004 has had little if any influence on the activities at Fond Gens Libre. A strategic link has not yet been forged with the status of the World Heritage Site. In a study conducted by Nicholas (2007) assessing stakeholders' perspectives of sustainable tourism development in the PMA it was found that almost none of the residents (99 per cent) in Fond Gens Libre were involved in the management, tourism or decision-making related to the PMA. Therefore, it is important that residents be sensitised to the meaning and implications of World Heritage status for the community. These recommendations unveil the need for an integrated plan inclusive of a feasibility study aimed at empowering the community to manage a sustainable, viable community-based enterprise.

Conclusion

The development of tourism in a community, especially an undeveloped one, can galvanise many impacts – both positive and negative. However, tourism is generally embraced by communities and perceived to be a potential gateway to alleviate some of the socio-economic problems in the area. In the context of Fond Gens Libre tourism development has undoubtedly changed the everyday lives and livelihoods in the community for many residents. Tourism has been a key catalyst to empower residents to benefit in a direct economic way. Residents have also enjoyed an upgrade of the community as a main tourist attraction with improved amenities. Fuelled by ethnodevelopment, several community residents, particularly women and the youth, who, partly due to their ancestral roots as descendants of the runaway slaves were traditionally marginalised and exploited, have now gained financial independence. Despite these benefits, the management structure of tourism development, previously characterised by a lack of accountability and transparency and still today characterised by limited resident involvement in decision-making, may potentially generate conflict within the community and ultimately threaten the sustainable development of tourism in Fond Gens Libre.

In summary, redesigning the management arrangement to facilitate collaboration, consultation and negotiation is strongly proposed. Tourism development should be undertaken on an inclusive basis, with the involvement of a wide spectrum of community residents playing various roles in activities such as catering, tour guiding, cultural performances, designing souvenirs, farming and lodging services. This benefits management, in collaboration with governmental and non-governmental agencies, to extend the training opportunities available to community residents. The success and sustainability of community-based tourism in Fond Gens Libre therefore hinges strongly on inclusive participatory management and decision-making, increased training opportunities and community mobilisation to capitalise on opportunities for sustainable tourism development. It is to this end that a participatory model to foster greater inclusion of community residents has been proposed. However, the actualisation of such a model will require increased self- and community determination and continued empowerment and ethnodevelopment within the community.

Community-based tourism (CBT) as a winning formula can be achieved when locals benefit directly from the tourist dollars flowing down the local economy, thereby creating a greater multiplier effect due to reduced leakages. This contributes to the alleviation of poverty and declining unemployment. The direct involvement of locals also promotes inclusion with an increased sense of ownership and support for the tourism sector which ultimately results in less resentment towards tourists and consequently more satisfied visitors.

The scope of this study was constrained by the lack of access to data on revenues and investments. With a more accountable management structure, future studies in Fond Gens Libre may seek to measure tourism benefits derived at the community level over time based on data such as the revenue earned and the redistribution of profits into development activities. Empirical research can also be subsequently conducted to determine the average household dependency on Gros Piton in comparison to similar communities in the developing world. Finally, this research makes an original contribution to scholarship by thoroughly assessing the possibilities for community empowerment and ethnodevelopment in a small island Caribbean state.

Notes

1. The population of Saint Lucia is approximately 183,000 residents.
2. Among a total of 19 World Heritage Sites in the Caribbean, 14 are designated as cultural and 5 as natural sites.
3. In 2005, a total of nine tour guides (40 per cent) were female as well as the administrative assistant in the office.

References

Agrawal, A. and Gupta, K. (2005) Decentralization and participation: the governance of common pool resources in Nepal's Terai. *World Development* 33(7), 1101–14.

Aref, F. and Redzuan M. B. (2009) Community capacity building for tourism development. *Journal of Human Ecology* 27(1), 21–5.

Ashley, C. and Garland, E. (1994) *Promoting Community-based Tourism Development*, Research Discussion Paper No. 4. Windhoek, Namibia: Directorate of Environmental Affairs, Ministry of Environment and Tourism.

Blackwell, A. and Colmenar, R. (2000) Community-building: from local wisdom to public policy. *Public Health Report* 151(2/3), 161–6.

Buckley, R., Pickering, C. and Weaver, D. B. (2003) *Nature-based Tourism, Environment and Land Management*. Cambridge: CABI Publishing.

Cahyanto, I., Pennington-Gray, L. and Thapa, B. (2013) Tourist-resident interfaces: use of reflexive photography to develop responsible rural tourism in Indonesia. *Journal of Sustainable Tourism* 21(5), 732–49.

Caribbean Natural Resources Institute (CANARI) (2009a) *Fond Gens Libre: Who Benefits from the Gros Piton Trail?* Laventille, Trinidad: CANARI.

Caribbean Natural Resources Institute (CANARI) (2009b) *Report on the Fourth Meeting of the Forests and Livelihoods Action Learning Group*. Laventille, Trinidad: CANARI.

Central Statistics Office (2011) *2010 Population and Housing Census: Preliminary Report*. Retrieved online from: http://www.stats.gov.lc/StLuciaPreliminaryCensusReport2010.pdf (accessed 25 November 2011).

de Lima, I. B. and Kumble, P. (2015) Intervenções etnoterritoriais e sociais: os avanços no desenvolvimento comunitário Kalunga com o (eco)turismo (Social and ethnoterritorial interventions: the advances on Kalunga community development through (eco)tourism). In M. G. de Almeida *et al.* (eds), *O Território e a Comunidade Kalunga (The Territory and Kalunga Community)*. Goiânia, Goiás, Brazil: Gráfica UFG, pp. 191–229.

Dhakal, B. and Thapa, B. (2015) Buffer zone management issues in Chitwan National Park, Nepal. *Parks Journal* 21(2), 63–72.

Drumm, A. and Moore, A. (2005) *Ecotourism Development: A Manual for Conservation Planners and Managers*. Arlington, VA: Nature Conservation Agency.

Eagles, P., McCool, S. and Haynes, C. (2002) *Sustainable Tourism in Protected Areas: Guidelines for Planning and Management*. Gland, Switzerland: IUCN.

Humes, A. (2008) *St. Lucia's Moment*. Retrieved online from: http://www.cntraveler.com/islands/2008/07/St-Lucia-s-Moment (accessed 25 November 2011).

Kala, C. P. and Maikhuri, R. K. (2011) Mitigating people-park conflicts on resource use through ecotourism: a case of the Nanda Devi Biosphere Reserve, Indian Himalaya. *Journal of Mountain Science* 8, 87–95.

Larson, P., Cumberbatch, J., Fontaine, M. and Nolan, M. (1998) *Environmental and Coastal Resources Project (ENCORE): Lessons Learnt to Date*. USAID.

Lima, I. and Weiler, B. (2015) Indigenous protagonism in tourism operations and management in Australia, Brazil, and New Zealand. *ASR: CMUJ of Social Science and Humanities* 2(1), 7–37.

Mehta, J. N. and Kellert, S. R. (1998) Local attitudes toward community-based conservation policy and programmes in Nepal: a case study in the Makalu-Barun Conservation Area. *Environmental Conservation* 25, 320–33.

Moswete, N. and Thapa, B. (2016) An assessment of community-based ecotourism impacts: a case study of the San/Basarwa communities of the Kalahari, Botswana. In K. Iankova, A. Hassan and R. L'Abée (eds), *Indigenous People and Economic Development – An International Perspective*. Abingdon: Routledge, pp. 223–36.

Moswete, N., Thapa, B. and Lacey, G. (2009) Village-based tourism and community participation: a case study of the Matsheng Villages in southwest Botswana. In J. Saarinen, F. Becker, H. Manwa and D. Wilson (eds), *Sustainable Tourism in Southern Africa: Local Communities and Natural Resources in Transition*. Clevedon: Channel View Press, pp. 189–209.

Nicholas, L. (2007) Stakeholder Perspectives on the Pitons Management Area in St. Lucia: Potential for Sustainable Tourism Development. Unpublished PhD dissertation, University of Florida, Gainesville, FL.

Nicholas, L. and Thapa, B. (2006) Community-based tourism: a case study on the Fond Gens Libre community in St. Lucia. *Proceedings from the 12th International Symposium on Society and Resource Management: Global Challenges and Local Responses*, Vancouver, Canada

Nicholas, L. and Thapa, B. (2010) Visitor perspectives on sustainable tourism development in the Pitons Management Area World Heritage Site, St. Lucia. *Environment, Development and Sustainability* 12(5), 839–57.

Nicholas, L. and Thapa, B. (2013) The politics of World Heritage: a case study of the Pitons Management Area, St. Lucia. *Journal of Heritage Tourism* 8(1), 37–48.

Nicholas, L., Thapa, B. and Ko, Y. (2009) Residents' perspectives of a World Heritage Site: the Pitons Management Area World Heritage Site, St. Lucia. *Annals of Tourism Research* 36(3), 390–412.

Nyaupane, G. and Thapa, B. (2004) Evaluation of ecotourism: a comparative assessment in the Annapurna Conservation Area Project, Nepal. *Journal of Ecotourism* 3(1), 20–45.

Parker, P. and Thapa, B. (2011) Distribution of benefits based on household participation roles in decentralized conservation within Kanchenjunga Conservation Area Project, Nepal. *Environment, Development and Sustainability* 13(5), 879–99.

Parker, P. and Thapa, B. (2012) Natural resource dependency and decentralized conservation within Kanchenjunga Conservation Area Project, Nepal. *Environmental Management* 49(2), 435–44.

Persha, L., Agrawal, A. and Chhatre, A. (2011) Social and ecological synergy: local rule-making, forest livelihoods, and biodiversity conservation. *Science* 331, 166–8.

Plummer, R. and Fennell, D. A. (2009) Managing protected areas for sustainable tourism: prospects for adaptive co-management. *Journal of Sustainable Tourism* 17(2), 149–68.

Ribot, J. (2002) *Democratic Decentralization of Natural Resources: Institutionalizing Popular Participation.* Washington, DC: World Resources Institute.

Robbins, P., McSweeney, K., Waite, T. and Rice, J. (2006) Even conservation rules are made to be broken: implementation for biodiversity. *Environmental Management* 37, 162–9.

Romero, C. and Andrade, G. (2004) International conservation organizations and the fate of local tropical conservation initiatives. *Conservation Biology* 18, 578–80.

Scheyvens, R. (2000) Promoting women's empowerment through involvement in ecotourism: experiences from the Third World. *Journal of Sustainable Tourism* 8(3), 232–49.

Singh, S., Timothy, D. J. and Dowling, R. (2003) *Tourism in Destination Communities.* Cambridge: CABI Publishing.

Thapa, B. (2007) Issues and challenges of World Heritage Sites in Nepal. In R. White and J. Carman (eds), *World Heritage: Global Challenges, Local Solutions*. Oxford: Archaeopress, pp. 23–7.

UNESCO (2011) *Pitons Management Area.* Retrieved from the official website of UNESCO: http://whc.unesco.org/en/list/1161/documents/ (accessed 21 July 2011).

Wager, J. (1995) Developing a strategy for the Angkor World Heritage Site. *Tourism Management* 16(7), 515–23.

Zappino, V. (2005) *Caribbean Tourism and Development: An Overview*, Discussion Paper No. 65. The Netherlands: European Centre for Development Policy Management.

15 Ethnodevelopment in Kalunga's community-based tourism

From a past marked by slavery to ethnic group struggles for empowerment and recognition

Thaís Alves Marinho

Introduction

The growing cultural appreciation for maroon communities – African enslaved descendants in Brazil – has been evidenced from the current relationships established in the Kalunga community, the biggest maroon community of the country, located in the northeast of Goiás State. A traditional local organisation and some public policies allowed the formation of a new ethnic-cultural market, the essence of which is to refresh the past in the present and is also motivated by the lack of rural elements in the modern-technological routines of the cities. This factor, combined with people's interest in a culturally black enclave in a land surrounded by natural and scenic attractions, has been a drive for tourism development. Despite the fact that ethnodevelopment in this context favours the community's inclusion, it also brings new challenges to one's way of living developed in Kalunga territory as it adds a culturalist and essentialist requirement for the recognition of the value of the group. The results of an ethnographic study also demonstrate that the identity and territorial reinterpretations of Kalunga have also been part of an ethnodevelopment process. This chapter has to do with the struggles of Kalunga for empowerment moving from a past marked by slavery to an ethnic group recognition. It seeks to evaluate the elective affinities between the growing demands for an ecological ethno-cultural tourism, group empowerment and ethnodevelopment.

Since 1945, as stated by Sovik (2007), or 1960, as stated by Wieviorka (2003), many suppressed groups have appeared or reappeared, claiming their place in a multicultural world. Many of these groups begin the process of 'ethnicising themselves' so they become visible in public space, as pointed out by Wieviorka (2003: 19). In Brazil, this became evident from 1988, with the approval of a new *Carta Magna*, combined with other legislation and public policies that granted and reinstated ethnic groups in Brazil. This has been a milestone that champions the social and economic importance and incentives for ethnic groups opening up new possibilities for ethnic development.

Advances in this field with policies addressing ethnic issues seem to be a global trend which advocates the preservation of multiple identities, local cultures, ethnic lands and natural resources. Multiple subjectivities indistinguishable from tradition and localism are now taken as a basis for local experiments and projects aiming at promoting a segmented development. New paradigms emerge and concepts of ethno-development or self-development or 'development with identity' have been part of this new perspective to critically rethink assumptions that for decades have underlined conventional development models (Chernela 2011), so real long-lasting ethnic, social and economic changes can take place.

As pointed out by Yudice (2006), this trend works around assemblages, empowerments, entrepreneurship and performances of ethnic groups. Above all, ethnodevelopment has to do with the development of policies and processes that are sensitive to the needs of ethnic groups by creating the means for a decision-making process controlled by them and/or with their direct participation and intervention (Bonfil Batalla 1982; Wright 1988; Bengoa 1993; Stavenhagen 1990; Hettne 1996; Clarke 2001; Partridge *et al.* 1996; Davis 2002).

I argue in this chapter that institutional and organisational interventions in line with ethnic expectations and demands have been a critical resourceful empowerment source for the people of the largest traditional black community of Brazil, the Kalunga Community. However, despite the fact that ethnodevelopment favours the community's inclusion, it also brings new challenges to the Kalunga way of living in their territory. This is because the ethnodevelopment process introduced in Brazil adds a culturalist and essentialist requirement for the recognition of the value of the group.

As pointed out by Fuss, essentialism 'is most commonly understood as a belief in the real, true essence of things, the invariable and fixed properties which define the "whatness" of a given entity' (1989: 11–12). In Brazil, the expectation built throughout the time around the organisation of these traditional black groups is that they keep a specific identity founded on symbolic, economic and political African resistance. This belief sustains the idea that this 'black escapee' group have perpetuated an authentic African culture on Brazilian soil since the Portuguese colonial period. On this interpretation the present black communities were formed by slaves that escaped slavery, and that's the only possibility. This origin justifies today the integrity of their identity and the sustainable community way of living of the black communities. From this essentialist point of view the prerogative for ethnodevelopment policies is that these groups prove that they have an origin founded on escaped slaves. This became the guarantee for recognising the value of the group and for patrimonialisation, which compromises the possibility of self-determination.

The English word used to refer to this kind of community is 'maroon' and it contributes to the essentialism because it places the authenticity of the group at its origin as individuals who escaped slavery. According to Price (1979), the etymology of the word is surrounded by this meaning. Maroon derives from Spanish *cimarrón* – itself based on an Arawakan (Taino) Indian root. *Cimarrón* originally referred to domestic cattle that had taken to the hills in Hispaniola, and soon after it was also applied to American Indian slaves who had escaped from the Spaniards. By the end of the 1530s, the word had taken on strong connotations of being 'fierce', 'wild' and 'unbroken', and was used primarily to refer to African-American runaways.

It is commonly known that for more than four centuries the communities formed by such escaped slaves dotted the fringes of plantation America, from Brazil to the southeastern United States, from Peru to the American Southwest. Known variously as *palenques*, *quilombos*, *mocambos*, *cumbes*, *mambises* or *ladeiras*, these new societies ranged from tiny bands that survived less than a year to powerful states encompassing thousands of members that survived for generations and even centuries. However, that is not the whole story for most of the groups identified as *quilombos*, also called *quilombolas* (in Brazil) or as maroon groups (in English).[1] The essentialist assumption ignores the actual historical and territorial processes that each one of these groups faced as they configured their social organisation. The methaphorisation made by the legislators around the term *quilombo* (maroon) elucidates the multiple and complex reality of the traditional black communities in Brazil. But this understanding doesn't appear when using the terms *quilombos* or maroon groups. I choose in this chapter to use the word *quilombo* rather than maroon. To understand the dilemma of the Brazil scenario the focus should be on the metaphorisation around the word *quilombo* in the context of the twentieth century in Brazil, which did not happen to the word maroon at the same level.

Therefore, I propose in this chapter to reject the existence of an essence, an origin, an unchanging culture that can testify to the authentic existence of the Kalunga. As argued by Handler (1986) the ethnic ideologies conceive of authenticity as a function of the 'possessive individualism' as described by Macpherson (1962), where the existence of a collective unit (national or ethnic) depends on the property of an authentic independent culture that restates itself among others.

The results were obtained from an ethnographic study based on participant observation which took place in the Kalunga community in the west centre of Brazil between 2004 and 2012, with a literature review in 2015 and 2016. The results show that the Kalunga configuration contradicts the assumed essentialism of an authentic romantic origin for the group. Each of the Kalunga Afro-descendants intersects the collective memory they had access to during their life experience, founded on tradition, objectified by their habitus, with the legitimate formal logic, according to the intensity of the contact established with the technical-informational environment of the market and the bureaucratic-instrumentalism of the state. And this occurs in a discontinuous time and space, random and permeable, because it transits through different channels and media, crossing asymmetrically 'the here and now'.

Contrary to the ideal of authenticity founded by modern gnosiology, I argue that this fact does not invalidate the authenticity of such groups and individuals, since this is inaugurated by the creativity which emerges from the clash of these guidelines, as the residents of this community acquire the learning of sets of social symbols with their corresponding meanings of the knowledge of their ancestors, from which they acquire and elaborate fantasies, images and symbols to which they attach themselves, transforming them into the guiding principles of their conduct, behaviour and identity. It would be such internalised motivations, values and dispositions, objectified in their daily practices and actions, that formalise their own way of life, and which gives them the feeling of the normal, essential and natural, although such authenticity is contingent and varies in time and space, from individual to individual and from group to group.

Maroon community recognition: empowerment

Since the advent of the 68th article of the Brazilian Transitory Constitutional Device of 1988 the remaining *quilombos* communities occupying their lands begin to be recognised with the right of definitive property ownership delegating to the state the responsibility to provide them with the just titles of appropriation. The *quilombo* recognition, though formalised by the constitutional text, was already being discussed in academic circles from 1950, and in the black movement from 1970. The main purpose of these groups was to demonstrate that the Afro-descendant population also contributed in an original and authentic way to the construction of the national process through the already known *quilombos*, as understood in colonial terms (according to the definition of the Ultramarian Council), as a redoubt of 'black escapees'.

Initially, the proposal of valorisation of these communities was founded on the argument of 'black resistance' at one time adopting a certain 'revolutionary communist' meaning (Carneiro 2011), at another time by supporting a meaning in terms of physical, social and particular cultural characteristics (Ramos 1953). The prerogative behind those two concepts is that the proper way of life developed by the Afro-descendants becomes associated with any group tolerated by the dominant political elite that perpetuated themselves through their developed secular knowledge of sustainable familiarity with territory and nature. Thus there is an understanding that the current *quilombo* communities do not necessarily have an origin from the historical *quilombos* (groups of black escapees, or maroons groups).

Under this principle the Brazilian state, black movements and relevant institutions have acknowledged the *quilombo* as a Historical and Cultural Brazilian Patrimony, a recognition officially promulgated by the Brazilian Constitution of 1988, serving itself as a kind of commemoration of the centenary of the abolition of slavery, a sad dimension of a past mercantile transatlantic human trafficking.

The expectation around this organisation that recognises the *quilombo* community, beginning from Article 68, is that such groups sustain a specific identity founded on symbolic, political and economic resistance, exercised since the colonial period by the 'black escapees' that perpetuated an authentic African culture or, at least, an Afro-descendent one. In this romantic tale, the historical origin is responsible for the integrity of identity and the current sustainable way of living of members of the *quilombo* communities, giving the necessary authenticity to this recognition and to the formal patrimonialisation.

This posture shows itself to be essentialist, culturalist and romantic in that it ignores the actual historical and territorial processes that each one of these groups has faced as they configured their social organisation. On the contrary, it defends the existence of an origin, of an immutable culture that can attest their authentic existence, composing the ethnic ideologies conceptualised by Handler (1986). In these perspectives authenticity is a function of 'possessive individualism' (Macpherson 1962), where the existence of an aggregate unity (ethnic or national) depends on the possession of an authentic and independent culture that reassures itself over other cultures.

The Kalunga community is located in the northeast of the state of Goiás (middle west of Brazil), and it became a pioneer in the struggles for institutional recognition, concession of rights and ownership vis-à-visa an occupied land; these territorial claims started with the initiatives and participation of Baiocchi, an anthropologist who in 1982 had her first contact with the community. She actively participated together with local leaders in realising such objectives. This pioneer action culminated in the recognition of the community at state-district level through the state law (No. 11.409/91), with the title of 'Historic Siege and Cultural Kalunga Patrimony'. The law was based on a study carried out by a team from the Kalunga Project of the People of the Land – a subproject of the 'Historical Revival of the Quilombos' linked to the Federal University of Goiás; it was formulated and coordinated by Baiocchi and initiated a long journey in the search for community recognition and the benefits warranted by law. The Kalunga Project began in 1991 and became public in II National Seminary 'Historic Siege and Black Monuments' in 1992; it was adopted by the IDAGO (Institute of Agrarian Development of Goiás) (no longer functioning) that awarded land property rights documents to the Kalunga with the transfer of 241,300 hectares as a first step towards land recognition.

Recognition at the federal level was achieved by the insertion of public policies (Quilombola Brazil Programme) focused on the remaining *quilombo* communities from 2004, which had the Kalunga community as a pilot plan for social policy (Kalunga Action) and for the regulation of land implementation. This decision was published in the Official Diary of the Union on the 20th day of December 2009, with the allocation of an area of 261,999 hectares, 69 ares and 87 centiares, situated in Cavalcante, Teresina de Goiás and Monte Alegre municipalities in Goiás state. Meanwhile, about 100,000 hectares continued to be occupied by farmers and squatters who had lost their rights of land usufruct due to titleholder concessions to Kalunga by the government. To finish this process it is still necessary to remove the invaders of the territory and indemnify the farmers that were dispossessed and those occupants that hold rights.

Thus we can observe a certain disposition of the Federal Government and the civil society to press ahead with the development of the *quilombo* communities, according to what is demonstrated in the Pluriannual Plan (PPA) of 2000–3, 2004–7 and 2008–11, with the Quilombola Brazil Programme. The compromise made by the federal government agencies can clearly be seen in the efforts made towards integrated action in the development of projects with a focus on *quilombo* communities. The priority for public polices has been to promote and achieve local sustainable development aiming at opening and expanding markets for handicrafts and traditional products, local culinary products and the marketing of cultural and heritage sites, and it encompasses the production and commercialisation of organic food at the national and international level. This trend follows a growing demand for ecotourism and ethnic-cultural tourism through which, with regard to the Kalunga community, visitors can appreciate tangible and intangible ethnically conceptualised products and experiences *in situ*. This is another dimension of ethnodevelopment pointed out by Clarke (2001) and Willis (2005), 'ecological sustainability'. Within the Brazilian perspective and public policies, this dimension has to do with local sustainable development which is combined with sustainable use of local natural resources, the adoption of appropriate technologies and the democratisation of the decision-making process (with local population as protagonists of development) to improve the overall quality of life of the population, particularly unprivileged people – e.g. specific ethnic groups, black and indigenous ones – living in rural areas.

Ethnodevelopment, empowerment and tourism

Various actions have been taken to promote and strengthen ethnic tourism and local production concomitantly with Kalunga community capacity-building through the Sustainable Kalunga Project, Kalunga Association and CET/UNB Tourism Observatory, managed by the Tourism Study Center of Brasilia University. Their proposal conceptually resides in the thinking that Kalunga community autonomy can be achieved by locally managed tourism activities for income generation with government bodies and civil society support and partnerships. More recently tourism in the Kalunga land has contributed to an increase in income of some families in the community; they have also already benefited from several projects and social policies. These initiatives provide evidence that Kalunga – as an ethnic group – has moved from a backward and marginalised situation to a more promising context at a family and community level. These facts reveal that ethnic development has taken place in advancing and improving Kalunga life.

Since the inhabitants have received instructions about these touristic activities through workshops, they can decide whether to invest in touristic activities and the creative sector. They began to organise ethnic tourism allied to ecotourism, especially in Engenho II community,[2] the region closest to Cavalcante. Tourism packages offer a series of ethnic-based attractions and experiences for the visitors, such as being hosted and having traditional meals served with savanna's fruit juice at the house of 'Seu Cirilo', literally Mr Cirilo, who is one of the oldest residents and main Kalunga leader; other experiences include hiking, enjoying the canyons (Ave-Maria e Capivara) and the waterfalls (Santa Barbara, Capivara, Candaru) with an opportunity to go diving, riding a donkey as far as Cavalcante town, picnics, the contemplation of a pristine landscape and other outdoor recreations and relaxation.

The Sustainable Kalunga Project is managed by 'Seu Cirilo', ex-president of the Quilombo Kalunga Association, and 'Bell', both inhabitants of the Engenho II community; the Project has been financially supported by the Development and Citizenship Programme of Petrobras whose focus is sustainable tourism activities and cultural valorisation. As part of the Project, workshops for local capacity-building, cultural revival and expansion of trade for Kalunga products have been provided. The Kalunga residents also receive advice about the touristic impacts and tutorials on how to improve the activities chosen. Other benefits of the project include investment in tourism infrastructure, the construction of communal spaces, and vehicle acquisition and maintenance for the transportation of products and people.

As widely observed and discussed in the literature, tourism has been a double-edged sword; at the same time, it promotes a place, landscapes, natural attractions, people and their culture; it also negatively impacts on species and their habitats with the development of infrastructure built to serve the tourists' demands, as well as it impacts on local culture. Because tourism development demands planning, impacts can be mitigated while local communities can be economically rewarded. In Ruhanen's words (2007: 239), 'it has been advocated that tourism planning is vital to offset some of the negative impacts that tourism can have on the destination community.'

After all, to ally the patrimonialisation process and tourism development and yet generate a sustainable development for a local population requires the articulation of the cultural, political and economic spheres, within the ambit of the institutional designs and the coordination of the politics of regulation. One of the local strategies has been the participation in what is called solidarity tourism that has been generated in the Kalunga Historical and Cultural Heritage Site. The aim is to ally voluntary tourism with work combating social inequality, and at the same time to address the negative aspects of the activity.

To do this, the project has to be based on close knowledge of the individual person and the reality of families and communities that live in a region with the purpose of collaborating for the improvement of the quality of life and community development (Travessia Ecoturismo 2011). The visitors and participants can offer different kinds of help according to their skills and resources, such as social services and/or donations; on the other hand, the visitors can take positive outcomes from this contact with nature and learn about the customs and the simple life of the community. Solidarity tourism (Etienne and Jolin 2013: 107), according to their proponents, is an excellent way of integrating tourists and the communities, where both have the opportunity to teach and to learn from each other, 'a form of alternative tourism in which the central goal of the travelling is to make a positive contribution to the communities visited' (Cater *et al.* 2015: 305). The Kalunga Community participated for the first time in this activity in 2008, in partnership with Crossing Ecotourism.

These actions have contributed to the touristic organisation of the region of Engenho II community that now can receive the tourists with a basic tourism infrastructure. Yonder the Guide Association, properly equipped and capable, the village of the Engenho II has four restaurants whose the owners are Seu Cirilo, Seu Cesário, Januário and Lucinha, and a camping site managed by Isabel (known as Bel) regularised and in permanent operation.

The recognition and the opponents: the culture and self-determination in question

The recognition and concession of the territorial rights on behalf of the Kalunga did not occur without a reason, once the prerogative for the recognition was based on the Kalunga's authentic contribution to national construction; this alone would have justified the title of Brazilian Historic and Cultural Heritage and the subsequent investment in touristic activity. Thus during the whole process of fighting for recognition and for the registration of the territory the community has searched to reject the critiques in relation to a fictitious linking with the *quilombos*, on the one hand, while searching to demonstrate the authentic cultural aspects, on the other. This critique in relation to the maroon origin, as well as in relation to an original Afro-descendant culture, is usually led by the opponents of the recognition comprising a majority of the politically active members of the rural-based group, who belong to such political parties as the Democrats (DEM) and the Brazilian Social Democratic Movement (PMDB), because they have agrarian interests in the lands occupied by the community.

This is Ronaldo Caiado's case (DEM-GO) in that in 2004 he submitted to the Supreme Federal Tribunal a direct Action of Unconstitutionality (ADIN, n. 3.239), claiming the unconstitutionality of the Federal Decree No. 4.887/03 that regulates Article 68. He attacked the criterion of self-attribution to the *quilombos*' identity as necessary to the recognition and also the delimitation of a territory that embraces not only the dwelling areas with a limit to the necessary areas for physical, social and cultural reproduction and titling through expropriations and indemnities. Another example, is the law project 1.836/2011 signed by Deputy Valdir Collato of the PMDB/SC. This law project continues Caiado's argument that argues that the Decree 4.887/03 has gaps as it is unconstitutional. Collato uses as justification the action moved for Caiado as proof of the problems that this unconstitutional Decree has been causing to the *quilombos*' regulations. This law project seeks to administer the land regulation as proposed in Article 68, following a culturalist perspective, that establishes as the criterion to recognition 'the culturally specific link, that identifies them as descendants of black ancestors that during the slavery regime, has grouped together to form rural communities of resistance'.

In his doctoral thesis de Brito Neto (2005) advocated the idea that the only Kalunga singularity is the fact they have been treated 'especially ethnically' because they have never been isolated; he adopts a conception whereby the isolation and the original culture would be the criteria for their ethnic status, nor according to him do they present links with African culture; they are common Brazilians, marked by social exclusion, as are so many other Brazilian groups.

Where did the Kalunga come from?

This divergence of opinion in relation to the origin and the symbols of identity, motivated me to research the origin of the dwellers of the region of the Vão do

Moleque community (literally, Valley of the Brat community), in the villages of Taboca, Capela, Curriola and Maiadinha. Through this study it was possible to rebuild the genealogical tree of the families that lived in those villages up until the mid-nineteenth century and undertake an ethnographic study; the results of this research were presented for the Master's degree of the post-graduation programme in Sociology by the Federal University of Goiás (2008), entitled *Identity and Territoriality Among the Kalunga of the Vão do Moleque*. By means of participant observation, despite the apparent homogeneity of identity and daily routine, I found that the community reveals important differences which are related to the way each individual has internalised the social structures that have constrained them since the colonial period until their constitutional recognition. In other words, the guidelines that universalise what was aimed at consolidating a national identity and the economic development of the country, initially founded over the racist ideal of whitening and miscegenation and that sustained the myth of the racial democracy, were internalised in different ways by these Kalunga individuals, generating distinct perceptions over territory, over nature and over themselves.

Such differences refer to the way each individual perceives the logic of territorial appropriation and how they perceive themselves racially from such a nexus. It is possible to classify the Kalunga in terms of four categories: on the one side there are 'owners of land' and 'true negroes', and on the other cattle owners and husbandmen. These divergences frustrate the state, the black movement and the academic expectation of the present integrity of identity founded in the *quilombos* phenomenon, feeding the denunciation about a myth of identity present in the speech of liberal and conservative sectors that have agrarian interests in the lands occupied by such communities and therefore opposed to the recognition of identity. Even the Kalunga present doubts concerning their authenticity, as demonstrated in the testimony below of a 45-year old resident from Diadema in Teresina, Goiás:

> Here people are not Kalunga. There were not *quilombos* nor slaves around here, no, they say that only there after the Funil (Funnel) are the true negro. Researchers have already come here and they have said that the people here are not Kalunga. Even my 'woman' [wife] was from the other side, she came here with the family that has bought land here so they became 'owners' of the land that they live on. I came here because I married her, and even me, I am not Kalunga.

This vagueness as to the Kalunga identity and the *quilombo* origin are frequently expressed. An informant, when asked if she was Kalunga, was an example of someone with a similar reaction or 'reaction formation': 'I am not Kalunga, I am not black! I am not an animal to have a name. The name can be of the place, but not mine', and on the other hand, 'I don't know anything about slavery, this kind of thing was on the other side there.' Sometimes, they make themselves unwilling and humble 'I don't understand the letter [written communication], I am silly'

(Marinho 2008). The main difference which I perceived refers to ethnic classifications and is usually concerned with the differences over territorial occupancy between the dwelling in the Vão do Moleque community and those of the Vão de Almas community (literally, Valley of Souls community), both Kalunga groups in the Kalunga Heritage Site. The deposition below, gathered during the field research, elucidated this differentiation:

> There was an epoch that 'slaves' have existed but later on they have run away and they went to *Ribeirão dos Bois* village near Monte Alegre, eight leagues from here, it is before *Morro do Chapéu* village those really are the true negroes, our people here we are from another filiation, we are the 'landowners', we were always here and that's it. (Interviewee, male inhabitant, 84 years old)

The deposition indicates the reference area of the supposed *quilombo* at the time of slavery, between the municipality of Teresina de Goiás and Monte Alegre, next to the region of Vão de Almas in the village of Sucuri located on the north side of the Paranã River, where it is yet possible to find ruined buildings according to the depositions. Also explicit is the differentiation between those who originate from the *quilombo* (the true negroes) and those who have appropriated the land using other means (the landowners) considered legitimate.

This differentiation is utilised by the majority of the families that live in the Vão do Moleque, because they orient their occupation, permanence and legitimate rights to the land by the filiation with a white slave master, 'Luciano Alves Moreira', indicated as great-great-great grandfather and great-grandfather of the majority of deponents or other variations of this filiation (Marinho 2008). In this perspective, they would be 'owners of the land, everywhere there, and that's it'. The fact that the territory has been inherited from a legitimate land proprietor serves to inform the inhabitants of the region that their status is superior to those that do not have such dominion.

In the great majority of cases the landowners, although they practice subsistence shifting agriculture, only move their fields between cultivation seasons, but not their residence. This residential stability is enabled because these are traditionally cattle farmers and this provides wider economic possibilities, with contacts with the cities and with the bureaucracy. The agriculturists, although they also consider themselves 'landowners', are often associated (by cattle farmers) with the ownership realised by 'the true negroes', that is to the individuals considered 'more black', who would have occupied the territory via *quilombo*, or other kinds of occupation not considered legitimate from a bureaucratic point of view (following the colonial framework) as additions, squatters or invaders of unoccupied lands.

Economic activity based on subsistence agriculture is also sustained by keeping small animals such as hens, pigs and goats; it produces a semi-sedentary life because of the need to shift the site of cultivation in opening up new fields or swiddens (called in Portuguese *roça*). The activity is maintained with no irrigation, no fertilisers and no machinery, and therefore they need to leave previously cultivated land and move to new fertile sites. To avoid the long route from the house to the fields, they also change their place of residence. Such a system of shifting residence means that they may lose the territory that they have occupied previously – even if they were to move back to it subsequently; they are taken advantage of by land-grabbers and other farmers that have gained land by buying it or occupying it by legitimate or illegitimate means.

These classifications are extremely dynamic and sometime ambiguous. While the *molequeiros* (those living in Vão do Moleque) associate the 'true negroes' with the inhabitants of Vão de Almas, at the same time they also associate this criterion with the 'agriculturalists'; while inhabitants of the *Vão do Moleque* refer to themselves as 'landowners' and cattle owners, they do not relate 'true negroes' with themselves; rather, they relate this 'African origin' to those individuals who have belonged to the Vão de Almas community by reason of the ruins of a historic *quilombo* found in their locality. On the other hand, in spite of the economic activity exercised (cattle husbandry or agriculture) and the individual colour (negroes or those with lighter skin colour), no inhabitants of the Vão do Moleque community referred to themselves as 'true negroes' when this research was undertaken between 2006 and 2007.

The interesting finding is that the same occurs in the Vão de Almas community, because whatever the economic activity (agriculturalists or cattle rearers) most of them refer to themselves as 'landowners' and associate the 'true negroes' with the Vão do Moleque. In this dynamic we perceive that there is not a transcendental entity that seems to guide the identity of these individuals when they claim *quilombo* status because it frequently uses the notion of authenticity as it is currently employed as the foundation of the definition of such *quilombolas* groups. A joke within the community reflects this dynamic of negation of the *quilombo* or slave origin that the Kalunga term attempts to indicate.

> A traveller that was looking for the Kalunga, has arrived in Vão de Almas community, and wanted to be sure that he was in the right place. – Is this the Kalunga community? He asked an individual inhabitant of the region, who then answered: – [this place x] it's not the Kalaunga, they are in Vão do Moleque community! Arriving there, the traveller, asked the same question to an inhabitant of the region, and with a great surprise, he got a similar answer: – [this place y] ... The Kalunga, they are in the other direction, there in the Vão de Almas ...

The main strategy adopted by the group until then was based on the negation of the *quilombo* origin; in the case of the Vão do Moleque's dwellers the purpose was to acquire more social status and for that very reason they kept away from the colonial matrix, since this involved direct conflict and a crisis of identity, and also provoked homogenisation of the group.

Kalunga social organisation and territoriality

The pressures brought to bear in the political arena have resulted in the adoption of an essentialist, culturalist and pragmatic conception of identity by the Kalunga themselves. The Kalungas were led to believe that to stake a claim for their contribution to Brazilian society this pragmatic and essentialist version of identity was the only way. This tendency is especially shown by the Kalungas' leaders. They are more and more open and disposed to 'performatise' African culture, so they participate in and promote workshops to appropriate this culture, including dancing and costumery in workshops that were offered during the I and II Kalunga Meeting of Cavalcante. Beyond the African cultural complex, they use cultural tourism with a bias towards its sustainable development as a promotional activity and a strategic delineator of the Kalunga cultural patrimony.

Nevertheless, in spite of such 'performatisation', the evidence relating to Kalunga identity and social organisation suggests that is not possible to identify an object of limited contours, like colour, much less 'race' or African culture or maroon origin, or ecological sustainability with which individuals are confronted. There is therefore not an original 'locus' of authentic content. The acquisition of substance is inaugurated, constructed and maintained by means of contact with the 'other', in a dialogic way (Bourdieu 1989; Taylor 1998). Thus in contrast to what is affirmed by the essentialist and culturalist position, the culture is neither static nor does it comprise unique criteria which can be used to identify an ethnic group (see Barth 1969; Cohen 1969; Oliveira 2003; among many others).[3] Therefore we understand that the I-identity and the We-identity do not establish themselves once and for all, but they are liable to constant transformations, related among other things to a particular environment, territory and social process (Elias 1994).

Territory therefore must not be excluded in this process of identity production; it is not only a dimension of physical space that shelters communities. After all it is in the territory that the individuals rescue facts, histories and daily practices of such communities (Deleuze and Guattari 1997). As social practice the territory is a field that constitutes itself in simultaneity to the inhabitants' collective identity. The culture is a means to express this identity in between the socio-economic possibilities. Adding to this conjunction of elements we have multiple variables that signal a common 'status', that is a repertory of practical knowledge and abilities contained in the territory, in the same way that territory is contained within this knowledge and these capabilities (Bourdieu 1989). The common *habitus* of territoriality then structures cultural relationships in a territory which in turn establishes group identity.

The space of territoriality as a supporting element of identity has two dimensions: the meaning of social formation and the collective production of space. From these dimensions the territory of the Kalunga community becomes a product of social and political practices and is constituted by a set of rules and codes, norms and dispositions, instituted by the system of representation validated in the group, which dynamises and provides a specific status for the population that inhabits it.

The Kalunga occupation of the territory is achieved through domicile and shifting agriculture, providing an original mark or status for this group. While other groups such as the Indians, who certainly used hunting terrain as a means to establish the boundary of territory, like the *Bandeirantes* with their mining areas, and agriculturalists with their pastures, the social dimension of territoriality among the Kalunga is built through the grouping of families, linked by their sense of locality, coexistence, reciprocity and religious activities.

The Kalunga spatial organisation is related to the spheres of family life, so we can identify three social spaces: the house and the garden, which represent the domestic sphere corresponding to the nuclear family; the village or localities (the domain of kinship or family nucleus), which represents the sphere of sharing, where a group of families live close to each other and establish bonds of local solidarity, preferably, but not exclusively, consanguineous; and the sacred spaces, representing the public sphere (cemeteries, courtyards and chapels intended for religious festivals and rituals), a meeting place for the community as a whole.

Ethnicisation and self-determination

The region within the study consists mostly of blacks, Afro-descendants. However, some families stand out for their lighter skin tone. Each family has a miscegenation trajectory. Most of them identify at least one white ancestor in their family – gold diggers, peddlers, merchants and slave masters, coming mainly from Bahia and interior Goiás. To a lesser extent, an Indian person is identified in the family and when mentioned it is invariably said that 'the grandfather had taken the Indian grandmother in the loop.' Because it is a community claiming its ethnic-*quilombola* identity, some may believe that such *quilombola* territories, to be 'legitimate', should use the criterion of black colour as a requirement for membership of African or Afro-descendant culture.

However, in many cases this criterion is not used. In fact, the racist heritage and whitening ideology have generated situations where the clearest colour is seen as advantageous in various regions of the Kalunga Community. The valorisation of miscegenation is the traditional way of processing racial relations for which Brazil is known, where antagonisms apparently are dissolved into everyday interracial sociability (Bento 1999). This apparent racial democracy can also be perceived among the Kalunga, especially up to the recognition of Article 68 and culturalist demands.

Thus the old strategy of the reproduction of the Kalunga identity, informed throughout the Brazilian historical constitution by the social structure, translated in the habitus Kalunga, was previously based on 'whitening'. The vainest Kalunga still boast that they are 'more qualified' (in the aesthetic sense), they call themselves 'landowners', 'proprietors', 'farmers' to the detriment of agriculturalists and 'true negroes'. These discourses demonstrate the negation of black skin colour as an attempt to escape conflict and as a strategy of upward social mobility in the Kalunga social structure. Such a strategy made it possible for these people to remain elusive in their territory, which culminated in their being made 'invisible' and isolated, guaranteeing local sustainability, cultural preservation and corroborating the myth of Brazilian racial democracy.

Therefore, while colour and African provenance are important to the life choices of these individuals, they are not the only directives that guide the social and cultural organisation of the group. The relationship with the territory and with the relatives marks a unique and particular territoriality, because control over the land is achieved in groups, being exerted by the collectivity. Such territoriality is defined, therefore, on the basis of ethnic boundaries based on kinship affiliation, co-participation in values, cultural practices and especially the specific circumstance of solidarity and reciprocity developed in confrontation in the context of alterity proposed by outsiders. The categories 'here' and 'outside' used by the Kalunga point to the ethnic boundary that defines this group, not the isolation, nor a specific culture, as proposed by de Brito Neto (2006) and other culturalists. The territoriality of the Kalunga community is featured in the ethnic identity of each group that constitutes it, with reference to the understanding of Barth (1969), considered the father of ethnicity theory, along with Cohen (1969). Landownership, regardless of its heritage, is used by the Kalunga community as a collective subject set up as an ethnic group observed by its system of kinship and 'belonging', beyond colour, inbreeding or African or Afro-descendant culture.

It is the land that provides the group, which benefits from it, with its own identification mechanisms. For example, when asked about the difference in the life of the Vain and the life of city-dwellers, they say: 'It's all the same … [but] people live here and do things differently, to our liking, right!' Another resident of Curriola tells us about this traditional and private way of doing things: 'Here, we cook on the wood stove, (laughs) it's just for the dough in the pot and to put embers on the lid, that's it.' And she goes on, 'But it's really good, green beans, string beans, *aff*, planted in the field, made in the iron pot, here on the stove, (laughs).' On another occasion, another 29-year-old Diadema resident says that being a Kalunga 'is to wake up early, pick up firewood in the yard and make coffee on the wood stove, to take care of the garden, sacting like a paraakeet behind a bird …' [*sic*]. Figures 15.1, 15.2 and 15.3 give a notion of the Kalunga daily routines, lifestyle, village and community layout and construction type, Kalunga food production and harvest, Kalunga art, etc.

The identity of the people that we now call Kalunga relates to a simple way of life relative to life in the hinterland of the central-west of Goiás, marked by the harshness of the peasant life and cattle-raising; it can be verified even before the Brazilian formal recognition of these black communities from the Constitution of 1988. The Kalunga individuals historically oriented their permanence in the territory by using external contrastive elements that internally organised a common feeling among the members of this group as belonging to the territory.

At first, such dispositions that guided the organisation of these black individuals are based on the memory of a hard life of suffering typical of farmers of the centre-west of Goiás, who sought to survive in a place marked by economic

Typical Kalunga House made of mud and straw. And a cattle enclosure at the back.

Kalunga Backyard

Kalunga House Style

Flour Mill

Figure 15.1 Kalunga community, village, houses, backyards and flour mill.
Credit: Thaís Marinho.

decline after the golden period of glory. As time went on, a group belief condensed, formalising the same origin, from identification with the territory, objectified by diverse denominations such as: the people of the S*ertão* (Hinterlands), of the Vain, the millers, the blacks of the C*hapada* (Veadeiros Plateau Area), the *Kalungueiros* and, finally, 'Kalunga'. As Weber (1991) points out, in his work on *Economy and Society*, where he devoted his thoughts to ethnic community relations, ethnic identity is based on a historical and collective construction of a feeling that individuals in a group nurture and that expresses a belonging to a common origin.

In these terms the social organisation is linked to the processes of ethnic identification. These do not derive from the psychology of the individuals, which are not by themselves conscious or unconscious, they depend on the constitution of spaces of visibility and on the forms of interaction with the 'external world' (Barth 1969). Therefore, when one speaks of *quilombola* recognition among the Kalunga, it refers to a specific historical moment of revealing to the world a perceived group identity. This justifies the association of other actors with these identity movements, such as the black/*quilombola* movement and representatives

Figure 15.2 Kalunga manioc (cassava) production, harvesting, pottery, bird trap and the ukelele, a traditional Kalunga wood guitar.

Credit: Thaís Marinho.

of the academy, as in the case of the anthropologist Baiocchi in the construction of Kalunga ethnogenesis.

In this way, even if the culture shows very little about the dynamics of ethnic construction, the difficulty of understanding this phenomenon and the methodological shortcomings of how to undertake this analysis mean that, in the spaces of interaction, the cultural attributes become expressive, become stereotyped and selective, not as revealing of a subjective or ineffable reality, but as a selection, as a public demand that needs to be validated at the moment of contact. This misconception would justify Kalunga 'ethnicisation' as a requirement or condition of recognition by the ethnic-*quilombola* field. This 'ethnicisation' 'refers to the formation of social boundaries aiming to protect the integrity of (presumed) ethnic-cultural heritages' (Milikowski 2000: 443) by ascribing ethnic and racial identities. It is part of the logical production of difference as described by Wieviorka (2003). Some postcolonialist writers, such as Spivak (1988) and Minh-Ha (1995), insist that some subversive, empowering force can come from the employment of essentialist strategies.

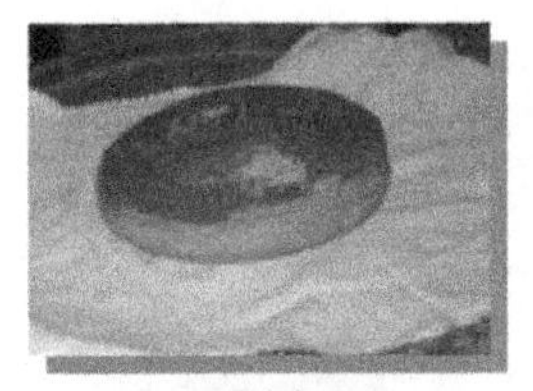

Baked Cake

Bake cooking process –
Traditional style

Broom made with a local
palm tree (*Buritirama*)

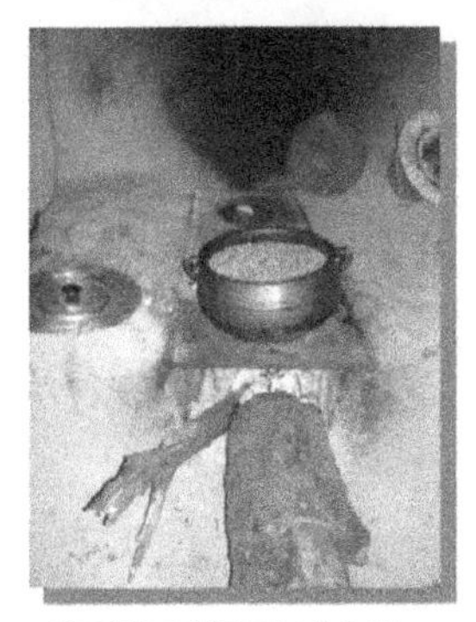

Traditional firewood oven.
Cooking green beans.

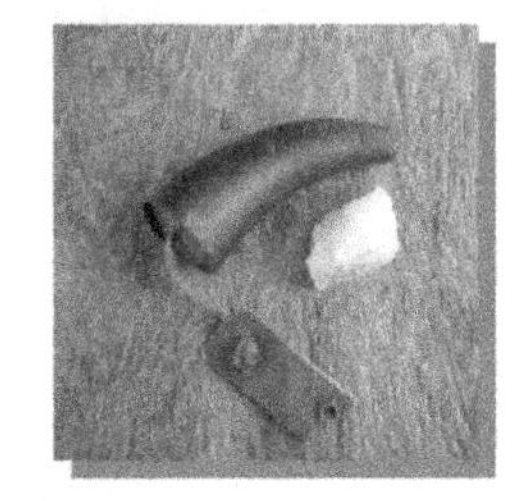

'Artifício' - It is an instrument made
of cattle horn, to make fire. It also
uses cotton, cork, a stone and a
piece of metal.

Figure 15.3 Kalunga food production, traditional rice harvesting, traditional firewood oven, brooms and the *artifício*, a traditional lighter.

Credit: Thaís Marinho.

Final considerations: territorial management and ethnodevelopment

Cultural valorisation (even though it may result in 'essentialist ethnicisation') and the local organisations erected from there, made possible the formation of a new market, whose essence is the translation of the past into the present. The focus of interest in this past way of life is consumed with nostalgia and romanticism by visitors, motivated by the absence of this authentic rurality in the ultra-technological routine of cities. Therefore the priority of the public policies of this sector has been sustainable local development, taking advantage of the opening and expansion of national and international markets for handicrafts, traditional products, local products, cultural products, as well as ethnic, ecological and organic ones.

This trend accompanies the growing demand for ecotourism and ethnic and cultural tourism, which includes promoting direct contact with the environment, rural activities, the local population and its routines, ways of being, thinking, acting and living, from where it is possible to apprehend their knowledge, customs and traditions. Especially in Engenho II there is the direct involvement of the local residents, who have the know-how as managers and owners of their cultural heritage. The ethnic group was certainly empowered and included within the ethnodevelopment process.

However, it is important to point out that this participation, still ongoing and growing, continues to occur thanks to the perception of the importance of the secular knowledge they hold, the territory they enjoy and work in, the houses they inhabit, the utensils they use, the special events they celebrate, beyond their African origin. This knowledge and involvement of the local community together with the participation of civil society can generate an environment of discovery of new solutions to the challenges imposed by a historical, political, social and cultural context. So, it is necessary that the Kalunga withhold the right to self-determination and to identify and promote their local own needs and interests.

The valuation of the intangible heritage of the Kalunga has multiple and beneficial results if well planned and practised. Such valuation can: (1) generate the preservation of traditional knowledge as a valuable way of life for future generations; (2) determine the 'physical survival' of the Kalunga Land as a unique territory, since traditional adaptation to the environment has made possible a sustainable lifestyle; (3) to allow the preservation of a way of life as a source of dignity, cultural pride and identity; (4) be used as a source of income generation through the development of tourism activity.

However, some challenges are compounded by ethnodevelopment and territorial management. Although ethno-tourism is a viable solution for the Kalunga, much of the Siege remains little known and explored by tourism. There are many factors that contribute to the lack of success of this activity, among them: long distances – some localities are six hours by truck on dirt roads, which may be impassable due to floods in the rainy season or to the damage to the roads caused by those floods; discomfort during travel and accommodation; the lack of infrastructure for the reception of tourists such as trails, guides, lodging, transportation; the unpreparedness and disinterest of the residents; weak associative bonds caused, among other factors, by the difficulty of communication among the residents, since their residences are distant from each other; and the lack of information and lack of knowledge regarding bureaucratic procedures. In other words there is no tourism organisation in all the localities of the Siege.

The lack of democratisation also prevails in the distribution of resources, actions and policies both among the residents and among the project implementers who leave it to the local leadership. In turn, the families of the leaders, having privileged access to information and coming into direct contact with local politicians, tourists, businessmen, academics, implementers, researchers and other professionals, have the position, capacity and influence to dispose of a large part of the investments for themselves. The fact is that greater contact with the 'outsiders' allows the leaders to have greater control of the resources invested in the community, and at the same time this privileged position generates recognition on the part of the other residents who come to see them as charismatic figures (Weber 1991).

Despite the apparent contradictions, the Kalunga leadership, especially of Engenho II where the activity is more developed, are fully aware that leisure and tourism constitute new forms of activities, products and services that can generate profit. But that's not all. If we analyse tourism only from the point of view of the consumption of space, the examination would be reductionist. Therefore, for ethno-tourism activities, emancipation becomes necessary, since its objective, besides increasing income generation, is to act as an element of connection between different worlds and cultures. From this perspective 'acculturation' and the lack of organisation and cohesion of the group would devalue the tourist site.

For Barretto (2000: 13), the construction of a solid social and cultural base is a fundamental step in the development of sustainable tourism, capable of withstanding the usual deterioration, as much due to natural factors as economic changes and those generated by tourism itself.

Notes

1. Historically, the maroon groups were formed by ancestors who were enslaved in farms, mining and heavy construction from 1600 to 1888, and escaped from slavery. On May 1888, the royal family approved the Gold Law (*Lei Áur*ea) which formally abolished slavery in the country. With the new Law, freed black individuals sought to join their fellows in isolated areas, forming black communities, most of them situated in the eastern and central regions of Brazil.
2. In this community we can observe with greater commitment the functioning of local initiatives and other groups of civil society; most of them seek to produce new leisure offerings as part of a sustainable development policy, which facilitate the increase in income generation for these residents. This is because the village of Engenho II has a specific character in relation to the other 61 villages of the community because it forms a village where the houses are close to each other, allowing social ties to extend beyond the home boundary. In this environment community ties are experienced with more enthusiasm, leading to greater local organisation and planning of tourist activities, such as ordering lunch, supplying guides, animals and equipment as well as medical assistance, among other possibilities. The proximity to the urban area of Cavalcante also becomes an asset for the flow of policies and actions aimed at economic solidarity and permaculture. Beyond this strategic position, the place has exuberant waterfalls, some with clear blue water, canyons and lively landscapes of native *cerrado*.
3. The culturalist requirement used as an ethnic criterion had been abandoned even in the 1960s by Fredrik Barth (1969) and Abner Cohen (1969). These researchers were inspired by the resurgence (or the visibility) of ethnic groups in Europe. And they provoke an epistemological rupture in anthropology when trying to analyse these groups by the ongoing dynamics of construction and restructuring of its borders, focusing the analysis on the limits and negotiations of these contours and not on the culture of the group in question, as it still seems to be deployed among the legislators in Brazil. The abandonment of the tribal paradigm that interprets culture only as a set of objective traits, observed from the outside, functioning in a closed regime, in isolation, is a critique of the 'ideal type definition' of an ethnic group, apprehended and analysed by cultural content (Barth 1969, 11). In this perspective, ethnicity would not be the inductive inventory of a series of collective representations such as territories, languages, customs or common values that define the ethnic state. This culturalist view presupposes, according to Barth (1969), first, an erroneous equation: a race = a culture = a language = a society; second, it assumes that this discrete formation (culture) is the social 'subject' or 'actor' responsible for accepting, refusing or discriminating against other similar formations, as if there were such a thing as cultural autonomy.

References

Almeida, J. G. (2005) Organização Espacial e Ocupação no Kalunga: a moradia como efetivadora. *Paranoá Periódico Eletrônico de Arquitetura e Urbanismo* 7.

Arruti, M. (2006) *Mocambo: Antropologia e História do processo de formação quilombola*. Bauru, SP: Edusc.

Barretto, M. (2000) *Turismo e legado cultural: as possibilidades do planejamento*. Campinas, SP: Papirus.

Barth, F. (1969) *Ethnic Groups and Boundaries: The Social Organization of Culture Difference*. London: George Allen & Unwin.

Bastide, R. (1975) *As religiões africanas no Brasil*, Vol. 2. São Paulo: Livraria Editora Pioneira/EDUSP.

Bengoa J. (1993) Development with identity: the issue of indigenous development in Latin America. In J. E. Uquillas and J. C. Rivera (eds), *Indigenous Peoples and Development in Latin America: Proceedings from the Second Inter-Agency Workshop on Indigenous Peoples and Development in Latin America*. Washington, DC: World Bank Regional Office for Latin America and the Caribbean, pp. 58–66.

Bento, M. A. S (1999) *Cidadania em preto e branco: discutindo as relações raciais* (*Citizenship in Black and White: Debating the Racial Relations*). São Paulo: Editora Ática.

Bonfil Batalla G. (1982) El Etnodesarrollo: sus Premises Jurídicas, Políticas y de Organización. In G. Bonfil Batalla (ed.), *América Latina: Etnodesarrollo, Etnocídio*. San José de Costa Rica: FLASCO, pp. 133–45.

Bourdieu P. (1989) *O poder simbólico*. Rio de Janeiro: Bertrand.

Carneiro E. (2011) *O Quilombo dos Palmares*, 5th edn. São Paulo: WMF Martins Fontes.

Cater, C., Garrod, B. and Low, T. (2015) *The Encyclopedia of Sustainable Tourism*. Oxford: CABI Publishing.

Chernela, J. M. (2012) Indigenous rights and ethno-development: the life of an indigenous organization in the Rio Negro of Brazil. *Tipití: Journal of the Society for the Anthropology of Lowland South America* 9(2). Available at: http://digitalcommons.trinity.edu/tipiti/vol9/iss2/5.

Clarke, G. (2001) From ethnocide to ethnodevelopment? Ethnic minorities and indigenous peoples in Southeast Asia. *Third World Quarterly* 22(3), 413–36.

Cohen, A. (1969) *Custom and Politics in Urban Africa: A Study of Hausa Migrants in Yoruba Towns*. London: Routledge.

Davis, S. (2002) Indigenous peoples, poverty and participatory development: the experience of the World Bank in Latin America. In R. Sieder (ed.), *Multiculturalism in Latin America: Indigenous Rights, Diversity and Democracy*. New York: Palgrave Macmillan, pp. 227–51.

de Brito Neto, J. C.(2005) L'informations des exclus: l'expériance des calungas au Brésil (Information of the Excluded: The Experience of Calungas in Brazil). Unpublished doctoral thesis, Université Paris 8 Vincennes – Saint Denis, France

Deleuze, G. and Guattari, F. (1997) *Mil Platôs: Capitalismo e Esquizofrenia*, Vol. 3. Rio de Janeiro: Editora 34.

Elias, N. (1994) *A Sociedade dos Indivíduos*. Rio de Janeiro: Zahar Editor.

Etienne, C. and Jolin, L. (2013) Case study: the International Organisation of Social Tourism (ISTO) working towards a right to holidays and tourism for all. In L. Minnaert, R. Maitland and G. Miller (eds), *Social Tourism: Perspectives and Potential*. London and New York: Routledge.

Fuss, D. (1989) *Essentially Speaking: Feminism, Nature and Difference*. New York: Routledge.
Handler, R. (1986) Authenticity. *Anthropology Today* 2(1), 2–4 (February).
Hettne, B. (1996) Ethnicity and development: an elusive relationship. In D. Dwyer and D. Drakakis-Smith (eds), *Ethnicity and Development: Geographical Perspectives*. Chichester: John Wiley, p. 36.
Macpherson, C. B. (1962) *The Political Theory of Possessive Individualism: Hobbes to Locke*. Oxford: Oxford University Press.
Marinho, T. A. (2008) *Identidade e Territorialidade entre os Kalunga do Vão do Moleque*. Goiânia. Dissertação (Mestrado em Sociologia), Faculdade de Ciências Sociais- Universidade Federal de Goiás.
Marinho, T. A. (2012) *Subjetividade, Identidade e as Redes de Consumo Kalunga*. Brasília. Tese (Doutorado em Sociologia), Departamento de Sociologia, Universidade de Brasília.
Marinho, T. A. and Pinto, J. G. (2012) Turismo etnocultural e patrimônio cultural kalunga, In A. F. Lucena, D. C. Dias, C. R. R. Carvalho and L. O. Dias, *Desenvolvimento Sustentável e Turismo: análises e perspectivas*. Goiânia: Editora PUC Goiás, pp. 159–85.
Milikowski, M. (2000) Exploring a model of de-ethnicization: the case of Turkish television in the Netherlands. *European Journal of Communication* 15(4), 443–68.
Minh-Ha, T. T. (1995) Writing postcoloniality and feminism. In B. Ashcroft, G. Grifiths and H. Tiffin (eds), *The Post-colonial Studies Reader*. London: Routledge, pp. 264–8.
Oliveira, R. C. de (2003) Reconsiderando etnia. *Sociedade e Cultura* 6(2), 133–47.
Partridge, W. L., Uquillas, J. E. and Johns, K. (1996) *Including the Excluded: Ethnodevelopment in Latin America*. Paper presented at the Annual World Bank Conference on Development in Latin America and the Caribbean, Bogotá, Colombia.
Price, R. (1979) *Maroon Societies: Rebel Slave Communities in the Americas*. Baltimore, MD: Johns Hopkins University Press.
Ramos, A. (1953) *O Negro na Civilização Brasileira*. Rio de Janeiro: Casa do Estudante Brasileiro.
Rubim, A. A. C. and Rocha, R. (ed.) (2012) *Políticas culturais*. Salvador, Bahia: EDUFBA.
Ruhanen, L. (2007) Strategic planning for local tourism destinations: an analysis of tourism plans. *Tourism and Hospitality Planning and Development* 1(3), 239–53.
Schwartz, S. (1995) *Segredos internos: engenhos e escravos na sociedade colonia*. São Paulo: Companhia das Letras.
Sovik, L. (2007) Cultura and identidade: teorias do passado e perguntas para o futuro, In G. M. Nussbaumer (ed.), *Teorias and Políticas da Cultura: visões multidisciplinares*. Salvador, Bahia: EDUFBA.
Spivak, G. C. (1988) Subaltern studies: deconstructing historiography. In R. Guha and G. C. Spivak, *Selected Subaltern Studies*. Oxford: Oxford University Press.
Stavenhagen, R. (1990) *The Ethnic Question: Conflicts, Development and Human Rights*. Tokyo: United Nations University Press.
Taylor, C. (1998) *Multiculturalimo. Examinando a Política de Reconhecimento*. Lisbon: Instituto Piaget.
Travessia Ecoturismo (2011) *Turismo Solidário na Chapada dos Veadeiros*. Available at: http://www.travessia.tur.br/pt-br/ (accessed 8 July 2012).
Weber, M. (1991) Relações comunitárias étnicas. *Economia e Sociedade*, 1, 267–77.

Wieviorka, M. (2003) Diferencias culturales, racismo y democracia. In D. Mato (ed.), *Políticas de identidade y diferencias sociales em tiempos de globalizacion*. Caracas, Venezuela: FACES–UCV, pp. 17–32.

Willis, K. (2005) *Theories and Practices of Development*. New York: Routledge.

Wright, R. (1988) Anthropological presuppositions of indigenous advocacy. *Annual Review of Anthropology* 17(1), 365–90.

Yudice, G. (2006) *A conveniência da cultura: usos da cultura na era global*. Belo Horizonte: Ed. UFMG.

Conclusion

16 Tourism and ethnodevelopment

Advances in the field and concluding highlights

Victor T. King and Ismar Borges de Lima

This volume has been designed to help fill a gap in research on tourism development and the ways in which ethnic identity and culture integrates with and supports this enterprise. Although much has been written on tourism and socio-cultural and economic development, there has been a noticeable lack of detailed ethnographic, on-the-ground research and analysis on tourism used as a development tool among marginalised, minority or ethnic populations within the context of nation-states and globalisation, and specifically in relation to such initiatives as community-based ecotourism (CBET) and 'mission-tourism' (see, for example, Eerang Park, Toulakham Phandanouvong, Phouvanh Xaysena and Sangkyun Kim on CBET in Laos in Chapter 7, and Shirley Worland on mission tourism' among Karen refugees in Thailand in Chapter 6). The volume contains rich case study material from Central and South America, Asia and Europe, which is of significant value in comparative studies, and demonstrates the problem of conceptualising communities and target populations as in some sense socially and culturally homogeneous (see, for example, Nantira Pookhao, Robyn Bushell, Mary Hawkins and Russell Staiff on Thai case studies in Chapter 4, and Thaís Alves Marinho on the Brazilian 'maroons' in Chapter 15). What research has been undertaken has often been too simplified and generalised, as Gerda Warnholtz and David Barkin argue in Chapter 2, in their study of tourism-based sustainable development interventions in Mexico, and tourism presents opportunities for local populations, but if not handled in the correct way it also poses threats to cultural identity and viability and to natural resource sustainability.

Ethnodevelopment (like ethnicity) and ethnic groups are intellectual constructs, and as constructs or concepts they are only useful if they help us to explain certain social, cultural, economic and political phenomena and processes in a globalising world. One of the main issues with which we have to grapple is that without defining what we mean by ethnicity and ethnic group then it is extraordinarily difficult to formulate policies and put into practice programmes and projects of ethnodevelopment which stand some chance of success (see Thaís Alves Marinho, Chapter 15). And success has to be measured in terms of the benefits which are directed to and secured by those communities and groups which are the targets of development interventions and not benefits which accrue to outsiders or to representatives of the state.

In the case of ethnodevelopment we are usually concerned with marginal populations or those communities usually thought about in traditional and popular parlance as 'tribal' or 'minority' within the context of modern nation-states, and those which are relatively poor and deprived and require economic support, education and resources. The concepts and terms, in using tourism as a development intervention, and which surface frequently in this volume, comprise empowerment (social, economic, political and psychological), self-determination, autonomy, participation, inclusion, reciprocity, collective or community-based participation, self-confidence and respect, capacity-building, entrepreneurship, authenticity, sustainability and the sustainable management of biodiversity and socio-cultural integrity and identity. (Eerang Park *et al.* in Chapter 7 demonstrate these complexities in relation to their study of community-based tourism in the Lao PDR as does Marinho in her Brazilian case study in Chapter 15.) In other words, the targets of development interventions are people who have been excluded from the mainstream of national and globalised life as well as from the primarily economic, but also political benefits which are secured from participation in wider debates and policy-making and in the crucial decisions which are taken about the future direction of the nation-state. In addition, these issues are concerned with the contribution which the constituent populations of a given nation-state are expected to make, the ways in which these populations are conceived and constructed and the rights which they can expect to enjoy.

However, the crucial focus in policies, programmes and projects which are directed to the development of ethnic groups is what is defined, delimited and understood as ethnicity and an ethnic group. Several of the chapters in this volume address the problems engendered in the encounter between different stakeholders when different conceptions and definitions of an ethnic group are involved. For example, in Chapter 3 Carlos Alfredo Ferraz de Oliveira, Ismar Borges de Lima and Márcia Teixeira Falcão demonstrate that ethno-tourism has become part of an ethnodevelopment process that involves strategies formulated by the Pataxó people for their sustainability and their territorial management in the context of the Brazilian Policy for Environmental and Territorial Management of Indigenous Lands introduced in 2012. The concept and definition of 'indigenous' in this context is crucial.

Furthermore, Marinho engages with this problem directly in a study of the Kalunga community in the Brazilian state of Goiás – a maroon community descended from African-enslaved people – and the complexity of defining them and determining how they are to be included in and treated and administered in the modern Brazilian state. Here she examines the problems of 'culturalist' and 'essentialist' preoccupations in the conceptualisation of ethnicity which locates identity in terms of origins, authenticity, essence and an unchanging culture with fixed boundaries and straightforwardly defined, unique characteristics. This was a very common perspective in early anthropology, that culture and particular cultural traits, including language, behaviour and material productions, were in some way immutable and were handed down from one generation to another and that they served to define separate cultural units. Ethnic groups were seen, from a cultural-essentialist perspective as clearly defined, delimited and bounded cultural units; they were in some sense thought of as primordial and their roots could be traced back to a distant past, to an origin which was not only expressed in cultural terms but was also fixed in a particular territory and environment. In some cases, populations have adopted and used the definitions of ethnicity that are imposed from outside; in other cases, they contest them.

Clarissa Gagliardi and Rosana Bignami, in a related Chapter 13, in their study of the legacy of black people in relation to the development of cultural heritage tourism in Vale do Paraíba, Brazil also address the issue of the historical construction of identities (native Indian, African black and European white). In this case study they argue that Black history has been neglected; it has been marginalised in the process of creating a Brazilian nation-state, based on the concept of an ethnic-mixed country through the mechanism of miscegenation and 'whitening'. Tourism in the Vale do Paraíba focuses not on the role and contribution of the former 'dominated' black slave population there and its cultural heritage but on the 'dominant' landowners and political elite of European origin. Thus ethnodevelopment as a strategy within the context of heritage tourism to promote ethnic resilience and welfare is yet to be achieved there.

In the case of Brazil, rather than the concept of fixed 'racial' categories of Indian, black and white, more recent research on ethnicity has emphasised the constructed, fluid, flexible and ambiguous character of identities and the ways in which they are subject to what has been termed 'cultural politics'. The role of the Portuguese colonial state and the post-independent Brazilian state, in other words the role of those who have the power and influence to define, classify and administer ethnic groups, in this exercise of ethnic definition has served to include some populations and to exclude and marginalise others. It is a history built on sociocultural, economic and political inequality and one which has acted to stratify ethnic identities. Indeed Marinho, and Gagliardi and Bignami, demonstrate the constructed, shifting, contingent, contradictory and contested character of identity and the different conceptions of ethnicity created and deployed by different constituencies and stakeholders.

In a modernising, developing nation-state where not only economic resources such as land are constantly sought after in the interest of profit, but also security, livelihood and status, then the insecure minorities, often without sufficient levels of education, without access to bureaucratic support and without political leverage, are under threat. It is clear that often these marginalised communities are unable to secure enhanced livelihoods by themselves; they need economic support, technical and financial advice, infrastructural improvements, educational input, sometimes language training, and connections with external agencies, institutions and sources of information. This in turn can increase dependency rather than promote independence. But Kennedy Rolando Tapia Lomas, Carmen Trujillo and Ismar Borges de Lima in Chapter 5 demonstrate that the direct hands-on participation of the Fakcha Llakta community in Ecuador in the execution of the nine programmes of their Management Plan undoubtedly helped to increase a community sense of ownership, conservation and responsibility for the well-being of Cascada de Peguche and its cultural-historical elements. Positive government support was a vital element in this set of programmes. Furthermore, in giving support to indigenous populations in tourism development, such government policies as the certification of 'authentic' local products and services are of considerable importance in ensuring that appropriate financial rewards go to those who live and work within a particular tourist site rather than to external businesses and providers, as Cecilia Bernardi, Outi Kugapi and Monika Lüthje demonstrate in the case of the Sámi in the Nordic countries in Chapter 11.

But the vitally important dimension in this process of modernisation and building a nation-state is what constitutes ethnic identity, how groups and categories are defined and classified, and what rights, protection and status derive from political, legal and constitutional arrangements attached to particular identities? Oliveira, Lima and Falcão in Chapter 3, for example, examine the consequences for minorities of the important constitutional and legal changes which were instituted by the Brazilian government from 1988 in recognising indigenous rights. Given the fact that the context of cultural and ethnic politics is one in which the policy-makers and practitioners charged with programmes and projects in the field of ethnodevelopment make decisions on behalf of communities identified as needing support, then the balance between top-down and bottom-up policy-making and planning becomes problematical and complex. These complexities in turn help us to explain and come to terms with the failures of experiments in ethnodevelopment, but also the successes which deserve celebration (as in the case of Pataxó, Barra Velha, Bahia State, Brazil in Chapter 3, and Bang Na village in the Lao PDR, demonstrated by Eerang Park *et al.* in Chapter 7).

What is important is that there is communication between the various stakeholders: local communities as hosts, local entrepreneurs, tourist visitors (domestic and international), tour guides and agencies, representatives of government departments with an interest in tourism development, NGOs, development practitioners, volunteers, academic researchers and international bodies such as UNESCO. Furthermore, these stakeholders are themselves seen as complex, differentiated categories. Tuhina Ganguly and Mike Grimshaw in Chapter 12 demonstrate these complexities even in the category of overseas tourists depending on their culture and ethnicity, and the dilemmas and complications which this produces in encounters among tourists and between tourists and hosts. The various stakeholders also engage in relationships which are unequal; in other words, they access, enjoy and exercise different degrees or levels of power and influence, and it is usually those subject to development interventions who are in dependent or more disadvantaged social, economic and political positions. The balance between support and dependence on the one hand and resilience and independence on the other is a very delicate one.

In some cases local responses are positive and agency is clearly demonstrated; local people are willing to grasp opportunities and there is evidence of the development of entrepreneurial capacity and energy (see, for example,

Yang Ningdong and La Mingqing in Chapter 11 and the case in south-west China of Mosuo hand-woven textiles for the tourism market). But the constraints on the development of indigenous entrepreneurship are formidable and wide-ranging and not easily overcome (see, for example, Akhmad Saufi, Sacha Reid and Anoop Patiar in Chapter 9 on Lombok, Indonesia). In other cases, there is suspicion of tourism as a positive force and a partial or complete rejection of the opportunities offered. Some local people decide not to embrace the new development initiatives. Even when there are signs of success, the benefits may go to certain individuals and groups and not to others, and in the case of the Fond Gens Libre community within the Pitons Management Area World Heritage Site in Saint Lucia explored by Lorraine Nicholas and Brijesh Thapa in Chapter 14, the authors call for the need to seek much wider and deeper empowerment and involvement of more people in the tourism development process.

The complexities are increased enormously when tourism is identified as a policy instrument and an agent in development, as Warnholtz and Barkin demonstrate. They refer to development *through* tourism as presenting a paradox to planners. It is perhaps not sufficiently realised that there are considerable socio-cultural, economic and political difficulties which tourism generates as an agency of development. It has many stakeholders and unlike development interventions which are directed to the improvement in agricultural processes and technology or in developing social welfare and health systems, the tourism sector immediately links host populations into a potentially large international market; tourism, with its wide range of stakeholders, is a complex development tool. It also goes without saying that many development interventions are designed to generate increased tourist interest within a particular country and specifically within identified tourist sites, especially from the rapidly increasing middle classes (with income, leisure time and aspirations to indulge) to visit their own tourist attractions. But to succeed a tourist-oriented location will often seek a wider international audience, not only for additional income but also for international profile and a competitive edge.

Therefore, on the one hand, tourism is deployed as a positive agency of development and economic opportunity for the poor and marginalised, and, on the other hand, it acts to translate ethnic groups/minorities, culture and nature into commodities which can be promoted by governments and tourism agencies nationally and internationally. In other words, in a negative sense it is used to generate funds in the marketplace and to change the objects and services offered to the tourist market and the 'tourist gaze' into 'attractions', 'staged events' and 'performances'. Nevertheless, in certain circumstances the commodification of ethnicity and culture may not necessarily lead to negative outcomes, but may also provide a source of pride among the host community and be a means to economic development and empowerment and to an expression of ethnic identity (see, for example, Nantira Pookhao *et al.*, Chapter 4). Local communities are also capable of separating tourist-related activities (performed front-stage) from everyday practices (undertaken backstage).

These are some of the dilemmas explored in several of the chapters in this volume, and particularly the dangers of focusing too much on economic development, management and tourism as an industry rather than the social, cultural, heritage, ethical and identity dimensions of tourism development. What is also demonstrated are the problems generated by a lack of social and cultural knowledge and competence on the part of practitioners, like Christian mission volunteers (and the 'missionary gaze'), who are genuinely motivated by an altruistic impulse to help ethnic minorities but who are unaware of the complex situations in which they intervene (see Worland in Chapter 6). The imposition of Western concepts of entrepreneurship or of sustainability and ecotourism and the failure to take into account or understand local values and practices are also problematical in development interventions (see, for example, Ingeborg Nordbø in Chapter 8 on 'projectitis' in Lago Budi, Chile). We have to address complex communities, different forms of intra-community communication and local divisions based on socio-economic class, age, gender and ethnicity.

We hope that this volume, in the range of case studies provided from diverse locations, has provided some sense of the complexities involved in deploying tourism development as a means to address the economic and political disadvantages which indigenous and minority populations frequently experience. But the important advantage that local communities possess is their cultural and environmental knowledge which is an essential supporting element in their identity and distinctiveness, and it is these components of ethnic life and activities which have to be deployed as valued resources in the policies and practices which we have referred to in this volume as 'ethnodevelopment'.

Index